An Introduction to Human Resource Management

An Introduction to Human Resource Management

Second Edition

John Stredwick

ELSEVIER
BUTTERWORTH
HEINEMANN

AMSTERDAM • BOSTON • HEIDELBERG • LONDON • NEW YORK • OXFORD
PARIS • SAN DIEGO • SAN FRANCISCO • SINGAPORE • SYDNEY • TOKYO

Elsevier Butterworth-Heinemann
Linacre House, Jordan Hill, Oxford OX2 8DP
30 Corporate Drive, Burlington, MA 01803

First published 2005

British Library Cataloguing in Publication Data
A catalogue record for this book is available from the British Library

Library of Congress Cataloguing in Publication Data
A catalogue record for this book is available from the Library of Congress

ISBN 0 7506 6534 3

For information on all Elsevier Butterworth-Heinemann publications
visit our website at http://books.elsevier.com

Typeset by Charon Tec Pvt. Ltd, Chennai, India
www.charontec.com
Printed and bound in Italy by Legoprint S.p.A.

Contents

Preface to Second Edition

The main purpose of this book is to give a balanced introduction to the complex world of human resource management. Essentially it is intended for first degree students studying the subject as part of a modular degree course or for students on a foundation degree in Business Studies. It can also be valuable on post-experience courses such as Certificate or Diploma Courses in Management Studies or as part of the MCI series of qualifications.

The book combines the main theoretical underpinning for the subject area with a large number of practical examples and cases to assist the learning process. It is divided into 12 chapters to provide one topic a week on a modular course, but many of the chapters have sufficient material to allow work to be extended into two semesters if this is required.

The second edition has updated a large number of areas of legislation, especially in the field of equal opportunities, employee rights in flexible working and in employee relations generally. Many new cases and examples of research have been added. Chapter 1 has been extensively revised to place a greater emphasis on the role of human resources in improving organisational and employee performance. Chapter 12 has been rewritten entirely to take into account the quickly changing and rich sources of cases and research in the international field. I am grateful to my former colleague, Graham Symon, for his scholarship in this area.

At this stage, let us set out the many job titles that you will find advertised in the growing pages of a popular human resource publication which define the differing job roles. Below you will find some of the common ones, all defined in their managerial role. Staff working for or with them, where they exist, will support the activities will titles such as Officer or Administrator. It is very rare to have all these defined functions in one organisation. Where there is no dedicated person for such functions, they will be carried out either by the head of human resources or by a human resource generalist.

Human Resource Planning Manager. This is a rather rare animal today, who will be working for only the largest of organisations. They will be involved in producing, monitoring and evaluating the planning process for human resources. This will involve considerable analysis work relating to the external environment, the current systems, operations and human resources within the organisations and their interface with the organisation's strategic plan. Details of human resource planning are set out in Chapter 2.

Equal Opportunities Manager. Most large organisations have appointed a person within human resources to design policies and monitor the realities of equal opportunities. The job will also involve training and communicating to staff, carrying out investigations and dealing with high profile claims of discrimination and harassment. Details of the function are set out in Chapter 3.

Recruitment and Selection Manager. A common position where the key roles are defining vacancies, advertising, short-listing, interviewing, testing, selecting and appointing staff with the appropriate terms and conditions. Setting out the policy is also an important function to ensure the best and appropriate practices are in place, especially in terms of equal opportunities. Details of these activities are to be found in Chapters 4 and 5.

Employee Relations Manager. This position is concerned with building relationships with employees on a collective and individual basis. It deals with the collective functions of bargaining and negotiating, reaching agreements on terms and conditions of employment and handling major initiatives, such as improved flexibility, site relocation and redundancy. A major aim is normally to improve levels of involvement and participation by employees. The person will also deal either directly, or through line management, with individual issues which relate to grievances, discipline and dismissal. Setting out aims and policy is a key part of this position and making sure that the policy is agreed, understood and implemented consistently throughout the organisation. You will find details of these activities in Chapter 7.

Compensation and Benefits Manager. There are a number of names describing these activities which can be called Reward Manager and Manager, Payment Systems. A Pensions Manager is a specialist function within this general area. The principal concern here is the establishment of a system of pay and rewards which meets the needs of both the organisation and the bulk of the employees. This will involve establishing a basic pay structure and individual rates, systems of rewarding performance and generating a selection of benefits across the organisation appropriate to the circumstances. Setting out the policy behind the pay systems is essential as is monitoring the internal process and the external market to ensure sufficient comparabilities. All these areas are discussed in Chapter 9.

Learning and Development Manager. Sometimes still called Training Manager, this involves the analysis of training needs to identify where training is required and what form it is to take, setting up internal training facilities with the necessary resources, giving advice on the appropriate selection of external training courses and facilities and evaluating how successful the training has been. Training areas include initial induction, specialist skills training, supervisory and management training and any other areas that help the organisation achieve success in the initiatives it plans. In policy terms, if the organisation wants to apply for accreditation for Investors in People then the leading role in the application will be made by this function. Similarly, if the direction is towards being a 'learning organisation' there is a key role in planning, achieving and monitoring for the Training Manager. Further details are in Chapter 10.

Health and Safety Manager. Although this function does not always report to the human resources function, it is generally seen as a 'people' function, rather than simply a technical or engineering function. Defining policy on health and safety is the major function here, taking into account the legislative environment together with constant vigilance to ensure the policy is appropriate for changing circumstances, understood and operated by trained line managers and investigated where it is clear a breach has taken place. Monitoring safety statistics, staff training and communication and promoting health initiatives are other important activities. Details are to be found in Chapter 11.

International Human Resource Manager. A less common appointment which primarily has responsibility for the appointing, rewarding, performance managing and welfare arrangements for international staff in their differing locations and functions, together with the establishment of the policies that go with these areas. These areas are explained in more detail in Chapter 12.

The remaining two chapters are linked to all activities in human resources. Chapter 6 covers concepts and ideas on *effective ways of working* while Chapter 8 deals with *performance management* in its broadest sense. Human resource generalists are likely to spend a great deal of their time in work connected with both of these areas, working out with line management how to improve working systems and measure and raise performance of individuals, teams and the organisation as a whole.

How to get the best out of the book

At the start of each chapter is a short list of objectives and you should keep these in mind as you read through the chapter so that, by the end, you are confident of reaching those objectives. The summary at the end of each chapter should also help to reinforce the main issues, theories and body of knowledge discussed within the chapter. Also at the end of each chapter is a set of activities for you to carry out that will help you to bolster your learning.

A further intention is to encourage you to read up on research, so each chapter has one or more summaries of important research articles or publications, called 'Focus on Research', and some of the activities are related to these articles. The case studies are of two kinds. The majority are real-life cases from published sources or from the author's experience. There is also a linked case study around a fictitious company called 'Meteor telecoms' which is intended to demonstrate some of the experiences that occur within a human resources department. Again, some of the student activities are related to these episodes.

Introduction

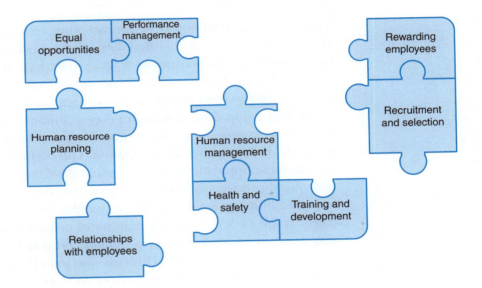

Objectives

By the end of this chapter you will be able to:

- Understand some of the influences on the business environment that has changed the approaches to employing people.
- Explain the origins of human resources (HR) and their development over the last 100 years.
- Evaluate a selection of HR models and appreciate their inherent contradictions.
- Identify the roles and purpose of HR in today's environment.
- Comprehend the links between HR management (HRM) practices and high performance.

■ Describe ways in which the effectiveness of a HR department can be evaluated.

Case study

Meteor Telecoms case study

Sarah was waiting anxiously in the reception area of the head office of Meteor Telecoms. It was her first day with the organisation as a Trainee HR Officer and she was not sure what to expect. Her 2(1) degree in Business Studies had pleased her with an especially good mark for her final year dissertation on the 'learning organisation'.

She had enjoyed the selection process 3 months before, which had involved an assessment centre spread over a very long day and had been overjoyed by being offered the position. This had sounded exciting with considerable opportunities for personal development and promotion in a quickly growing organisation, although the actual job description seemed a little vague. She had been told that her work load would have considerable variety, joining a number of project groups as well as getting involved in head office recruitment and training. She was to work for David Martin, Personnel Director who joined the company himself 6 months ago and has a department of six staff.

After a wait of 20 minutes or so, his secretary came down to meet her apologising for the delay and took her into David's office. He explained that he had to make a presentation to the Board on future strategy and this meeting had been brought forward so he had been making last minute preparations. He went on to say that he had obtained agreement from the Chief Executive that Sarah could sit in on this presentation which would give her a good introduction to the organisation.

Sarah had been doing her homework on Meteor Telecoms since her offer of employment. She knew that this company, set up 15 years ago, initially manufactured and installed telecommunication equipment but it had moved on to other associated businesses, such as helping companies set up call centres. It had around 2000 employees, spread over a number of sites around the UK. It went public 5 years ago with the two founding Directors retaining a minority stake. City reports indicated that it was well respected and had kept to its growth forecasts although the profits were taking longer to realise than had been initially expected.

An hour later, she was sitting in the board room and David had started his presentation. He began by going over the background to the company, its rapid growth, some of the difficulties this has produced and the current issues involved in recruiting, retaining, motivating and managing employees. He explained that the company has now reached a turning point in the way that people resources were managed. In its first 15 years, the growth rate had been such that there was a heavy concentration of recruitment and selection at all levels to get enough skilled employees on board. More recently, training and pay systems have had a higher profile but the activities are disjointed and reactive to the immediate circumstances. Given the tightening of the labour market, the highly competitive market for specific skills and a turnover rate higher than expected, it is time to put together an overall strategy in the people management area.

The proposal he put forward deals with the change from a tactical and reactive approach to one that puts people management at the heart of all business initiatives. He gave a number of examples of how this will lead to higher performance of employees and help the company achieve its corporate objectives. The introduction of a competence framework will encourage all employees to focus on the key skills and competencies that lead to business success. Linking these skills and competencies with a performance management programme will lead to the identification of training and development needs, and the rewarding of high-performing employees. Although trade unions had made little inroads into the business, David warned against complacency, pointed out the dangers inherent in the union recognition clauses of the recent legislation and advised a programme of greater employee involvement in planning, decision-making and innovation. He continued with further examples and some detailed proposals on each of the major proposals, emphasising that these were HR 'best practices' and would have a strong impact on improving performance in the organisation.

After the presentation, discussion ranged between Martin and some directors who remained unconvinced, pointing out the major uncertainties inherent in the business and the inability to plan too far ahead, certainly in terms of employment. David pointed out that, no matter which way the business turned, there would still need to be a sizeable core of skilled, flexible and committed employees and, without them, the business would flounder. At the end of the meeting, the Chief

Executive asked David to head up a small team to put up a fully detailed proposal for 2 months time, together with an action plan. Sarah left the meeting excited by the opportunities evident in influencing the course of the business.

Introduction

The opening scenario has taken place in board rooms up and down the country over the last 20 years ever since the term 'Human Resource Management' (HRM), was popularised by Beer and others in the mid 1980s (Beer *et al.*, 1984). In this chapter, we will firstly examine the economic and business context that has stimulated so much discussion on the role of employees in the organisation; this will be followed by a brief history of the personnel profession and then an analysis of the various models that have been put forward regarding the role and nature of HRM, including the role of HRM in improving performance. The chapter will end with some examples of HR strategy in theory and practice.

The economic and business context

The last 20 years or so has seen an unprecedented boom in most of the world's economies, but especially in the Western economies and none greater than in America. Apart from a brief recession in the early 1990s and a period of uncertainty brought on by the 11 September terrorist attacks, growth has been steady and reliable, inflation has been benign and unemployment has gradually reduced to levels that most economic commentators now call 'full employment'.

However, although actual unemployment is low, employment has a high degree of uncertainty. Levels of redundancy have been high throughout the period, brought about through structural changes in manufacturing and the service industries. The number of employees in manufacturing in the UK has reduced by almost a third since 1980. Although the numbers of jobs in the service industries have increased substantially to more than make up the shortfall in manufacturing, many of these jobs are poorly paid, part-time and temporary. The Finance sector has both created a great number of jobs but has also brought about huge redundancy programmes, often in the same organisations as the advances in technology replace face-to-face contact with automated, Internet and telephone service. Programmes of de-layering (reducing the levels of management and supervision), business process engineering (making processes more efficient and usually reducing administrative and other associated staff) and de-centralisation have all created waves of doubt, fear and mistrust amongst the mass of employees involved. Added to this is the constant flux through takeovers, mergers, buy-ins, buy-outs and float-offs, and it is not surprising that being employed is regarded as an insecure occupation.

Even in the public sector, uncertainty has been created with the massive privatisation programmes in the 1980s and 1990s covering coal, gas, electricity, water, rail, airports and telecommunication industries together with British Airways, British Aerospace and BP. Furthermore, direct government employment in the Civil Service, Local Authorities, Education and Health has been fundamentally altered by outsourcing, the creation of semi-autonomous 'Agencies' and the complex workings of compulsory competitive tendering and 'best value' programmes.

Change, therefore, has been the only constant. And, if most commentators are to be believed, the process of change will continue. According to Flannery *et al.* (1996) there are at least six major changes that are common to almost every organisation which will have a major influence on employment policies in the foreseeable future.

Rapidly Changing Technologies have probably had the biggest impact. In a few short years, the computer has fundamentally changed jobs. The spreadsheet alone has eliminated huge numbers of jobs. The work that had previously been carried out by roomfuls of mid-level analysts in finance, sales and marketing can now be handled by one clerical person on a personal computer. Information technology goes further than just making offices more productive. Organisational charts and rules are ignored by the cable that links employees, and information now flows more freely than ever before. Employees are linked in buildings, around countrywide units and around the world. Networking has moved beyond a technical definition to a way of employees working together, often in different locations and many from a home base.

Technology also leads to shorter and shorter cycle times. Cars that used to take 7 years from design to mass production now take only 3 to 4 years. The release date on computer games is crucial to a week or less, so lead times are often brought forward to steal a march on competitors. The demands created by just-in-time logistics operations has meant that gaps or delays cannot be tolerated, so urgency, time-directed performance and immoveable deadlines are part and parcel of employees normal working environment. The need for employees to work flexibly is crucial in this respect. They need to be able to move quickly from one task to another, to be able to service their own areas and to change their working hours and practices.

Technology makes it happen but it is *ever-demanding customer* that drives the process. Today's customers are better educated, more informed and have less time to want to wait about either for the service that is not good enough, or the new products that they can now afford and want today. This is partly because women, who have always taken more purchasing decisions, spend more time working now. A faster response, higher quality and a heightened, more personalised sensitivity to their needs are other customer demands while retaining accessibility, functionality and reliability. They want it their own way, not the way it has been presented to them in the past without a choice. To be successful, businesses and their employees have to make sure that they meet these demands in full or they will lose their client base. No excuses ('someone in head office will deal with that for you', 'they don't deliver after 3:30', 'we are short of staff today') are acceptable. This puts additional pressure on front-line employees who need to be able to solve, or better still, prevent customer problems by working closely together with employees who provide an internal service to them.

A poor product or service will not survive today because of the nature of *globalisation*. Markets have been liberalised throughout the world. The European communist block has imploded providing vast new potential markets. Trading agreements through the World Trade Association have allowed goods to be marketed in most countries with tariffs and barriers eliminated or vastly reduced. The Asian/Pacific region has grown at an extraordinary pace, especially China, providing a vast range of competitive or alternative goods for the world market at lower prices. This competition has lead to organisations taking far more care of their labour costs by either increasing productivity, eliminating wasteful bureaucracies and jobs which add no value, or outsourcing to cheaper suppliers. All of these actions affect the way people are employed. Handy (1994) created a new equation for success = ½ workforce, paid twice as much, producing three times as much.

With increased competition, organisations are finding that a good product or service alone does not ensure success. Instead, as Flannery *et al.*, puts it:

> '... they must distinguish themselves by focusing on fundamental competencies and capabilities that will set them aside from the pack. To achieve this, organisations must maximise ... competencies – those underlying attributes or characteristics that can predict superior

performance. These range from tangible attributes, such as skills and knowledge (technical know-how, for example, or the ability to operate a sophisticated computer) to intangible attitudes and values ... such as teamwork and flexibility. These competencies will become a part of the organisation's foundation and will be the focus of everything from hiring and training to marketing' (p. 11).

The sixth major change has been alluded to already and is a consequence of the other five, *namely what is required from employees.* Organisations no longer want robots, performing their job mechanically, working fixed hours. What is wanted is an intellectualised workforce, with employees making their own informed decisions, using good judgement and assuming more responsibility for the organisation's performance. Such a dramatic change requires that people accept new values, behave differently, learn new skills and competences and be prepared to take risks. This was made clear in another influential publication by Hamel and Prahalad (1994):

'Delegation and empowerment are not just buzzwords, they are desperately needed antidotes to the elitism that robs so many companies of so much brainpower' (p. 131).

The need to initiate changes in employee practices represents a major challenge for the HR department. This is their prime role and the place where they make their major contribution to the organisation. We will look again at these changes in respect of the models of HRM that have been put forward in recent years and in various chapters in the book which relate to selection, motivation, training, performance management and reward.

Origins of HRM

Modern day requirements of the HR department are a far cry from the origins of the profession which began in the mid nineteenth century through the early interventions of high-profile social reformers such as Lord Shaftesbury and Robert Owen. They became concerned at the exploitation of the factory workers, where the emphasis had been strongly on discipline and cost control, at the expense of the employee's health, welfare and personal living standards. Concentrating at first on the appalling working conditions, especially for women and young children, enlightened employers started to believe that if employees were treated humanely and rewarded fairly, they may work better and become more productive.

Their influence, plus the interests of public health and order, help to bring in a number of statutes relating to hours and conditions of work which were policed by factory inspectors. Alongside such regulation, a small number of paternalist employers, motivated by Christian beliefs (especially Quakers), appointed Welfare officers to provide individual and group support for employee's health, accommodation, financial and personal situations. In 1913, the Welfare Workers Association (WWA) was formed with 34 members, supported by six companies and sponsored by Seebohm Rowntree of the chocolate factory fame (IPD, 1999). It is a matter of interest that the Scottish Society of Welfare Supervisors, which was set up shortly afterwards, refused to join with the WWA because 'they did not wish to join with the ladies, whose problems are very different from the men's'. How times and attitudes have changed!

Five name changes followed over the next 90 years before becoming the Chartered Institute of Personnel and Development (CIPD) in 2000. By 2005, the Institute had over 115,000 members and had become the largest Institute in the world concerning the management of people.

The roles of practitioners have varied over this period as identified by Torrington (1992) in Figure 1.1.

Humane Bureaucrat	Setting up formal systems of recruitment, selection, appraisal, discipline and grievance.
Consensus negotiator	Bargaining with unions, creating systems of involvement and participation.
Manpower analyst	Providing a longer-term plan for employment numbers, together with programmes for skills, competence and career development.
Organisation man	Working strategically with top management to create organisation structures and management development systems.

Figure 1.1
Roles of HR practitioners. (Adapted from Torrington *et al.*, 2002)

The role of HR today

Introduction

There has been much dispute in recent years as to what HRM departments should actually do. For example, the earliest role, welfare, took a back seat in the 1960s and 1970s as management decided this was too 'soft' an activity and away from the mainstream corporate objectives. Personnel professionals saw their role as tough, masculine negotiators, dealing with hard-nosed unions. This has now been generally recognised as a bad mistake. The unions stepped into the breach and raised their profile and membership by taking time to look after their members personal, financial and occupational concerns. Through this period of confrontation, employees chose, in return, to follow the union leadership and oppose much of management's agenda which lead, inevitably, to poor productivity and lack of competitiveness. Although regarded as distant history now, the period of the late 1970s was as close as Britain ever came to a form of revolutionary shift of power.

Welfare, perhaps in a different guise, returned in the 1990s through concern for such areas as family-friendly and flexible benefits, with some evidence from the 1998 Workplace Employee Relations Survey (WERS) (Cully *et al.*, 1999) and elsewhere, that this concern from employers provides an increase in commitment and job satisfaction among employees.

By the end of the 1980s, it became important to differentiate between the established 'personnel' thinking and that of the *new concept of 'HRM'*. This was set out persuasively by Guest (1989) who set out four main areas where HRM can be identified and analysed, which makes it a different beast:

- *The policy goals of HRM.* These consist of a package of four main areas. Firstly, to encourage the commitment of employees to high performance and loyalty to the organisation as a whole. Secondly, an emphasis on quality of staff which, in turn, will produce quality goods and services. Thirdly, a concern to ensure that flexibility plays an important part in the way staff are organised, so that they are adaptive and receptive to all forms of changes – in their jobs, in the hours they work and their methods of working. Finally, and most important, that these goals are integrated into strategic planning so that HRM policies 'cohere both across policy areas and across hierarchies' (p. 49). They also need to be accepted and used by line managers as part of their everyday work.
- *The HRM policies.* Although using conventional personnel practices, such as selection and training, it is important that the practices are of high quality and that they go towards meeting the organisational goals. Employees need to be trained, for example, to be flexible and to respect high-quality work.

Communication should be goal-directed, that is, getting results, rather than simply concerned with getting out a monthly magazine on time.

■ *The cement.* To make these policies work, there needs to be support from key leadership from the top, a strong culture that can drive through the policies consistently and fairly with no sudden change of direction, and there must also be a willingness throughout the organisation to value the success that can come through the effective utilisation of HR.

■ *The organisational outcomes.* These include a low level of staff turnover, absence and grievances (individual or collective) together with a high-level change, problem solving and innovation.

Two examples of organisations that have clearly adopted an HRM approach to employment are TGI Friday's and Rhino Foods as shown in Case studies 1.1 and 1.2.

Case study 1.1

Employment philosophy at TGI Friday's

TGI Friday's is built on several key philosophies, including developing the attitudes of employees in certain directions. Here are extracts from their Employee Handbook, showing the emphasis they make on flexibility, empowerment and commitment:

'The owner who has invested his life savings in his business will no doubt strive to make his restaurant successful. He will make sound decisions, set high standards and work to achieve those standards, respond quickly to problems and possess an uncompromising commitment to quality. The concept of ownership at Friday's is simply this: Do the job as if you owned the restaurant! The concern for the Guest, commitment, effort, determination, decision-making, sense of urgency, attention to detail, care for the environment, quality of product and standard of performance that would result in a successful restaurant are all key components.

The results-oriented employee, instead of reacting to company decisions with the attitude of 'I hope they know what they are doing' or 'That will never work' will, instead, get involved with decision-making and confront any obstacle preventing the result. If you adopt this philosophy as your own, you will share in the success this 'pride of ownership' will bring.

You are the company's lifeblood. YOUR personality makes each of our stores unique. The company could not exist without you caring for the Guest's needs.'

Source: TGI Friday's Employee Handbook

Case study 1.2

People philosophy behind Rhino Foods

The founder of Rhino Foods, Ted Castle, believed he knew what a good company should look like and, early on in the company's history, wrote into the Purpose Statement a vital Employee principle:

> The employees and families of Rhino Foods are its greatest assets. The company's relationship with its employees is founded on a climate of mutual trust and respect within an environment for listening and personal expression. Rhino Foods declares that it is a vehicle for its people to get what they want.

This fundamental principle of encouraging empowerment has been put into practice in a number of ways. The teams of production employees make their own decisions about production, manufacturing, distribution and even recruitment. When business fell away in the early 1990s, employees went out in teams to negotiate additional work with local employers, hiring themselves out for temporary periods with a continuing guarantee of a job at Rhino, helping the company to avoid making redundancies. The company makes sure that any promises it makes are always carried out in full.

Source: Flynn (1996)

The operation of HRM in practice

HRM systems and practices have replaced personnel in the majority of organisations (in title, at least). There are a number of examples of models illustrating the varying roles and styles for the operation of HR departments and practitioners and here are three of them.

Karen Legge (1978) identified three HR practitioners ('Personnel' in those days) who were seeking to develop their power within the organisation. These were the *conformist innovator,* the person who works with the conventional organisational objectives and identifies with them, and come up with initiatives that help the organisation towards achieving those objectives through cost saving, productivity increases and reducing conflict. The *deviant innovator,* on the other hand, stands somewhat aside from the conventional organisation aims and adopts an independent professional stance. The initiatives they recommend tend to be unconventional and their adoption will depend on their individual status and conviction with the results somewhat unpredictable. Subject areas here could, today, involve proposals on work-life balance, empowerment or knowledge management. Their innovative ideas, which may face considerable opposition, can provide results which lead to the organisation obtaining clear competitive advantages. The third role is that of *problem-solver,* a more conventional role, one that looks to provide day-to-day assistance to the line management.

Storey's (1992) analysis set up a grid which contrasts, on one axis, how far the work undertaken is strategic or merely tactical and, on the other axis, the degree to which the HR manager intervenes in the management process. This is shown in Figure 1.2.

Working clockwise, HR specialists who fall into the *advisor* category are those who focus on strategic issues but are not themselves responsible for carrying out the actions they recommend. *Handmaidens* are

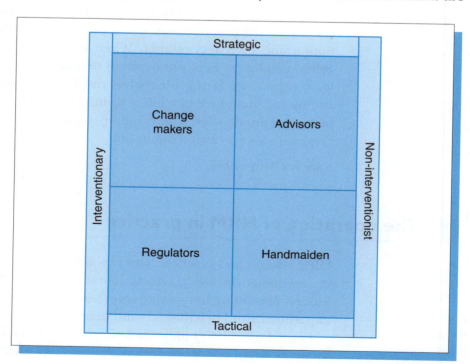

Figure 1.2
HR interventions.
(*Source:* Adapted from Storey, 1992)

those who also have little part in implementing policy but they only operate at a tactical level, dealing with administration and the provision of welfare, training and basic recruitment. *Regulators* are, again, involved only in tactical issues but they are more interventionary, trying to ensure that the HR policy is carried out properly in co-operation with line managers. The *change makers*, on the other hand, are both strategic and interventionary, concerned less with administration and more with the broader view of people management in their organisations. A change maker is expected to assess the organisation's needs, reach appropriate conclusions and then drive the required changes to completion. This is regarded, Storey indicates, as the proper role for an effective and senior HR specialist.

Ulrich (1998) followed a similar tack, but developed the model so that the x-axis measures the degree to which the HR practitioner manages the process and, on the other hand, manages the people involved, as shown in Figure 1.3.

The *administrative expert* manages the processes on a day-to-day basis, ensuring that policies on grievances, discipline, equal opportunities and incentive arrangements work effectively. This is not a role to be

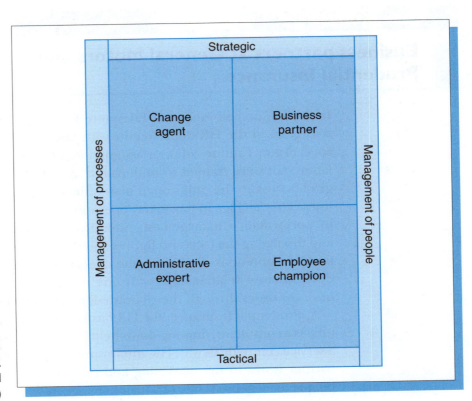

Figure 1.3
Role of HR
(*Source*: Adapted
from Ulrich, 1998)

derided because it is generally vital to the organisation's smooth running. Recognition, however, does not come easily from this role as it is only really noticed when things go wrong.

The *employee champion* acts as a voice for employees on a day-to-day basis, working for an improvement in their position, their contribution and their engagement with the organisation. This role is intended, by improving their engagement to improve their overall performance.

The *change agent* works from a strategic viewpoint attempting to ensure that employees go along with business changes, making sure that visions and values are translated into action and reality.

The *business partner*, the most senior of the roles, works with the board to ensure board strategy is developed and put into effect, identifying areas where action is required and instituting remedial initiatives.

The concept of the business partner has found many supporters in recent years, adopted by companies such as RBS, Shell and General Motors. It is interpreted in different ways but the central precept of the close relationships with business units, helping to solve practical problems and delivering real value to the organisation. Two examples are shown in Case study 1.3.

Case study 1.3

Business partners at General Motors and Prudential Insurance

In 2003, Vauxhall Motors at Ellesmere Port (part of General Motors) re-organised the HR departments with HR staff either outsourced to specialist or routine roles, or assigned to a business-focused role. The latter staff were trained to understand all aspects of the business and given a desk in the unit's open plan offices next to the car production lines. They engage in day-to-day operations, such as assisting managers in performance management, identifying training needs, coaching and discussing the facts and figures about people in her unit, their promotions, potential, disabilities and concerns. The main purpose was to develop close relationships with line managers and helping to solve business issues through their knowledge of people management.

At Prudential Insurance, the HR business partner works in a business unit as a consultant, drawing down help from centres of excellence while a service centre deals with HR administration issues. As an example, one partner works in the marketing and innovation function running the people management side of a major change initiative to improve how to deal with customer complaints. Having worked out with the unit manager what needs to be achieved, the partner pulls together an HR team for the project, uses the recommendations of the specialist HR group and co-ordinates the delivery of the project. This needs skills in relationship building and a good understanding of the business.

Source: Pickard (2004)

Purcell and Ahlstrand (1994), have taken a different approach, setting out the nine core activities that HRM departments should engage in to become fully influential in an organisation. They believe these to be applicable to most, but not all, medium to large organisations but it will depend on the nature of the business and the way the organisation in directed. Some are indisputable, such as HR planning and developing essential HR policies; others are more debatable:

- *Corporate culture and communications.* Organisations are bound together internally not just by common ownership or by everything being included on the balance sheet. Culture, 'the ways we do things around here' is difficult to define but easy to identify, especially when it is articulated well and often. It is normally up to the Chief Executive to set out or re-define the principle aspects, the philosophy, the set of values and the essential style of management but it is HR that must be responsible for championing and disseminating these cultural aspects around the organisation in an effective fashion.
- *HR planning in strategic management.* Developing a HR plan which emerges from the strategic plan is the second core activity. This is clearly a core activity but one where the link is not always made as tightly as it should be.
- *Essential policy formulation and monitoring.* Established policies and procedures remain an essential feature of an effective organisation and policies regarding the way people should act and be treated are no exception. Standards need to be set and monitored for compliance. The recognised difficulty here is striking the happy medium between a rigid bureaucratic set of procedures that deal with every eventuality but restrict innovation and empowerment and a set of vague guidelines that have many interpretations and are largely ignored.
- *'Cabinet Office' services.* This is a more unusual observation and based on the need for the Chief Executive to have advice from a trusted senior subordinate, one that is not linked to a major

department such as finance or sales which would be liable to defend their own territory and not be regarded as independent. The advice would be principally concerning the implications for staff in general, succession planning for senior executives but would also include the cultural development issues and some specific investigations set in place through issues raised by non-executive directors. This is a considerable source of power and influence for HR and emerged from their personal relationship, not from their specific position.

- *Senior management development and career planning.* This is another undisputed, important role, even when longer-term planning is more difficult to undertake. It is linked with the succession planning process and with the need to develop managers with wide experience so there is flexibility in place for strategic moves into new or existing market places.

- *External advocacy – internal advice.* As HR develop a close relationship with the Chief Executive, their 'cabinet' responsibilities may stretch to representing the organisation in the corridors of power. This is not just on local matters such as trade association committees but some political lobbying on crucial issues such as government legislation or interpretation of European directives. The internal advice is feeding matters such as this back to the executives in the organisation.

- *Information co-ordination.* This involves helping large organisations to co-ordinate necessary information across the group on pay, bargaining and general personnel statistics, such as headcount, turnover and absenteeism.

- *Internal consultancy and mediation services.* Included in this role are aspects of organisational design and learning. The introduction of competencies would be an example here.

- *HR for small units.* An extension of the internal consultancy to part of the larger group that have little or no HR presence.

Purcell and Ahlstrand (1994) recognise that this list does not indicate a comprehensive attention to all HR matters. Training, health and safety, recruitment and pay issues do not come to the fore on their own. In fact:

'Our research shows that the role and authority of corporate personnel departments is becoming more ambiguous and uncertain ... Much of the activity identified ... places a premium on political and interpersonal skills and 'corridor power'. In this situation, the authority of corporate HR staff comes more from their own expertise and style than from a clearly defined role and function. It has often been noted that HR managers need to be adept at handling ambiguity.'

Purcell and Ahlstrand (1994: p. 113)

An interesting model was developed in the Cabinet Office for reviewing the HR function in the public sector is shown in Figure 1.4.

The role of developing leadership skills is sometimes downplayed in UK writing but it is very strong in American versions of successful HRM ambitions. Rucci (1997) has set out six key requirements for HR departments to add value to the organisation and ensure its own survival:

- *Create change.* HR should move away from the control, standardisation and compliance model, and encourage the development of an organisational capability of flexibility, speed and risk-taking. This will mean eliminating unnecessary rules and giving greater emphasis to individual judgment and accountability for line managers.

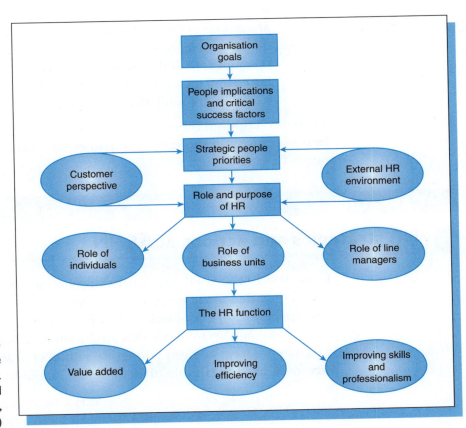

Figure 1.4
Reviewing the
HR function.
(*Source*: Adapted
from Cabinet Office,
1997)

■ *Develop principled leaders.* Top executives who ground themselves in a base of moral or ethical principles are few and far between but it is they who lead organisations to sustained long-term success. HR needs to set in motion systems to develop such talent, especially leaders who have the courage of their conviction and an unwillingness to compromise on ethical issues.

■ *Promote economic literacy.* Too much specialisation has lead to many managers not having the breadth of outlook to understand the 'big picture' within the organisation. HR should give more emphasis to ensuring managers learn all the skills and knowledge so they can contribute advice on big policy decisions.

■ *Centre on the customer.* HR should help to create boundary-less organisations where the customers' viewpoint seriously influences policy decisions and ensure that customer-directed activity is central in performance reviews, promotion criteria and reward decisions.

■ *Maximise services/Minimise staff.* HR needs to focus on its internal customers, identifying where it adds value and driving down its costs.

■ *Steward the values.* HR's role should not just be the organisation's conscience or the 'values police'. It should ensure that the values are understood and ensure that the progress is monitored and measured by embedding them in all HR activities – selection, training, performance management and reward.

These prescriptions reflect the nature of HR programmes entered into by progressive and successful companies. An example in practice is set out in Case study 1.4.

Case study 1.4

HR strategies and actions at AEHN

In the late 1990s, AEHN, an American acute care hospital was faced by what it regarded as a tumultuous and unpredictable period in its history and the new CEO undertook to transform it from one that was largely stable and complacent to one that was 'nimble, agile and change-hardy' or it may not have survived. Alongside a number of strategic changes in direction, five key HR initiatives were set in motion:

■ *Achieving contextual clarity* – AEHN went to great lengths to be quite sure that employees at all levels understood the CEO new vision for the organisation, the progress towards achieving that vision and the links between their individual and collective actions to raise organisational performance. Although using conventional methods, the messages were delivered in a fairly intense way with bulletin boards refurbished with a constant flow of relevant stories and reports, banners saying 'Are you ready for change? Are your skills ahead of the game?' and a steady flow of short courses and meetings to illuminate the organisation's progress for all to understand. Workshops included subjects such as 'survival tactics in times of change'.

- *Embedding core values* – Central to the culture change process, embedding and sustaining the set of core values became the fundamental driving force for the HR initiatives. Taken up by the top team after a year's debate, they were cascaded through the organisation with references weaved into all forms of communication and into HR practices. For example, the selection process was revised to add an assessment of applicants' core values by means of situational interviewing and the performance management scheme was heavily revamped to focus on behavioural manifestations of the values.

- *Enriching work* – a number of work redesign experiments were started to encourage much greater flexibility and empowerment. A position called Patient Care Associate was created to administer tests, take blood and do other duties that previously had been carried out by specialists; staff moved much more around units to fill gaps and to broaden perspectives and encourage social networks; self-managed teams were created to provide 'seamless, patient-focused care'.

- *Promoting personal growth* – employees were encouraged to take responsibility for their personal growth to help them perform better and be prepared for promotions. This was helped by the introduction of 360 degree feedback which generated more convincing reasons for personal development and change. Alongside this, there was an agreed policy of zero tolerance of employees who failed to pursue and eventually succeed in needed development.

- *Providing commensurate returns* – Not a great deal could be done on substantially improving salaries so the programme concentrated on non-financial benefits. The work enrichment was one important step and the 'Recognise, Appreciate, Celebrate' initiative as another. Staff received 'pat on the back notices' and a 'celebration of a risk taken award' (given for a good effort irrespective of result).

These initiatives were business-based and fitted together well so employees were able to understand both why the changes were necessary and also to see them as a coherent set which would benefit the patients, the staff and the organisation.

Source: Shafer *et al.* (2001)

Contradiction in the models

It is recognised widely that models, such as Ulrich's, do not paint a perfect picture of an ideal world of HR. There are some inherent contradictions which still need to be considered and clarified. For example, there is an emphasis on teamworking in most models. As set out in more detail in Chapter 6, the influence of technology and the need for co-operation and commitment in complex processes has made effective teamworking an essential ingredient of a high-performance organisation. Yet, alongside this in the HRM model, is the prescription of performance-related pay, which is overwhelmingly paid out on an individual basis.

The role of the HR specialist is similarly struck by ambiguity. If they are the professional advisers who stand back from the day-to-day personnel activities, such as recruitment and discipline, giving advice and counselling, how will they develop their skills in these areas to be able to give the advice? If they can do the job better, will not the hard-pressed line management want to 'dump' these activities back on HR?

Taking this form of empowerment further, there has been doubts expressed as to whether employees will perform better in organisations where this process has meant an overload of work and responsibility. This part of the model is seen as a covert way to save a great deal of money at the expense of an employee's health.

Furthermore, a unitarist viewpoint (see Chapter 7) is fine when the business is expanding as most employees can see the benefits of achieving the HR plans. But when difficulties occur which lead to massive job changes, re-location and redundancies, then it is difficult to act convincingly towards those employees who will lose out by these changes and convince them that their interests are identical to that of the organisation's. Even when business is on an even keel, it is sometimes difficult to reconcile the emphasis of individual development through empowerment and learning contracts (See Chapter 10) and the need to have a unitarist approach. Where there is a variety of individual developments, there is more likely to be a variety of different views, ideals and objectives.

Practitioners have also found Rucci's advice on reducing their own costs and staff difficult to stomach, especially where he places such great emphasis on simplifying standardisation and moving away from compliance. How can HR maintain the organisation's values and provide ethical leadership if there is no strict control over compliance in areas such as equal opportunities and grievance procedures?

The differing approaches to HRM are shown in both of the Focus on research 1.1, which examines strategic involvement, business contribution and devolvement to the line.

Focus on research 1.1

A Chameleon function – HRM in the 1990s

A 5-year longitudinal study was carried out in the UK in the early 1990s using evidence from eight large organisations, including Glaxo PLC, Lloyds Bank and a NHS Trust. Detailed audits of their HR practices in one business or region were carried out, including a review of how their policies and procedures were conducted in practice. Data was gathered from focus groups, semi-structured interviews and questionnaires.

The findings concerned three main areas. HR involvement in strategic decision taking was strong at the divisional level but weak at the overall group level. Integration of HR practices with strategic direction occurred through personal influence of the HR management with their senior operational managers in an interactive, emergent and informal fashion. HR contribution to business performance was difficult to measure as each organisation had a mantra that 'people were the source of competitive performance' but there was an increasing awareness of this mantra throughout the organisations and understanding that some purposeful management of people needs to be designed and enacted by line management. There was strong evidence that HR generalist staff were being moved out of the central function to the business units with devolvement of responsibility to the line. Line management had much more control over HR decisions and budgets. Where HR performed the role of an adviser/coach well, then they were less regarded as a rule enforcer.

Source: Hope-Hailey *et al.* (1997)

The role of HR in raising performance

Although there may be considerable doubt concerning the actual role HR should perform and how it should be done, HR established a place at the senior management table by the early 1990s through their ability to identify and solve practical problems in fields such as recruitment, employee relations and training. HR professionals and researchers then turned their attention to interpreting and reinforcing the maxim that '*people make the difference*'. This has been approached in three different ways:

- Firstly, researchers have attempted to identify whether adopting HR practices can make an observable difference in practice to organisational performance in measurable terms. This has often been referred to as '*opening the black box*'.
- Secondly, a number of projects have been set up to examine what makes up a truly exceptional collection of HR practices, often called '*bundles*' that raises performance in the organisation.
- Thirdly, there has been a considerable debate, one that is still very much alive, as to whether such a collection of practices (called '*best practices*') will work in every situation, or whether the context and nature of the organisation puts different demands upon the practices to be operated (called '*best fit*').

Opening the 'Black box'

In attempting to examine the impact of HR practices on organisational performance, a number of researchers have discovered some impressive and direct impacts and influences. This is referred to by Ramsey *et al.* (2000) as 'the 'high road' approach to management, in which organisations choose to compete primarily on quality and rely especially on HR development and employee contributions to succeed in this (p. 502)'.

Much of this research has been carried out in America, with the best-known being Huselid (1995). He carried out in-depth surveys in top companies, matching the nature of the HR practices against performance measures, such as growth, productivity and profits. Using market value as the key indicator, he found that organisations with significantly above-average scores on using HR practices provided an extra market value per employee of between £10,000 and £40,000. He also found that the introduction of such practices lead to an immediate impact (Guest, 1998).

In the UK, a CIPD-financed project by the University of Sheffield's Institute of Work Psychology (West and Patterson, 1998) concluded that HR practices are not only critical to business performance but also have a greater importance than an emphasis on quality, technology and R&D in terms of influence on bottom-line profits. For example, effective HR practices were found to account for 19% of the variation in profitability and 18% in productivity while R&D accounted for only 8%. This led them to conclude that if managers wish to influence performance of their companies, the most important area they should emphasise is the management of people.

Patterson and his colleagues were studying a group of small- and medium-sized companies and an example of the type of practices implemented in the most successful company of the group (Zotefoams) is shown in Case study 1.5.

Case study 1.5

Zotefoams' HR practices

Zotefoams achieved the highest profits and productivity of all the companies taking part in the University of Sheffield research, resulting from a heavy investment in unlocking the employee potential, especially on the shop floor. Their HR practices included empowering the employees to determine work priorities, deal with quality issues and solve day-to-day problems. To support these changes, 75% of employees have received problem-solving training, flexibility is achieved through the extensive use of National Vocational Qualifications (NVQs) and developing skills are rewarded through skills-based pay. Team ethos has been promoted through a benefits harmonisation programme together with employee share options and profit-sharing schemes.

Source: West and Patterson (1998)

Some of these findings have arisen from broad surveys across sectors and others from selected industries. Thompson (2000), for example, investigated 400 UK aerospace companies and concluded that high-performing organisation, as measured by value added per employee, tend to use a wider range of innovative HR practices covering a higher proportion of employees. The greatest differentials between higher- and lower-performing organisations (as measured by value added per employee) was in the use of two way communication systems, broader job gradings and employees being responsible for their own quality.

'Bundles' of HR practices

At the same time that researchers were attempting to prove conclusively that successful and effective HR practices improved the bottom line performance, it became clear that a differentiation needed to be made between such practices: in effect, that some worked better than others and, more critically, that although individual practices may be relatively unsuccessful, when brought together in a 'bundle' their combined outcome was much greater than their individual contribution. A number of writers have formulated these bundles into what they call a system of 'High Performance' or 'High Commitment', indicating that using the full set will inevitably lead to improved organisational improvement. It is emphasised by all the researchers that these bundles have to be coherent and integrated to have their full effect with Wood (1995) explaining that 'it is through the combined effects of such practices that management can most hope to elicit high levels of commitment' (p. 52).

The *level of commitment* shown by employees is seen as key to high performance. Without such a commitment, employees will not be prepared to develop their skills and competencies, take on board the enhanced responsibilities for quality, work organisation and problem solving, and 'go the extra mile' to come up with improvements and innovations or improve the customer's experience. That is why a number of researchers use the level of commitment as a key reflection of organisational success from a people management viewpoint.

For Purcell *et al.* (2003), a committed employee will use discretionary behaviour in that the employee can give co-operation, effort and initiative because they want to, arising out of the fact that they like their job and feel motivated by the systems in place, especially the HR ones.

Researchers have found that a high level of commitment comes about from the implementation of the following HR practices:

Employee involvement

The importance of involvement is explained more fully in Chapter 7, but the basic thinking is that it is impossible to gain the employees' trust if they do not both have the essential business information available to management and that they have at least the opportunity to be consulted on important issues that may affect their jobs and the way they are carried out. This passes the message that employees are treated as mature, intelligent beings, not just 'hands' or 'labour' who leave their brains in their lockers. There is a willingness, in fact a concerted effort, to involve employees in resolving work-based problems. The process of involvement can include briefing groups, staff surveys, focus groups or more sophisticated systems such as Quality Circles or recognition schemes. It can also extend to financial involvement through employee share-ownership. Marchington (2001) points out from his research that these practices are very popular with employees (80–85% of employees involved in such practices want them to continue), although he adds the disillusioning caveat that some employees enjoy working with them because it is 'better than working' or 'gives me a half hour off work'!

Employee voice

Millward *et al.* (2000), by using the data from the 1998 WERS, have shown the close association between positive responses in attitude surveys and direct voice arrangement. A 'voice' for the employees does not have to be through a formal trade union and it is certainly not just ensuring there is a formal grievance procedure. It can be through a works council or a staff representative committee working in a non-union environment. The importance of this practice is that the employer recognises the importance of employee group viewpoints and suggestions and that the employee does not feel isolated so important issues can be raised in a formal (or informal) setting without the employee themselves having to, in effect, raise their heads above the parapet.

Harmonisation of terms and conditions

'Everybody works for the same team' is a common form of encouragement from senior management but falls on deaf ears if there is a clear manifestation of differing benefits at varying levels in the organisation. When Japanese companies began setting up satellite operations in the UK in the late 1970s and early 1980s, one of the surprises to commentators was the degree of egalitarian symbols on display. In Nissan in Sunderland, for example, there was one canteen serving everybody and it was frequented by all staff including senior management; everybody was on the same level of holiday entitlement and wore the same overalls. Of the expected managerial hierarchy, there were few overt signs, although they were inevitable within the background culture. Employees, however, respected the equality and it fed the belief in the 'one company' ethos leading in turn to effective team working at all levels (Wickens, 1987).

Employment security

The 'jobs for life' culture evident some 30 to 40 years ago no longer exists. Rather, it never really existed in the first place, except in pockets of the public services, such as prisons and the Post Office. Even in the large banks and multi-national corporations, employees may have had a clear, well-trodden career pathway set out, but the precise directions, both geographically and occupationally, may have worked out very differently to expectations and preferences. In the last 20 years, the global and business environmental changes have caused such changes in employment that the pathway has become one made up of crazy paving and employees have to lay it themselves!

So how can any business promise employment security? The theorists indicate that the security is of a different dimension. There may be short-term guarantees of employment, such as 12 months or of the life of a large-scale contract or, more usually, it is the cultural imperative of the organisation that redundancies will only take place as a very last resort. Internal transfers, skills re-training, short-time working will all be alternatives to try to extend the employee's contract as long as possible to get over difficult times. It is, in effect, the opposite of the tough employer's 'high and fire' short-term employment policy. It keeps to the HRM thinking that the employee is a critical asset, not a cost to be reduced.

Alongside these practices to encourage commitment, there are a group of practices that integrate with the *organisation's business strategy*.

Sophisticated recruitment and selection

The essence of what 'sophisticated' means in this context will be explained in Chapters 2, 4 and 5. It is essentially the combination of recognising the importance of bringing into the organisation the right people with the right skills and personality (having a strategic approach to HR planning), and carrying out careful and detailed recruitment and selection procedures. These procedures especially refer to using psychological tests and structured interviews that match people effectively to the organisational culture, to the job and the team requirements. It is also associated with using the latest technology such as on-line recruitment.

Extensive training and development

It is clearly not enough to select the right people, as will be set out in Chapter 10. In the swiftly changing world, employees need to constantly learn new jobs, which involves developing their skills and knowledge. They must also be prepared for enlargement of their jobs and to be ready for promotion opportunities. The emphasis switches in a subtle way from the organisation organising training courses to the organisation encouraging employees (individually or in groups) to undertake learning experiences, which can take many forms. As employees take greater control over their own learning, their level of commitment is likely to rise. The 'ideal' form of this item in the bundle is of employees undertaking self-directed life-long learning with the framework of a 'learning organisation' as explained in Chapter 10.

Self-managed teams

The practice of allowing teams to have greater control over their work is a relatively recent one, although theorists, such as Mayo and his colleagues at the Hawthorne production plant in America in the 1930s, have been advocating it throughout the twentieth century. It is linked closely to involvement and, in a fully fledged system, team members are involved in decisions concerning work rotas, breaks, changes in production processes, leave and sickness arrangements. Moreover, they are encouraged to think about and promote local improvements on an individual and team basis. It is quite an adventurous concept because it involves reducing the power and day-to-day authority of local management, but, at the same time, retains their accountability. It requires very careful training and monitoring for all parties concerned but the research has shown that, when it works well, it is closely associated with high productivity and overall performance. Geary and Dobbins (2001) study of a pharmaceutical company found that:

> 'For some employees who had enjoyed little autonomy (previously), the extension in their discretion made a substantial positive impression in their sense of achievement and job satisfaction' (p. 17).

Extensive systems of flexibility

If constant and rapid change is the norm, then successful organisations need a workforce that is flexible enough to respond quickly to the required changes. They need to be multi-skilled, willing to work hours that suit the customer (such as over a 24 hour cycle in supermarket retailing) and willing to switch jobs and locations when necessary. The organisation also needs to have in place facilities to increase and reduce the employee numbers when required through systems of annualised hours or use of temporary and short-term contracts or by outsourcing work. More details are given of these systems in Chapter 6 which shows examples of how such practices can lead to improved performance.

Performance pay

The emphasis on high-performance outcomes inevitably has meant that pay systems are geared to reflect the level of performance. Employees' pay at all levels is contingent; in other words, it has an element that varies depending on the success of the outcomes. Examples of these systems can include bonus schemes for production employees and call centre staff, performance related pay for managers and administrative staff, incentive systems for sales and service staff, and executive bonuses for directors. Commitment should be encouraged by aligning the pay of employees with organisational performance, through share options, profit sharing and gainsharing. Details of all these systems, and the associated performance management processes that must support them, are set out in Chapters 8 and 9.

Figure 1.5 summarises the identification of high-performance HR practices as reported by a number of researchers.

Each of the research studies indicate additional practices that they regard as 'high performance'. For example, in the EEF/CIPD study, the list includes comprehensive induction, coherent performance management systems with wide coverage, job variety and responsibility, use of quality improvement teams, market competitive pay and policies to achieve an appropriate work-life balance. The US Department of Labour study adds a focus on the customer and developing measures of success while West and Patterson stress the need for 'favourable' reward systems and job systems that promote problem solving.

Given that a bundle of HR practices leads to improved performance, then it follows that using this bundle is the best thing to do. In theory, it becomes a set of 'best practices' which can be universally applied.

Best practice or best fit?

When reading the previous section and looking at Figure 1.5 it may have occurred to you that there does not appear to be much consensus as to what HR practices make up the full set. Each item of research comes up with a different set of best practices, some of which overlap with other research but each has a special leaning. In America, Boselie and Dietz (2003) have reviewed 10 years of research in this area and have found little that recommends a common approach although the practices reported more extensively were training and development, participation and empowerment, performance pay and information sharing through involvement.

As the extensive research reveals such a varied set of bundles, considerable doubt has been shed on whether the application of the set of bundles or best practices will lead inevitably to improved performance. Many writers, therefore, have taken an alternative view that there is no 'holy grail' of practices which will magically improve organisational performance. What works well in one organisation may fail dismally in another where the context may be totally different. In a private sector organisation (e.g. a manufacturing company), you may well expect performance pay to be widespread and to form the bulwark of

	Pfeffer (1998)	US department of labour (1998)	West and Patterson (1998)	EEF/CIPD (2003)	Wood and Albanese (1995)
Employee involvement	X		X		X
Employee voice	X				
Harmonisation	X		X	X	X
Security of employment	X				X
Sophisticated selection	X		X	X	X
Extensive training/ development	X	X	X	X	X
Self-managed teams	X	X	X	X	X
Extensive flexibility			X	X	X
Performance pay	X			X	X

Figure 1.5
HR practices associated with high-performance organisations

performance management and motivation systems; however, in the voluntary sector (e.g. a hospice charity), it is highly unlikely that any of the staff would work under a performance pay scheme. The context, the vision, the values – they are so different.

Huselid himself comes down firmly on the side of a range of possible bundles, based on the reasoning that sustained competitive advantage depends partly on being able to develop arrangements that are hard to imitate. If the 'holy grail' was quite distinctive, then every organisation would immediately adopt it and the competitive advantage would be lost. He calls the practices that would work for the organisation in question to be a set of 'idiosyncratic contingencies', those that happen to fit well into the specific strategy and culture of the organisation (Guest, 1998).

Thompson (2000), similarly, is reticent in recommending wholesale adoption of the innovative HR practices associated with high-performing aerospace companies:

> 'That is probably too simplistic a message… There is certainly a risk in encouraging businesses to adopt particular sets of working practices if they are not ready for them or if they do not fit with existing strategies' (p. 19).

Purcell (1999) is even more dismissive, claiming that:

> 'The search for bundles of high-commitment work practices is important, but so too is the search for understanding of the circumstances of where and when it is applied, why some organisations do and others do not adopt HRM, and how some firms seem to have more appropriate HR systems for their current and future needs than others… Our concern should be less about the precise policy mix in the bundle and more on how and when organisations manage the HR side of change' (pp. 36–37).

Marchington and Grugulis (2000) adopt the same viewpoint:

> 'Best practice, it seems, is problematic. When unpacked, the practices are much less 'best' than they might be hoped, there are times when they appear to be contradictory messages, they are not universally applicable and they tend to ignore any active input from employees' (p. 1121).

How do you know which HR practices an organisation should adopt? Only by a combination of knowing and understanding the true nature, and strengths of the organisation, so you can eliminate those practices that have little chance of success, and then by experiment.

For Claridges, the luxury hotel, the bundle of HR practices that supported their turnaround strategy was quite specific to their unique context, as shown in Case study 1.6.

Case study 1.6

HR initiatives supporting Claridges' turnaround

In 1998, Claridges, the luxury hotel group, was battling to maintain its place in the market with occupancy down, complaints up and 73% staff turnover rate. The staff satisfaction survey was returned by only 47% of staff, indicating widespread distrust of management and only 67% said they felt proud to work for the hotel. The response by senior management was to create a transformation, putting employees' attitudes and performance with customers at the top of the list. This was encapsulated in the new core values:

Passion, team spirit, service perfection, responsibility for actions, communication, interpersonal relations and maximising resources.

The aim was to embed these new values, through lively, participative and sometimes amusing training, involving acting out sketches indicating the working of the new core values which became memorable 'events'.

The main elements of the HR initiatives included a new *reward and recognition scheme*, where staff who demonstrated excellence in implementing the new values would have the chance to win prizes ranging from a limo home to an overnight stay in the penthouse (worth up to £4000). The new *performance management scheme* was based on measuring the employee's contribution to the new values with individual and general training based on the gaps that the PM scheme identifies. Sideways experience is encouraged with staff receiving *training in a collection of different skills. Internal promotion* is now much more common with a natural progression from kitchen porter up to waiter and beyond. The *quarterly newsletter* and staff surveys attempt to enhance the communication quality and draw the teams together.

Within 3 years, the staff turnover had dropped to 27% and pride in working for the organisation increased to 99%, as shown by the 100% staff return on the survey, a sure indication that trust in management had returned.

Source: Edwards (2004)

In the knowledge-intensive firms, the best fit of practices have been found to be the kind that develops intellectual and social capital needed in order to acquire business and manager customer relationships. Here, the crucial aspect is the development of knowledge-sharing processes, not just the knowledge and skills of the workforce (Swart *et al.*, 2003).

Purcell's (1999) distinct preference for 'best fit' has led him to urge a much greater emphasis on sharing employee knowledge throughout the organisation. If organisations have unique circumstances that require unique sets of HRM practices, then it is vital that the knowledge and understanding of both circumstances and practices are held in common by all employees:

> 'The key point about those firms which adopt high-commitment management successfully and adopt it to their unique circumstances is that this codified knowledge, this ability in the passing game, has to be shared among core members of the organisation. If the organisation is to…keep on managing the transition from the current to the future state and avoid sharp punctuated change, then roles become diffuse and 'belonging' becomes important' (p. 37).

Although there appears to be extensive evidence of HR practices adding to organisational improvement, there are a number of critics who doubt the close association. The greatest is Legge (2001) whose scepticism has been consistent and vociferous for many years. She points out the vagueness of definition of the 'best practice', such as performance pay, and the appropriateness of the measures used for organisational success. She also doubts whether the use of the practices actually influence the performance (the lack of causality).

There have also been studies that demonstrate that HRM practices can lead to a deterioration in working life. Danford *et al.* (2004) researched the high-performance HR practices introduced in an aerospace company but found some major negative impacts on the employees, such as substantial downsizing, a superficial implementation of empowerment and a lack of trust between the parties.

Resource-based view of the organisation

Alongside these investigations, theories have been developed regarding the nature of HR whereby they can be regarded as uniquely valuable to the organisation because they are a collection of assets (skills, competencies and experience), that are much more difficult to imitate or replicate, unlike other conventional assets such as land or capital. This is associated with the resource-based view (RBV) of the organisation where competitive advantage is associated with four key attributes – value, rarity, a lack of substitutes and difficult to imitate.

- ■ HR are seen to be *valuable*, looking at employees of football teams, for example, the very skilled ones are certainly seen to be extremely valuable and some senior executives transfer to new organisations with an upfront payment. The cost of replacing employees who leave organisations is often high, especially if they are experienced and are seen by customers as important. As explained by Boxall and Purcell (2003):

'(organisations) can never entirely capture what individual … (employees) know. Some of what we know – including many of our best skills – cannot be reduced to writing or to formulas. When we leave the firm, we take this knowledge with us. When whole teams leave … the effects can be devastating' (p. 83).

- ■ *Rarity* is associated with the value as there will always be a labour group which is in short supply. IT staff in the 1980s and 1990s, nurses and teachers in the early 2000s, plumbers most of the time. Organisations that have a steady supply of skills in short supply will have a competitive advantage.
- ■ It is possible to *substitute for labour*, through automated call centres and production lines but those organisations that possess skilled employees where such substitution is impossible (most service organisations, consultancies, etc.), should be able to gain an advantage. It has been argued that the UK's competitive advantage has been maintained because of our very large service sector whereas Germany's large manufacturing sector has been constantly chipped away by international competition and automation.
- ■ Similarly, it is difficult to *imitate* the skilled work of employees. Cheaper versions of services can be available (self-service in restaurants) but the market for high-quality service by skilled employees is normally in a state of constant growth.

Having recognised the importance of people as a resource, it provides encouragement to employers to identify and then improve the quality of their 'Human Capital'. In terms of identification, the CIPD (Brown,

2003) put forward a proposal in the form of a framework so organisations could report on the way that they:

- Acquire and retain staff, explaining how the firm sources its supply, the composition of the workforce in terms of diversity and employment relationships and its retention policies.
- Develop staff, including details of skill levels and development strategies.
- Motivate, involve and communicate with employees.
- Account for the value created by employees including how they manage the bank of employee knowledge and the methods of determining team and individual performance.

An example of this approach at RBS is shown in Case study 1.7.

Case study 1.7

Accounting for people at RBS

As part of its vision for the future, RBS has set a goal of being the 'most admired bank' in the world. The board have accepted that the contribution made by its 115,000 individual employees around the world will be vital in achieving this accolade and have set up a system of monthly reporting on a range of people-based information. These include conventional measures such as labour turnover, absence and labour costs against targets but additional features include an analysis of answers provided in a series of regular surveys. There are employee opinion surveys, joiners and leavers surveys and irregular 'pulse' surveys. This information is combined with measures of organisation performance, such as customer service and business centre profitability to obtain overall figures on employee performance.

All of this information is used for two purposes. Firstly, to monitor the performance of staff and secondly to measure the degree of staff engagement which RBS regards as crucial to the health of the organisation. It sees engagement as measuring how much employees 'want to and actually do improve our business results' and is a much more focused measure than employee satisfaction or commitment. 'Engaged' employees are likely to be those that:

- Consistently speak positively about RBS to their colleagues, potential employees and customers.

■ Have an intense desire to remain a member of the RBS group.

■ Put in extra effort and engage in behaviours that contribute to business success.

RBS sees the role of HR to improve these people measures through initiatives that support the business plan and raise the engagement level of employees.

Evidence of using the system has shown that there is a positive correlation between increased engagement and rising productivity and a negative correlation between increased engagement and staff turnover. All the data gathered is utilised in a joined-up way, flagging up trends and issues that need attention.

The model for RBS is about influencing the future performance of the organisation, allowing the group to demonstrate a link between its people, the factors influencing their engagement and business performance.

Source: IDS (2004)

Barriers to high performance

Finally in this section, a quick look at research that identifies how HR practices are not easily implemented. Kim and Mauborgne (2003) from Boston Consulting group, in a study of 125 US companies, have identified four main hurdles that consistently prevent HR professionals from effecting high performance, as shown in Figure 1.6. Although the prescription applies to any change process, the perceived lack of natural influence of HR practitioners makes the prognosis more compelling in terms of HR processes improving overall performance.

Barrier	How to overcome barrier
Cognitive hurdle – managers cannot see that radical change is required	Pointing out the numbers is insufficient. Managers need to be put face to face with the problems – with dissatisfied employees or customers.
Resource hurdle – insufficient resources available to implement the practice successfully	Reduce HR resources that are not adding value (cold spots) and transfer resource to those practices which have a high potential performance gain (hot spots).
Motivational hurdle – that discourages and demoralises staff	Work on the major influencers, the champions of change. Bring problems out into the open and ensure everybody follows the improving story line.
Political handle – that brings internal and external resistance to change	Identify and silence internal opponents by building alliances with natural allies. Isolate external opponents.

Figure 1.6
Barriers to high performance (*Source*: Kim and Mauborgne, 2003)

Auditing and benchmarking HR performance

Having established the role and operation requirements of the HR function, it is wise to carry out a regular evaluation of its effectiveness. As we have seen, the ultimate test is whether it contributes to the achievement of organisational business objectives and this can be measured internally, albeit in a subjective format. An alternative external method is by benchmarking, that is by comparing the overall performance with broadly similar organisations and departments which has six main stages (see Figure 1.7).

By carrying out each of these stages, a thorough analysis is completed for the activity being considered. A practical example is shown in Case study 1.8.

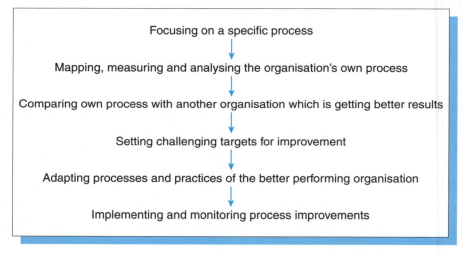

Focusing on a specific process

Mapping, measuring and analysing the organisation's own process

Comparing own process with another organisation which is getting better results

Setting challenging targets for improvement

Adapting processes and practices of the better performing organisation

Implementing and monitoring process improvements

Figure 1.7
Benchmarking
process

Case study 1.8

Benchmarking internal vacancy filling at the Employment Service

In 1996, the Employment Service decided to benchmark their internal vacancy filling process, the specific objective being to achieve a radical reduction in the time taken from the notification of a vacancy to the post being filled, which currently took 12 weeks. The benchmarking took place against 44 other organisations who were sent a questionnaire relating to the vacancy filling process and the individual times taken at specific stages. From the answers, five organisations were chosen for follow-up visits. The team also decided to encourage radical thinking by exploring processes that had parallels with vacancy filling. Following a brain-storming session, the team chose shelf filing in a supermarket as an 'off-the-wall' comparison process.

As a result of studying the existing process closely, exploring parallel processes and benchmarking, the team were able to reduce the overall vacancy-filling average to 8 weeks, an improvement of 33%. A number of specific changes were made, including:

- Using IT to facilitate same day dispatch of advertisements.
- Including the date of interview in the advertisement.
- Streamlining the interface of personnel and line management in the sifting and interview process.

Source: Employment Service – internal research

Benchmarking can also take place against the whole HR function. This can be a mix of quantitative and qualitative measures, as shown in BP Chemicals project (see Case study 1.9) which can lead to a wholesale change in the way the department is organised and focused.

Case study 1.9

Identifying 'Best-in-class' HR operations at BP

In the early 1990s, BP Chemicals Hull manufacturing and Research site conducted an in-depth benchmarking study aimed at identifying 'best-in-class' chemicals manufacturing management worldwide. Arising from this highly influential process, it was considered that the HR team had to change its ethos, attempting to transform itself from a functionally-based organisation to one focused on high-quality service provision. This change required not just the normal internal assessment but by focusing on best practice outside the organisation.

This comparison took three routes. Firstly, a list of comparable performance measures which included:

- HR staff as a ratio of total employees.
- Training days per head.
- Trainers as a proportion of total employees.
- Training spend per head.
- Absence rate.

- Staff turnover rate.
- Dismissal rate.
- Tribunal rate.

On comparison with 10 other similar organisations, it was found that BP sat firmly in the middle of the measures, both positive (such as training days) and negative (dismissal rate). However, some of these measures were crude and mechanistic and only provided a one-dimensional view of performance. So the second route was to select a number of 'activity drivers' which assessed the extent to which an organisation's current priorities in turn generated work for the HR function. These included unionisation, age profile, growth rate and staff development culture. Discussions took place with comparable organisations as to the implications of these activity drivers and the way the HR department worked and the drivers were further refined as the discussions developed. The final route was to interview selection of employees for their views on the operations of the HR department, where some honest insights revealed gaps and misunderstandings.

The outcome of the exercise was to identify features of what was regarded as 'best practice' for HR operations and the key messages were:

- The best HR functions had already become client-focused, while managing to retain functional expertise.
- Teamwork and flexibility was regarded as vital in coping with the large peaks inherent in any HR function.
- They generally had smaller corporate HR functions.
- Business objectives were clearly spelt out and understood by the workforce.
- There was a strong commitment to training and many had transformed their reward system to be competency rather than performance based.
- Much traditional HR activity had been devolved to line management so HR staff had to tolerate and manage diversity.
- Great efforts were made to simplify HR systems, making them more relevant to business needs.

Many changes were made arising from this exercise, including changing HR from the role of gatekeeper to that of coach and making substantial moves in the area of devolving HR to line management.

Source: Holt (1994)

Summary

■ Recent world-wide economic and social developments have brought closer the impact of the global economy, dependent largely on the skills, initiatives and abilities of employees.

■ HR have had many different roles in the past but the major role today is to initiate change in employment practices that support the successful operations of the organisation.

■ There is a major role for HR in improving organisational performance through identifying ways that bring out the best performance in individuals and teams.

■ There is considerable debate as to whether there are a set of 'best practices' that can be applied universally or whether it requires a different set of practices which 'fit' the organisation's culture and context.

Student activities

1   Compare and contrast the HR profession with that of law and medicine in respect of characteristics such as professional knowledge, ethical considerations, local expertise required, status in the organisation and views of the general public.

2   Set out some of the opportunities presented to Sarah in the Meteor case study. How would she best take advantage of them?

3   If you were an employee of Rhino Foods (Case study 1.2), suggest ways that you would expect the organisation to put into practice its espoused aims regarding its employees.

4   The move to devolve HRM to line managers has advantages and difficulties. Set out a case for and against in the example of recruitment and selection.

5   Read the BP article and consider how valuable the benchmarking process was in practice.

6   How would you best sell the HR function to the rest of the organisation?

References

Beer, M., Spector, B., Lawrence, P., Quinn Mills, P., Walton, R. (1984) *Managing Human Assets*. The Free Press.

Boselie, P., Dietz, G. (2003) *Commonalities and Contradictions in Research on Human Resource Management and Performance.* Paper presented at the Academy of Management Seattle, 2003.

Boxall, P., Purcell, J. (2003) *Strategy and Human Resource Management.* Palgrave.

Brown, D. (2003) A capital idea. *People Management,* 26 June, 42–46.

Cabinet Office (1997) *Consortium Project – The Changing Role of the Human Resource Function.* Cabinet Office.

Cully, M., O'Reilly, A., Millward, N., Forth, J., Woodland, S., Dix, G., Bryson, A. (1999) *The 1998 Workplace Employee Relations Survey – First Findings.* DTI.

Danford, A., Richardson, M., Stewart, P., Tailby, S., Upchurch, M. (2004) High performance work systems and workplace partnership: a case study of aerospace workers. *New technology, Work and Employment,* **19**(1): 14–29.

Edwards, C. (2004) Five-star strategy. *People Management,* 8 April, 34–35.

EEF/CIPD (2003) *Maximising Employee Potential and Business Performance: The Role of High Performance Working.* EEF/CIPD.

Flannery, T., Hofrichter, D., Platten, P. (1996) *People, Performance and Pay.* The Free Press.

Flynn, G. (1996) Why Rhino won't wait until tomorrow. *Personnel Journal,* July, 37–40.

Geary, J., Dobbins, A. (2001) Teamworking: a new dynamic in the pursuit of management control. *Human Resource Management Journal,* **11**(1): 2–23.

Guest, D., Conway, N., Briner, R., Dickman, M. (1996). *The State of the Psychological Contract in Employment. Issues in People Management* No. 16. IPD.

Guest, D. (1989) Personnel and HRM: can you tell the difference? *Personnel Management,* January, 48–51.

Guest, D. (1998) Combine harvest. *People Management,* 29 October, 64–66.

Hamel, G., Prahalad, C. (1994) *Competing for the Future.* Harvard Business Press.

Handy, C. (1994) *The Age of Paradox.* Harvard Business School Press.

Holt, B. (1994) Benchmarking comes to HR. *Personnel Management,* October, 32–35.

Hope-Hailey, V., Styles, P., Truss, C. (1997) A Chameleon function: HRM in the 1990s. *Human Resource Management Journal,* **7**(3): 5–18.

Huselid, M. (1995) The impact of human resource management practices on turnover, productivity and corporate financial performance. *Academy of Management Journal,* **38**: 400–422.

IDS (2004) The Royal Bank of Scotland group. *HR Studies Update 769,* March, 14–17.

IPD (1999). *Petition to the Privy Council.*

Kim, W., Mauborgne, R. (2003) Tipped for the top. *People Management,* 24 July, 26–31.

Legge, K. (2001) Silver bullet or spent round? Assessing the meaning of the 'high commitment management/performance relationship. In: Storey, J. (ed.). *Human Resource Management: A Critical Text.* Thomson Learning.

Marchington, M. (2001) Employee involvement at work. In: Storey, J. (ed.). *Human Resource Management: A Critical Text.* Thomson Learning.

Marchington, M., Grugulis, I. (2000) 'Best Practice' human resource management: perfect opportunity or dangerous illusion? *International Journal of Human Resource Management,* **11**(6): 1104–1124.

Millward, N., Bryson, A., Forth, J. (2000) *All Change at Work: British Employment Relations 1980 to 1998 as portrayed by the Workplace Industrial Relations Survey Series.* Routledge.

Pfeffer, J. (1998) *The Human Equation.* Harvard Business School Press.

Pickard, J. (2004) One step beyond. *People Management,* 30 June, 27–31.

Purcell, J. (1999) Best practice and best fit: chimera or cul-de-sac? *Human Resource Management Journal,* **9**(3): 26–41.

Purcell, J., Ahlstrand, B. (1994). *Human Resource Management in the Multi-Divisional Company.* Oxford University Press.

Purcell, J., Kinnie, N., Hutchinson, S. (2003) Open minded. *People Management,* 15 May, 30–33.

Ramsey, H., Scholarios, D., Harley, B. (2000) Employees and high performance work systems: testing inside the Black Box. *British Journal of Industrial Relations,* **38**(4): 501–531.

Rucci, A. (1997) Should HR survive? A profession at the Crossroads. *Human Resource Management,* **36**(1): 169–173.

Shafer, R., Dyer, L., Kilty, J., Amos, J., Ericksen, J. (2001) Crafting a human resource strategy to foster organisational agility. *Human Resource Management,* **40**(3): 197–211.

Storey, J. (1992) *Developments in the Management of Human Resources.* Blackwell.

Swart, J., Kinnie, N., Purcell, J. (2003) *People and Performance in Knowledge-intensive Firms,* CIPD.

Thompson, M. (2000) *The Competitiveness Challenge: Final report: The Bottom Line Benefits of Strategic Human Resource Management.* Society of British Aerospace Companies.

Torrington, D., Hall, L., Taylor, S. (2002) *Human Resource Management,* 5th edition. Financial Times Prentice Hall.

US Department of Labor (1998) *Government as a High-Performance Employer,* SCANS Report for America 2000.

Ulrich, D. (1998) *Human Resource Champions: the Next Agenda for Adding value and Delivering Results.* Harvard Business School Press.

West, M., Patterson, M. (1998) Profitable personnel. *People Management,* 8 January, 28–31.

Wickens, P. (1987) *The Road to Nissan: Flexibility, quality, teamwork,* Macmillan.

Wood, S. (1995) The four pillars of human resource management: are they connected? *Human Resource Management Journal,* **5**(5): 49–59.

Wood, S., Albanese, M. (1995) Can we speak of a high commitment management on the shop floor? *Journal of Management,* **32**(2): 1–33.

Further reading

For a detailed report on the role of the HR department, read:

Tamkin, P., Barber, L., Dench, S. (1997) *From Admin to Strategy: The changing Face of the HR Function.* Institute of Employment Studies Report 332. IES.

For an alternative approach to Benchmarking, see:

Carter, A., Robinson, D. (2000) *Employee Returns: Linking HR Performance Indicators to Business Strategy.* Institute of Employment Studies Report 365. IES.

For a detailed article on human resource management and the bottom line see:

Baron, A., Collard, R. (1999) Realising our assets. *People Management*, October 14, 38–45.

Robinson, D., Perryman, S., Hayday, S. (2004) *The Drivers of Employee Engagement*, IES Report 408.

For a balanced view of outsourcing HR and the use of shared HR services, see:

Reilly, P. (2000) *HR Shared Services and the Realignment of HR*, IES Report 368, July.

Reilly, P., Williams, A. (2003) *How to Get the Best Value from HR: The Shared Services Option*, IES Report, February.

Web sites

HYPERLINK http://www.cipd.co.uk
www.ipd.co.uk
The website for the Chartered Institute of Personnel and Development.

HYPERLINK http://www.hrworld.com/
http://www.hrworld.com/

Major US site concerned with all aspects of Human Resources. – free registration.

HYPERLINK http://www.shrm.org
http://www.shrm.org
The American equivalent of the CIPD.

HYPERLINK http://www.hrisolutions.com/
http://www.hrisolutions.com/
This site has a large number of links to HR web pages.

CHAPTER 2

Human resource planning

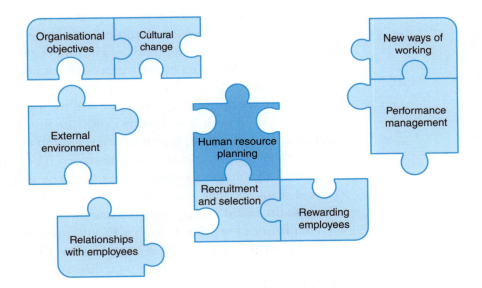

When you have read this chapter and carried out the activities, you will be able to:

■ Understand the purpose of human resources planning (HRP) in an uncertain world.

■ Identify the main issues that influence the way HRP is approached.

- ■ Draw up an outline plan by following the three-stage planning approach.
- ■ Conduct simple mathematical calculations to identify demand and supply data.
- ■ Identify the necessary implementation strategies and practices to achieve success.
- ■ Assess the extent to which HRP can improve organisational effectiveness.

Introduction

Manpower planning in large UK companies was once the centre of influence for human resource (HR) professionals. A period of 2 to 3 years in the department that collected and processed vast amount of internal and external staffing and market data, identified the labour needs for 5 years ahead and then produced a master plan of recruitment, training and career development to meet all those needs, was considered an essential milestone on the road to high office. The influence of the staffing master plan, just as in the Soviet equivalent, could not be under-estimated as it guided the majority of HR activities in a predictable world.

Today, as set out in Chapter 1, we are no longer sure of what the future will hold even 2 or 3 years down the line. Large organisations still have strategic plans, but these are set out in more general terms of shareholder returns and competitive stance. They provide for flexibility to take advantage of opportunities that arise and to cope with unexpected dangers that may befall. They are rarely written precisely because the world's competitive environment is no longer precise.

That is not to say that planning should not take place. On the contrary, in uncertain times, those organisations that know where they are and have a good idea of their general direction will, like the sailors who learnt to calculate the latitude, be more likely to be the survivors than those who never learnt those required skills. There is less emphasis on the single-scenario plan and more on the development of trained and competent staff that will thrive in a number of scenarios. The main thrust, according to Sparrow (1992), is that:

'Human Resource Planning picks up the issues that are at the heart of the business, such as acquisition, decentralisation, empowerment, internationalisation or technology, and investigates their human resource management implications. HRP therefore requires a strategic approach to the recruitment, development, management and motivation of the people in the organisation, in the context of a pressing business issue. It is a systematic process of linking human resource practices with business demands in order to improve an organisation's abilities. It establishes the plans, courses of action and targets for the range of policies needed to enable the organisation to influence the management of its human resources.'

Sparrow (1992: p. 253)

So the emphasis has turned away from the rigidity of detailed long-term planning towards greater flexibility and towards viewing planning as a continuous process of diagnosis and action planning (Iles, 2000). Having said this, there are some major sectors where old-style planning remains absolutely essential. For example, the National Health Service (NHS) with its 1 million plus employees, operates in a largely predictable, non-competitive environment. It can plan its staffing in the light of longevity and other demographic forecasts matched with likely technological advances and macro-employment conditions. Even here, as Frank Dobson, Health Minister at that time, commented (Today Programme, 2 August 1999) 'decisions we take today to increase the number of consultants will take around 15 years to come to fruition – you must plan for improved staffing in highly skilled professions many years in advance'.

Research also seems to indicate that detailed planning helps the business. Koch and McGraph's (1996) American study found that productivity tends to be better in firms that formally plan how many and what kind of people they will need, and that superior HRP skills will enhance the quality of the firm's investment in human capital, providing a form of resource-based advantage.

Reasons for lack of planning

Rothwell (1995) distinguishes four main reasons why many organisations put few resources into the HRP process. Firstly, the belief that planning is so problematical as to be useless due to the rapidly changing technology, new forms of government policies or regulation, or competitive environment. The need for planning may, in fact, be in inverse proportion to its feasibility.

Secondly, within the organisation, there are a 'shifting kaleidoscope of policy priorities and strategies which depend on the policies of the powerful interest groups involved' (Rothwell, 1995: p. 178). Taken together with the weak power base of the HR function, especially at times of economic recession, the planning process will be skimped with merely a 'spin' applied to justify the political requirements.

A third reason is that UK management in general does not have the best records with long-term plans, preferring a pragmatic adaptation over conceptualisation and a distrust for theory or planning. This viewpoint very much reflects the attitude of the City, where short-term gains often take preference over long-term investments – the so-called City 'short-termism'. This is contrasted with German and Japanese approaches which, while lacking a degree of flexibility, have a clear view of the future longer-term direction and the need for detailed planning to get there. A survey of HRP in America in 1984 (Burack, 1985) found a predominance of the 'quick-fix' and 'reactive management' being applied at the people side:

> 'This short term way of thinking ... can be seen in the lack of employee/management development programmes, feedback and actions to develop critically needed skills, hire/fire cycles rather than careful employment planning ... and incentives directed at short-run rather than long-run objectives.'
>
> Burack (1985: p. 140)

Rothwell adds a fourth explanation that HRP is often difficult to identify although it may take place at an operational level and then be rationalised *post hoc* as successful strategy.

To these can be added a further reason which is the change in nature of organisational structures. Traditional bureaucratic structures have presented a series of stepping stones for career progression, allowing individual's careers to be mapped out. With the downsizing and de-layering that has taken place in the 1990s, opportunities for traditional promotion routes have been much reduced and planning far more uncertain. In fact, many HR managers have spent much of the early 1990s making redundant senior staff who arrived at their current positions over 20 or 30 years through such a process. Having gone through such an unpleasant experience, enthusiasm to continue such career planning processes has naturally waned amongst HR staff.

When the organisation operates in a rapidly changing international environment, it becomes impossible to centrally plan all the training, development and potential career moves for large numbers of management. Standard Chartered Bank, for example, moved from a global manpower planning approach to devolving responsibility to managers in individual countries. The group head office continued to play a role in planning for succession at the highest levels, as well as setting standards for HRP around the world but the actual practice is now a local operation. The pace of change was so quick with regular re-organisations that the data collected at the centre became out of date too quickly (Speechly, 1994).

Purpose of HRP

The main purpose of HRP is to support the organisation's objective of securing a competitive advantage. Donald Burr, the Founder of People Express, set out a long-term HRP at a early stage of his company's development to stay non-union, pay lower salaries, and have broad job categories and work within teams. This has led the organisation to compete successfully through lower people costs and has given a sustained competitive advantage (Ulrich, 1987).

There are four main general objectives in developing an HRP:

- *Continuity flow*: To get the right people in the right place at the right time with the necessary skills. This involves policies in respect of recruitment, succession planning and training.
- *Maintenance*: To retain the stability in the workforce through pay and benefits, and individual career planning.
- *Response to change*: To put into effect changes that come about from major operational strategies. These can involve re-location, re-training or re-deployment.
- *Control*: To ensure that staff move in the right direction through the establishment of standards, performance control systems and building long-term employee relationships.

The detail and direction of each of these will be fashioned by the organisation's overall strategic plan. If the strategic plan indicates a development of new products or services, then the continuity plan is crucial in ensuring that staff are recruited, trained and motivated in time for the launch. If divestment of certain activities is decided, then a strategy and detailed plan needs to be in place to prepare for the change, be it through redundancy or transfer of undertakings. If the strategic plan focuses on increased productivity or improved workforce relationships, then the HRP needs to be in place to accomplish this objective.

Dimensions of HRP

Figure 2.1 shows a model of the two main dimensions of HRP. These are vertical and horizontal integration (described in Chapter 1) and how the planning fits internally and externally.

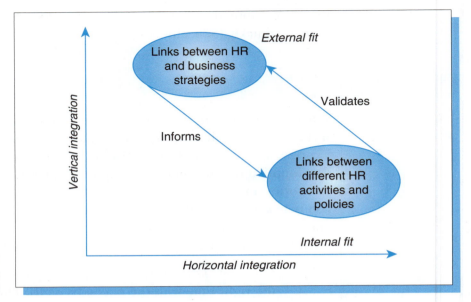

Figure 2.1
Key dimensions
of HRP

This linkage cannot be emphasised too much. As explained by Barney and Wright (1998):

'Sustainable competitive advantage stems from HR systems rather than a single practice. Any practice is good – until it gets copied by a competitor. … It requires a change in the mind-set from traditional sub-functions (selection, training, appraisal) to the view of human resources where all these independent sub-functions are viewed as inter-related components of a highly inter-dependent system.'

Barney and Wright (1998: p. 40)

This viewpoint has been supported by quantitative research by Youndt *et al.* (1996); this found that firms with highly integrated systems seemed to have a major source of competitive advantage.

Planning for specific purposes

Taylor (2002) puts forward a number of types of planning that are aimed at achieving practical organisational objectives.

Micro-planning deals with forecasting supply and demand for specific groups, such as the example of nurses (you will find later in this chapter). It is especially relevant when dealing with tight labour markets or where there major organisational developments, such as a bank moving into Hedge Funds, or where there needs to be a swift change to meet a new environmental challenge, such as a new competitor or the introduction of regulation.

Contingency planning covers the situation where possible scenarios are examined and the implications assessed before major decisions are taken. An example here would be the plans for the development of a major manufacturing plant where the implications for various levels of expansion would be considered in terms of shift systems, labour availability, employee relations and payment systems. These implications would influence the decision as to whether to expand on site or elsewhere.

Succession planning is a third type where the objective is to focus HRP activity on the recruitment and development of individuals to fill managerial and top positions. As the future leadership of the organisation is probably the most crucial aspect of its potential and continuing success, then resources set aside to search out and train potential board members is a vital HR activity. Through graduate or management trainee entry, plans can be set out for promotions every few years, plan their experience in a range of organisational projects and activities, ensure they have both line and staff responsibilities, and support the plan with a regular infusion of management training. Given the essential requirement of having top-quality management in today's world, it is all the more strange that the 1990s saw a sizeable reduction in this process and more concentration on 'buying-in' the necessary skills and experience in the international marketplace. This was reversed in the early 2000s, according to Simms (2003), when organisations began to appreciate the statistics that 80% of organisations with above-average financial performance have strong succession management systems. Moreover, regulatory institutions, such as the Financial Services Authority, have imposed the requirement on organisations to prove they have sufficiently robust succession schemes in place. An example of a successful succession planning system (GKN PLC) is set out in Case study 2.1.

Case study 2.1

Succession planning at GKN

GKN is an large engineering company with operations in 30 countries. Since the mid-1990s, the organisation had adopted a more rigorous and systematic approach to management appraisal and development, arising from a major concern that too many good people were leaving the organisation. As a result, GKN was recruiting too many people from the outside to fill vacancies higher up in the organisation.

Working closely with line managers, the HR department identified 75 key roles across GKN's international spectrum, the skills needed for these roles and a talent pool of around 200 potential successors. From this point, a number of 'Emerging Leaders', people at the top of the talent pool, were picked out to be prepared for promotion over the longer period. Twenty-five of these went through an intense assessment and development programme with a major consultancy and were then sent to Columbia Business school in America for a week's programme called 'Emerging Leaders'.

Although the graduate intakes are tracked well, the organisation has also been concerned that non-graduates with potential have not been identified early enough. Systems to pinpoint such employees were put in place including a 'buddy system' to encourage employees to stay in touch with others in different divisions and each of the six executive committee members actively mentor three or four younger executives – a system that is cascaded down the organisation.

While graduate retention in most organisations is 50–55% after 5 years, GKN's is closer to 70% and, among its 200-strong team of executives, the ratio between home-grown and bought-in talent is approaching 80:20.

Source: Simms (2003)

A further type of planning focuses on *developing skills and competences*. This is not just identifying the volume and types of skills required but to work out ways that these can be met from both within and outside the organisations. Taylor (2002) uses an example of the skills needed in the computer software industry where the skills can be sourced from temporary or agency employees, or outsourced to independent organisations.

The final type concerns the 'soft' areas of HRP which deal not with numbers but with *cultural and behavioural objectives*. The most well known of these are longer-term campaigns to transform staff attitudes towards quality and customer-care issues. Planning in this area has shown a very rapid rise since the mid-1980s and has proved a necessary and crucial part in improving the competitive position of many organisations.

A different approach to the subject is taken by Armstrong (1996) who sees the practical side of HRP as a series of implementation strategies consisting of the following:

- ■ *Acquisition strategies*, defining how the resources required to meet forecast needs will be obtained.
- ■ *Retention strategies*, which indicate how the organisation intends to keep the people it wants.
- ■ *Development strategies*, which deals with skills and competency requirements.
- ■ *Utilisation strategies*, identifying how productivity and cost-effectiveness can be improved.
- ■ *Flexibility strategies*, evaluating how various flexible working practices can lead to improved organisational effectiveness.
- ■ *Downsizing strategies*, defining what needs to be done to reduce numbers to those the organisation needs.

The need to ensure that the plan is not just a collection of disjointed ideas but an integrated whole is emphasised by Mark Huselid with his concept of *'bundling' HR practices* (Guest, 1998). In his research on successful US companies who use high-performance work practices (i.e. progressive HR practices), he found that it was not the specific practices themselves that led to success. The key lies in having the right 'bundle' of practices, as explained in Chapter 1. As the secret to competitive success is having an advantage that is difficult to imitate, then the bundle must be specific to one organisation. If it were not, then it would be easy to copy and nobody would have an advantage.

He calls the practices 'idiosyncratic contingencies' which fit with the business strategy and the organisational culture. The bundle of practices have to complement and support each other. Benchmarking, therefore, is of little value. Finding the right fit is a difficult matter and often happens by chance or experiment. So, although a plan that includes certain practices, such as linking pay to performance, a high degree of involvement, sophisticated selection processes and extensive training, may work with some companies, this is not guaranteed. An example of an organisation that has used a combination of HR initiatives in response to the need for changes is shown in Case study 2.2.

Case study 2.2

Cultural change at the CERT group

CERT, a major multi-site logistics company, employing around 500 staff, faced a loss of profitability that led to the need for a major re-organisation in 1998. It took advantage of this opportunity to identify factors that could differentiate the company from its competitors and provide the basis for financial recovery. Investment in training and other personnel practices were seen as key factors and two of the initiatives chosen were CERT College and CERT Challenge.

CERT College aimed to involve every employee in lifelong learning and provide financial and material support for both job-related training and broader personal development. A learning centre was set up in each depot with a designated training co-ordinator plus employees who have been trained as trainers and mentors.

CERT Challenge was centred around the re-organisation which gave greater emphasis and support to customer-facing staff. Quality improvement teams were set up in each depot and the CERT Challenge has identified more than 50 actionable areas for improving customer service.

These actions have helped to create a more motivated workforce and have already helped to win new business.

Source: IRS (1999)

Carrying out HRP

The numerical or 'hard' aspects

In dealing with the traditional version of HRP, there are three main stages in producing a realistic plan. There is an assessment of the *future demand* for HR, taking into account the current situation, the external environment and the organisation's business plan. This is followed by the analysis of the *likely supply* of HR, both internal and external, taking into account the internal labour movement and the external forces. The final stage is to *draw up a plan* detailing the actions necessary to reconcile the first two parts so that organisational needs can be met. Figure 2.2 illustrates this process.

However, forecasting is a notoriously uncertain activity in all fields of life. There are a number of sources which can assist the process but none of them are, in themselves, reliable. There is no guarantee that what has happened in the past will be repeated in the future. Information on the macro-economic front is often confused with as many different economic forecasts as there are forecasters, and official figures on economic growth and employment regularly revised in retrospect. Even the information provided by employees through surveys

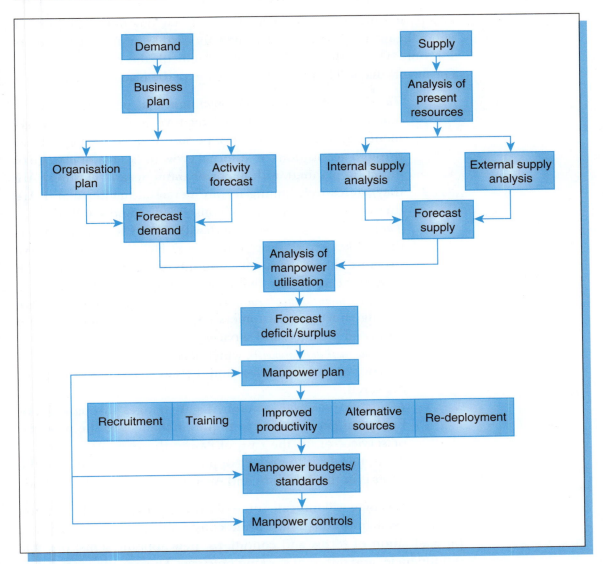

Figure 2.2
The process of HRP (*Source:* Armstrong, (1996))

cannot be totally relied on as the basis for their responses (such as trust, commitment and economic well-being) may swiftly change.

Assessment of future demand

The starting point for any forecasts is the organisation's *business plan* which sets out the way the preferred, realistic scenario for the period ahead.

This period may be 1, 2 or 5 years, which may vary depending on for whom the plan is produced: major investors, banks or internal consumption only. The further ahead, the more difficult the planning process. The factors that will influence the direction of the plan can include:

- *The driving forces behind the organisation,* as personified by the major shareholders, Chief Executive and senior management. Are they engaged in a period of rapid change, either through acquisitions or internal growth? Is a major change of direction planned, with major divestments and closures? Are they aggressively aiming for an increased market share? Are they content for a period of consolidation and stability?
- *The competitive environment,* both within the UK and overseas. Is the market growing or contracting? How is the competitive structure changing with new entrants or consolidation through mergers? Is there any change in the regulatory environment?
- *The need to introduce new products,* the product life cycles are getting shorter as customers continue to demand new and improved products and services.
- *Technological developments,* which lead to changes in the products or services themselves and the way that they are made or delivered.
- *Legislative framework,* whereby legal changes through UK or European law may lead to required changes to the products or services or, in the case of easing the regulatory environment, may lead to greater opportunities. An example of the latter is in the Telecoms and Airline environment in Europe.

The business plan will indicate some of the changes in the HR requirements. New acquisitions will provide considerable activity in terms of rationalisation of terms and conditions, new appointments, possible redundancies and different working practices. The introduction of new technology may reduce the number of production or administrative employees required. A set of new products may increase the requirements. The drive for increased productivity of, say, 5%, may insert into the plan a reduction by that amount in the staffing required. The introduction of legislation of health and safety or the minimum wage may require a planned change in working practices or payments systems.

All these changes are likely to be considered first in general terms and then refined by way of more sophisticated methods. These include *computerised modelling,* where all the variables can be inserted to produce 'what–if' forecasts and the most likely one is selected. The alternatives are substituted to produce a revised plan at a later date should external factors change. *Statistical techniques,* especially time series, can be utilised to look at how the demand has varied over an extended time period. *Work study and organisation and method techniques* can also be utilised to help indicate where improvements in labour utilisation and operation can be implemented.

Student activity 2.1

Forecasting demand

Here is a scenario for you to calculate the numerical demand for certain staffing groups in an NHS hospital trust in the northern home counties over a 4-year period. The current number of employees is shown in Figure 2.3.

	Permanent	Temporary
Nurses	576	24
Sisters	48	6
Administrative support staff	240	16
Administrative supervisors	30	2
Total	894	48

Figure 2.3
Current staff

The *business plan* includes the impending re-organisation of hospital services in the entire region which will involve the transfer of a number of services to the trust and a closure of a major unit in Year 3. This will mean the following changes in demand:

Year 1	Year 2	Year 3	Year 4
+6%	+4%	−30%	+5%

The introduction in *new technology* affects labour requirements in two ways. A new computer system should produce an increase in staffing of six administrators in Year 2, but the following year a reduction of 16 staff will occur. New medical technology planned has a higher labour content and will produce an increase in the requirement from Year 2 onwards of 16 nurses and one sister.

It is planned that the introduction of annual hours and other flexible working arrangements will lead to *productivity increase* of 2% in Year 1.

The requirements arising from the *government targets* for improved customer service will lead to the need for an increase in administrative staff of 3% for Year 1. A *flatter organisation structure* is planned which will change the ratio of sisters to nurses as follows:

	Current	Year 1	Year 2	Year 3 onwards
Sister:nurse ratio	1:12	1:14	1:14	1:16
Administrative supervisor: support staff	1:8	1:10	1:10	1:14

Action required

Take each year in turn, starting with Year 1, and calculate the staff required in each category. You may be able to put this onto a spreadsheet to help your calculations (see Figure 2.4). You may need to make certain assumptions as you go along, make sure you keep a note of these. The first calculation for nurses in Years 1 and 2 have been carried out for you.

	Year 1	Year 2	Year 3	Year 4
Starting point	600	624	665	
Business plan	+6% = +36	+4% = +25		
New technology		+16		
Productivity improvement	−2% = −12			
Total	= 624	= 665		

Figure 2.4
Demand for nurses

Demand for nurses (Existing staff = 576 + 24 temps = 600 total)
You will need to complete Figure 2.4 and draw up a similar table for the other three staff categories.

Assessment of future internal supply

Staff turnover has a critical effect upon the supply of labour to an organisation. This turnover can be put into the categories of voluntary or compulsory turnover.

Voluntary turnover includes:

- Leaving to take up a job elsewhere.
- Leaving to raise a family, set up a business or enter full-time education.

- Leaving due to partner's re-location.
- Retirement (although the organisation may enforce a compulsory retirement age).
- Leaving due to ill health.

Compulsory turnover includes:

- Dismissal for misconduct.
- Dismissal due to ill health.
- Dismissal due to redundancy.

Staff turnover, sometimes called 'wastage', can be calculated for the organisation as a whole or by specific job or skill categories, which is more useful. The *wastage index* is calculated as follows:

$$\frac{\text{Number of staff leaving in a year}}{\text{Average number employed in the same period}} \times 100$$

For example, the number of staff leaving in a year may be 60 while the average number employed in that period is 200 giving a wastage index of 30%. Although this is a useful comparative measure, it may hide considerable variations. In this example, the wastage rate appears very high, indicating a regular turnover of all staff. However, the reality may be that, of the 60 leaving, many have stayed only a few weeks while the bulk of employees remain throughout the period. For this reason there is an alternative calculation called a *stability index*, calculated as follows:

$$\frac{\text{Number of employees with 1 year service at December 31}}{\text{Number employed 1 year ago}} \times 100$$

Thus, in the above example, if the organisation employed 200 staff at the start of 2000 and, of these, 170 were still employed at the end of the year, then the stability index would be 85%. This gives a more positive spin on the situation than quoting a turnover rate of 30%.

A final method of analysing turnover is the *half-life index*. This is to take a cohort of employees who all started either at the same time or all within the same 3- or 6-month period. This might be, say, a group of trainees or new employees at the start-up of an operation. The index is calculated by the time taken for the cohort to be cut in half through turnover. For example, if the cohort of 30 trainees started in 2003 and was reduced to 15 by 2009, then the half-life is 6 years. This is a useful way of comparing the stability of different cohorts.

There are a number of possible employers' responses to labour shortages as shown in Figure 2.5. The strategic activities may take longer to put into effect but will be more likely to move towards resolving the difficulties faced.

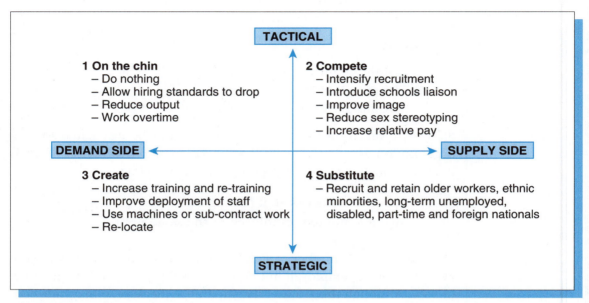

Figure 2.5
Employers' responses to labour shortages (*Source*: Morris and Willey, 1996)

Labour turnover is one of the critical measures in HR and much research takes place into its prevalence and causes. In Focus on research 2.1, details are given of the 2003 CIPD Survey.

Focus on research 2.1

Labour turnover, 2003

The Chartered Institute of Personnel and Development (CIPD) carries out a survey each year into labour turnover and the 2003 report, based on information from around 1000 respondents, includes the following findings:

- The average turnover was 16% compared to 26% in 2000.
- Those working in a sales and service environment had the highest turnover at 18% with rates in call centres especially high at 51%.
- Management, professional, technical and scientific staff had the lowest turnover at 12%.

- The private sector (20%) had a higher turnover rate than the public sector (12%).
- Hotels and catering (46%), retailing (27%) and communication (27%) were the sectors with the highest turnover while utilities (9%), paper and printing (9%), chemicals (12%) and local government (12%) were the lowest.
- The average estimated cost per leaver was £4807 for managerial staff and averaged £4301.

Source: CIPD (2004)

Another important aspect of internal supply is the *absenteeism rate*. If this deteriorates in the course of a year, then the supply of labour reduces by the amount of the deterioration. The supply will increase, of course, if absenteeism improves. As much of the responsibility for sick pay schemes has been transferred to employers in recent years, the cost of absenteeism is very high so there is a considerable incentive for employers to aim to reduce absenteeism.

Internal transfers and promotion also need to be considered in the equation as they affect the numbers in specific job categories.

These are all ways of analysing the current situation but may not necessarily be a reliable guide to the future. Each area needs to be assessed on what is likely to happen on current information. A sustained campaign on absenteeism may lead to a sizeable reduction. Staff leaving for domestic reasons may be persuaded to return quickly if child care facilities or flexible hours practices are in place. Voluntary turnover needs to be analysed through an exit interview with each leaver. A number of employees may be lured to a rival organisation because of better terms, conditions or working practices so there is a need to assess what, if anything, can be changed and the costs involved, together with the costs of not doing so. Employees may be taking early retirement because they want to work reduced hours. Similarly, some employees with a high-sickness record may benefit from the same remedy. The organisation needs to examine if this is possible and beneficial in the circumstances.

Assessment of external supply

If it is considered that internal supply factors are difficult to determine, then those for external supply present even greater problems.

Here it is the larger issues of economics and sociology which have the greatest influence in determining whether the right potential staff will present themselves at the gate, so to speak, to fill the available vacancies.

Economic factors include:

- *Local unemployment rates.* High unemployment rates should provide a greater source but this is not always the case as often the local unemployment is high because the skills level is low. Should specialist skills be wanted then these may only be available in specific locations, especially London and other big centres.
- The *level of interest rates* can have an effect in that high rates may encourage the second earner in a family to wish to extend their hours to fund the higher mortgages.
- The *infrastructure* which influences the ability to travel easily to the place of work.
- The *degree of competition* for labour in the area.

Sociological factors include:

- The *density of population* in the surrounding areas, their age structure and the availability of specific groups (full-time, part-time, graduates, school-leavers, etc.).
- *Patterns of immigration and emigration in and out of the area.* New Towns have been very popular start-up sites because of the immigration of young families and skilled or semi-skilled workers into those towns. The New Towns are attractive because their facilities – shopping, housing and leisure – are usually of high quality and readily available. Inner city areas, on the contrary, are unpopular because such labour is generally moving out, being replaced by unskilled labour.
- The general *skills levels* in the area and the degree of government-backed support for improving skills generally.

General factors include:

- The *attractiveness of the company* as a place to work both in terms of its national 'brand' (IBM or Virgin carry a particular caché and tend to attract more applicants than average) and the facilities in the workplace. A gleaming new office block with a health club, extensive car parking and haute cuisine restaurant will also tend to increase the supply of labour.
- The *links with educational establishments* and other sources of recruits.

The external factors are usually only considered in detail when organisations are considering re-locating or setting up a new site. The sources of required labour are an important element in the decision process along with land or rental cost, accessibility and any government assistance.

Student activity 2.2

Forecasting supply

Continuing with the scenario set out in Activity 2.1, this exercise asks you to calculate the likely supply of labour at the hospital. Here are some of the internal factors that will influence the forecast:

Staff turnover (voluntary). The average turnover for the last 2 years are as follows:

Nurses	Sisters	Administrative supervisor	Support staff
20%	12%	10%	16%

In addition, three sisters and two administrative supervisors have been promoted to higher positions within the organisation on average over the last 4 years.

Retirements. There will be two retirements each year in each of the groups for the next 4 years.

Promotions. When positions of sisters or administrative supervisors become vacant, they are filled internally on 80% of occasions.

Trainee nurses. Each year, 35 trainee nurses are recruited for a 3 year programme of which 80% usually complete the training programme.

Absenteeism has been a particular problem in respect of nurses, running at 10% on average. A new agreed procedure has been introduced with the aim of reducing this to 6% from Year 1.

In terms of *external factors*, temporary nurses can be recruited through local agencies, but local sources of recruitment are becoming more difficult due to the recent opening of a private hospital in the area. Recruiting overseas, especially in the Far East, is being considered in principle.

Action required

Take each year in turn, starting with Year 1, and calculate the effect on the staffing in each category. You may be able to put this onto a spreadsheet to help your calculations (see Figure 2.6). You may need to make certain assumptions as you go along and make sure you keep a note of these. The first calculation for nurses in Years 1 and 2 have been carried out for you.

Internal supply of nurses (Existing staff = 576 + 24 temps = 600 total)

	Year 1	Year 2	Year 3	Year 4
Starting point for year (Figure *b* from previous year)	600	624	665	
Voluntary turnover	−20% = −120	−20% = −125		
Retirements	= −2	= −2		
Trainees completing	= +28	= +28		
Improved absenteeism	+4% = +24	= +24		
Total (*a*)	= 530	= 549		
Number required (see demand) (*b*)	= 624	= 665		
Shortfall to be recruited in period (or surplus) (*b* − *a*)	= 94	= 116		

Figure 2.6
Internal supply of nurses

You will need to complete this table and draw up a similar table for the other three staff categories. So for nurses, you will see the very high recruitment required, although you will find that this may alter by Year 4.

Producing the HRP

Having carried out the analysis of the right numbers and skills required (the demand for labour) and the factors that influence their supply, the HRP reconciles the two and indicates how the shortfall can be met. On a few occasions the plan indicates a surplus so the plan will indicate how that surplus is to be shed.

The plan will consist of the traditional methods of dealing with the shortfall or surplus which will involve a recruitment or disposal plan. However, the plan will also include ways in which recruitment or disposal can be minimised in the future through recommendations on

HR initiatives. Many of the proposals that could be included are set out in the relevant chapters on recruitment, training and other areas so the following will only be a short summary with indications of further reading.

Recruitment/selection plan

This will cover the sources and methods of recruitment/selection including advertising campaigns, selection testing and proposals for dealing with particularly difficult recruitment areas. You will find examples of recruitment/selection issues and initiatives in Chapters 4 and 5.

Retention plan

Exit interviews, which take place immediately before staff leave, can provide detailed information as to the causes of staff turnover and can be the catalyst for the introduction of new initiatives. Some of the information yielded from exit interviews can include:

- The payment systems can be inappropriate or not match up to that offered by the competition.
- The hours of work or shifts may not fit individuals' personal lives.
- Employees may be uncertain as to what is required of them or dissatisfied with the way they are assessed.
- The nature of the work, or the way it is organised, can be boring, undemanding or too stretching and in need of re-designing.
- The management processes may be criticised for being too controlled or too lax.
- The physical conditions may be unpleasant or unsafe.
- The opportunities for training, development and promotion may be too limited.
- Employees may have a sense of unfairness in the employment situation on the grounds of discrimination or through lack of communication or representation.

All of these complaints can stimulate discussion and proposals for change. Included within the plan, therefore, can be proposals on reward, effective ways of working, training, performance management and the employment relationship. You will find a full discussion on these subject areas in the appropriate chapter together with ideas on how initiatives can be constructed to ameliorate the problems.

Disposal plan

In the case where there is an identified surplus of labour, then the plan to eliminate that surplus needs to be in place. That can include details of timings, legal consultations, and whether redundancies will be voluntary or compulsory. If compulsory, then the selection procedure needs to be proposed and agreed. Alternatively, the surplus can be reduced through transfers, early retirement and natural wastage.

The 'soft' aspects

This final area concerns initiatives that may need to be introduced to meet strategic elements of the organisation's strategic plan. These deal with the need for organisational, cultural and behavioural changes, and are essentially long-term processes. These include the drive to introduce a more flexible working environment, a greater concentration on quality through Total Quality Management and Quality Circles, an emphasis on team-working and empowerment, and encouraging employees to work more closely with the customers through customer care campaigns. You will find more details of these subjects in Chapter 6.

Introducing these initiatives is an activity not to be taken lightly. They have implications far beyond their immediate aims and have close links with other HR initiatives. In all of these areas, there needs to be planned links with recruitment and selection where tests can be formulated to identify employees who are more likely to adopt flexible behaviours or those related to quality awareness, team-working or customer care. Extensive communication and training needs to be planned for all parties concerned with effective and regular evaluation. The integration of pay mechanisms to reward the desired behaviours also needs to be considered carefully and, if agreed as policy, carefully planned so that it acts effectively but does not disturb the existing (probably complex) pay system. There will also need to be a performance management scheme to support such pay mechanisms. Practical employee involvement is another requirement for potential success. As put by Bramham (1994):

> 'There is a fundamental need to recognise that quality comes from *commitment and co-operation* and not coercion. It is perhaps possible to reduce costs and improve productivity by force but it is unlikely that customer care and quality will emerge by force and management edict. For this reason, the customer-quality focus requires the third aspect, employees, in order to be achieved.'
>
> Bramham (1994: p. 22)

Finally, it is now quite common for there to be the introduction of a competency framework throughout an organisation where flexibility, customer care, etc. are required competencies. Such a framework is a very long-term project which needs highly detailed planning.

To improve the quality of HRP, Boxall and Purcell (2003) suggest the following principles should apply:

- *Stakeholder principle*: The HRP does not belong to the HR team and it should clearly meet the needs of all levels of line managers. In particular, it is vital to focus on those employees most affected by the outcomes of HRP.
- *Involvement principle*: Only through dialogue with those centrally involved in managing people in the organisation can the quality of HRP be improved. It should be driven by senior management but facilitated by the HR department who use their specialist expertise in research and communication to ensure that all sections of the workforce are involved in some way in the planned processes.
- *Rivalry principle*: Labour markets are competitive and intelligent rivals will attempt to recruit the best people and build the best processes. So it is crucial to understand what competitors are doing in the HR area.
- *Dynamic principle*: This recognises the need for short- and long-term planning but also that constant changes and adaptations are necessary. Scenario planning is important here, looking at 'what–if' situations and moving from 'Plan A' to 'Plan B'.
- *Integration principle*: Ultimately, HRP is only as good as its degree of constant integration with the business plan and its regular updates.

Conclusion

No HRP will be a valuable tool unless there has been *involvement and consultation* with the managers who will be implementing much of the programme. Nor should a plan be produced without the *main costs* being evaluated and a timescale place on the constituent parts. A detailed plan involving heavy recruitment, training and a number of 'soft' initiatives will be expensive. HR sometimes have a reputation for inadequacy over effective costing and this is a major defect. Unless it is possible to demonstrate that a HRP is going to add value to the organisation and lead eventually to bottom line improvements, then the plan is unlikely to be accepted or effective when operated. It has to be delivered with conviction, even some passion or it will carry little weight. For this reason, the rolling-out of the plan needs to take place with the overt *support of the Chief Executive* with the funds clearly committed. Having said that, when the plan has proved to be successful, it can add considerably to the credibility of the HR department, as shown in the Case studies 2.3 and 2.4 concerning Essex County Council and Heathrow Express.

Case study 2.3

Planning to solve social workers staff shortages at Essex County Council

With employee numbers running beyond 40,000 and a budget of more than a billion pounds, Essex County Council was keen to ensure it had up-to-date workforce planning in place, which it achieved through a dedicated oracle system held in departmental databases. It became clear in the early 2000s that the perennial problem of shortages of qualified social workers was deteriorating with vacancies at 25%, more than twice the national average. Without a clear action plan, this problem could not be resolved.

Without a substantial increase in salaries and benefits (impossible in most cash-starved local authorities) it was unlikely to be able to make up the shortfall by recruiting from other authorities, so a more drastic solution was investigated to focus on the capacity of existing staff. The council carried out a survey of the time spent on 'skilled' social work activity, and how much on ancillary work, particularly administration, to identify how possible it was to switch the administrative tasks to support staff, where recruitment was possible.

The survey also gave an opportunity for social work staff to buy into the proposal by suggesting how the service and their role could improve through changes in the way they carried out their work. A workshop took place before the survey was issued to explain the exact purpose of the survey and to dispel any fears about 'snooping'. Another workshop took place when the returns and analysis was completed to discuss the way forward. Many good ideas emerged and a number were implemented to release time for social workers to better use their skills and professional expertise, both in handling cases and in transferring skills to other staff, especially those in residential homes.

Source: IRS (2003)

Case study 2.4

How HRP helped turn round a disaster for Heathrow Express

On Friday, 21 October 1994, three parallel tunnels being constructed as part of the Heathrow Express link collapsed. This led to a huge increase in the cost of the project, a Heath and Safety Inspectorate successful prosecution and a long delay in the project. Rather than blame each other for this disaster, British Airports Authority (the developer) and Balfour Beatty (the contractor) set up a 'solutions team'. Initially this was to examine technical problems but it led quickly to a £1 million staff development programme being set up. The emphasis at the earliest stage was to encourage all the staff to forget their differences and difficulties, and work together as one team rather than two suspicious warring factions. The plan was put into place not just as a routine training exercise but to help change the culture and way of working in the light of the severe difficulties.

This programme included a series of strategy workshops involving managers of both companies, extensive training in managing people skills for supervisors and a monthly information exchange meeting with groups involving suppliers. The latter meetings fostered an atmosphere of openness and supported the way the two main companies worked together. The front line training sessions took place as close as possible to the tunneling sites. A number of 'champions' were identified – people who volunteered to take an active role in influencing the single-team culture and in leading discussion groups. They benefited from a personal development programme and were instrumental in deepening the culture change. Despite initial cynicism, most of the staff came to approve of and support the culture change. In turn the two companies made every effort to meet the immediate needs and requests of the staff if they co-operated with the programme.

BAA estimated that the single-team approach made a saving of atleast £1.5 million, chiefly from non-duplication of roles between the two organisations but also from the way staff approached the management of people and the problem-solving techniques learnt on the development courses. The programme won the 1997 People Management Award.

Source: Thatcher (1997)

Meteor case study

Putting together an HRP

After her 2-month orientation course at head office, Sarah joined the team at Forstairs, which was the new factory site in the throes of being built. The completion date was in October, 5 months ahead, but the management team had been appointed and all the planning was under way. HR at the site consisted of herself and Scott Hammond, HR Manager, who was 29 and had joined the organisation as a graduate 5 years ago and had experience of a similar unit together with 2 years in the head office function as a training specialist.

In the first week on site, they set a day aside to start to draw up the HRP. Scott had already discussed the Forstairs business plan with the site director, so he had a clear view of the planned culture for the site, the operations labour force, its skills and objectives. Scott suggested that they divide the day into two. The first part would be concerned with the 'number-crunching' side, working out the number of employees needed, their skills, profiles and training programmes. The second part would be concerned with the strategic elements, including the details of pay, incentives and benefits, the performance management system, the communication and involvement policy for the workforce and equal opportunities arrangements. From the start, Scott emphasised that the HR policies would have to fit together into a coherent collection, or 'bundle' as was the current phrase.

The first part was dealt with smoothly with Sarah given the job of producing a Gantt chart that summarised the plan. She drew it up as shown in Figure 2.7.

Employees would be phased in over the 3-month period in batches of 20. Sarah would produce a similar chart for all other groups of employees and these charts would be prominently displayed in her office and on the main noticeboard, and the progress to date would also be indicated. She also agreed to carry out a thorough pay survey to confirm that the original data collected 12 months ago as a basis for the project proposal had not changed greatly. A final set of proposals would encompass the equal opportunity aspects of recruitment, selection, training and promotion, which would take into account the nature of ethnic mix in the locality.

The discussions on strategy and policy took a good deal longer. They were required to work within a competence framework that had been designed by consultants some months back. This framework was divided into core competencies that all employees should develop,

Operatives	June	July	August	Sept	Oct	Nov	Dec	Jan	Feb
Finalise job design	—								
Complete training schedules	——								
Liaise with partners (job centres, agencies, etc.)	———								
Advertise		——		——					
Interview, test		—	———	——	——				
Reference, select			——	——	——	——			
Induct and train. Start prototype production					——	——	——		
Promote and train team leaders						——			——
First assessment at end of probationary period							——		
Start incentive scheme								——	

Figure 2.7
Meteor Gantt chart

including problem solving, quality focus and innovation plus sets of specific competencies for departments and roles.

Scott considered that this framework should be the lynch-pin for many of their activities. For example, he wanted to test applicants to see how they matched the core competencies. How close the resulting match came out would influence selection decisions. He also suggested that the performance management scheme should have a very clear focus on employees' performance in line with the competencies. Sarah was less happy with the proposal that decisions on wages and salaries should be a direct outcome of such an assessment. She considered that a period of 'bedding-in' for the framework was required before too much was weighted on it. It might crumble if it was not found to be sufficiently robust. She proposed instead a system of skills-based pay for the operatives with simple and transparent increases when individual skills modules had been achieved. Scott could see the merit in this proposal and asked her to put up a scheme in the next month although he wanted a continuous stress on performance as part of the culture of the unit.

They needed a further meeting to discuss the system of employee representation, communication and involvement. Scott had some unhappy experiences of working with unions and wished to avoid having to recognise them. He proposed setting up an influential Employee Council from the start that had a strong role in consultation, a 'Kaizan-style' employee recognition scheme to encourage employees to join in the innovation process and briefing groups, and regular departmental meetings as an important part of communication process. This 'bundle' would, he felt, direct the employees towards positive support of the company's activities rather than the more negative aspects he associated with trade unions. Sarah agreed with the main drift, but pointed out the difficulties associated with this approach that may cut across representation rights recently legislated.

They felt this was a good start and Scott agreed to arrange a meeting at the end of the month with the general management team to discuss them in detail.

Student activity 2.3

In Activities 2.1 and 2.2, you have calculated the demand for staff and the internal supply factors, which produce a deficit to be recruited or a surplus to reduce. In Activity 2.3, you need to put together the HRP. This will set out how you plan to remedy the deficit and deal with the surplus. You will have seen in the text that the report should be in two parts. The first part will deal with the immediate policy of recruitment and disposal, in other words the methods and sources of recruitment and the decisions to be made over disposal. Both issues are linked because you may decide to make redundancies, engage a policy of recruiting on a temporary basis or keep the surplus and reduce by natural wastage. In your report, set out which policy you adopt and why.

The second part will be your recommendations on how to avoid being faced with such large recruitment numbers in future years. In other words, the policies you would use to reduce staff turnover or the improved training you would implement to ensure a larger supply of nurses for the future. Make sure your recommendations are relevant to this case study.

Summary

- HRP can be divided into the 'hard' aspects, which deal with quantitative data, such as the numbers and skills of employees required, and the 'soft' aspects that are involved with corporate culture and organisational development.

■ Planning now has a much shorter timescale than in previous decades due to the unpredictable changes that organisations face and the need to respond in a flexible way.

■ Aspects of planning include contingency planning, succession planning, developing skills and competencies, and behavioural objectives.

■ Planning involves identifying future demand and internal supply, identifying the gaps between the two and planning to fill them.

Additional student activities

1   In the CIPD Labour turnover research, the cost of replacement of employees who leave is high. Why is this?

2   In the Meteor case study, Sarah has put together a comprehensive HRP. Think about what could go wrong or what difficulties could be faced and work out how you could deal with these problems.

3   Read the article about the staff shortages in Essex County Council. Think of other areas where there are shortages of professional staff (accounting, legal, planning and hospitals) and suggest ideas how these shortages could be reduced through changes in job design.

References

Armstrong, M. (1996) *A Handbook of Personnel Management Practice*. Kogan Page.

Barney, J., Wright, P. (1998) On becoming a strategic partner. The role of human resources in gaining competitive advantage. *Human Resource Management*, **37**(1): 16–46.

Boxall, P., Purcell, J. (2003) *Strategy and Human Resource Management*. Palgrave Macmillan.

Bramham, J. (1994) *Human Resource Planning*, IPD.

Burack, E. (1985) Linking corporate business and human resource planning: strategic issues and concerns. *Human Resource Planning*, **8**(2): 133–145.

CIPD (2004). *Labour Turnover Survey 2003*, CIPD.

Guest, D. (1998) Combine harvest. *People Management*, 29 October, 64–66.

IDS (1999) The CERT group. *Employee Development Bulletin*, **113**, 9–13.

Iles, P. (2000) Employee resourcing. In: Storey, J. (ed.) *Human Resource Management: A Critical Text*. Thomson Learning.

IRS (2003) Planning. *Employment Review 790*, 19 December, 43–48.

Koch, M., McGrath, R. (1996) Improving labor productivity: human resource policies do matter. *Strategic Management Journal* **17**: 335–354.

Morris, H., Willey, B. (1996) *Corporate Environment.* Financial Times Pitman Publishing.

Rothwell, S. (1995) Human resource planning. In: Storey, J. (ed.). *Human Resource Management: A Critical Text.* Routledge; pp. 167–202.

Simms, J. (2003) The generation game. *People Management*, 6 February, pp. 26–31.

Sparrow, P. (1992) Human resource planning at Engindorf plc. In: Winstanley, D., Woodall, J. (eds). *Case Studies in Personnel.* IPD; pp. 252–259.

Speechley, N. (1994) Uncertainty principle. *Personnel Today*, 31 May, pp. 19–22.

Taylor, S. (2002) *People Resourcing*, CIPD.

Thatcher, M. (1997) Digging for victory. *People Management*, 6 November, pp. 28–31.

Ulrich, D. (1987) Strategic resource planning: why and how? *Human Resource Planning*, **10**(1): 37–56.

Youndt, M., *et al.* (1996) Human resource management, manufacturing strategy and firm performance. *Academy of Management Journal*, **39**: 836–866.

Further reading

For a detailed guide to using computerised human resource planning see:
Peter Kingsbury's. (1997) *IT Solutions to HR Problems*, IPD.

The Institute for Employment studies have produced two reports concerning human resource planning:

- Reilly, P. (1996) *Human Resource Planning: An Introduction.* Report 312.
- Hirsh, W. (2000) *Succession Planning Demystified.* Report 372.

For detailed research on integrating HRM with Strategic Management, see:
Bennet, N., Ketchen, D., Schultz, E. (1998) An examination of factors associated with the integration of human resource management and strategic decision making. *Human Resource Management*, **37**(1): 3–16.

Web sites

http://www.hrps.org/html/index1.htm
This is the web site of the US-based Human Resource Planning Society.

http://mansis.com/hrp.htm
A short human resource planning text.

Equal opportunities and managing diversity

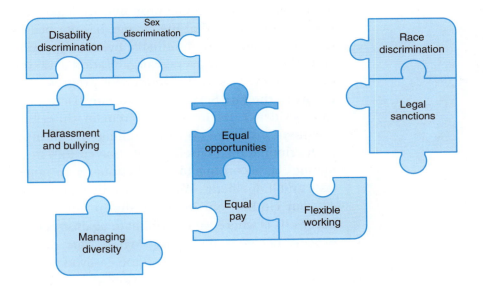

When you have studied this chapter, you should be able to:

■ Understand the business case for equal opportunities (EO) and be able to identify how it applies in differing organisations.
■ Explain the outline of the legislation relating to EO.
■ State the main differences between a policy of EO and that of managing diversity.
■ Identify the signs of sexual harassment and the ways it can be countered.

■ Assess the implications of putting a policy into practice and evaluating the success of initiatives in this area.

Introduction

In the 1970s, three new laws came into effect that were intended to bring about a 'sea-change' in the social, economic and cultural relationships in the workplace. There has been no doubt that the Equal Pay Act, Sex Discrimination Act and the Race Relations Act all made a massive contribution to the reduction of discrimination and the promotion of equality. Subsequent legislation covering age, disability, religion and sexual orientation have served to fill in remaining gaps in discrimination so that a comprehensive legal framework exists in the UK. Few will argue that the change has not been significant or that it has not produced an identifiable overall improvement in the attitudes and efficiency of the average organisation. Differences of opinion continue, however, as to the amount of progress that has been made. A report by the Fire Service Inspectorate (Delgado, 1999), for example, shows evidence that fire brigades remain white, male-dominated macho organisations where overt discrimination continues to exist.

Discrimination, in itself, is not always wholly negative. To be 'discriminating' is, according to the dictionary, an adjective 'showing good taste and judgement'. We all discriminate, for example, in the food we eat, our clothes, our interests, the furniture and decorations in our houses. It is where we discriminate against people, however, that this process becomes damaging. Where this discrimination is on the grounds of race, it can lead all too easily to violence and crime, as the history of segregation and race riots in America showed. In the UK we have had our share of race disturbances, especially in the 1950s and 1960s, which arose from deprivation and discrimination over housing and employment. Discrimination by one religious or ethnic group against another can tear nations apart as we are reminded by the horrific events in Palestine, Northern Ireland, Yugoslavia and Ruanda.

Sex, age and disability discrimination is less overt but still has an insidious and restricting effect upon society, and serves to waste precious skills and abilities. We no longer have advertisements for 'bright young men' to train to become bank managers, nor do we have prohibitions on men becoming midwives or women to crew submarines. Instead, most appointments and elections have been made on merit alone and there is some satisfaction that, in recent times, we have had a blind cabinet minister, a female chief constable and a black leader of our second biggest trade union. In 2004, the first woman was appointed to command a UK naval ship.

There is not universal success, however. Women still make up the vast majority of employees in many badly paid sectors such as hotels, catering, cleaning, care services, unskilled and semi-skilled assembly work while only 18% of MPs are women (Equal Opportunities Commission, 2004). The idea of 'women's work' and 'men's work' remains with the latter often regarded as an extension of domestic duties leading to it being valued less and subsequently paid less. Female earnings as a percentage of male earnings, having climbed from 71% in 1975 to 79% in 1993, has stayed at that plateau for most of the 1990s, reaching only 81% by 2004. The gap between male and female pay is at its widest in professional occupations. For example, women in bank and building society managers earn 36% less than men in similar posts (Overell, 1997a).

The unequal nature of men and women in the workplace can still be extensive. In the study by Collinsons (see Focus on Research 3.1) the detailed case histories of harassment do not make comfortable reading. Equal Opportunities Commission (EOC) have estimated that only 5% of employees who experience sexual harassment file a formal complaint and, of that minority, only 10% get as far as a tribunal hearing (EOC, 2001). In a detailed investigation, Cockburn (1991) found that men's social power gives them a degree of 'social authority' in the workplace which conveys the message:

> 'You are only a women… and at that level, you are vulnerable to me and any man.'
>
> Cockburn (1991: p. 142)

Focus on research 3.1

Sexual harassment

Margaret Collinson and David Collinson carried out a study of four women who had achieved promotion to management status in an insurance company. Each of them suffered extensive discrimination and harassment both before and after promotion and the research describes the nature of the harassment, verbal and physical, in considerable detail. It was not just their own manager at fault. Harassment came from their peer group, their subordinates and from clients. Each of the four women coped with their treatment in different ways.

One continually fought it off, attempting to freeze it out, and became very isolated and a source of disparagement within her own team. Another swam with the tide, joining in the male-oriented humour and sexual behaviour to the extent that she was honoured at one conference by being awarded the title of an 'honorary man'. However, she knew this was a dangerous course of action and was faced on more than one occasion by having to physically fight-off men who had misread the signs of her behaviour. The third went into denial, using this as a career-centred strategy disguised to protect her personal reputation within the male managerial heirarchy. The fourth did not complain, but just handled it professionally and competently, refusing to be provoked.

Source: Collinson and Collinson (1996)

For older workers, especially men, employment trends have worked against them. In the period 1980–2000, total employment rose by over 2 million but employment of men aged 50–64 fell by 10%. Employers, advised by their pensions departments, estimate that over-50s cost more to hire and many organisations believe that physical vigour, uncluttered minds and unsullied records of youth are more valuable than the wisdom and judgement that should spring from experience.

Legislation has been shown to be a powerful driver of social change, especially on the macro level, but it is not enough to complete the task. Other arguments have been put forward which explain why providing EO makes economic sense. In this chapter, the following areas will be examined:

- The business case for EO.
- A summary of the legislation to date on sex, race and disability.
- Discussion on the alternative approaches, including managing diversity.
- Implications for EO Policy and Practices.

The business case for EO

In their attempt to influence a radical change of policy within organisations in the 1970s and 1980s, both the EOC and the Race Relations Board focused on the individual and their rights. By being threatened with legal sanctions, it was thought that organisations would change their policies and practices overnight. It certainly did produce some change but of a more compliant sort but did little to change attitudes, especially in the areas of performance management and promotion.

In the 1990s, however, it began to be realised that substantial *demographic changes* were occurring which would inevitably lead to skills shortages. The birth rate had fallen dramatically in the 1970s and there was little sign of recovery in the next 20 years so it was known that the number of 16–25-year olds would take a sharp fall. If the traditional sources of labour (young, white, qualified and full-time males), became much reduced, then organisations realised that they would have to re-think their HR Policies and look for untapped sources of expertise. Job descriptions would need to become more flexible to accommodate part-time working; specifications would have to be altered to eliminate unnecessary requirements on height and lifting ability, and broadened to envelope all sections of the community; working conditions and benefits would have to change to allow wheelchairs, language classes, career breaks and child-care facilities.

A second reason relates to the *changing nature of the workplace*. There was a sharp decline in industrial and manufacturing jobs in the 1980s (2 million jobs were lost in this period) and this ran alongside a growth in the service sector. Whereas a large proportion of industrial jobs were held by men, the opposite was true for a majority of the service sector employment. A forecast today is that 80% of all new jobs to be created between 2005 and 2020 are expected to be taken by women. Companies in this sector have a positive incentive to encourage the best applicants by providing career opportunities and a supporting environment for all.

The growing emphasis on *customer relations* in a competitive economy is another reason for focusing on wider opportunities. Active diversity management can open up new opportunities and improve market share by broadening the customer base. This has been seen particularly in the financial sector where banks and building societies are focusing on diversity issues in the way they target their products and services. They are becoming much more user-friendly to women, taking on board the increasing spending power of the female professionals and they are also addressing the needs of ethnic minority businesses. As a manager of GrandMet PLC put it:

'Customers are increasingly looking through the front door of the companies they buy from. If they do not like what they see in terms of social responsibility, they will not go in.'

Quoted in IPD (1997a)

The Halifax Bank recognised this opportunity by specifically targeting the Chinese community in Manchester which was substantially unrepresented in the Bank's employees. The business benefits of having a group of mandarin on Cantonese speakers in the branches led to an immediate increase in mortgage business of around 40% (Merrick, 2001).

Conveying an image as a '*good employer*' also has repercussions on equality issues. Companies seen to have high-ethical stances, with such policies as 'dignity at work' which prevent harassment and bullying, become more attractive to both customers and potential employees. On the other hand, those seen as dominated by a white, male culture may not appear to provide the environment required. Moreover, in the case of equal pay, there is no greater de-motivating force in the workplace than a sense of injustice over pay by a large section of the workforce. Internal equity, including fair pay and treatment for men, women and minority groups, is a vital part of the perception of 'fairness'.

All these reasons have encouraged organisations to raise their profile on equality issues. Littlewoods, the retail store group, for example, created an Equal Opportunities Strategy Committee in 1995, headed by the chairman, which meets twice a year. One initiative arising from this committee was the decision to approach community groups, the Racial Equality Council and disability advisors when opening their Oldham store and this led to twice as many applications as normal (Clark, 1998). The Halifax Bank launched an internal campaign 'Fair's Fair' in 1999 with a video-based training programme emphasising age diversity. Age-related questions have been removed from the application form and pictures in recruitment brochures have been revamped to show a much wider span of ages for all jobs. By 2000, a survey showed that 98% of staff have a good understand of EO and one of their staff recruits that year was a 60-year-old lawyer (Glover, 2001).

An example of a comprehensive approach using a business case is shown by Hertfordshire County Council in Case study 3.1.

Case study 3.1

Tackling glass ceilings and sticky floors at Hertfordshire County Council

Hertfordshire County Council (Herts CC) is the largest employer in Hertfordshire with 25,000 employees, 80% of whom are part-time and 55% full-time. An EO Policy has been in place since the early 1980s which was reviewed in 1994 as part of a general review of HR strategy. The important question was how the organisation measured up to their public statements that 'We are an equal opportunities employer' and 'positive about disabled people'.

Their actions fell into a number of categories. On *disability*, the Council introduced awareness training, access audits and employee's forum, and became accredited as a 'two ticks' user. They also changed the stress on their policies to 'ability'. On *race*, they instituted a black employees' group and designed a specific development programme for black employees together with a full audit of their performance against the CRE Standards. For *women*, they were the first local authority to join Opportunity Now and developed a wide range of flexible working initiatives alongside a women's development programme.

Other initiatives included the development of staff support schemes, mentoring programmes, a work place nursery and a reassessed harassment at work policy.

They were conscious that all of these actions needed ongoing assessment and this was carried out through an annual DDA audit and a set of specially designed performance indicators. Interviews with leavers included questions on their own assessment of the value of the EO Policy. Four years on, an overall assessment showed success in most areas, although there were pockets where awareness was low and where management considered that EO was a job for the Personnel department, not for them.

Source: Hertfordshire County Council internal documents

There have been two employers' organisations set up to encourage the business case. Opportunity Now was set up in 1991 to increase the quality and quantity of women's participation in the workforce. The Employers Forum on Age, launched in 1996, had 160 members in 2004 which represented 14% of all the UK's employees. Ruth Jarrett, Development Director commented at the launch that:

> 'The spate of early retirements has been like a period of temporary amnesia, where the whole business sector forgot the value of long-standing employees. Now people are starting to remember again.'
> Pickard (1996: p. 10)

EO legislation

As with much of the legislation relating to individual rights, an additional stimulus was given by our entry into Europe (then the Common

Market) in 1973 when our signature to the Treaty of Rome required national legislation to match that of our partners relating to equal pay, and discrimination on the grounds of race or sex. Each of the relevant acts will be considered, followed by the remedies open to aggrieved employees and then the crucial discussion on the differing forms of discrimination will take place.

Sex Discrimination Act 1975

In essence, this act consists of one main clause, making it unlawful to discriminate in employment and other areas on the basis of sex or marital status, or to treat less favourably any employee on the ground of sex. There is one limited exemption to this where sex is a genuine occupational qualification (GOQ), such as in the pursuit of authenticity (acting or modelling), to preserve the privacy and dignity where people may object to the presence of someone from the opposite sex or where the job is in a single sex establishment. Even here, the application of GOQ is being narrowed each year. For example, in Etam plc v Rowan (EAT 301/88) it was held that being a woman was not a GOQ for a sales assistant's job in a woman's clothing shop. A further example of sex discrimination is given in Spotlight on the law 3.1.

Spotlight on the law 3.1

Sex discrimination

Richard W. Carr was facing a downturn in business which caused the organisation to declare redundancies. When it came to the method of selection, Earl was chosen because she had a young child and it was considered that she would, therefore, be unable to make the required overnight trips.

The Tribunal held that this was direct discrimination on the basis of sex, arising from the company's traditional view of a mother's responsibilities.

Source: Earl versus Richard W. Carr and Co. COIT 4680/92

The act set up the EOC which has three main functions:

- To monitor the implementation of the Sex Discrimination Act and the Equal Pay Act.

■ To promote the equal treatment of women and men at work
and to eliminate discrimination.

■ To draw up codes of conduct.

■ To make recommendations to government for improvements
in the working of the Act and to advise on how the Act should
be revised to help meet the other goals.

The EOC has commissioned and published extensive research, made
videos, and other information and communication publications, drafted
codes of practice (see later in the chapter) and supported a number of
high profile tribunal cases relating to equal pay and sex discrimination. They have also carried out a number of investigations into policy
and practice in certain companies including an investigation into sexual harassment of women employees in the Royal Mail business unit in
2004 (EOC, 2004).

Employment equality (sexual orientation) regulations 2003

This regulation extends all the provisions in the Sex Discrimination
Act to the treatment of people on the grounds of their orientation,
such as gays or lesbians.

Race Relations Act 1976

This act makes it unlawful to unfairly discriminate on the grounds of
race, colour, nationality or ethnic origin. Again, GOQs are allowed only
in very limited cases for authenticity, such as an acting role and in the
provision of personal welfare services. However, even these GOQs are
declining with a successful tribunal claim in 2003 by a white Englishman
who was turned down for a job as a waiter in a chinese restaurant. The
definition of 'race' is broad as shown in Spotlight on the law 3.2. It also
covers employees of Jewish and Irish origin.

Spotlight on the law 3.2

Race discrimination

An English applicant was turned down for a position with the NJPB, a
Scottish police authority, on the grounds that he was not of Scottish

origin. The subsequent tribunal held that the English and the Scots could be regarded as separate racial groups by reference to their national origins and this decision was upheld by the Employment Appeals Tribunal.

Source: Northern Joint Police Board v Power. EAT 27-08-97 (535/97)

In another case, an Irish Lecturer working at Northumberland College of Arts and Technology was subjected to what the tribunal called, 'a particularly appalling case of discrimination upon discrimination' which included being called an 'Irish prat' by a fellow lecturer. He was awarded £29,000 of which £13,000 would have to be paid by the College, £2000 by the Principal, £6500 by his line manager and £5000 by his colleague who made the remark.

The Commission for Racial Equality is a publicly-funded, non-governmental body set up under the 1976 Act to tackle racial discrimination and promote racial equality. Their main activities are:

- Providing information and advice to people who think they have suffered racial discrimination or harassment.
- Tackling the major causes of discrimination in the public, private and voluntary sectors by promoting good and best EO practices.
- Increasing awareness of racism and prejudice, and of ethnic minorities positive contributions to a successful, diverse Britain through public education and awareness programmes.

They have published reports, commissioned research and supported applicants in their legal actions. They have taken action against a handful of organisations. They began proceeding (section 62 of the Race Relations Act) against Bradford City Council in 1991 after industrial tribunals had upheld nine complaints of race discrimination against the council over a 3-year period. Four years later, following an independent report, it was decided to drop the action when the council agreed to implement the report's recommendations in full, including reviewing its compliance with the CRE Code of Practice, introducing a thoroughgoing corporate policy against discrimination, a commitment to discipline managers and other employees who were responsible for unlawful discrimination and to improve ethnic monitoring of employees, applicants and grievances (Equal Opportunities Review, 1995). Other formal investigations undertaken by the CRE include racism in the Prison Service (2000) and in the Police Service (2004).

Disability Discrimination Act 1995 (DDA)

The DDA has two main provisions. Firstly, it is unlawful to discriminate against employees or applicants because of their disability. Secondly, it is an obligation on all organisations to make reasonable adjustments to the workplace to accommodate the needs of a disabled person and ensure they are not disadvantaged. The legislation was introduced to help to protect the 2.9 million disabled people in employment (Sly and Risdon, 1999). It is clear from recent tribunal decisions that the definition of a disability, which can be both mental as well as physical, is being applied in a broad-brush way, as long as it has a substantial and long-term adverse effect upon the person's ability to carry out their normal duties. Tribunals have decided that there are limits to the adjustments that an employer is required to make. They do not always have to provide personal caring services for an employee that might need them, for example, but regulations introduced in 2004 reduce the ability of the organisation to argue that they cannot afford to make the adjustments. A Disability Rights Commission was set up in 1999 with essentially the same powers and the EOC and the CRE.

Two examples of important cases are given in Spotlight on the laws 3.3 and 3.4.

Spotlight on the law 3.3

Disablement discrimination

Cambridge was employed in a hospital and was off work for a long period due to ill health. She tried coming back to work but was only able to work short hours and was adversely affected by the office conditions in which she was required to work. She was eventually dismissed on the grounds of incapacity due to ill health. She won her tribunal claim on the grounds that the employer had not made a sufficient assessment of either her condition and prognosis and the effect of the disability on her and her ability to perform the duties, together with and assessment of what steps may have been taken to reduce the disadvantages to which she was subject.

Source: Mid-Staffordshire General Hospitals NHS Trust versus Cambridge 2003 IRLR 353

Spotlight on the law 3.4

Disablement discrimination – reasonable adjustments

Palmer was employed in a factory making electric showers and found increasing pains in her shoulder causing absence and slower work performance. She suggested to the management that a bench, that could be adjusted for height, would help to alleviate the situation and improve her performance. It would cost around £500. The company chose not to take up this suggestion and she was subsequently dismissed after prolonged absence. The tribunal found that the organisation had not attempted to make a reasonable adjustment to the work place in the case of a disabled employee.

Source: Palmer versus Caradon Mira Ltd, 1998 1400115

Equal Pay Act 1970

The legislation lays down the principle that men and women working for the same organisation are entitled to the same rate of pay if they are carrying out the same work. There must be no discrimination over pay. The nature of the comparisons is refined under three categories. Firstly, 'like work' the work which is the same or broadly similar. Secondly, work rated as the same under a non-discriminatory job evaluation scheme operating in the organisation. Thirdly, work that is of 'equal value'.

This last refinement arises from the 1983 Equal Value Regulations which were introduced following a judgement by the European Court of Justice that the UK had failed to properly implement Article 119 of the Treaty of Rome regarding equal pay. This amendment has attempted to close a loophole where a lower paid woman regards the work she carries out to be of equal value as different work that a man carries out but there is no internal mechanism (i.e. a job evaluation scheme) that serves to carry out that comparison. (You will find how job evaluation schemes work in Chapter 9.) Under the Equal Value Regulations, she has the opportunity to make the equal value claim and the tribunal will commission an independent expert to investigate the claim and produce what is in effect a brief job evaluation report. The expert will compare the jobs considering aspects such as skills, responsibility and supervision. However, this process is very complex in practice and few employees take up the challenge of putting in a claim unless they are supported by their union or EOC.

There are a few exceptions allowed which relate to situations where the employer claims there is a 'Genuine Material Defence'. This is where a difference in pay is accepted by the employer but justified by a reason which is *not related to sex*. For example, it could be because the higher paid male has a higher performance rating than a woman doing the same job or have better qualifications relevant to the job.

Employment equality (religion or belief regulations) 2003

Arising from the European Union (EU) Equal Treatment in Employment Directive, these regulations prohibit discrimination on the grounds of religion. The regulations define religion simply as 'any religion, religious belief or similar philosophical belief' and it will be up to the courts to clarify and interpret this definition. They will take into account such factors as collective worship, a clear belief system or a profound belief affecting the individual's way of life or view of the world. Discrimination in recruitment, selection and employment applies across the board but exceptions to the regulations can apply to churches and other public or private organisations whose ethos is based upon religion or belief. Such organisations may be permitted to recruit and employ staff on the basis of their religion or belief as long as they can show it as a 'genuine occupational requirement'. An example would be in employing school teachers in a school with a religious character.

Age discrimination

Legislation prohibiting age discrimination becomes effective in the UK from October 2006. The likely implications of this legislation are dealt with later in the chapter.

Remedies for the employee

Under each of these acts, applicants and employees have the right to apply to a tribunal if they believe that they have been the subject of discrimination. They need to show that they have been treated differently and less favourably because of their sex, race, disability, etc. This can apply in the recruitment and selection process where they are unsuccessful in obtaining employment or, for employees, in any aspect of their employment. If they are successful in their claim, then they are entitled to compensation, which has no limit (unlike unfair dismissal compensation – see Chapter 7). The highest awards have been made to women in the armed forces who, between 1978 and 1990, were forced to resign when they became pregnant. In 1981, the MOD conceded that this policy was unlawful and in breach of EU Equal Treatment Directive. By 1994, £22 million had been paid out in compensation to around 2415 ex-service personnel who had suffered because of this policy (IDS, 1994).

The compensation in equal pay claims is calculated in respect of the loss of earnings between the pay received and the level of pay that should have been received. In sex and race cases, a payment can be made for injury to feelings which can be a high as £21,000 where a black prison officer had been the subject of racial harassment for 18 months (Armstrong, Marsden, HM Prison service v Johnson, quoted in Korn, 1997).

The statistics for applications are shown in Figure 3.1.

	Cases received	Settled before tribunal	Withdrawn before tribunal	Tribunal cases heard
Sex discrimination	4740	2215 (47%)	1670 (35%)	615 (13%*)
Race Relations Act	3157	1242 (39%)	1064 (34%)	600 (19%*)
Disability Discrimination Act	2573	1256 (49%)	824 (32%)	374 (15%*)
Equal Pay Act	1337	605 (45%)	405 (30%)	278 (21%*)
* The remaining cases were either struck out by the tribunal or were out of scope.				

Figure 3.1
Statistics on formal Industrial Tribunal claims concerning equal opportunities in 2002–2003 (*Source*: ACAS 2004)

In each tribunal claim, Advisory, Conciliation and Arbitration Service (ACAS) has a statutory duty to conciliate between the parties to help them to reach a settlement before the case gets to a tribunal. This involves a conciliation officer talking to each side, ensuring they both know the realities of a tribunal, clarifying the areas of differences and attempting to get the sides to agree on a satisfactory solution. As the figures show, a solution was achieved in almost half of the cases and a further one-third of the cases were dropped, leaving only one in six claims to actually arrive at the tribunal. Tribunal hearings have resulted in less than one-half being successful.

Many cases take an inordinate length of time to be settled. Pam Enderby, a speech therapist, started her claim for equal pay with her chosen comparator, a clinical psychologist in the same health authority in 1986. It was a complex case with a number of significant issues and was only successfully settled in 1997 following hearings at the House of Lords and the European Court of Justice (Enderby versus Frenchay Health Authority and Secretary of State for Health. ECJ 1993 IRLR 591).

Defining discrimination

Discrimination was defined in both the Sex discrimination Act and in the Race Relations Act and can take three forms:

Direct discrimination. An instance here would be to advertise for a 'Girl Friday' or to use different criteria for selection for promotion. In the case of race discrimination, it may relate to an employer indicating to a recruitment agency that they do not want black casual workers; or an employer may turn down a deaf a partially sighted applicant specifically because of this disability. In each case, an individual or group is treated less favourably than another on the grounds of sex, race or disability. The employer has no defence even if they genuinely believe what they are doing is right. The motives are irrelevant.

Indirect discrimination. This occurs where the employer treats all applicants or employees the same but a practice, condition or policy adversely affects one sex, or race more than another, or if it affects the disabled more than the able-bodied. The way it normally adversely affects that group is because the proportion of people from a particular group able to meet the condition or policy is considerably smaller. Moreover, the employer cannot objectively justify the practice, policy or condition. If the employer cannot convince the tribunal that the defence is genuine and substantial, then the employer will lose the case.

Two examples are shown in Spotlight on the laws 3.5 and 3.6.

Spotlight on the law 3.5

Indirect discrimination – age limit

The University of Manchester advertised for candidates to fill the post of careers adviser, indicating that they wanted a graduate aged 27–35 with a record of successful relevant experience. Mrs Jones, aged 44, applied for the position. She was a strong candidate and was already occupying a similar temporary post, having entered the profession at the age of 38 as a mature student but she was not selected for interview because of her age. At the subsequent tribunal hearing, Mrs Jones argued that the age limit adversely affected mature students who would not be able to meet the requirement on experience. Most of these were women who had brought up a family so this adversely affected the female group. She used statistical evidence to support her case.

In defence, the University justified the requirement on the grounds that the department contained a high proportion of older employees and an age balance was required. The case was eventually decided at the Court of Appeal who held that the discrimination caused by such a requirement should be balanced against the benefits that the requirement should bring. In this case, they agreed with the tribunal that the hardships outweighed the potential benefits. Mrs Jones was successful and was awarded compensation.

Source: Jones versus University of Manchester. Court of Appeal 21.12.92 – Report in IDS Brief 489, March 1993: pp. 2–4

Spotlight on the law 3.6

Indirect discrimination – location of applicant

A firm of household furnishers in Liverpool stipulated that they did not want job applicants from the city centre because experience had shown that their unemployed friends tended to gather round the shop and discourage customers. As a result of this stipulation, Hussein was refused an interview and he claimed race discrimination at a subsequent tribunal. The tribunal held that the employers had unjustifiably, if unknowingly, discriminated against Hussein since 50% of the city centre population was black as opposed to 2% of the Merseyside population. The Employer's condition therefore excluded a significantly higher proportion of black applicants than white applicants.

Source: Hussein v Saints Complete House Furnishers 1979 IRLR 337, ET. – report in IDS Handbook on Race Discrimination (1999): p. 18

Other tribunal examples have included:

1 The requirement to restrict applicants geographically by residence to a specific area which discriminated against ethnic minorities, whose representation in that area was slight.

2 Recruiting only through word of mouth in an employment site dominated by white males.

3 Giving too much weight to family relationships when apprenticeships were chosen.

Victimisation. This takes place when an employer treats somebody less favourably because they have taken action in making an allegation or have brought proceedings under any of the discrimination legislation.

A fourth area, which has now been included within this general area, relates to Harassment within the workplace. This can take a number of highly unpleasant forms such as insults or ridicule based on sex or race, unwanted sexual attention or withholding career progression. Two examples of harassment and victimisation are detailed in Spotlight on the law 3.7 and 3.8.

Spotlight on the law 3.7

Sexual harassment

Mrs Clayton was one of the first two women to join the fire service when she joined the Hereford and Worcester Brigade in 1989 after an exemplary career in the Womens Royal Army Corp. Over the next 5 years, she was the subject of continuing harassment and verbal abuse together with victimisation which included forcing her to take a turntable ladder to 100 feet and spin it for more than an hour. She was also made to carry out dangerous drills which male firefighters do not have to do. The tribunal decided that her personality and self-confidence had been totally destroyed and her career shattered. The brigade had done little or nothing to prevent sexual discrimination and its management was totally ineffectual. She was awarded substantial compensation.

Source: Graves (1995: p. 3)

Spotlight on the law 3.8

Racial harassment

An Asian postman, Mahmood Siddiqui, suffered a 4-year campaign of racial abuse before taking sick leave and eventually retiring through ill health in 2002. Following his tribunal hearing in 2004, he was awarded total compensation of £180,000 made up of:

- ■ £104,142 for loss of earnings,
- ■ £20,000 in interest,
- ■ £8,000 for legal costs,
- ■ £46,400 for personal injury and injury to feelings.

The tribunal ruled that Siddiqui was subjected to a 'vicious campaign aimed at removing him from the shift'. The abuse included offensive graffiti, threats to burn him, damage to his car, and threats to his wife and children. Despite repeated complaints, management took no action and, in fact, his immediate manager gave 'tacit support' to the campaign. It was only when a hidden camera was put in place recording specific racial abuse from colleagues, that action was taken to stop the campaign.

Source: Martin (2004)

Approaches to EO Policy

The combination of legislative requirements and the arguments behind the business case detailed earlier should be sufficiently convincing for most organisations. It is not enough simply to stamp 'we are an equal opportunities employee' on advertisements or even just to adapt one of the toilets so they can be used by disabled employees. In recent years, there have seen a number of debates as to the make-up of 'best practice' approaches. What form should *positive action* take and how far can *affirmative action* go to remain both legal and ethical? How much can an EO approach succeed on its own without effecting a *cultural change* approach? Should *managing diversity* take the place of a conventional *EO* approach.

The original acts gave indications that positive action was to be encouraged under certain conditions. Section 48 of the SDA and Section 37 of the RRA allowed employers to direct training and experience to under-represented groups where the number of persons of that sex or race doing that work is comparatively small. It has never stretched to preferential offers of employment which remains a form of illegal discrimination.

In their 1996 'Guidance Notes for Employers on Setting targets for Gender Equality' the EOC set out two types of targets, as set out in Figure 3.2.

Qualitative targets	Quantitative targets
To incorporate equal opportunity objectives into management appraisal	To raise the application rate of black and ethnic minority men and women from 2% to 10% over 2 years
To implement a flexible working/part-time/job sharing policy and special leave arrangements within 2 years	To raise the proportion of females taking part in management development training from 40% to 60% over 2 years
To implement a sexual harassment policy this year	To improve the return rate of women from maternity leave from 60% to 70% within a year

Figure 3.2
Equality targets (*Source:* EOC, 1996)

They go on to differentiate between the examples of quantitative targets and an illegal 'quota' system (e.g. to promote women to 80% of vacant supervisory posts).

Affirmative (or positive) action aims to provide a workforce that reflects the composition of the community from which the organisation draws its labour force. The belief is that it helps those that are disadvantaged to 'get to the starting line' or that it helps create a 'level playing field'. It involves the setting of targets and a positive programme of communication within the geographical areas concerned. But experience in America has been mixed and the Supreme Court took an influential decision in 1995 to reduce the scope of federal programmes which targeted contracts at firms that employed large number of women or ethnic minority staff. Commentators reflected that there were indications that black Americans no longer see affirmative action as either necessary or desirable (Merrick, 1995).

In the UK, the high profile Macpherson Report into the murder of black teenage, Stephen Lawrence, has led to the Home Secretary announcing the introduction of targets for the recruitment of ethnic minorities into the Police Service, followed shortly afterwards by similar targets for the fire, immigration, probation and prison services (Blackstock, 1999). Positive discrimination overstepped the mark in ACAS versus Taylor (EAT 11-02-98) where a male employee of ACAS suffered unlawful sex discrimination during a promotion exercise because the employer practiced positive discrimination in favour of female candidates.

Stand-alone campaigns to improve EO are rarely successful on their own. By definition, action needs to be taken because the cultural ethos of the organisation has remained traditionally linked to unequal opportunities, with privileged groups having preferential opportunities to jobs and promotion.

A successful strategy will need to harness the authority of those directors who have achieved success under the traditional culture and encourage a fundamental shift in their approach to the subject. Hertfordshire County Council (see Case study 3.1) followed this path using the model shown in Figure 3.3.

Cultural change approach	Equality programme approach
Perceived as a high status project	Perceived as a low status project
Involves all stakeholders	Responsibility rests with HR department
Success linked to business strategy	Introduced to meet legal threats
Lead by top management with their continual support	Initial support from top management but involvement occasional and perfunctory
Stirs positive emotions	Stirs negative emotions
New language matching the change process	Language and reality do not match
Clear goals and standards set	Steeped in generalities or vague goals
Aims to change behaviour	Aims to protect or divert unsuitable behaviour
Communicated to all parts of the organisation	Communicated only to limited areas

Figure 3.3
Cultural change versus equality programme (*Source*: Hertfordshire County Council internal paper)

While traditional EO approaches rely on removing the barriers to equality for disadvantaged groups through legal sanctions and firm targets, an alternative approach is through the concept of managing diversity. This is based on the theory that people should be valued as individuals for reasons related to business interests, as well as for moral and social reasons. Kandola and Fullerton (1998) defined managing diversity as:

'The basic concept of managing diversity accepts that the workforce consists of a diverse population of people. The diversity consists of visible and non-visible differences which will include factors such as sex, age, background, race, disability, personality and workstyle. It is founded on the premise that harnessing these differences will create a productive environment in which everybody feels valued, where their talents are being fully utilised and in which organisational goals are met.'
Kandola and Fullerton (1998: p. 146)

Managing diversity is a much subtler process than an EO drive. Employees are not selected or promoted on the basis of ethnic or gender calculations but because of their individual and varied contribution they can make to their job and the organisation. Part of the thinking is that too much of a concentration on disadvantaged groups may eventually lead to a backlash from majority groups so the emphasis is on inclusion, fairness and relevance to all employees.

The inherent differences between the two approaches is shown in Figure 3.4. and the Meteor Case Study at the end of chapter looks at the practical implication of these concepts.

Equal opportunities	Managing diversity
Seeks to remove discrimination	Seeks to provide opportunities for all employees
A major issue for disadvantaged groups	Seen as relevant to all employees
Sets clear targets	Does not rely on positive action
An issue driven by HR activists	Inclusive of all management and employees
To meet potential and actual legislative threats	Driven by business needs

Figure 3.4
Equal opportunities and managing diversity (*Source*: Kandola Fullerton, 1998)

A 10-year research project carried out by occupational psychologists Pearn Kandola showed that firm targets and positive action by organisations had started to drop substantially, especially in targets on sex and race. However, this was not to say that the managing diversity approach had taken over. Only 25% of organisations considered that they would make progress on diversity and less than 8% provided diversity training for all staff (Overell, 1997b).

Further evidence that managing diversity is a complex process has come from a report (CIPD, 2004) which found that impressive progress had been made in finding ways of accessing diverse talent and using different perspectives and ideas to increase creativity and innovation to gain economic advantage. However, different kinds of diversity – social- and knowledge-based for example – impact on the organisation in different ways in different contexts and can cause conflict if not handled appropriately.

The two policies are not entirely contradictory. Removing discrimination can lead to opportunities for all employees. Like a good school teacher, a good employer will want to encourage and develop all employees but realise at the same time that some will need that little bit more extra help. A policy initiated by human resource (HR) activists can be led by all the directors and serve to include all sections and interests. It is possible, however, that the subtleties of managing diversity may disguise a policy of inaction or that a strident EO campaign can dichotomise viewpoints into two armed camps. In the next section, the implications for necessary action in HR areas are discussed with recommendations based on a fusion of the two viewpoints.

Implications for EO practice

This section will look at the following areas where action is required:

- Finding out the facts including carrying out EO audits
- Generating and communicating EO Policies
- Recruitment and selection
- Working practices
- Disability requirements
- Health and safety issues
- Performance Management issues
- Handling harassment
- Equal pay issues.

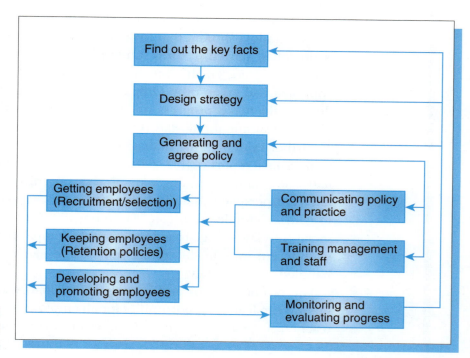

Figure 3.5
Action on equal opportunities

Note: For further reading on Codes of Practice, please see details in Further Reading at the end of this chapter.

A diagrammatic indication of action required is shown in Figure 3.5.

Finding out the facts

Policies and practices cannot be effectively constructed without a systematic *audit* of where the organisation finds itself. The *audit* will be based on two issues. The first is the external relationship with the community at large. How does the employment structure mirror the community in terms of age, sex, race and disability? Does it vary at different management levels or by department? It is not unknown for an organisation to have a well-balanced total workforce but for the vast majority of the management and supervisory grades to be white males. Another factor to consider is the contacts with the community, especially where there is strong ethnic presence. Does the organisation play a part in supporting community activities such as by sponsoring social or sporting events or, in larger organisations, seconding managers to work in the community for short periods as part of their personal development?

The second audit concerns the internal relationships. This should examine the number of sex, race, disability and age grievances reported, and a survey of initiatives that have taken place in the period under review, such as access training, explicit policies on harassment or elimination of age criteria. Indications of a lack of success would be a lack of knowledge or indifference from employees, managers complaining of 'too much political correctness' or lack of applications from women or minority groups for promotion. Customised audits can be commissioned from specialised organisations that will find out the views of specific employee groups to the operation of EO Policies.

In 2003, the British government required government departments to carry out periodic equal pay audits.

Generating and communicating EO strategy and policies

Further decisions will have to be made on where the organisation stands in respect of the EO or managing diversity approach and whether the objectives will be veer towards the quantitative or the qualitative. The policy statement should include the following features:

- Commitment to equal treatment throughout the organisation.
- Justification of why it is important for the organisation and its employees.

- Assignment of organisational responsibility. (Somebody with authority and ability to achieve results.)
- Incorporation of EO objectives into the competency framework (if one exists) or individual performance objectives.
- Outline of the nature of training initiatives to assist the achievement of the objectives.
- Outline of recruitment, promotion and other key EO initiatives and practices.
- How grievances will be dealt with quickly and effectively.
- How monitoring is going to take place.

Not only does it need board-level commitment but it is also vital that there is a 'champion' who will take hold of the policies and ensure they are effectively implemented throughout the organisation.

It is not advisable to rely on non-verbal means of communication of this policy (and any revisions). Putting the policy onto the intranet may be necessary but will play little part in changing attitudes or culture. A series of meetings should be held (plus a corporate video from the managing director in a large organisation) so that the real message can be consistently applied across the whole organisation. Meetings should also allow questions to be asked and revealing comments to be made.

Grievances concerning EO should be dealt with through the organisation's grievance procedure although those concerning harassment need to have especially careful consideration as we shall see later.

Recruitment and selection

This is probably the most significant area for policy and practice to ensure that all sections of the community have EO for gaining employment and that decisions are taken on merit alone. In *advertising*, it is unlawful to publish an advertisement which may be understood to indicate an intention to discriminate (S.38 of SD ACT, S.29 of RR Act). Job titles must be sexless, such as 'operator' or 'telephonist', or an indication must be given that applications from both sexes are welcomed. In EOC versus Eldridge McFarlane-Watts (COIT 17256/90), an advertisement for a secretary was headed 'The Secretary's prayer' and took the form of a poem seeking a secretary 'willing to listen to her master's voice on eternal tapes'. The tribunal held that this wording gave a clear indication of an intention to discriminate against men.

A picture 'speaks a thousand words' so, if there is space, an illustration in an advertisement depicting men, women and a mix of races, and disabilities clearly indicates a welcome to all applicants. Consideration should also be given as to where advertisements are placed. Choosing a magazine with predominantly male or female readership is unwise unless used as part of a balanced choice of media. Likewise, using ethnic minority media can be valuable for broadening the sources of recruits but should not be used on its own.

Sources of recruitment must be broad and not restricted simply to word of mouth, relatives, trade union sources or simply filling vacancies through unsolicited letters.

Selection processes run up against a set of potentially difficult problems:

- The job specification must not be unnecessarily restrictive or unjustifiably demanding to the extent that it may exclude large numbers of applicants in terms of sex, race or disability. Care needs to be taken here in terms of the level of skills, use of written and spoken English, mobility and years of experience required. The application form should only contain questions that are relevant to the job and working generally at the organisation. The Code of Practice on sex discrimination recommends that questions on marital status and number of children should not be included (they can be asked after selection for pension purposes).
- A number of organisations use systems of ethnic monitoring which provide additional sheets for applicants to complete which are separated from the application form.
- Short-listing should be carried out without consideration of sex, race, age or disability. This is formalised by some organisations who extract the names and ages of applicants before the short-listing process. Under the Disability tick symbol, employers give guaranteed job interviews to disabled applicants.
- Only those selection tests that are free from racial bias (some older tests were standardised on all-white groups) should be used and that sufficient additional help is given in preparation where this is required. Disabled applicants may need special assistance in taking the tests.
- Interviewing needs to be carried out in a way that all candidates are treated equally and fairly. Preparation and using a carefully worked-through structured interview system is the best protection against claims of discrimination. It is probably unwise to ask questions about domestic arrangements, even if they are asked of all candidates except to point out positive features of the organisation's family-friendly benefits.

A record of reasons for rejection must be kept in case of a subsequent claim.

- The special needs of interviewees need to be considered. When Val Milnes, a disabled HR manager who is paralysed from the waist down, attended interviews, numerous difficulties presented themselves in terms of parking, access, room suitability and interviewer reaction. Moreover, it was clear that many interviewers were just going through the motions to fulfil their requirements under the disability tick symbol requirements (Glover, 2002).

For further examples of innovative recruitment policies, see the Asda Case study 3.2 and the Penguin Books Case study 3.3.

Case study 3.2

Asda's recruitment policy

When Asda announced plans to set up a new store in Hulme, Manchester, which had a large ethnic population and high unemployment, it was not made welcome with open arms. Many local businesses had moved out and new ones recruited from outside the area so the area had little experience of benefits from incoming enterprises. Initially, there were fears that they would be a typical white, prejudiced employer but Asda was determined to work with the local community and recruit locally. After an extended consultation, including a business information day, helped by the local Commission for Racial Equality representative, they decided to advertise only in the local paper and not in the Manchester Evening News and also to link up with community groups and those supporting the unemployed. Help was given to the unemployed (the local figure was 70%) with training provided at recruitment fairs in interview skills.

The result of the drive was that 90% of the stores staff were recruited locally and that 50% were of ethnic origin compared to Hulme's 32%. Each new employee is given a Colleague Handbook which outlines policy and what it means for them, including what to do if they experience unacceptable behaviour, including a confidential help line to a senior HR manager.

Source: Equal Opportunities Review (1999)

Case study 3.3

Improving racial equality at Penguin books

In response to a concern that Penguin, a London-based publisher, was not reflecting the overall London ethnic population, which is estimated to make-up 30% of the capital's population, an internal investigation indicated that people from ethnic minorities were not getting entry level positions. It was not institutional racism, just a lack of pro-active policies on recruitment. In the early 2000s, the company developed a number of initiatives. Firstly, it started to spend much more time going out to Universities and working with career services to target ethnic minority students. It had particular success with its open days, to which it invited young people from 'under-represented groups'. Secondly, it started offering a number of paid internships each summer, working hard to ensure a diverse mix of people, and expanded the number of unpaid work experience schemes. It was expected that these temporary staff would provide a good pool of potential permanent employees in the future. Finally, the organisation worked much closer with its agencies to ensure a representative list of potential candidates so that the proportion of ethnic candidates rose from 12% to 22% within 2 years.

Source: Edwards (2004)

Retention policies

Family-friendly and *Cultural Diversity* Policies have extended rapidly in recent years (see Chapter 6) and these make a real difference to the equality environment. Providing part-time or flexible hours contracts, offering job shares, creches or child-care vouchers, career and caring breaks and out-of-school schemes all provide support and assistance to those with family responsibilities (still mostly women but a growing proportion of men) who wish to balance the demands of work and home.

Cultural diversity includes the provision of specialised foods, choice over holidays and festivals, and freedom over dress and uniform. There is a need, however, to include all these freedoms within the requirements of health and safety and the public image for those meeting the public. Clarification was eventually reached on dress in the case of Smith versus Safeway PLC (1996, March 5, *the Times*). In this Court of

Appeal case, Mr Smith, who worked in the delicatessen, had objected to having to cut his hair when it became shoulder length, when women were allowed to tie their long hair back. The Court rejected his claim, deciding that organisations can have different requirements of men and women, taking conventional attitudes into account. But, when viewed as a whole, it should not have a less favourable impact on one sex. In a similar case, the Employment Appeal Tribunal decided that a female nurse was required to wear a cap even though this did not apply to men who had their own uniform requirements (Burrett, H. versus West Birmingham Health Authority – detailed in IDS Brief 511, February 1994, p. 17).

Care will have to be taken in the case of requests on the grounds of religious belief. Requests by Muslims for facilities and time off for prayers at specific times will have to be carefully considered, for examples.

Disability requirements

The DDA lays down the need for 'reasonable adjustments' to be made to employment arrangements to compensate for practical problems faced by a disabled person. Apart from wheelchair access, this can include altering the working times, accepting additional time off for treatment (disabled employees generally have excellent attendance records so this is a small burden on the employer), providing a reader or special braille equipment and paying for specialised training where transfers to other occupations are required. The 'reasonable' nature of the adjustments relate to the cost of the adjustments in relation to the organisation's resources, the current situation in relation to the employment of disabled persons in the organisation and the ease or difficulty and ultimate benefits or making those adjustments. The emphasis is on two situations. Firstly, for existing employees faced with a developing disability or one arisen from a serious accident. Secondly, where an employer receives an application from a disabled person. In general, there is a greater onus on the employer in the case of an existing employee but where the organisation has a very low proportion of disabled persons, then the onus on making reasonable provisions grows larger.

Health and safety

The issues here include the need for multi-language safety signs, documents, training and testing, and necessary adjustments for disabled employees. Care should also be taken in relation to the Manual Handling Operations Regulations 1992 (see Chapter 11) to ensure warehousing and other operations can be manageable by both sexes.

Performance management issues

It is vital that all employees have the opportunity to carry out their work to their best ability and to share in career-progression opportunities. The much-used expression 'glass ceiling' indicates that women have promotion limitations placed on them. The importance of 'role models', examples of successful women or members of ethnic minorities who show what can be achieved and are examples for others to emulate, cannot be under-estimated. However, there is considerable opposition to the concept of 'tokenism' where women have been appointed to senior management positions simply so that the organisation can appear satisfied that they have carried out their EO obligations. A 'glass escalator' policy, where promotion criteria is transparent and fairly operated, should be the preferred option.

Courses limited to women, such as 'Women into Management' or 'Assertiveness Training', were popular 10 years ago but have far fewer takers today. This may be a healthy sign as more women believe that they do not need such courses and can achieve their goals without specific help. Women may also feel uncomfortable at being identified as needing such support. Mentoring has an important place here with role models providing the personal help and examples in cultivating future management and supervisory skills to aspiring trainees. A good example in the Halifax bank is shown in Case study 3.4.

Case study 3.4

Giving confidence to women to climb the ladder in Halifax Bank

Twice a year, about 60 women gather at Halifax headquarters to take part in a 'glass ceiling' event. Since the launch of their 'Fair's Fair' diversity programme in 1998, the number of female senior managers has increased from 7% to 26% while the presence of women at middle management has risen from 26% to 42%. The meetings are primarily to boost the confidence of the women so that they believe they can take the next step up the ladder. Encouragement is given to networking skills and the ability to display ambition and assertiveness without being aggressive.

Source: Merrick (2001)

Within the performance management scheme itself, it is important that targets are seen to be fair and equitable across all groups, as are the resulting training and reward outcomes. Developing disabilities would need to be taken into account. For example, it would only be fair to adjust the individual targets for an employee working as a word processor or customer call centre operator if they developed debilitating illnesses.

Handling harassment and bullying

We have already seen some examples of the incidence of harassment that have finished up at tribunals. The Chartered Institute of Personnel and Development (CIPD) describe harassment as:

> 'Unwanted behaviour which a person finds intimidating, upsetting, embarrassing, humiliating or offensive. It is essential to remember that it is not the intention of the perpetrator that is key in deciding whether harassment has occurred but whether the behaviour is unacceptable by normal standards and disadvantageous'.
>
> IPD(1997b: p. 1)

Harassment can also take the form of stalking, offensive jokes, wide use of 'pin-ups', gratuitous swearing and, especially in Northern Ireland, the singing of sectarian songs and the flying of bunting and flags. The inevitable outcome for the victim is fear, stress which can lead to anguish and depression, and under-performance. For the general employee environment, it can lead to an unpleasant rift between those who cause and support the harassment and those who support the victims or are victims themselves. It is an exhibition of power over those who tend towards vulnerability and has no place in an organisation that wishes the culture to be one of commitment, teamworking and support.

Although bullying is not protected per se in equality legislation, claims can be made by victims under a number of headings. Employers are under a duty of care to provide a safe environment; they have an implied duty to maintain mutual trust and confidence; finally, employees can claim that the lack of protection was sufficient to bring about constructive dismissal. It is the lack of action by the employer which enables the claim to be made against them.

The main aim of policy in this area is complete prevention. It should start with a policy statement which explains the different forms of harassment and bullying, and the damage they cause to the organisation and its employees. It should stress the need for mutual respect at all levels and the need for all employees to feel valued. The way that allegations will be treated should be set out, that they will be speedy, fair and confidential, and promise protection from victimisation for the complainant. It should be made clear that individuals are liable to pay compensation to the victims as well as lose their jobs. This statement should be communicated to all employees in a clear and unambiguous way, giving opportunities for discussion and for questions to be asked.

Procedure for handling harassment

It is becoming more common for the organisation to provide independent counsellors to whom victims can turn for advice in the strictest confidence and without pressure. They will help the victim decide whether or not to take their complaint forward although they will be encouraged not to ignore behaviour, which makes them, and probably other members of the department, uncomfortable. They will also be encouraged to be able to produce evidence, in the form of diary entries or notes of witnesses present. Without any action, it is not likely to stop.

Unless the incident is very serious, complaints should generally be dealt with internally and informally so as a solution can be reached quickly and without too much embarrassment. What is difficult in these circumstances is the maintenance of confidentiality. The alleged harasser, having been told of their actions by a third party, often regarded as an appropriate role for a member of the HR department, and why they cause distress, has the right to know who is making the allegation. Hopefully, once the issue has been raised, then the harassment will stop and no formal punishment need be exercised. At this stage, a solution may be the agreed transfer of one of the parties.

However, if it is a one-off serious incident, or harassment continues after informal discussions, then the process will need to be taken through the official grievance or disciplinary procedure. In Midland Bank, the procedure is that a trained investigator from another area will be appointed to carry out interviews and produce a report. On the basis of this report, the HR department decide if formal disciplinary proceedings are to take place (Crabb, 1995). During the procedure, it is likely that neither party will want to continue to work in the same office or near locality within which most harassment occurs. In some procedures, the accused is suspended on pay, pending investigation, but this can be regarded as judgemental. Overall, it is probably better to allow both parties to take garden leave but, because of the sensitivity of the issue, to proceed as quickly as possible.

If the complaint is upheld, then the outcome depends on the severity of the offence. It can stretch from immediate dismissal to a warning and/or transfer to another position, sometimes at a reduced grading. The incident should be used to examine existing arrangements and to set changes in motion so it will, hopefully, not be repeated.

Equal pay issues

The EOC Code of Practice on Equal pay suggests that there are opportunities for discrimination on all aspects of pay:

- On the basic rate, women can be on lower grades because the jobs in which they predominate have not been evaluated fairly.
- Women may not have been represented properly on the job evaluation committee or the factors chosen in the scheme may favour men (supervision, strength required and technical skills).
- They may also be appointed at lower starting points on the pay scale.
- They may also move more slowly to the top of the scale if movement depends on achieving competencies or performance. This may be because of the unfair rating system which is skewed against women.
- On performance pay, women may have targets which are too demanding compared to men or the assessments made by managers (still mainly men) may be unfair towards women.
- Women may have reduced access to benefits, such as allowances and company cars because of the way their jobs are graded or because decisions are taken in a discriminatory way by management.

When an organisation sets up pay systems or evaluates existing ones, it is important that these potential problems are open to investigation and rectification. A transparent and accessible appeal system is also essential to help women put their case before having to turn to legal redress.

Age discrimination

The changing demography, explained in Chapter 1, will result in the over-45s dominating the workforce in the twenty-first century. By 2021, 46% of the workforce will be over 45 and, taking Europe as a whole, the number of people aged 50–64 will have increased by 20% in two decades. Despite the growing importance of this section of the workforce, ageism remains entrenched in society and the workplace. Discrimination is displayed principally at recruitment when age limits are often overtly or covertly used by describing the ideal candidate in an advertisement as 'between 25 and 35' or using more indirect descriptions as 'a recent graduate' or 'with 1–3 years experience'.

The new expression '*glass precipice*' indicates that older employees may be constrained from career-development activities where employers see a limited investment return from training while redundancy selection can often work against older employees, especially in non-unionised establishments where no formal selection procedure is agreed. The extent of this overt discrimination is shown by the huge reduction in economic activity rates of older men in the last 50 years, as shown in Figure 3.6. In the 1950s, over 90% of men over 55 were in paid employment but this had fallen to just over 60% by 2000.

	1951	1961	1971	1981	1990	2000
Men aged 55–59	95.0	97.1	95.3	89.4	81.4	74.9
Men aged 60–64	87.7	91.0	86.6	69.3	54.6	50.3
Men aged over 65	31.1	25.0	23.5	10.3	8.8	7.9
Women aged 55–59	29.1	39.2	50.9	53.4	54.8	57.6
Women aged 60–64	14.1	19.7	28.8	23.3	22.7	25.9
Women aged over 65	4.1	4.6	6.3	3.7	3.4	3.4

Figure 3.6 Economic activity rates of men and women 1950–2000 (*Source*: OECD 2001 quoted in Duncan, 2003)

As with all other discrimination, it is counter-productive in that it limits the sources of available competent candidates and may result in the loss of essential skills and company operating knowledge when large numbers of older employees are encouraged or forced to leave. Having a low-activity rate puts a large burden on the state through benefit payments, especially invalidity benefit and public sector early retirement pensions. It has also been one of the causes of the early twenty-first century crisis in private pension funds, where older employees have been persuaded to accept redundancy or early retirement through generous provisions paid by the funds.

In 1999, the government introduced a voluntary Code of Practice on Age Diversity in Employment. This warns employers to avoid ageist practices in advertising, cautions against asking only older applicants for medical references and baring older staff from promotion and suggests that age diversity in the employment context provides many benefits. This voluntary code did not go far enough for many activists and there have been pressures throughout Europe in recent years from such organisations as The Employers Forum on Age, for legislation to be implemented in this area. This finally arrived with the EU Equal Treatment in Employment and Occupation Directive 2000.

Legislation takes effect in October 2006 introducing the principle of equal treatment into all aspects of age. Currently, age discrimination is enshrined in law in areas of redundancy and unfair dismissal where no claims can be successful if the employee is over 65 and all employees have a fixed retirement age. These elements may need to change to meet the requirements of the EU Directive. Direct discrimination in job adverts will be outlawed as will age-related promotion decisions. It is likely that interview questions, such as 'When do you intend to retire' will be held to be discriminatory as will expressions like 'we went for the younger person – they have more enthusiasm and are less of a health risk'.

Having said all this, Article 6 of the Directive allows different treatment on the ground of age if objectively and reasonably justified, setting out the following examples:

- Maximum age limits for recruitment based on training needs of the job or the need for a reasonable period before retirement. This will apply, presumably, for jobs such as airline pilots.
- Protection of young workers, such as restricting their employment on night work or on dangerous machinery.
- Encouraging or rewarding loyalty by paying long service awards.
- Allowing employment planning to ensure a workforce that is age-balanced to a reasonable degree.

There will be a continuous debate over how much difference the legislation will make, given the broad exceptions that may allow organisations to continue to discriminate, albeit in a less overt fashion (GMB, 2001). Legislation has the tendency to 'creep' and loopholes to be closed, either in the UK courts or at the European Court of Justice.

On the more positive side, there is good evidence that some employers have little respect for age discrimination. On the contrary, there is the well-known case of B and Q superstores, who have specifically recruited a large proportion of older employees on the grounds that they know something about do-it-yourself and have more patience with customers (Worsely, 1996). This has been copied by most of their competitors who have also appreciated the cost advantages of employing older people. Sainsburys has also operated a much more age-friendly since the mid-1980s (see Case study 3.5).

Case study 3.5

Age diversity at Sainsburys

Sainsburys began to develop plans in 1986 to target older employees and, by the early 2000s, 15% are over 50 and 1% over 65. It produced a retirement plan and pension protection mechanisms, enabling members to draw partially on their pension to top up a reduced salary. Employees can reduce their hours without significantly decreasing their net income and they can continue to contribute to their pension up to the age of 75. Age has been removed from the application form and is requested for monitoring only.

The company have reported that their mixed age workforce has led to improved customer satisfaction by more accurately reflecting the profile of their customers. It also believes that the new approach has contributed to a better-motivated workforce which feels more valued and more willing to contribute to business success.

Source: DTI website

Monitoring and evaluation – the role of HR

This final section reverts back to the starting point:- Where does the organisation stand in terms of its own agenda and objectives? We emphasised in Chapter 1 that two of the major strengths of HR should be its reputation for an independent viewpoint and an ethical approach and these areas should be fully utilised to examine and monitor what is going on and how effective initiatives have been. The central feature of an effective HR intervention is to have an overall strategy. This can be the most useful device, apart from the statistical targets that may be utilised, is an employee attitude survey which asked employees to give their viewpoint on EO issues, especially whether they are improving or deteriorating. Another approach is through benchmarking, in other words to find out how the organisation is performing in relation to similar companies or those professing to operate best practice.

Ensuring that employees responsible for recruitment, selection, performance management, and health and safety are all knowledgeable is a further important role for HR, as is the consideration of changing working practices to enable a better balance to be achieved between home and work. HR should also be in the best position to make fair investigations into accusations of discrimination, victimisation and harassment.

A further examples of a concerted, organisation-wide approach is detailed in Case study 3.6.

Case study 3.6

Agreed programme of action on EO at a Beaverbrook College*

Strategic and financial management

- Integrate equality considerations within the strategic and financial planning process.
- Recognise that equality arrangements could be financially rewarding as well as achieving corporate objectives.
- Accept that there is a direct link between equality arrangements, access, increasing students numbers through recruitment and retention and achieving corporate goals.

Ethos and Philosophy

- Continue to reflect the need for strong and positive links and partnerships between the College and the community within the corporate strategies, policies, vision and mission statements, personnel and staffing guidelines.

■ Reward achievements in the promotion of equality targets where appropriate.

■ Encourage all staff and students to contribute to good practice and to accept responsibility for the promotion of equality arrangements.

Advertising, marketing and promotion

■ Advertising in community media and distribution of publicity through community organisations and businesses owned by ethnic minority.

■ Make full use of ethnic minority network.

■ Target schools, clubs and centres with large ethnic minority users.

Food, Personal services, cultural and religious needs

■ Encourage multi-cultural activities within and outside the College.

■ Engage counsellors/guidance officers with reasonable understanding and knowledge of the cultural needs of the large ethnic groups and a strong commitment to equality, diversity and multi-culturalism.

■ Provide a wider choice of food including vegetarian and Halal dishes.

Staffing and recruitment issues

■ Carry out awareness training for staff dealing with enquiries and interviews.

■ Ensure applications are re-designed to capture required equality information.

■ Appoint more visible ethnic minority governors and staff.

■ Ensure bilingual staff are available to help with visits by ethnic minority parents and relatives to the College to help them to understand what is going on.

■ Target recruitment advertisements using the ethnic minority facilities.

Environment and communications

- Display positive images of students, staff and communities.
- Establish a complaints policy and a grievance policy which includes an anti-racist perspective.
- Deal firmly with racist graffiti, all forms of harassment, violence, abuse, bullying and provocation.
- Ensure that staff are made aware of their responsibilities towards equality at planning and operational levels.

*The name of this College has been changed to preserve confidentiality but the action programme is real.

It is not always the case that policies and procedures achieve the results that are required as shown in the Meteor case study.

Meteor case study

EO in practice

Sarah sat down to draft her EO Policies and Practices document ready for the management meeting the following week. She had studied the debate between the Managing Diversity approach and the traditional EO approach, knew the arguments from both sides and considered both had value. She was therefore determined to put in place a system that had the best of both worlds.

She knew the locality had a strong ethnic element, mostly Pakistanis, making up around 8–10% of the population and that the workforces of most factories in the area were male dominated. An objective was set in her mind to recruit at least 8% from ethnic minorities and to include a substantial number of females into the short lists.

There was a thriving publication so she included it on the list for advertising vacancies and designed an advertisement where the illustration included males and females, white and ethnic minority employees working together. However, she made no mention in the advertisements of an EO policy or any special wording to encourage it.

The recruiting team consisted of a number of line managers and she made sure that those who had not attended an EO awareness course did so before the recruitment started. She also put forward a proposal for courses to be designed to help prepare employees for promotion. Although directed at all employees, she planned to ask managers to give special consideration to minority groups. If she could ensure that a number of women and Pakistanis had the ability, aptitude and drive for promotion to team leader and made a success of it, then they would act as role models. A small number of jobs on the site had been identified as possibilities for disabled employees. She planned to make contact with the Pakistani community group and arrange for a translator to be present on each of the occasions where application forms had to be completed and interviews took place. Finally, she contacted the external caterer to ensure that there was a sufficient range of meals suitable for all groups of employees.

Another set of proposals she made covered family-friendly benefits. She put forward a plan for employees to job share throughout the site. This would need to be arranged between two employees who both wanted to work part-time. They would need to work with their team leader to ensure the shifts and skills needed were covered. Given the complexities of the shift system in the factory, flexible hours and flexitime would be very difficult to organise but this would be possible in the offices.

At the management meeting, she was closely questioned by two production managers regarding the overall plan. Although not overtly racist, they indicated a small degree of hostility towards specific proposals, specifically the interpreter. They considered it essential that all applicants had a firm grasp of English so they could follow instructions, including those in Health and Safety. All the work was semi-skilled and skilled, requiring judgement and effective communication within the team. After considering the issues, Sarah agreed to drop that proposal.

They also could not see the point of encouraging variable hours, having the viewpoint that this would simply lead to all female employees wanting to go part-time. Sarah was not happy to concede on this issue but took Scott's advice to give way here, as it was not a key component, and made a note to raise it again in a year's time.

The recruitment process was not straightforward. Despite having a reasonable response from minority groups, there were objections from the two managers to a number of female and ethnic applicants going onto the short list. Sarah answered most of their points by indicating that organising an interview do not mean a commitment to select. When it came to the interviews themselves, the proportion of rejections for female and ethnic applicants was particularly high from the same two managers. The reasons given were petty and illogical and discussing the cases took up a considerable amount of time. Sarah did not want to make an appointment over their heads and it needed a round-table meeting with Scott and the site manager to reach compromise decisions where a proportion went on to the final selection stage.

Towards the end of the first batch of selections, Sarah received two letters of complaint. One was from a Pakistani who had not been selected for interview. She pointed out that her neighbour had been selected but had fewer qualifications and less experience than she had. She threatened action unless the matter was re-considered. The second was from the husband of an applicant who claimed that his wife had been insulted by a number of questions at the interview concerning her previous experience and aspects of her personal life, such as caring responsibilities. Sarah had not been involved in either of these cases; both interviews had been carried out by the two hostile managers.

Sarah was very concerned that her ambition to introduce 'best practice' in the unit did not seem to be progressing very well.

Summary

- There are two strong cases for eliminating discrimination from the workplace. These are, firstly, the obligations from laws outlawing discrimination on the grounds of race, sex and disability and, secondly, the business case which is based on changing demography, the need to improve relations with all customers and all communities and to be seen as a good employer.
- Indirect discrimination occurs where a condition or policy affects adversely members of one race, sex or the disabled.
- More attention is now given to cases of victimisation, bullying and harassment to ensure that vulnerable employees receive better protection.
- Organisations need to consider carefully whether an approach of managing diversity is preferable to that of a traditional EO approach.
- Champions are required to drive EO through the organisation and to ensure that it is correctly applied in recruitment, selection, retention, pay and employee development activities.

Student activity

1 You have been asked to conduct an EO survey in an organisation of 1000 employees on one site. How would you carry this out?

In your answer, design a questionnaire and indicate how you may use it. You may also want to explain how focus groups may provide useful information.

2   Read the research article by Collinson and Collinson (Focus on the Law 3.1) and discuss which you believe to be the most appropriate of the four different courses of action.

3   Look up the case in Spotlight on the Law 3.2. Discuss how you would respond, as a Tribunal member, to a claim by a citizen of Leeds that they have been discriminated against because of their location and accent.

4   Read the source of Spotlight on the law 3.4 and compare their decisions over reasonable adjustment with more recent cases. Has the position changed as more decisions have been made at higher courts?

5   Role play interviews from the two complainants in the Meteor case studies. Decide on what would be Sarah's best course of action.

References

ACAS (1998) Annual Report 1998. ACAS.

Arkin, A. (1995) Big firms unite to put an end to ageist practices. *People Management*, 7 September, p. 12.

Blackstock, C. (1999) Straw to set job targets for minorities. *The Guardian*, 5 July.

Central Statistical Office (1995) *Social Focus on Women*, HMSO.

CIPD (2004) Diversity: stacking up the evidence. *Executive briefing*. CIPD.

Clark, S. (1998) Fair progress. *Personnel Today*, 21 May, pp. 21–24.

Cockburn, C. (1991) *In the way of Women*. Macmillan.

Collinson, M., Collinson, D. (1996) 'It's only Dick' The sexual harassment of women managers in insurance sales. *Work, Employment and Society*, **10**(1): 29–56.

Crabb, S. (1995) Violence at work: the brutal truths. *People Management*, 27 July, pp. 25–29.

Delgado, M. (1999) Damning new report criticises 'racist and sexist' fire service. *London Evening Standard*, 17 September.

Duncan, C. (2003) Assessing anti-ageism routes to older worker re-engagement. *Work, Employment and Society*, **17**(1): pp. 101–120.

Edwards, C. (2004) Do the write thing. *People Management*, 17 June, 36–38.

EOC (1987) *Formal Investigation Report: Dan Air*. Equal Opportunity Commission.

Equal Opportunities Review (1995) *Accord ends CRE three-year Court Action*. No 61, *May/June*, 7–8.

Equal Opportunities Review (1993) *Sexual Harassment at Work Widespread*. No 51, *January/February*, 5–6.

Equal Opportunities Review (1999). *Opportunities for Ethnic minorities.* May/June, 16–17.

Equal Opportunity Commission (1996). *Guidance Notes for Employers Setting Targets for Gender Equality.*

Equal Opportunities Commission (EOC) (2001) *Sexual Harassment is No Joke.*

Equal Opportunities Commission (EOC) (2004) *Women and Men at Work.*

Glover, C. (2001) Generation Xtra. *People Management,* 22 February, pp. 40–42.

Glover, C. (2002) Ticked off. *People Management,* 24 January, pp. 38–39.

GMB (2001) *Memorandum to Select Committee on Education and Employment. House of Commons.*

Graves, E. (1995) Woman firefighter's career destroyed by 'culture of hostility'. *The Guardian,* 1 April, p. 3.

IDS (1994) IDS Brief 525, September, 1.

IPD (1997a) *Managing Diversity – an IPD position paper.* Institute of Personnel and Development.

IPD (1997b) *Key Facts – Harassment at Work.* Institute of Personnel and Development.

Kandola, R., Fullerton, J. (1998) *Diversity in Action: Managing the Mosaic.* IPD.

Kirton, G., Green, A. (2000) *The Dynamics of Managing Diversity.* Butterworth Heinemann.

Korn, A. (1997) EAT rules on pay-outs for wounded feelings. *Personnel Today,* 10 April, 15.

Martin, N. (2004) Asian postman awarded £130,000 for race abuse. *Daily Telegraph,* 26 May, 8.

Merrick, N. (1995) US Court ruling halts affirmative actions schemes. *People Management,* 29 June, 9.

Merrick, N. (2001) Minority interest. *People Management,* 8 November, 52–53.

OECD (2001) *Labour Force Statistics.*

Overell, S. (1997a) EOC: equal pay is still years away. *People Management,* 2 February, 16.

Overell, S. (1997b) Firms turn away from employment targets. *People Management,* 6 March, 19.

Pickard, J. (1996) Firms rally against age discrimination. *People Management,* 16 May, 10.

Sly, F., Risdon, A. (1999) Disability and the labour market. *Labour Market Trends,* September, 455–466.

Worsely, R. (1996) Only prejudices are old and tired. *People Management,* 11 January, 18–23.

Worsely, R. (1999) The age of forgetfulness. *People Management,* 30 June, 31.

Further reading

For essential policies in developing Equal Opportunity Policies see:

Davidson, M., Cooper, C. (1992) *Shattering the Glass Ceiling.* Paul Chapman.

Ingham, J. (2003) How to implement a diversity policy. *People Management,* 24 July, pp. 44–45.

For a practical guide to harassment issues, see:
Stephens, T. (1999) *Bullying and Sexual Harassment*, IPD.

A further example of a comprehensive approach to initiatives to foster age, disability, race and sex equality at British Telecoms to be found in Steele, J. (1998) Itemised bill. *People Management*, 8 January, 36–38.

A further example of a CRE Investigation (into the RME Union) is given in:
Racial Equality right down the line (1998) Commission for Racial Equality.

For a general introduction to the subject see:
Daniels, K. and MacDonald, L. (2005) *Equality, Diversity and Discrimination*. CIPD.

The EOC publications include:

- Code of Practice on Equal Pay
- Code of Practice on Sex Discrimination
- Guidelines for Equal Opportunities Employers
- Job Evaluation Schemes Free of Sex Bias
- The Sex Discrimination Act and Advertising
- Sex equality and Dismissal and Redundancy
- Sex Equality and Sexual Harassment.

The CIPD give excellent advice on dealing with disability in:
Adapting to Disability: It wasn't so difficult after all. (2003) Change Agenda. CIPD

Web sites

http://www.eoc.org.uk
Equal Opportunities Commission website which includes their substantial list of publications.

http://www.disability.gov.uk/
Government information on the Disability Rights Task Force and the Disability Discrimination Act.

http://www.agepositive.gov.uk/
Government information on tackling age discrimination with numerous case studies.

http://www.efa-agediversity.org.uk/case-studies
Employers Forum on Age case studies.

CHAPTER 4

Recruitment

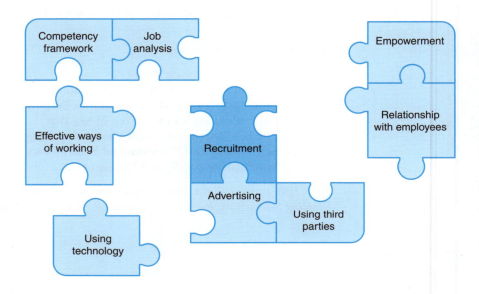

Objectives

When you have read this chapter and carried out the activities, you will be able to:

- Identify the key aims of the recruitment process.
- Write a recruitment policy incorporating equal opportunity procedures.
- Plan a recruitment campaign.
- Understand the difference between job analysis, job description and person specification.
- Design a job advertisement.

Introduction

In Chapter 1, it was shown that the recruitment remains one of the most crucial activities of human resource (HR) specialists in the organisation with the central purpose of attracting suitable applicants for vacant posts. Increasingly, however, it is also seen as very much a public-relations exercise, giving the opportunity to sell the organisation to the public and to present a desirable public image to successful and unsuccessful candidates alike. A further aim is to ensure that there is compliance with the growing legislation on discrimination set out in Chapter 3. On a more practical note, it has been estimated that the average cost of replacing an employee is close to £4300, rising to £6800 for a manager (CIPD, 2003b) so the bottom line is immediately affected if recruitment is not handled well.

In this chapter the four main stages in the recruitment process will be examined:

- *Drafting a recruitment policy*, as a foundation on which the whole recruitment process will be based.
- *Determining whether a vacancy exists*, or whether the apparent gap can be filled in another way.
- *Defining the details of the vacancy*, including the job description and person specification.
- *Attracting the applicants* through advertising and other methods.

Drafting a recruitment policy

A recruitment policy represents the organisation's code of conduct, including the rules to be followed and the standards to be reached. It should include the following areas:

- The importance of considering internal applications and developing existing employees to enable them to be considered for promotion.
- Handling and processing applications with due speed, diligence and courtesy.
- Ensuring that the successful applicants will be chosen without regard to sex, race, age, disability, marital status, religion or any other factor unconnected with their ability to carry out the job.
- Making sure that no false or exaggerated claims are made in recruitment literature or job advertisements.

Does a vacancy exist?

Vacancies can occur either through an existing occupant leaving the organisation or through the creation of a new post through expansion or re-organisation. In either case, it is all too easy to opt for recruitment without first thinking through all the alternatives that could be considered, especially as substantial savings can be made by not recruiting or replacing. Here are some alternatives:

Doing away with the work altogether

Although less likely in these competitive times, there are still some positions where the work carried out adds insufficient value to the organisation to justify a replacement. This may come about through the changing nature of the business, a reduction in the activity that this position services or simply because the job was created in the first place without sufficient thought or justification. The arrival of business process re-organisation has often, through a thorough and detailed examination of each business process, weeded out jobs where the main function may be to process figures or write reports that are no longer required.

Automate the work

The number of employees working in manufacturing industries has drastically reduced over the last 30 years as their work has been replaced with new technology. The latest industrial revolution is in the offices where computer developments have rapidly changed the face of communications and information processing. Although it is seldom possible to replace one employee through mechanisation, the arrival of a vacancy can present the opportunity for a re-think of the work structure.

Contract-out the work

Sub-contracting (or outsourcing, as it is more commonly called today) is becoming more frequent at all levels. Employers are seeing the advantages of avoiding employment costs and making overall savings, especially where the work is put out to competitive tender. It is very common in the building industry and in information technology (IT) but can equally well apply to work done in or outside the organisation's premises. There are, however, potential hazards of having much less control as well as, in some cases, the complexities of TUPE legislation, which deals with the legal aspects of transferring employees from one business to another as the work is outsourced. The work can be contracted to a specialist organisation, such as a facilities maintenance company, or to an agency which will deal with a large number of unskilled or semi-skilled operations and who will recruit, train and supervise the staff themselves. An example of the latter is at the Xerox Corporation plant in the Forest of Dean where much of the production operations are outsourced to Manpower PLC (Stredwick and Ellis, 2005).

Re-organising the work

This can take the form of replacing the post by separating different parts of the work, eliminating those that are unnecessary and farming out the rest within the department or even to other departments. It can also take the form of *job enrichment*, which is to extend the work of existing employees to cover more responsibility and decision making. An example of how this was carried out for airline reservation clerks is given in Parker and Wall (1998). Additional sources dealing with this important area are shown in Further Reading at the end of the chapter.

Re-organising the hours

It may be possible for other members of staff to work overtime to carry out the work, especially if it can be shown that it does not justify a full-time post. This has the advantages of avoiding the recruitment exercise and providing additional salary for those staff willing to work the overtime. It is not, though, a recommended viable long-term alternative as overtime costs are high and it can help to create an overtime culture where work is extended simply to justify working overtime. A second alternative is to re-jig the shift system to partly increase the overall hours or to spread out the work in a more even way. Finally, the post can be converted into a part-time position that should bring cost savings and also allow a degree of flexibility should the volume of work increase in the future.

Defining the details of the vacancy

When it has been decided that a vacancy exists, the specific details of the position need to be agreed. This is carried out in three stages which will be looked at separately:

- Investigating the nature of the work and its key features. This is carried out through *job analysis*.
- Agreeing a summary of the job and the nature of the person who will best fit the post. This means drawing up a *Job description* (or, in some cases, a *Job profile*) and a *Person specification*. Alternatively, a competency profile can be drawn up which will define the nature of the job and the competencies required to carry out that job efficiently. If competencies are used, they will be part of a wider competency framework in use in the organisation.
- Deciding on the terms and conditions of the post, including hours of work, salary and benefits. This is known as an *employment package*.

Job analysis

Purpose of job analysis

Analysing jobs is central to the people management process. Establishing and defining jobs correctly is the starting point for not just the recruitment process; it plays a major part in the way employees are managed and motivated, becoming the basis for the performance management process (see Chapter 8); it helps to establish how employee's training needs are analysed (see Chapter 10) and has a major input into the design of pay systems, especially the comparison of one employee's pay with another (see Chapter 9).

Job analysis can take place in a number of situations, all of which are associated with organisational change. In the event of a merger or takeover, it is not uncommon for an analysis of some of the critical jobs to be commissioned to see if changes need to be made in the light of the new business imperatives. This may result in the work being re-designed, often with fewer employees. When a major expansion takes place and many more staff are required for one or two posts, job analysis may take place to correctly define the posts for recruitment purposes or to re-design them so there is greater efficiency. A third situation is when redundancies are necessary and jobs may be analysed in terms of workload and purpose. Business process engineering, where organisations closely examined every activity and process within the process, taking out those which did not add value, was very common in the late 1980s and early 1990s, and used job analysis extensively.

The size of the organisation can influence the process of job analysis. In large organisation, where hundreds of recruits are sought each year, such as in defence or banking, it is worth undertaking rigorous job analyses as the consequences of selection mistakes can be very costly to the organisation. For example, employing an unsuitable candidate in a control room of a nuclear power station could result in millions of pounds worth of damage. Similarly, as recruiting and training a police officer can cost £100,000, it is vital to get the job design right and match this with the recruitment processes and methods so fewer trainees leave before their training is completed (Cooper *et al.*, 2003).

An important element to remember, although it gets very blurred in practice, is that the aim of job analysis is to analyse the job, not the performance of the employee carrying out the job.

How to carry out job analysis

The analysis starts with a *definition of what information needs to be gathered.* This can include the instructions given as to how to carry out the work, the processes that lead to the job holder's actions (communications, flow of work, etc.) the nature of the mental and physical processes required, the degree of flexibility in the work itself and in the employee's thought patterns, the targets and required outcomes, the relationships with other employees – superiors, peers and subordinates – and the general terms and conditions attached to the work.

The next stage is to decide on the format for collecting the information required. For a full description of this topic, see Taylor (2002) but here is a summary of a number of ways that this can be done:

- *Asking employees to complete a questionnaire.* This can be designed by the organisation, with or without the help of specialist consultancy services, or there are a number of standard questionnaires available on the market. The questionnaire needs to be able to be readily computerised from which job descriptions and person specifications can be readily drawn. The advantage of using this system is that the questions are standard and, if tested properly, will be user friendly. The difficulty is that filling in questionnaires about their job is not always a favourite pastime of employees and they may choose to exaggerate the importance of some aspects of their work.

■ *Asking employees to keep work diaries.* This method, if carried out properly, will get a very accurate picture of what actually happens over an extended period, say a week or month. However, many employees will be generally reluctant to carry out such a demand and those that do it properly may not be typical. Again, it is possible to build up the job beyond its actual importance.

■ *Observe the employee.* A realistic picture can certainly be drawn up using this method. However, a one-to-one observation is very expensive and time consuming, and may need to be spread over a period of time for it to be representative. It would not be very appropriate for work in accounting offices, where there is a monthly cycle, an annual cycle and often a quarterly cycle as well. It may well be that employees behave differently when they know they are being observed but this may have less truth these days following so many 'fly on the wall' television programmes. Even in today's more compliant workplace, it is unlikely (and unethical) to consider using video recorders for this purpose.

■ *Interview the employee.* Sometimes carried out in groups, this provides the opportunity to get the full picture of the post by using probing, clarifying and reinforcing questions. With a group of employees, it may be possible to obtain a more consistent all-round picture, especially in the areas of responsibility and decision taking. Through interviewing, two specific techniques can be used to produce an outcome. The first is the *repertory grid* technique where, through questioning, a grid is constructed of the tasks carried out and the skills and competencies required to carry out those tasks, scored from, say, one to five. This is of considerable assistance in producing an accurate person specification.

The second technique is that of drawing out a set of *critical incidents* to examine which parts of the job are crucial to its success or failure. Starting from a study of key job objectives, the employee is asked to set out anecdotal incidents which resulted in achieving or not achieving those objectives and the part they played in these incidents. This process assists in being able to draw up the skills required to be successful in the job.

Job description

Although principally drawn up for the purpose of recruitment, job descriptions are used for a number of other purposes. They are an integral part of the job evaluation process, where grading and salary decisions are taken on the basis of carefully sculpted job descriptions. They are also used as a basis for training programmes, where training is focused on the elements of a job and how employees can perform better in their job. They are also key to the performance management process where an employee is measured to a larger or smaller extent against the requirements of the job set out in the job description.

Job descriptions come in many shapes and sizes. There are simple versions which give a basic description of the main tasks (see Figure 4.1). There are more complex (and useful) versions which indicate

Job Title	Secretary, Sales Office
Reports to	Sales Office Manager
Location	Head Office
Hours	Full time

Summary of position

To carry out secretarial duties, including word processing of letters and sales reports, telephone work, filing, essential hospitality and general assistance with meetings.

Main activities

1	To produce sales reports from information provided by the regional sales teams.
2	To word process letters, circulars, etc. for the sales managers and supervisors.
3	To deal with essential e-mail circulation to sales staff.
4	To handle telephone queries relating to the sales report and commission issues.
5	To file documents, letters and reports and any other items for the department.
6	To help with hospitality at times of conferences and weekly meetings.
7	To take minutes of sales meetings and help initiate any action pending from these meetings with the appropriate manager.
8	To carry out any other necessary duties associated with the sales office.

Figure 4.1
Task oriented job description

accountabilities and standards as shown in Figure 4.2. The decision on which format to use will be contingent on the current size and complexity of the organisation and the purpose for which the job descriptions are being drawn up. If it is only for recruitment of basic clerical employees, then a simple version will suffice. If it is for supervisory or managerial employees or if the descriptions are also being used for other purposes, then a more complex version is necessary.

The essential ingredients of every job description are:

- Job title
- Job location
- The superior to whom the job holder reports
- The staff who are responsible to the job holder
- The overall purpose of the job
- Whether it can be full time or part time
- Most frequently performed duties with some indication of their importance (Figure 4.2).

Job Title	Senior Library Assistant
Reports to	Senior Librarian
Location	Main Library
Hours	Total of 38 per week on shift rota basis

Main accountability

To implement library procedures in respect of book ordering, cataloguing and loans within the appropriate time span and within costs allocated.

Key result areas (extracts)

1　　*Book Ordering*. To place orders for books as requested, to check their arrival within the agreed time span, to complete the certificate and pass all documentation to the senior librarian to authorise payment within.

2　　*Cataloguing*. To ensure that books delivered are catalogued correctly and on the shelves within 8 working days.

3　　*Library Loans*. To handle applications for, and safe return of all inter-library loans within the stipulated time period. To chase up any non-returned books if more than 2 days overdue, recording accurately all transactions.

Figure 4.2
Accountability oriented job description

Job profile

There has been much discussion in recent years on the restrictive nature of job descriptions. It has been argued that modern day working practices serve to make descriptions outdated and superfluous. The pace of change is so great that the work that an employee actually carries out can alter within months, even days, of their starting date: so job descriptions need constant updating which can take up considerable time and effort. Furthermore, as we have seen in Chapter 1, employees are now encouraged to work beyond contract; in other words, to do anything that helps them, their unit and their organisation to achieve results quickly, efficiently and in the interests of the customers they serve. This *modus operandi* is difficult to write into a job description and limits to the description can only be tested by practice and experience. The profile, therefore, will only indicate the main tasks and accountabilities, and use more generalised statements as to the nature of the work. At Abbey National Building Society, they combine a job profile with key aspects of the specification, relevant competencies and indicators of performance and call this a job statement. An extract (excluding the specific competencies) is shown in Figure 4.3.

Person specification

The specification has three objectives. Firstly, to provide a focus for the organisation to agree on the traits of the person who is likely to be successful. This is an internal process to ensure that HR and line management are reading, so to speak, from the same hymn sheet. Secondly, when incorporated into advertising material, it communicates the required information to potential applicants. This should help to reduce the number of applications that are quite unsuitable. Thirdly, the specification can be used as a selecting aid whereby a scientific and objective method can be used to select applicants for the short-list by means of measuring them for proximity to the specification.

Before the era of equal opportunities legislation, person specifications followed closely the models laid down by either:

- Rodger's seven-point plan (1952) – Physical make-up, Attainments, General Intelligence, Special Aptitudes, Interests, Disposition and Circumstances.
- Munro-Fraser's fivefold framework (1954) – Impact on others, Qualifications and experience, Innate abilities, Motivation and Emotional Adjustment.

JOB STATEMENT FOR
Job Statement for Administrative Assistant, Personnel

Job Purpose: To deliver a range of administration support services within Personnel

	ACCOUNTABILITIES	PERFORMANCE INDICATORS
1. **Administration**	Undertake broad range of administrative processes; input data onto computerised systems; check for accuracy and completeness. Provide *ad hoc* information.	Workload targets met on time
2. **Communication**	Initiate contact with others in order to commence/complete processes, gather information by face to face, telephone or in writing. Feedback regularly to customers/line managers on progress.	Accuracy of work
3. **Respond to Enquiries**	Resolve standard queries received either face to face, by telephone or letter; refer promptly and accurately enquiries requiring additional expertise; access and annotate records.	Effectiveness at processing enquiries, accurately assessing when to refer, annotating records accurately
4. **Work planning**	Prioritise and plan tasks to be completed. Clearly communicate areas where you are unable to meet requirements.	Work planned effectively, customers kept well informed
5. **Service standards/compliance**	Ensure that procedures are in place to meet all statutory requirements so that internal and external customers are given quality service. Contribute ideas to improve service/processes.	Compliance with processes/regulatory requirements and legislative work completed to schedule

KNOWLEDGE, SKILLS AND EXPERIENCE	COMPETENCIES
1–2 years in admin. experience Good knowledge of range of systems Keyboard, WP & telephone skills Team Focus Focus on customer care Numerate Problem Solving Ability to work under pressure.	

Distinguishing features: There is a diverse range of jobs requiring differing levels of specialist knowledge across the personnel function

Figure 4.3

An example of a job profile at Abbey National Building Society

JOB STATEMENT FOR
Job Statement for Administrative Assistant, Personnel

(This page describes differences from the CENTRAL level of the job statement and needs to be read in conjunction with the first page)

COMPREHENSIVE

ACCOUNTABILITIES	PERFORMANCE INDICATORS
Handles complex admin. work.	Effectiveness at handling more complex admin. work and problems
Is autonomous in planning own work	Accuracy of completed tasks to service standards
Provides more complex management information reports and analysis	Prompt completion of accurate reports
Undertakes day-to-day supervision, more systematic coaching and development of core/central levels	Effectiveness of coaching/development support
Proposes improvements to admin. processes and local systems	Successful implementation of new processes
Covers for professional management level	
Keep abreast of current legislation	
Technical advice	

KNOWLEDGE, SKILLS AND EXPERIENCE	COMPETENCIES
Good knowledge of systems/procedures and how they need to be applied	
Keyboard, telephone, spreadsheet and WP skills	
Thorough understanding of how software needs to be applied	
At least 2 years in admin. role	
Ability to prioritise own and others work	
Awareness of policy/legislation information	
Numerate	
Interpersonal skills	
Problem solving	
Ability to work under pressure.	

Figure 4.3
(continued)

JOB STATEMENT FOR
Job Statement for Administrative Assistant, Personnel

(This page describes differences from the CENTRAL level of the job statement and needs to be read in conjunction with the first page)

CORE

ACCOUNTABILITIES	PERFORMANCE INDICATORS
Works on less complex and closely defined clerical admin. processes Generation of standard correspondence to customers Resolves basic information enquiries and refers where necessary Input of data onto computerised systems likely to be a focus of the job Receives close supervision when processing work	Speed and accuracy of completed tasks to service standards Adherence to standard documentation, referral where appropriate Effectiveness at resolving enquiries, accurately assessing when to refer Speed and accuracy of input Learns from instruction and supervision

KNOWLEDGE, SKILLS AND EXPERIENCE	COMPETENCIES
Ability to learn procedures and systems Keyboard, telephone and WP skills Ability to assimilate basic data and information Numerate Ability to work under pressure.	

Figure 4.3
(continued)

Neither of these models remain safe or satisfactory today. General Intelligence and Innate Ability is impossible to quantify, given the demise of the IQ test which leaves only a vague and unworkable statement of 'a good level of intelligence'. Most practitioners accept that Interests are irrelevant and likely to be discriminatory, especially if they wish, as was often the case, to draw out interests in male activities such as golf or shooting. Questions on circumstances are especially discriminatory, referring to ability to work shifts, to be geographically mobile or likelihood of length of time before the applicant starts a family. Even physical make-up has been steadily eroded as a required specification, with few occupations able to justify height, strength or even manual dexterity in their specification on grounds of equal opportunities. Even 'ability to lift heavy weights' is a doubtful requirement since the introduction of the Manual Handling Operators Regulations 1992.

This leaves qualifications, knowledge, skills and experience plus certain personal qualities which should make up the conventional person specification. Personal qualities have a more subjective element but psychometric testing (see Chapter 5) provide a more solid objectivity as long as the qualities required are based on well-defined and justified organisational requirements rather than the personal preferences of the recruiter.

A conventional person specification will take the form of Figure 4.4 with characteristics distinguished by the 'essential' and 'desirable' tags. It is important that the levels of qualifications, skills and experience is not over-rated as this will have a double negative effect. It will both discourage a number of suitable applicants from applying and then discourage the successful application when they find that their skills and experience may not be put to best use.

Using a competency framework

Up to a certain level, conventional person specification methodology can be acceptable in providing the framework for the short-list selection process, but it does have a glaring omission. It fails to focus on the elements that are likely, in the end, to provide success in the job, namely the competences that applicants will bring to the job – not what they have done and what qualifications they bring, but how they have performed, as measured in terms of outputs and standards of performance.

Since the late 1980s, there has been a gradual growth in the number of organisations that have started creating competency frameworks. They have been established as part of the enhanced performance management process to enable the organisation to obtain, manage, develop

Requirement	Essential	Desirable
Education and qualifications	❏ Educated to A level standard	❏ Good grades in English and Maths
Work experience	❏ 2–3 years experience in a supervisory role within a customer service or sales environment	❏ Agency experience ❏ Sales experiences ❏ Managerial experience
Abilities	❏ Good verbal communication ❏ Managerial skills ❏ Analytical skills ❏ Planning and organising skills	❏ Good written and numerical skills ❏ Computer literate ❏ Good business acumen
Motivation	❏ Self-motivated ❏ Competitive ❏ Results oriented ❏ Prepared to invest in staff development	❏ Desires career advancement ❏ Ambitious
Personality	❏ Socially confident in all situations ❏ Empathetic ❏ Persuasive ❏ Able to cope under pressure ❏ Adaptable ❏ Creative and innovative	❏ Diplomatic ❏ Able to direct and control others
Circumstances	❏ Commitment to overcome difficulties in meeting work requirements	❏ Lives within 1 hour's travel from the branch

Figure 4.4
Person specification – branch manager, employment agency

and reward people who can ensure the organisations meet their goals. Part of that process is to change the emphasis from *a job description* which simply sets out what employees do to a *competence profile* which lays down the essential competencies required for effective performance in that job. To these organisations, these competences are indivisible from the jobs.

For all jobs, the organisation will have a set of organisational or *core competences* which will apply to all positions. These are usually linked to the organisation's core values and include such areas as customer care, flexibility, effective communications and attention to quality. There will also be *specific or technical competencies* applying to certain jobs or occupations. For each of these competences, there will be a series of levels setting out the degree of depth or importance as it may apply to each position.

Having established the framework, the final stage is to draw up a competency profile for each position, setting out the competencies applicable and the level of application.

A simple version is shown in Figure 4.5 where a set of six competencies have been drawn up for Magistrates Clerks and Figure 4.6 which details one of these competencies.

Competence 1	Build and maintain an effective working relationship with magistrates
Competence 2	Facilitate the business of the court
Competence 3	Contribute to the aims and objectives of the court
Competence 4	To advise and work in partnership with administrative staff
Competence 5	Train and develop magistrates and staff
Competence 6	Organise and support statutory and other committees

Figure 4.5
Magistrate Court Clerk Competencies

Competence title: Build and maintain an effective working relationship with magistrates

Outcome   Magistrates' decisions are appropriate and legally correct

What does the court clerk do?	What is the required standard?
Facilitates a structured decision-making process	■ Advice to magistrates is accurate, objective and communicated in a way which is structured, clear and comprehensible
	■ Occasions when it is appropriate to intervene are anticipated, relevant issues are identified and necessary information is obtained
	■ Interventions address the specific issues decisively and clearly advice is given whether elicited or not
Liaises with magistrates	■ Respective roles are clearly identified and agreed
	■ Pre-court consultation with magistrates is carried out on every occasion
	■ Other opportunities are taken to encourage open dialogue with magistrates; for example, attending training sessions and bench meetings
	■ Feedback is sought and given with magistrates regularly

Figure 4.6
Court Clerk Competence 1 (*Source*: Lord Chancellors Office)

The set of competencies act as an effective job description and can also be used to specify the applicants required. They should either already possess the competencies detailed or be capable of being trained to achieve them. These precise definitions are used as the basis of the required training and also to assist in monitoring performance in the job.

Figure 4.7 gives a more complex example of how the overall framework has been constructed for management at the Whitbread Beer

---

Breaking down roles into measurable, bite-sized pieces

Fingerprints are unique, as are the various management roles in the Beer Co.

A job fingerprint takes each overall competence label; for example, leadership or business awareness and sub-divides it into more specific sub-categories.

Each Competence ends with a 'summary of importance' section. This is used to simplify outputs. The greater detail made possible by sub-categories is available as and when required.

Examples:

Behavioural	**Technical (e.g. sales)**
3. PERSUADING AND INFLUENCING *(LABEL)*	**L-NEGOTIATION**
(DEFINITION) Seeks to sell ideas rather than impose them, using rational and logical argument. Adopts an appropriate style according to the situation. Argues a point in a compelling yet unemotional way and is comfortable when dealing with conflict.	Able to effectively negotiate agreements, satisfying both company interests and customer needs.
(SUB-CATEGORIES) a. AUDIENCE b. STYLE c. CONFLICT d. DEPTH OF ISSUES e. RESPONSIBILITIES f. ROLE RELATIONSHIPS g. CONSULTATION h. SUMMARY OF IMPORTANCE	a. INVESTMENT AND FACT FINDING b. PLANNING AND FINANCIAL AWARENESS c. KNOWLEDGE AND APPLICATION OF TECHNIQUES d. NEGOTIATED IMPACT AND OUTCOME e. CREATIVE SOLUTIONS f. COMPLEXITY OF THE NEGOTIATIONS g. SUMMARY OF IMPORTANCE

pointing the way to continuous improvement

Figure 4.7
Example of competencies at Whitbread Beer Company

Once this is done each sub-category is ranked on a scale of 1–5 in terms of **how much is required** by the role (Role Profile) or **how much is demonstrated** by the individual (Individual Profile)

Examples:

Behavioural

3. PERSUADING AND INFLUENCING

Seeks to sell ideas rather than impose them, using rational and logical argument. Adopts an appropriate style according to the situation. Argues a point in a compelling yet unemotional way and is comfortable when dealing with conflict.

a. AUDIENCE

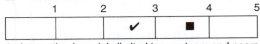

1. Interaction is mainly limited to own team and peers.
3. Interaction is often cross functional, involving other managers.
5. Interaction is mainly with Board and Senior Management or cross divisional.

b. STYLE

1. Typically one style of influencing (selling, negotiating, telling, etc.)
3. Maybe required to vary style.
5. An ability to constantly vary style and approach.

c. CONFLICT

1. Minimal challenge or conflict.
3. Some challenge or conflict.
5. A high degree of challenge or conflict.

Key: *Role* ■ *Individual* ✔

Technical (e.g. sales)

L-NEGOTIATION

Able to effectively negotiate agreements satisfying both company interests and customer needs.

a. INVESTIGATION AND FACT FINDING

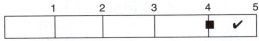

1. Has a basic understanding of the customer structure and can identify key decision makers.
3. Can identify specific customer needs and wants and understands the business context.
5. Has a detailed understanding of the customer's marketplace and strategies and is able to identify the strategic value to WBC.

b. PLANNING AND FINANCIAL AWARENESS

1. Is able to identify low cost/high value concessions and their financial implications at a basic level.
3. Is able to identify and cost more complex sanctions and incentives which may fall outside functional guidelines.
5. Is able to identify the strategic value of the negotiation/relationship.

c. KNOWLEDGE AND APPLICATIONS OF TECHNIQUES

1. Can identify the common ground in a straight-forward negotiation.
3. Can identify how to manage more complex negotiations by summarising and testing the understanding of others, being able to make tentative proposals and identifying how to manage 'low reactors'.
5. Is able to manage very complex negotiations by identifying how to avoid 'spirals' and how to deal with hard bargainers.

 pointing the way to continuous improvement

Figure 4.8
Example of competencies in detail

Company. Figure 4.8 details how one of the competencies, Persuading and Influencing, has a sub-group category, Negotiation, which has a five-scale ranking which can be applied to every applicable position.

Selecting the employment package

The position offered has to be attractive to potential applicants so the package on offer must aim to meet a number of needs. Setting the salary range can be a complex process and is dealt with in detail in Chapter 9. Briefly, it has to be in tune with the marketplace but also to be congruent with the internal pay system. Although general terms and conditions, such as holidays, pension and sick pay, are likely to be standard across positions at that level, their may be certain terms which need finalising. For example, does a company car go with the position? What are the actual hours of work, if they are defined? Is there any opportunity for flexibility associated with those hours? Are there any optional benefits that the successful candidate can sign up to, such as private health insurance?

Attracting the applicants

A number of general issues are involved at this point. Will internal candidates be encouraged to apply? Will the entire recruitment process be handled by the organisation or will third parties be brought in to assist? Will the advertising process be a traditional one involving local or national newspapers or will more innovative methods be used involving, for example, the Internet? What alternative methods of attracting applicants will be used besides newspaper advertising? How will the requirements of equal opportunity legislation, as detailed in Chapter 3, be met successfully? Who deals with the various stages of the process – HR or line management? These issues will be dealt with in turn.

Internal candidates

There are numerous advantages in recruiting internally. The candidates' performance is known well, as are their attendance records and their strengths and weaknesses. Hopefully, as set out in Chapter 10, an effective career development plan will be in place which can identify employees who are ready to be promoted or who are available to take up project-style positions. From an employee's viewpoint, an internal promotion is normally a far more satisfying move than the risk involved in moving to another organisation when service rights are lost and a mass of cultural and technical information has to be learnt in a very short time. A promotion generally gives a healthy signal both to the individual, who will feel valued but a signal is also given to the rest of the workforce who will be encouraged to stay, all being well, with the hope of following in the successful employee's footsteps. Moreover, an existing employee knows the organisation, its systems and procedures, and should find it easier to adjust and settle in the position. Finally, internal recruitment is normally short, except in the largest public sector organisations and it is certainly cheaper than external advertising. The vacancy can be advertised through internal advertising on notice boards and in newsletters to denote that it is open to all employees and to support a culture of transparency. Nothing is more de-motivational than the sudden announcement of internal promotions without the position being advertised.

Given such advantages, why has external recruitment continued to grow so strongly at the comparative expense of internal promotion? There are two main reasons. Firstly, the pace of change has become so great that organisations are wary of creating a 'cloned' labour force which follows policies and procedures that have been successful in the past. The belief is strong that a flow of new blood into organisations is essential and that external applicants will bring different experiences into play. The second reason is that there is no conclusive proof that internal appointments are actually more successful; employees may be promoted because they do their job so well but find the new job beyond them. This is known as the Peter Principle – employees are always promoted one step above their competence. Some employees also find it difficult to achieve the necessary respect when they had started a few years back as the office junior.

A balance, then, is usually required with a careful analysis of both internal and external applications to determine whether their existing skills and experience will allow a prediction of future competent performance in the advertised position.

Using third parties

Before advertising is considered an important decision needs to be taken whether to use third parties in any way in the recruitment process. Third parties take the following forms:

- Recruitment agencies, who will handle the entire recruitment process up to short-listing, providing candidates from their own sources or advertising on your behalf. These are used by 71% of employers (CIPD, 2003a), up from 64% in 2002.

- Advertising agencies, who help devise a single advertisement or complete campaign and advise on the advertising media.
- Executive Search agencies (sometimes known as 'head-hunters') who will search for senior staff on your behalf, approaching suitable candidates directly, often under considerable secrecy. The extent to which such agencies are used is growing, having risen to 40% in 2003 (Redman and Allen, 1993; CIPD, 2003a).
- Job centres can give energetic support, especially if the organisation is either moving into the area or has an expansion programme with multiple vacancies, particularly at operative or clerical and administrative level. Use of this facility has been slipping in recent years, down to 46% in 2003 (CIPD, 2003a).
- Educational establishments – schools, colleges, universities – can help provide a willing, if often inexperienced, source of applicants. Forty-five per cent of employers keep up this link (CIPD, 2003a).

All these sources can be valuable but have certain disadvantages as Figure 4.9 shows:

Whether third parties are used or not depends entirely on the nature of the vacancy and the context of the organisation. Here are

Third party	Advantages	Disadvantages
Recruitment agencies	Can provide candidates at speed using their database.	Charge a fee from 10% to 20% depending on level of vacancy and competitive situation.
	Save considerable time on dealing with large numbers of applications.	May not provide appropriate candidates especially if they have not been briefed adequately.
	Some specialist agencies have a very good knowledge of the vacancy market. This applies to accounting and IT staff especially.	Staff recruited through agencies have a tendency to move on quicker. Although the agency that provided them cannot supply them with further job details for ethical reasons, they are almost certainly bound to be on the books of other agencies who are under no such restriction.

Figure 4.9
Use of third parties (*continued*)

Advertising agencies	Experts in copy writing, especially with eye-catching headlines, use of colour and house style.	Charge fees for the service although less than may be expected as they negotiate discounts on the actual advertisement space with the media concerned.
	Provide high-quality art work which the media cannot usually provide.	May persuade you to spend more on the advertisement than you originally intended.
	Know the media options well with up-to-date prices.	
Executive search	When secrecy is important due to internal reasons, such as a re-structuring, they are a discrete agent.	They charge high fees, from 25% to 50% of the first year salary. Some of the fees are chargeable even when the appointment is not made.
	They know where to look in a very limited market, such as for a Head of Research for a Pharmaceutical company.	They can be of variable quality so it is important to use one referred to you who is of high reputation.
	They save on all the time and effort involved in responding to advertisements.	
Job centres	A central and convenient place for applicants to use providing a high response rate.	No sifting takes place so much of the response can be unsuitable.
	They offer a venue for mass interviewing.	Response can be weighted towards the unemployed rather than a wider marketplace.
	They usually do not charge a fee.	
Educational establishments	They provide a free service.	Applicants may not be experienced.
	Where the demand is regular, such as in graduate trainees or trainee computer operators, Colleges or Universities can provide a regular supply.	

Figure 4.9
(*continued*)

examples of situations where organisations are likely to use third parties:

- ■ *Example 1*

  A large organisation setting up a satellite operation in an area new to them which needs a variety of semi-skilled and unskilled labour will use an advertising agency to design a series of job advertisements and the job centre where candidates will respond to the advertisements and where interviews can be held.

- ■ *Example 2*

  A organisation recruiting a senior director will be likely to use an Executive Search agency to approach potential candidates on a confidential basis and to draw up a short-list. The head of the Crown Prosecution Service was recruited in this way in 1998 (Mills, 1999).

- ■ *Example 3*

  A organisation that has a regular need for 'year-out' sandwich students to carry out project work in marketing or personnel will build up a relationship with a number of universities so suitable students can be easily recruited at minimal cost.

- ■ *Example 4*

  A organisation with an uncertain longer-term administrative requirement will build up a relationship with a recruitment agency who will provide them with a combination of temporary staff and short-listed permanent staff on both a full-time and part-time basis.

Designing and placing advertisements

Newspaper advertising is a costly business. Although a single insertion for a small advertisement on a limited circulation local newspaper may cost less than £100, this can rise to over £10,000 for a substantial, full colour advertisement in a national quality newspaper. With an average cost moving towards the £1000 mark, it is vital that the right results are obtained.

The three key objectives of a good advertisement are that it:

- ■ *Attracts attention* – to successfully compete with other job advertisements in that media.
- ■ *Creates and maintains interest* – it has to communicate accurate information about the job, the company, the rewards, the

nature of the job and the type of person wanted and do all this in an interesting and attractive way.

- *Stimulate action* – the message must be sufficiently strong for potential applicants to read it to the end and then make the time and effort to respond in the required way. It should also have the negative effect in that unsuitable applicants will be discouraged from applying (Armstrong, 2003).

One of the many common misunderstandings that occur in the field of recruitment is that the success of the advertisement is measured by the volume of the response. Quite the reverse is true in reality. It is only the *quality* of the response that matters – how many applications are received from candidates that have the necessary requirements to fit the specification. Taken to the extreme, a response of one applicant can be a perfect response if that applicant is right for the job and the company. A response from 100+ applicants can, on the other hand, be a complete failure if none have those necessary requirements.

Attracting attention can be achieved by a number of means:

- Using bold and unusual headlines (see Figure 4.10 for examples).
- Salary and location clearly displayed.
- An effective illustration or striking artwork (e.g. see Figure 4.11).
- Using full or part-colour, although there are cost extras involved here.
- Agreeing with the publisher a prominent location of the advertisement, again with a supplementary cost.
- Prominent display of a high-profile corporate image, where that applies.
- An unusual free gift – Consultants Price Waterhouse added a packet of Refreshers to one magazine advertisement in 1998.

- If you do not raise your eyes, you will think you're at the highest point.
  (HH Human Resources – for a selection of vacancies)

- So how many jobs do you want?
  (Gardner Merchant – HR Manager)

- Work over Christmas. Travel round the world. Spread joy and happiness. Wear a red suit.
  (Virgin Atlantic – Cabin Crew)

Figure 4.10
Selection of unusual headlines (*Source*: Advertisements in *People Management*)

Increase turnover

Team Manager (Hygiene)
c.£30,000

Our name strikes terror in the hearts of roaches, rats and vermin all over London. From pest control and the mortuary service to clinical waste collection, we're one of the biggest forces in hygiene – and we want to be the best. As a professional business manager who's seen pest control 'action', you'll lead a hungry, motivated team of 35 into areas teeming with opportunities.

It's a target-driven environment, so here are yours: achieving ISO 9002, generating more income than last year's £1 m??, and maintaining impressively high standards. We're not necessarily looking for a public sector background, but we do insist on customer-focused performance management experience in a large, income-driven hygiene business. This is the opportunity to expand our successful business in an environment where only skill and professionalism are allowed to thrive.

 For an informal discussion call Roy Merchant on: 0181 356 4968 or write to him at Regulatory Services, London Borough of Hackney, 205 Morning Lane, London E9 6DC. Please quote ref: 7728/G3. Closing date: 29 June 1998.

One of the core values of transforming Hackney is an unequivocal commitment to the principle and operation of equality in terms of how we deliver the best service to our customers and all the people of Hackney, how we recruit and how we support our staff. We welcome applications from people who can make the principle a reality.

Transforming Hackney

Figure 4.11
Example of eye-catching advertisement

Creating and maintaining interest has a number of important issues to consider:

Does the advertisement concentrate on stressing the positive or is an element of the realistic included to avoid applicant disappointment either at interview or after appointment? Given the natural sceptical tendency of the public towards advertising, there is always a danger that a quotient of realism will deter good applicants who may suspect that this is the tip of the iceberg. It is useful, however, to make clear if the job is a new one and why it has been created. For example 'We have recently initiated an empowerment programme which has given more commercial responsibilities to local managers' … or 'An expansion phase has led to a further x posts being created …'.

Is the image of the company matched by the tone of the advertisement? A bright, breezy advertisement which would suit an informal, opportunistic company would probably be inappropriate for a regulatory public body (Fowler, 1990).

How much is said about salary? Research indicates that advertisements with a salary included provides a better quality of response (City Research Associates, 1988). Without a salary, a number of potential applicants do not apply, thinking that they may be wasting their time and a number of applicants whose current salary is either too high or too low making them unsuitable, actually do apply. There is general agreement here, so why are there so many positions advertised without a salary? This can be explained in part where organisations do not have transparent salary structures and believe they run the risk of alienating current employees by showing what is on offer for the vacant position. Others may follow the unfashionable and indefensible line that they will 'see who turns up and seems suitable and then negotiate an appropriate rate'. This is scarcely a professional approach and one that may well lead to discrimination on top of a confused salary structure. The way the salary is framed can be an important factor. Public sector advertisements can be unduly complex, such as 'PO3 (pay award pending)' which is acceptable for those working in that environment but will be unlikely to attract outsiders. The most common indicator currently used is to place a guide salary in the lower headline such as 'c £22K–24K' or 'salary to £24K'. An alternative method used where bonuses are common, such as in the sales or management environment is to state 'salary OTE £30K' where OTE stands for On Target Earnings which includes the bonus element.

How genuinely meaningful is the text? In the description of the ideal candidate, for example, how often are phrases used like 'excellent communication skills', 'computer literate', 'commercially focused' 'with an energetic, hands-on approach'. Due to their vagueness, they neither attract candidates nor put off the unqualified so it is difficult to justify their inclusion. It is better to either make clear specific qualifications required or make it clear that applicants will need to demonstrate these competencies at an early stage of the recruitment process. For example, 'leading a team of 10 engineers and analysts in the design and testing of manufacturing software'.

It is essential to include the *location of the post* in the advertisement, especially if it is a national advertisement, and the re-location package should be mentioned. Any necessity for regular travel should also be included.

Should the level of benefits be spelt out? The inclusion of benefits should be cautious, stressing only those which are essential features of the job (such as a company car), or make a real difference to the attraction of the post (such as subsidised mortgages/loans in the financial sector, private health insurance and subsided housing). Any family friendly benefits, such as flexible hours, job share or subsidised child care, can also be crucial. However, nobody was very attracted by the pension scheme, or life assurance and one should treat with reserve those applicants attracted by the sick pay scheme or holidays!

An example of research into various aspects of recruitment advertising is given in Focus on research 4.1.

Focus on research 4.1

Recruitment advertising

This research set out to examine how well a wide set of advertisements for managers matched the prescriptive models laid down by a selection of writers. A cluster sample of 1106 advertisements were used and prescribed items at varying levels of importance, such as location, salary, qualifications, job description and personal qualities, were identified. For salary, experience and job title, the match was high but qualifications were only specified in 32 of advertisements, although considered as vital by most of the prescriptive literature. Personal qualities, on the other hand, were specified in 81% of advertisements but featured as much less importance in the literature. Advertisements in the public sector came out better in salary, location and closing date while those in the private sector gave clearer instructions as to how to respond to the advertisement and in specifying the required experience.

Source: Redman and Matthews (1993)

In terms of *stimulating action*, there are a number of methods by which applications can be made, which will depend on the nature of the vacancy, the number of expected applications and the technology available. Options include:

- The applicant calls a dedicated number/person for a job pack including an application form.
- The applicant is invited to an open day interview event.
- The applicant responds by sending a curriculum vitae (CV) and covering letter by post or e-mail.
- The applicant is invited to call a specified person for an informal discussion.
- The applicant calls a dedicated number for a short-listing telephone interview (see Chapter 5 for telephone screening).

There are evenly balanced arguments for asking applicants to complete an *application form* or to send in their *CVs*.

Applicants would generally prefer to simply send in their CVs with a covering letter, believing that all the relevant information is included. They may select organisations that make an application easier rather than one that insists on the laborious process of completing a four-page application form.

Organisations may prefer to insist on an application form because it is simpler to select a short-list from a set of identical application forms. CVs may leave out negative areas such as no current driving license, or having been dismissed from previous employment. There may also leave out their age or not put their experience in a chronological order that could hide a crucial time gap. If candidates are not prepared to complete an application form then they show little commitment to the application. In general terms, public sector organisations tend to insist on a consistent approach to recruiting through an application form. It is also argued that the more common process these days of including a photograph may lead to a discriminatory approach to short-listing and should be discouraged.

A further difficulty is the truthfulness of the CV. Research by the Association of Search and Selection Consultants (ASSC) in 1998 found that a quarter of job applicants lied about their qualifications and career records or attempted to hide their previous misdemeanours (People Management, 1998). An extreme situation was the exposure of 16 nurses at Ashworth top security hospital in Merseyside who were found in 1997 to be practising without being properly qualified.

Providing information to applicants

An advertisement can only provide a limited amount of information. The provision of a 'job pack' is therefore important both to fill in as many gaps as possible and also to show evidence of an efficient and responsive employer. The job pack may include any of the following, depending on the level of the vacancy:

- Brochure on the organisation's activities.
- Job description.
- Person specification.
- Organisation structure showing how the vacancy fits into this structure, especially if it is a new job.

■ A handbook showing the benefits of working for the organisation, such as SAYE Share options or Profit Sharing, Private Health Insurance, etc.

■ Application form (if applicable).

The application form

The purpose of a application form is to provide full, relevant and consistent information on which to base decisions on recruitment and selection. It should also be designed to be user friendly, with a clear and simple layout, unambiguous questions and not too lengthy. It should allow the applicant to give a full and fair account of themselves. Meeting these requirements is not always easy and there are a number of issues to consider.

Will one form be sufficient for the organisation?

For a straightforward clerical position, the information required in general is essentially factual – personal details, education, qualifications and work experience is usually sufficient. This can be achieved in a two-page form. In more senior positions, it is usually necessary to allow the applicant to reflect on their experience to date, explain their motives and ambitions and explain why they believe they can match the requirements of the advertised post. This usually necessitates a four-page form. Having two forms can create some confusion, however, especially when jobs are on the border of seniority. Keeping to one long form, however, means requiring all applicants to plough through the sections on motives, ambitions and justifying their applications which can well put off a number of good applicants.

What questions should you not ask?

Equal opportunity requirements have meant a changing format where questions on whether the applicant is married and the age of their children, for example, should be avoided as this information does not have a bearing on their ability to carry out the job.

Do you link it to competency framework?

One of the benefits of a competency framework is that it integrates a number of HR areas – recruitment included. Having defined a job in relation to the competencies, it makes sense to try to match applicants to those required competencies so questions on the application form should reflect this. For example, where leadership is a required competency, the form should ask such questions as 'Can you demonstrate how you have exercised leadership skills in your current position'. The problem here, however, is that the competencies and their levels vary for different jobs and an application form which asks for a response on each competency will be very long indeed. A way round this is to use a basic form for key personal data and then a supplementary form specific to that position.

An extract from Wine Rack's lively application form that tries to reflect the company culture is shown in Figure 4.12.

Other methods of attracting applicants

The recruitment strategy may include a number of other methods used alongside or instead of newspaper or magazine advertising. They may have clear advantages at times but there are also hazards as summarised in Figure 4.13.

Employers' views on the most effective sources for attracting applicant

In the CIPD 2002/2003 recruitment surveys, local newspaper advertisements easily topped the poll, as shown in Figure 4.14 but word of mouth has a surprisingly high showing, given the nature of the high-profile organisations that tend to take part in such surveys. Advertisements on the organisation's website and Intranet are growing in popularity but the most interesting aspect of this survey was the breadth of choice which clearly supports the view that there is no single right choice of recruitment system. A number of different media and systems have to be used as a bundle, varying the choice depending on the nature of the vacancy.

Innovative recruitment methods using new technology

Recruitment has moved a long way in the last few years. A variety of techniques have arisen, making use of the Internet and telecommunication technology. Many organisations, including Shell and John Lewis Partnership have set up an interactive web page for graduate recruitment and Shell recruited 1 in 20 of its graduates by this means in 1998 (Welch, 1998). Tescos went a stage further when a panel, headed by its

STORE MANAGEMENT
APPLICATION FORM

CONFIDENTIAL

Wine Rack

Please return to THRESHER Human Resources, Recruitment Unit,
Ellis Ashton Street, Huyton Industrial Estate, Liverpool L36 6JB.

Vacancy ref:	TBM/0045
Candidate ref:	

Personal Details

Surname:	Maiden name:	First names:

Address:

Telephone (home):
Telephone (work):
Can we contact you at work?
YES/NO

Age:	Date of birth:	Sex: Male/female	Marital status	Children's ages

YOUR HEALTH – Please give details of any health problems or disability and state your Reg. D.P. No. if applicable:

Have you ever held a Justices Licence?   YES/NO
If so state when and where:

Do you have any civil/criminal convictions, past/current/pending?   YES/NO
Please specify:

This information is required in order for you to obtain a Justices Licence to sell alcohol.

Do you own a vehicle? YES/NO	Do you have a current driving licence? YES/NO

Please give details of any endorsements:

Do you own your own home? YES/NO   Rent?   YES/NO   Live with relatives?   YES/NO

Are you willing to work evenings?   YES/NO   Weekends?   YES/NO

Are you prepared to relocate?   YES/NO

Please tick the area(s) where you would be prepared to work:

☐ Scotland   ☐ South West   ☐ North East   ☐ South East

☐ North West   ☐ Greater London   ☐ Midlands   ☐ Central London

Are there any areas where you would not work? Please specify:

Figure 4.12
Application form for Wine Rack

Your Employment History

Please begin with your current or most recent job.		
From:	To:	Job title:

Name and address of employer:	Main responsibilities:
Nature of their business:	Main achievements:
	Reason for leaving:

Starting salary per annum £	Final salary per annum £	

Please give details of your second most recent job.		
From:	To:	Job title:

Name and address of employer:	Main responsibilities:
Nature of their business:	Main achievements:
	Reason for leaving:

Starting salary per annum £	Final salary per annum £	

Please list any jobs before those mentioned above.					
From	To	Employer	Job title	Starting salary	Final salary

Figure 4.12
(*continued*)

Your Education & Training

Full-time secondary education

From	To	Name of school	Examinations taken	Results with grades

Further education

From	To	Name of College/University	Subjects studied	Qualifications

Please give any other qualifications, membership of professional bodies or courses attended:

Other Information

Please describe your favourite interests and leisure activities:

Career plans: Describe briefly the development of your career, your plans for the future and the particular attractions of Store Management with Wine Rack.

Figure 4.12
(*continued*)

Wine Rack is committed to equal opportunities in employment and assesses job applicants without regard to disability, martial status, race sex. To enable the Company to monitor this policy, please indicate to which ethnic group you belong.

☐ Caribbean   ☐ Oriental   ☐ Other (please specify)

☐ African   ☐ UK European

☐ Asian   ☐ Other European

Do you require a work permit to be employed in the UK?   YES/NO

Have you ever previously applied to Wine Rack or any part of Whitbread P.L.C?   YES/NO
If so please give details:

Do you have any relatives who work for Wine Rack or any part of Whitbread P.L.C?   YES/NO
If so please give details:

What is your salary expectation?   What is your notice period?

Please state any dates when you cannot attend an interview:

Please state where you heard of this vacancy:

References. (These will not be taken up unless an offer is accepted).
Name: Name:
Position: Position:
Company and address: Company and address:

Wine Rack is part of Thresher Wine Merchants and as such, your terms and conditions are as those operated by Thresher Wine Merchants.

I certify that the information I have given is true in all respects. I understand that any offer is subject to satisfactory references, medical acceptance and obtaining a licence which will entail references to the Police and Excise Authorities. I also understand that if subsequently any of these conditions are not met, the Company reserves the right to withdraw its offer or cancel any agreement made.

Signature: Date:

FOR COMPANY USE ONLY – DO NOT COMPLETE THIS SECTION

Area Sales Manager's assessment of applicant's suitability:

ASM Signature: Date:

Figure 4.12
(*continued*)

	Advantages	Hazards and Difficulties Encountered
Word of mouth including relatives	❑ Very cheap and simple. ❑ Can be bolstered by offering a bonus to a member of staff you introduces a successful applicant. ❑ It is likely that the applicant will have a reasonable knowledge of the organisation and the job. ❑ Should fit easily into the culture and ways of the organisation. ❑ No need to plough through a large response.	❑ If used as a sole method of recruitment, then the staff will only come from a narrow range. ❑ Outside applicants may not know about opportunities so the source is limited. ❑ Can, and has, been regarded as a discriminatory approach in practice as females (or males) and ethnic minorities can be excluded from the process in predominately white, single-sex organisational environment.
Approaching previous applicants	❑ Very cheap and simple ❑ Applicants may already have been interviewed but just missed being selected on the last occasion so an appointment can be swift.	❑ The post and its conditions may have changed since the applicant applied. ❑ The applicant may no longer be interested having been suited elsewhere. ❑ It is necessary to maintain an effective database of such applicants with a time cut-off point.
Local mail shot through commercial leaflet distributor	❑ Can be targeted at specific areas in the locality which are convenient for travel and have produced quality applicants in the past. ❑ Relatively low cost.	❑ Cannot be certain of 100% delivery rate. ❑ Not necessarily thought of highly by potential applicants.
Milk round to universities and colleges and job fairs	❑ Can target quality universities and colleges.	❑ High cost in time, travel and accommodation. ❑ Suitable only for graduate recruitment.
Open days and hotel walk-in	❑ Good for recruiting large numbers.	❑ Uncertainty of response on the day makes resourcing difficult.

Figure 4.13
Alternatives or additions to newspaper/magazine advertising

Sources	%
Local newspaper advertisements	24
Recruitment agencies	14
Specialist journal/trade press	11
Word of mouth	9
Own website	8
Job centre	7
National newspaper advertisement	7
Intranet	6
Speculative applications	4
Links with schools/colleges	3
Executive search	3
Others – work placements, promotional events, commercial job-board internet sites, secondments, job-preview experiences, etc.	5

Figure 4.14
Most effective sources for attracting applicants (*Source*: CIPD 2003a)

Chief Executive, ventured online to answer questions from 100 students at 12 Universities who were prospective applicants. There are a large number of generic web sites that carry a range of vacancies.

A survey by the National Online Recruitment Audience Survey in 2002 reported 817,000 had visited Fish4jobs, with 627,000 visiting Totaljobs and other sites not far behind in 1 month (Tulip, 2003). It was calculated that 44% of Internet users over 15 had looked for jobs online, around a third of the UK working population.

Another company making use of the Internet is Cable and Wireless, as shown in Case study 4.1.

Case study 4.1

Cable and Wireless recruit on the Internet

Cable and Wireless, the communications giant, began advertising its vacancies online with the independent recruitment site, 3-year-old Top

Jobs on the Net (www.topjobs.net) in September 1998. Within 6 months, it received 500 applications and filled five vacancies in this way. A spokesman believed that online recruiting is ideal for positions in IT and finance although he was less certain on other professions, such as HRs and legal positions. As a result of their early success into cyberspace, the company launched in 1999 featuring all their vacancies. It was considered that the Internet provided an additional advertising stream that allows for corporate branding alongside recruitment. All the information can be kept up to date and there is access to vast amount of descriptive space, whereas, in conventional media, space is expensive. However, it is still necessary to continue to advertise on a dedicated recruitment site to ensure jobseekers can be directed towards their own site.

Source: Merrick (1999)

Telephone screening is another new development. Here, an applicant calls a freephone number, day or night and keys in their unique personal identification number, which automatically sets up a file for them on the company's HR system. During the interview, typically lasting 15 minutes, the candidate answers multiple-choice questions using their telephone keypad. The computer scores and weights their answers and automatically sends them an application form or schedules a face-to-face interview if they are successful. The system then sends the HR manager an interview schedule. (Burke, 1998).

Considerable savings can be made by using these techniques. In Chapter 5, Case study 5.1, Standard Life claimed the saving of 143 working days on a recruitment exercise for 15 managers.

Despite the fact that the outcome of typing the words 'jobs' into a search engine produces a choice of more than 600,000 web sites, the UK has been relatively slow, however, in making use of the Internet as a recruitment tool compared to America (Sappal, 1998). Not all professionals are whole-heartedly behind these new recruitment techniques, believing that ethical and practical issues remain unanswered. These include:

- Online applications make unreasonable demands on the time of the applicants, especially graduates who will need to make multiple applications to get their first job. Often the candidate only hears that the position has been filled when the extended form has been completed.
- The applicants may not always want to be judged quite so quickly and mechanically. Unless they have bought-in to the computer processes (and IT staff probably have) they may prefer to apply to organisations with a more human face.

- Online psychometric tests that are part of the application process, are used to screen out 90% of the candidates, which 'smacks of organisational expediency', according to Dulewicz (2004).

- Organisations are aware that some candidates get friends to complete the form for them or try under several names for practice (Harry Potter is very common).

- The judgements may enter into the realms of discrimination, in terms of age particularly, and will encourage a form of stereotyping when the specification cannot be over-ridden, as it can if handled by humans.

- Applicants may not be prepared for telephone interviews with instant forced choice judgements to be made which cannot be reversed, unlike in an interview situation where, if a question is not understood, it can be repeated or explained in another way.

- Sites do not keep their promises. A study by the consultancy The Driver Is (Welch, 2003) found that only nine out of 33 companies who allowed jobseekers to register for e-mails alerting them when new jobs were posted had actually sent out alerts within 3 months of the candidate registering.

Some organisations have attempted to overcome these difficulties. Marks and Spencers have eliminated competency-based tests because they take up too much time (Czerny, 2004) and clear with candidates first whether they are prepared to work shifts, weekends, be mobile and are eligible to work in the UK. Only then do they online tests in numeracy, verbal reasoning and a 'talent screener' which judges their motivation. Successful candidates then move to the final stage, which is an assessment centre. The organisation believes that the online process has improved success rate overall from 27% to 37%.

Who carries out the recruitment and selection processes?

The ability to recruit and select successfully is seen as a core skill by personnel professionals. Indeed, it was the failure of line management in this task that was one major influence in allowing the transition from welfare officer to personnel officer 60 or more years ago. It is generally at the heart of the HRs department and yet a number of organisations, mostly larger ones, have recently questioned why this should be so, pointing out that this activity should be a core management skill.

The main argument here is that managers have the ultimate responsibility for their staff, that it tends to be their greatest cost and that there needs to be a close bond from the outset between the manager and a new member of staff to make an effective partnership. This viewpoint is sometimes backed up by the time taken by HRs to carry out a recruitment exercise and their over-concern with paperwork and bureaucracy.

An effective partnership between HRs and line management is therefore essential. In the research carried out by Sue Hutchinson and Stephen Wood (1995) (see Figure 4.15), this balance was best met by HRs concentrating on those areas which carried a specific skill – commissioning advertisements from a recruitment agency, negotiating rates with newspapers, psychometric testing – and allowing the generic skills of interviewing and selection to be carried out either by the line management or jointly by the two parties. HRs would also activate the administrative

Issues	Line manager	Line in consultation with personnel	Personnel in consultation with line	Personnel department
Authorising vacancies	10	12	2	1
Job descriptions	5	16	3	1
Selection of media	2	4	12	7
Selection of agency/consultant	0	2	11	11
Screening applications	3	11	6	5
Arranging interviews	2	6	6	10
First interview	3	11	7	3
Subsequent interviews	4	13	5	1
Short-listing	6	15	4	1
Selection	8	15	1	1
References	1	0	6	17
Individual salary	1	9	9	5
Other terms and conditions	0	5	10	9
Induction	10	4	6	5

Figure 4.15
Balance of personnel and the line in the recruitment and selection process (completed by personnel managers in 25 organisations) (Source: Hutchinson and Wood, 1995)

tasks such as arranging interviews and obtaining references which will be dealt with in the next chapter.

A example of a complex recruitment exercise is shown in the Meteor Case Study.

Meteor case study

A major recruitment exercise

Today was the big day and Sarah had been at work since 6.30 a.m. The first of the recruitment advertisements was out in the regional newspaper and she had to make sure the team was all prepared. It was 2 years after she had joined Meteor and helped set up the original factory. She now needed to fill an additional 60 positions within a 6-month period with new employees joining an induction programme every 2 months. The 60 positions were as follows:

- 30 production operatives.
- 15 service engineers and support personnel.
- 8 Office support staff.
- 3 Sales representatives.
- 4 staff for a new team to advise organisations in setting up call centres. Two, as senior advisers, would act as consultants/account executives and two would be involved in actually setting up the centres, although the roles would be flexible ones.

The call centre team was a new initiative that was being piloted at her site, run by Gary Hands, an experienced manager head-hunted from a similar organisation.

From the original recruitment exercise, Sarah had accurate job descriptions and specifications for all the jobs except the new call centre positions. Together with Gary, she developed a set of competencies for each of the four jobs which matched their specific requirements. For the senior advisers, they centred on consultancy skills, such as persuasion, planning and presentation; for the operational/training roles, they centred on leading, training, problem solving and delegation.

The recruitment team

For such a large recruitment, Sarah recognised that she would normally work with a recruitment agency, selected for their knowledge of the area. This had been the process when the site was initially set up. However, she was aware that the economy of the area had been hit over the last year by a series of plant closures so recruitment itself should not be too difficult. She wanted to see if she could avoid the inevitable high costs of agency fees (in the region of £80,000 plus) and had not been completely satisfied with the service provided on the original recruitment. However, she could not handle it all on her own. She had therefore put together a small team consisting of a 'year-out' Business Studies student who had been taken on for a variety of projects 3 months ago and who had quickly shown a grasp of the business and its key requirements; an early retired ex-personnel manager she had met at through the local IPD branch who was happy to take on a 6 month part-time brief at reasonable cost; finally, a staff member who was returning from maternity leave and had asked for the opportunity to carry out part of her work at home. Other clerical staff would be seconded for short periods and agency staff would be used when necessary.

Sources of recruitment

Internal advertising. In the company magazine 3 months earlier, Sarah had informed all the staff of the site expansion and the bulldozers were already at work. With the next magazine, she included a complete breakdown of the positions and details of how staff could apply giving deadlines and approximate selection timings. She also gave details of the recruitment bonus scheme whereby employees who put forward names of friends and relatives who were eventually successful in obtaining employment, would receive a Marks and Spencers voucher for £60 after the employee's probationary period had been completed. It was made quite clear, however, that applications made through this route would receive no special preferential treatment in the final selection process, although they would be guaranteed an interview.

External advertising. The main gate on the site was onto a main road so Sarah made arrangements for a large signboard to be displayed with the vacancies detailed and an information packs available at reception. Also detailed were the dates of the open evenings/Saturday mornings when informal discussions could take place.

Through local networking, Sarah contacted the HRs managers of the local companies who had recently *shed labour*, sending them information packs to pass on any potential applicants. She arranged a meeting with the manager of the local *job centre* and gave her details of all of the operative, technical and clerical vacancies together with information packs. She had trawled through *previous applicants* but the pace of recruitment over the past 2 years had drained that source dry.

Two months earlier, she had arranged a meeting with her *advertising agency* to draw up a series of advertisements in the regional and local presses. There were some advertisements involving all the positions and others specialising in the sales, technical or administrative ones. Sarah knew that the site was under-represented for employees from ethnic minorities, so one of the advertisements was to go into a small regional magazine produced mostly for the Indian, Pakistani and Bangladeshi communities. The advertisements were to be phased over an 8-week period in a careful programme and cost a total of £20,000, including production costs. The agency suggested that radio advertising be considered as the local companies were currently competing fiercely and fees were not unreasonable. Sarah agreed to try a pilot exercise with a limited budget.

Dealing with the response

Sarah had made special arrangements with the Telecom company to rent additional lines for the period of the advertising campaign and these lines were manned according to the strength of the expected response. Two of the lines had a direct switch to the homes of two employees. From the telephone calls, the recruitment team placed the applicants details onto a database and the source of their response. This was downloaded on e-mail to the home of the employee returning from maternity leave who printed out the appropriate letter and stuffed the information packs. Twice a day, the packages were collected by courier to be posted.

For most of the vacancies, applicants were asked to complete standard two-page application forms but, for the call centre team posts, an additional supplementary form was necessary to capture their match with the required competencies. Applicants were discouraged from simply sending in CVs given the volume of applications that needed to be processed.

Three-thousand calls were taken in total over the campaign and 95% of the information packs were sent out within 2 days (a case of mumps causing a short delay for the other 5%!) 900 application forms were received through the advertisements and the other sources.

When, later on, Sarah carried out the evaluation of what was essentially a very successful campaign, she found that the advertisements produced the highest response to selection ratio and the job centre and open days the lowest response. However, in cost–benefit terms, without counting processing time, the reverse was true so she felt that it was worth the additional effort. The radio advertisements prove to be quite unsuccessful but she was not sure whether this was due to her rather half-hearted approach in this case. Twelve positions were filled through being referred by existing employees.

Summary

- There are many alternatives to filling a vacancy by recruiting a replacement for the person who has left. These include re-organisation the work, re-designing the job and contracting out the work.
- Job descriptions can be task oriented, accountability oriented or designed as a broader profile or statement.
- Person specifications are crucial to the recruitment process but contain pitfalls, especially in the area of equal opportunities.
- Organisations are increasingly using competency frameworks that can be utilised for recruitment, amongst other important areas.
- Third parties are increasingly used in the recruitment process, chiefly because of their expertise and their knowledge of the market.
- Technology is developing to assist the recruitment process, especially through the Internet.

Student activities

1 In groups of two or three, select two job advertisements from a national newspaper and produce a short comparative report on how the advertisements meets Armstrong's three criteria.

2 Individually design a job specification for a university lecturer in marketing, then compare results in groups of five. Produce a final version taking the best parts of each of your efforts.

3 As a class, list the possible sources when recruiting the following: a labourer in a sawmill; a laboratory technician for a hospital; a manager for a retail shop; a design engineer for a car component company.

4 Compare the Abbey national Job Statement with a conventional job description. In what ways does it differ and how valuable may it prove for the employee?

5 In the Meteor Case Study, pick out three examples of innovative practices, explain why Sarah decided to use them and identify any difficulties she could have encountered in using them.

6 Consider this scenario: you have a vacancy which you know can be filled internally by a suitable candidate but they may not be interested. Is it ethical to try to encourage them to apply and, if so, how would you go about doing so?

7 Read the article on Cable and Wireless and draw up a list of advantages and disadvantages of recruiting on the web.

8 Read the Redman and Matthews article on recruitment advertising. What major conclusions can you draw from their research?

References

Armstrong, M. (2003) *A Handbook of Human Resource Management Practice*, 8th edition, Kogan Page.

Burke, K. (1998) Automatic choices? *Personnel Today*, 22 August, 27–28.

City Research Associates (1988) *The Price Waterhouse Recruitment Advertising Survey*. Price Waterhouse.

Clark, T. (1993) Selection methods used by executive search consultancies in four European countries: a survey and critique. *International Journal of Selection and Assessment*, **1**(1): 41–49.

CIPD (2003a) Recruitment and retention survey 2003. CIPD.

CIPD (2003b) Labour turnover 2003. CIPD.

Cooper, D., Robertson, I., Tinline, G. (2003) *Recruitment and Selection: A Framework for Success*. Thomson Learning.

Czerny, A. (2004) Not so quick and easy. *People Management*, 26 February, 14.

Dulewicz, V. (2004) Give full details. *People Management*, 26 February, 23.

Fowler, A (1990) How to write a job advertisement. *Personnel Plus*, October, 31.

Fowler, A. (1997) *Writing Job Descriptions*. IPD.

Hutchinson, S., Wood, S. (1995) 'The UK experience', In: *Personnel and the Line: Developing the New Relationship*. IPD London.

Merrick, N. (1999) Super hire way? *People Management Review*, 15 July, 34–37.

Mills, E. (1999) The Mr. Big of crime comes clean. *Sunday Times*, 4 April, 5.

Munroe-Fraser, J. (1954) *A Handbook of Employment Interviewing*. Macdonald and Evans.

Parker, S., Wall, T. (1998). *Job and Work Design*. Sage.

People Management (1998) CV Deception Warning. 25 June, 12.

Redman, T., Allen, P. (1993) The use of HRM consultants: evidence from manufacturing companies in the north-east of England. *Personnel Review*, **22**(2): 39–54.

Redman, T., Matthews, B. (1993). Job marketing: an evaluation of managerial recruitment advertising practice. *Human Resource Management Journal*, **4**(4): 14–29.

Rodger, A. (1952) *The Seven-point plan*. National Institute of Industrial Psychology.

Sappal, P. (1998) The changing face of recruitment. *Human Resources*, March/April, 19–24.

Stredwick, J., Ellis, S. (2005) *Flexible Working Practices*. CIPD.

Taylor, S. (2002) *People Resourcing*. CIPD.

Tulip, S. (2003) A flying start. *People Management*, 7 August, 38.

Welch, J. (1997) Forced job losses still the norm. *People Management*, 18 December, 17.

Welch, J. (1998) Internet technology lets firms filter out students. *People Management*, 28 May, 14.

Welch, J. (2003) In the hiring line. *People Management*, 26 June, 30–31.

Further reading

Job analysis/job design.

For more detailed examples of *Job Design and Empowerment*, see:

Crandell, N., Wallace, M. (1998). *Work and Rewards in the Virtual Office*. Amacom.

Manz, C., Sims, H. (1993) *Business Without Bosses: How Self-managing Teams are Building High Performance Companies*. Wiley.

Advertising and recruitment

Roberts, G. (1997) *Recruitment and Selection: A Competency Approach*. IPD.

Kerrin, M., Kettley, P. (2003) *e-Recruitment: Is it delivering?* IES Report 402.

Web sites

http://www.u-net.com/bureau/employ/
UK Business Employment & Recruitment pages from the Business Bureau.

http://www.fres.co.uk/
The Federation of Recruitment & Employment Services.

CHAPTER 5

Selection

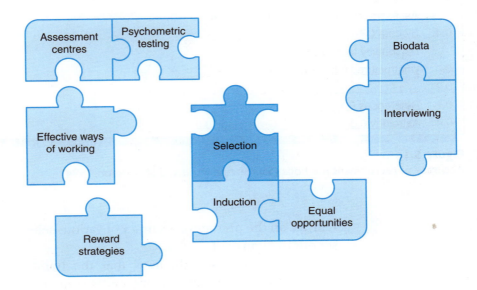

When you have read this chapter and carried out the activities, you will be able to:

- Explain the aims of the selection process.
- Identify the different methods employed in the selection process.
- Understand the purpose, value and drawbacks of the interview.
- Carry out an interview and review its success.
- Demonstrate the difference between ability and personality tests.
- Assess the value of references and understand the circumstances where they may be successful.

Before we move into these areas in detail, let us examine, as a snapshot, the research carried out by Mike Smith and his colleagues at

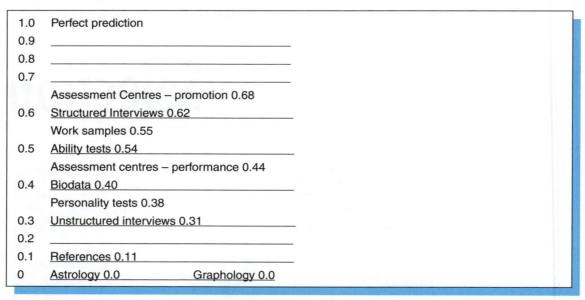

Figure 5.1
Accuracy of recruitment methods (*Source*: Anderson and Shackleton, 1994)

UMIST on the predictive accuracy of various selection methods. This is set out in Figure 5.1.

It can be seen straight away that the traditional approach using unstructured interviews and references come out of this research very badly. (Incidentally, early research published in 1989 showed the conventional interview at an even more lowly 0.18!) Testing in one form or another achieve much better results. Having said this, it is worth reflecting on the fact that even the best methods achieve success in only around three out of four cases. We will look at each of these methods in this chapter except astrology and graphology, which will not be mentioned again.

Aim of selection

Having followed a structured approach to attracting a pool of applicants for a vacancy, the next step is to follow a similar approach to selecting the right person for that vacancy. The right person can be defined as:

- somebody who matches the requirements set out in the job specification;
- has had satisfactory references;
- where future predictions indicate their success in the position;

■ has expressed sufficient interest in the position at interview to indicate that they wished to be offered the position.

The aim of selection is to find such a person who accepts the position and who gives satisfactory service and performance in the long term.

Systems approach or processual approach?

The systems approach to selection starts from the position of a well-defined job and a clearly analysed person specification. It assumes that there is one best way to carry out a job and a more or less 'ideal' candidate whose own history and personality will predict that she/he will perform very well in that job. It also tends to assume that the job will not alter a great deal in the future.

An alternative approach has been put forward by Herriot (1984) which puts a much greater emphasis on the *process of negotiation* between the parties where there is much more flexibility in the nature of the position. As explained by Newell and Rice (1999):

> Both of the parties have a set of expectations related to their current and future needs and values. Selection is portrayed as a series of episodes in which increasing amounts of information are exchanged to determine whether there is indeed compatibility between the organisation and the individual. Negotiation is possible because neither the organisation nor the individual is seen as having fixed characteristics, although the underlying values and needs of both sides are seen to be more stable. The outcome of this process, if successful, is that a viable psychological contract is negotiated that encapsulates congruence between the expectations of both parties. However, if the process of negotiation breaks down because the parties are unable to develop this sense of congruence, this can be construed as positive.... Because, in this way, the organisation avoids employing someone who will not fit within the organisation and the candidate avoids taking on a new position for which they are not suited.
>
> Newell and Rice (1999: p. 133)

This description portrayed here certainly fits most executive management selection today. Finding a Chief Executive for a large organisation has a strong element of adjusting the position around the ideas and strategic vision of a candidate as much a finding somebody who is able to carry out the detailed job description. Much negotiation takes place over performance targets, remuneration and other terms and conditions before both sides are happy that they have a deal that has a good chance of working.

It is not so common at more junior levels, except when positions are difficult to fill, when a job can be adjusted to meet the needs and abilities of candidates who are otherwise suitable.

This chapter will concentrate on the systems approach, setting out the logical steps in the selection process. This is not as a criticism of the processual approach but because the systems approach is more commonly used and more related to the great majority of human-resource-initiated selection practices. However, throughout this chapter the essential dilemma between the two processes will become apparent. Using a processual approach may open the doors to accusations of discrimination as the process lacks the objectivity associated with the systems approach.

Steps in the selection process

Selection is not just a question of interviewing, although this remains the most popular device in use. Selection is very much a process of de-selecting, that is, gradually eliminating candidates until finally one is left on the list for a vacancy. (Sometimes there is nobody left on the list and the process has to be started again.) No one has yet identified any one single watertight process of selecting a candidate that is totally infallible. Some methods are more reliable than others but, to a large extent, selection is about trying to minimise risk and maximising the certainty of making the right decision.

Starting from the position where the recruitment process has produced a number of applicants, the important steps in selection are as follows:

- short-listing the candidates for the next stage;
- setting up tests for the short-listed candidates, sometimes in the form of an assessment centre (although tests do not take place on every occasion);
- interviewing the candidates (and giving them feedback on the tests) and allowing the candidates to interview the selectors;
- choosing the successful candidate;
- obtaining references (although this is sometimes carried out before interview);
- offering the position, confirming in writing and gaining acceptance;
- organising the induction process;
- evaluating the result.

Each of these steps will be explained and analysed in this chapter.

Short-listing

Short-listing involves reducing the number of applications received down to an appropriate sized list of candidates to be invited for interview. The process varies in time depending on the ratio of application to vacancies. In recent years, as the number of graduate traineeships has stayed static, the number of graduates has increased by around 25% so the current ratio of applications to vacancies has increased, in some cases, to over 200:1. On the other hand, the number of vacancies for experienced software programmers has mushroomed so the ratio of applications to vacancies can be as low as 1:1. In the former case, there is much short-listing work to be done by the human resources department; in the latter, sadly, not a great deal usually resulting in more telephone calls to agencies to help in the recruitment process.

The aim would normally be to produce a short list of five or six candidates for interview for each vacancy.

There are two approaches in this reduction process. Firstly, there is the *screening* approach where unsuitable applicants are rejected until only the required number of applicants for interview is left. Applicants may be rejected for lack of experience or qualifications but it is not unknown for arbitrary decisions to be made involving the age, place of birth, handwriting or the inclusion of a photograph. Outright discrimination can also occur over the marital status, sex or ethnic background. Apart from being illegal, these methods are profoundly unfair and unreasonable as tribunals have continued to report.

The second method is one of *inclusion* where each applicant is compared with the requirements set out in the person specification and given a score through a pre-set scoring system. For example, a maximum of 10 points could be awarded for experience, 8 for qualifications, 15 for demonstration of certain key skills or competencies and 7 for other factors, giving a total of 40 points. It would also be agreed that a minimum number of points would need to be scored in certain categories to be able to be included in the list. The scoring would be carried out independently by two people, perhaps the line manager and the human resources manager, and, the results compared. Any discrepancies would be discussed. This process avoids discrimination and is much fairer to all the candidates, if taking a little longer.

Short-listing by phone is a relatively new process and takes several forms. Applicants can be asked to call a dedicated number where a member of the recruitment team will ask a series of pre-determined questions, the answers to which will be scored. If the target points are reached by the end of the interview, the applicant will be invited there and then to an interview on an agreed date. Alternatively, when application forms are received, the applicant will be telephoned, usually at home, with the same result. A final, more sophisticated process is when the questioning is automated. The applicant is asked a series of multi-choice questions by a recorded message and asked to use the keypads to indicate their answer. Their choices are automatically scored and totalled and an interview offered if appropriate. Short-listing by phone is only suitable where the organisation is very sure indeed of the necessary requirements for the position and where relatively large volumes are being dealt with. For example, it has been used often when starting up a call centre and the quality of the candidates telephone manner can be assessed along with the answers to the specified questions.

An example of telephone screening is given in Case study 5.1.

Case study 5.1

Telephone screening at Standard Life

Applicants for vacant positions have first had to get through an automated telephone screening interview. The company sorted through 561 candidates before taking on 15 recruits and claimed that the screening system saved 143 work days. The phone lines were open 24 hours a day, 7 days a week. The system, developed by Gallop, was tested on 100 existing staff and looked for six generic performance attributes: achiever, conscientiousness, responsibility, agreeableness, numeracy and stability.

Source: People Management (1998)

A further example of automated short-listing is the use of equipment to *electronically read CVs* using OCR (Optical Character Recognition) software. The system's artificial intelligence reads the texts and, by using search criteria such as qualifications, job titles and companies where the applicant has worked, will produce a ranking list of applicants against the mandatory and optional aspects of the person specification.

This system is quicker and more consistent than if it were carried out manually but will only be efficient as the search engine and will certainly miss many potential candidates, let alone the difficulty the technology faces in trying to understand poor handwriting.

An interesting argument in favour of telephone screening is that it can actually reduce discrimination, as the example of Nationwide Building Society's system shown in Case study 5.2.

Case study 5.2

How screening by 'phone' can reduce discrimination

The Nationwide Building Society believes that screening applicants by telephone is helping to eliminate the risk of assumptions being made on the basis of appearance, age and qualifications. The company, a founder member of the Employers Forum on Age, has developed the system since 1993 and is now applying it to a wide range of appointments at all levels, that is from customer advisers to senior branch managers.

Denise Walker, Head of Personnel, explains that the society records basic details when candidates first call and asks 'knockout' questions covering areas such as security and availability. Arrangements are then made for the candidate to be called back. The interviewers are provided only with the applicant's name and number, and the candidates do not need to prepare anything before the interview. Subsequent research indicated that successful applicants say that they found telephone interviewing a positive experience and, although those who were unsuccessful were not quite so enthusiastic, they still tended to feel better about the process and the criteria on which the short-listing decisions had been made.

Nationwide also found that, while the method does not entirely eliminate the need for face-to-face final interviews, it can be a more cost-effective way of short-listing when there are a large number of vacancies to be filled. Recruitment Manager, Sarah Davies says: 'This method has enabled us to recruit people in their 50s who traditionally might have been rejected at the short-listing stage.' Line Managers, she added, had admitted that previously they might not have considered these individuals, but once they had conducted a face-to-face interview, they had realised age is irrelevant.

Source: Employers Forum for Age Newsline (1997)

Biodata

Another technique used in short-listing, biodata, is to make a very detailed examination of the candidate's biography, comparing it to the biography of a group of successful incumbents in the position. As with all forms of selection, the technique depends upon the assumption that your past will assist in predicting your future. Candidates are asked to complete a detailed form which examines their previous and existing work record and also includes aspects of their personal lives. Just as with selection tests (see later) the questions are often in multiple-choice form so they can be computer analysed. When completed, it is scored and the short list selected from the candidates who have achieved more than the agreed threshold points. A more recent development is for the questions to be asked over the phone. It is not a commonly used technique; only 5% of large organisations use it (IRS, 1997) and it does have a number of drawbacks:

- Developing the questionnaire is a costly process involving research into the backgrounds and competence of current job holders. It will also need to be revised on a regular basis.
- A separate questionnaire has to be devised for each job; the biodata for successful sales employees can be very different to those of customer service employees.
- Candidates can be offput by the completion of such detailed information on top of the standard application information required.

The biodata technique, then, is only used in practice where there are a large number of applications to a standard position, where there are also a large number of current employees from which to draw up the biodata criteria.

Selection testing

You will recall that recruitment and selection is essentially about accuracy in prediction. The aim is to take on board a candidate who is going to succeed and perform well. The table at the start of this chapter showed that several forms of selection testing had much higher predictive success than conventional recruitment methods. Internal assessment centres are top of the league, while ability tests, assessment centres for external candidates and personality tests all do better than the traditional interview. That is why so much attention has been directed in recent years into analysing and refining tests and their results.

The first advocate of selection tests was Samuel Pepys, the famous 17th century diarist who, when secretary to the navy, proposed and outlined a more systematic assessment of ability than the nepotism currently rife. It was some time on from here before they began to be developed and adopted, firstly in America in the early part of the 20th century before they began to be more widely utilised in the Second World War in the UK when soldiers were people selected for officer potential. After the war, the ideas and methods were applied in the Civil Service but Figure 5.2 shows that the explosive growth in their use did not begin until the late 1980s.

Year	Percentage use by large employers
1973	7
1986	21
1989	37
1991	50
1997	75
2004	82

Figure 5.2
Use of selection tests

There are more than 1000 tests available on the market today which can be divided up into the categories of *measuring ability, aptitude, performance and personality*. Each of these will be dealt with in turn, together with common features of what makes up a good test and the correct way to use them. Then the benefits of using tests will be examined, followed by criticisms and difficulties involved in their use. Assessment centres follows the section on interviewing as they utilise a number of techniques involved in the selection process: personality tests, exercises and interviews.

Ability tests

These are tests that measure a candidate's existing ability, both mental and physical. They can measure a variety of areas such as verbal reasoning, numerical ability, sensory or motor skills, spatial or mechanical ability. Such tests can be constructed entirely related to the job concerned, such as wiring, assembling, bricklaying, typing or even lecturing. These are sometimes called *performance* tests or, in the case of the performing arts, *auditions*; alternatively, they can be general paper and pencil tests of mental or numerical skills.

When window surveyors are recruited into Everest Double Glazing, a mock-up window is constructed on their branch site and they are given a performance test to measure up the window, and point out any difficulties in installing the proposed replacement window, writing a short report subsequently.

Aptitude tests

These are also measures of ability that examine whether a candidate is likely to be able to acquire the skills and knowledge necessary to perform

Choose the pair of words which best completes each sentence. See how many you can do in 4 minutes

1   The .... invoice must be paid by ....

A	B	C	D
originall	original	original	originel
instalments	installments	instalments	installments

Each star represents a missing letter. You have to find the missing letters and write them down on the lines on the right. PRINT the letters in capitals. Here is one that has been done for you. In this one, the second word of each pair is the first word spelled backwards.

Don	nod	pit	tip	bag	gab	tub	***		<u>BUT</u>

Now do these yourself

1	me	meat	us	user	in	inch	**	once	....
2	her	there	his	whisk	***	shade			....

Figure 5.3
Examples of ability/aptitude questions

the job. Again, they can be set up as strictly job-related tests or a battery of published tests can be administered, such as those produced by Saville and Holdsworth or The Psychological Corporation. For example, a number of computer programming aptitude tests are available. These are typically presented as multiple-choice questions or for a gap to be filled in as shown in Figure 5.3.

Student activity 5.1

Discuss the advantages and difficulties of using ability, aptitude and performance tests.

Discussion of Student activity 5.1

You may have come up with some of the following advantages:

- Research has shown a reasonable prediction rate in comparison with other selection methods (0.54).

- Tests are usually not too difficult to design for specific jobs and relatively easy to judge especially on a comparison basis.
- The tests provide objective and predictive data to be followed up at the subsequent interview.
- Fair employment policies are demonstrated by introducing objective data into the proceedings.
- By using an effective test, it provides a professional image for the organisation.
- For off-the-shelf tests, large quantities of comparative data are available to aid judgement.
- Paper and pencil tests can be taken up at any location and are generally not too expensive.
- The test can be identified as a useful forecast for the candidate of the nature of the work.
- It gives additional confidence to successful candidates who recognise that the selection process is professional.
- The test can eliminate candidates who are not easy to train, a facet that is difficult to identify otherwise.
- A number of tests have now been introduced in computer mode so that candidates simply press the appropriate key for their answer. This means that the test is assessed very quickly indeed.

Here are some of the difficulties which may be encountered:

- Many tailor-made tests are amateur and untested themselves, utilised to justify personal decisions.
- Tests continue to be found to be discriminatory by tribunals, especially where understanding English is crucial to success in the test. The verbal reasoning test in Figure 5.3 would be more difficult for candidates where English is not a first language.
- It is necessary for the assessor to be trained in the use of off-the-peg tests.
- Feedback to poor performers is not easy.
- There is some evidence that candidates can improve their test performance by practice. Research is mixed here but veers towards a marginal improvement through practice. This has been believed for some time as the author remembers the many days at school at age 11 in the early 1950s when endless intelligence tests were practised before the 11+ examination and the subsequent high results in our year.

Personality tests

Personality tests are a type of psychological questionnaire that are designed to measure the more permanent emotional tendencies people have that make up their personality. Their prediction rates are surprising low at 0.38% but this may reflect to a large extent the way they are used (or misused) as much as the inherent defects of the tests themselves. Taylor (2002) sets out the basic assumptions on which the validity of personality testing ultimately rests:

- Human personality is measurable or 'mappable'.
- Our underlying human personality remains stable over time and across different situations.
- Individual jobs can be usefully analysed in terms of their personality traits that would be most desirable for the job-holder to possess.
- A personality questionnaire, completed in 30–60 minutes, provides sufficient information about an individual's personality to make meaningful inferences about their suitability for a job. (Taylor, 2002, p. 201)

The most well-known tests are Saville and Holdsworth's OPQ series, The Personal Profile Analysis, the California Psychological Inventory and the Myers–Briggs-Type Indicator. Cattell's 16PF (primary factors), has been in use for nearly 50 years and revised four times and this test has been chosen to give a more detailed explanation (see Figure 5.4). It sets out to describe personality in terms of 16 primary source traits (factors) or dimensions. These source traits are functionally different underlying characteristics and each is associated with not just one single piece of behaviour but rather is the source of a relatively broad range of behaviours. Proponents of the test argue that the advantage of measuring source traits is that you end up with a much richer understanding of the person because you are not just describing what can be seen but also the characteristics underlying what can be seen. It analyses how a person is likely to behave generally, including, for example, contributions likely to be made to particular work contexts, aspects of the work environment to which the person is likely to be more or less suited and how best to manage the person (Lord, 1994).

There have been criticisms of traditional personality tests, (and recent syntheses of these tests, such as the 'big five model': emotionality, extroversion, openness, agreeableness and conscientiousness, Iles, 2001) by psychologists who have pointed out that one-dimensional exactness is

Low score description	1	2	3	4	5	6	7	High score description
Reserved, detached, critical								Outgoing, warm-hearted
Less intelligent, concrete thinking								More intelligent, abstract thinking
Affected by feelings, easily upset								Emotionally stable, faces reality
Humble, mild, accommodating								Assertive, aggressive, stubborn
Sober, prudent, serious								Happy-go-lucky, impulsive, lively
Expedient, disregards rules								Conscientious, persevering
Shy, restrained, timid								Venturesome, socially bold
Tough minded, self-reliant								Tender minded clinging
Trusting, adaptable								Suspicious, self-opinionated
Practical, careful								Imaginative
Forthright, natural								Shrewd, calculating
Self-assured, confident								Apprehensive, self-reproaching
Conservative								Experimenting, liberal
Group dependent								Self-sufficient
Undisciplined, self-conflict								Controlled, socially precise
Relaxed, tranquil								Tensed, frustrated

Figure 5.4
16PF traits

a Western approach based on Cartesian logic (Trompenaars and Woolliams, 2002). They suggest that tests should include options to reconcile opposites that position people on bi-polar scales. For example, rather than people being forced to choose between:

(a) A job that is part of a team and the organisation, where everyone works together without bothering about individual credit. OR

(b) A job that allows everyone to work independently and where credit is given for individual performance without restrictions.

There should be the opportunity to reconcile these two positions through additional options:

(c) A job where everyone works together in teams to help the organisation as a whole, but where teams encourage, stimulate, reward and celebrate individual contribution. OR

(d) A job which allows everyone to work independently for personal recognition, but where credit and acclaim come from the team and the organisation.

The most important element in personality tests is the interpretation of the results. Candidates are not differentiated by whether they have scored highly or 'passed' the test. They are differentiated by how closely their test profile meets the requirements of the tested job profile. An example of how such tests can change the entire nature of the selection process is set out in Case study 5.3.

Case study 5.3

Selection testing for managed pubs

In the late 1980s, a well-known brewer became dissatisfied with the performance of their managed pubs. There were contrasting profits from pubs in comparable areas and the staff turnover and level of fraud was unacceptably high. They entered into an exercise to try to improve their recruitment and selection. Firstly, they set out to profile the high performers and a group of 100 or so landlords (and their partners) were given a battery of tests including Cattells 16PF. The results were a surprise to them. They had expected that a successful publican would have strong features on traits such as outgoing, warm-hearted, lively, relaxed and socially bold. This was not the case. Their strongest features were being practical, careful, controlled, socially precise, tense, conscientious, persevering, restrained, sober, prudent and reserved. Just the sort of profile you would expect from an accountant!

From these surprising results, they carried out a careful job analysis and profit investigation. They found that the high profits were made through efficiently serving a capacity house at the key times of the week: Friday, Saturday evening and Sundays. To be efficient they needed to be good at planning and organising, so nothing ran out, there was a ready supply of clean glasses and they motivated and controlled their temporary staff so nothing disturbed the correct takings. Availability of food was also crucial so teamwork between the partners was essential. When talking to the customers of the successful houses, the personality of the landlord came some way down the list below the general ambience and convenience of the pub, its quality of beer, cleanliness and food. The landlord needed to be efficient and friendly but not too friendly. He also needed to be good at preventing trouble or sorting it out quickly.

Following this exercise, the company completely altered the person specification. Each of the short-listed candidates (and they looked for couples) completed PF16 and the test results were used to confirm (or at times, to decide against) the appointment. By choosing candidates, many of whom did not actually drink, who closely matched the profile of their successful landlords, the company increased their profits by 40% over the next 3 years, reduced staff turnover by 60% and made a substantial reduction in cases of fraud.

Source: Author's case study

Tests need to be interpreted against the 'norm' and the results are expressed in the form of variation from the norm. A raw score tends to be fairly meaningless although psychologists are sometimes asked to make a general interpretation of a random test on a candidate for a client company.

Test format

There are three main formats of the tests. The ipsative or forced-choice question where the candidate has to choose between a number of statements or adjectives that describe themselves. For example, they may be asked:

Would you like to be regarded by your colleagues as agreeable ...
Or well-organised ...?

These are questions that are not liked by candidates as they find it difficult to distinguish between those choices. The results can show contradictions and confusion unless they are carefully interpreted.

A second format is to give a third alternative in answer to a question. For example:

I would prefer to go out with friends to the cinema in the evening rather than stay in and read a book.
Agree.........   Uncertain.........   Disagree ....

This format allows candidates a greater choice and can measure the candidate's degree of indecision.

A third format is to use the Likert scale where candidates have more than three choices:

Once I make up my mind, it is important not to change
Strongly agree … Agree … Uncertain … Disagree …
Strongly disagree….

Advantages of personality tests

■ They add an objective measure to the selection process in areas where interviewing alone may not tease out the salient features. A candidate may say that he is a good organiser, forthright, focused, caring, relaxed and a great entertainer but the test should give you a much clearer picture of which are the strongest traits.

■ Many of them have been around for a long time and have very well established norms for certain occupations so comparisons can be straightforward to operate.

■ There are usually advisers/consultants who will help in the administration and interpretation or provide you with the training to carry this out yourself.

■ Candidates, in general, regard the selection process has more rigour if selection tests are involved.

Student activity 5.2

Are there any difficulties involved in using personality tests?

Discussion of Student activity 5.2

You may have thought of some of the following difficulties:

■ The good tests have a commercial price to pay, either through an annual licence to use them or to pay for the interpretation or both. The cost of giving a test to 10 candidates works can cost over £200.

■ There are tests on the market which appear cheap but they do not have the validity and reliability required. Steve Blinkhorn, Chairman of Psychometric Research and Development, calls this the 'great underworld of psychometrics: shoddy personality tests and 10-minute quickies that tell you 'everything you need to know' (Smethurst, 2003).

- The risk of stereotyping candidates is all too easy. With the belief that personality is set in stone at the age of 30, some candidates may be labelled as unsuitable because they ticked a few wrong boxes. David Leeds, Head of Human Resources at Investac, avoids personality tests for fears of stifling variety. 'We are anxious not to stereotype or characterise people by putting them into different personality labels' (Butcher, 2004).

- Tests are sometimes regarded as the clinching factor in selection. Peter Saville has gone on the record to say that nobody should be selected just because of the personality test results; they must be used as an aid to selection (Money Programme, BBC television, 23 November 1996).

- Tests are often used wrongly, attempting to measure the unmeasurable or drawing inferences from results which are not justified. Of the 'big five' personality factors, most experts point to conscientiousness and emotional stability to be the best predictors of high-management performance but this is disputed by Ivan Robertson (2001) who has pointed out that the correlations between these two factors and high performance is weak and should not be relied upon.

- Candidates gain experience the more tests they take and can guess the kind of profile that the employers are looking for, ticking the appropriate boxes.

What makes a good test?

There are a number of essential features that make a test worth using. Firstly, it must be *valid*. This means it must measure the characteristic which the test is intended to measure. If it sets out to measure the aptitude for, say, bricklaying, then it must be tested to show that it actually does do so. Secondly, it must also be *reliable* in that the results are the same if the tests are given under identical conditions. Robust tests have themselves been tested effectively over a period of time before they are put on the market, usually with the help of volunteers. Details of validity and reliability are normally given in the test handbook. Thirdly, there must be *norms* available which have arisen from standardised interpretation. Fourthly, the tests must be *free of discrimination*. Care should be taken that a norm is not established from testing predominantly Caucasian males, as pointed out by the Commission for Racial Equality

The guide aims to ensure that:

- Proper consideration is given to the appropriateness of using tests.
- Tests are used in a professional manner which is relevant to the employment context.
- Equality of opportunity is ensured throughout the process.
- Test results are scored, interpreted and communicated by appropriately trained individuals.
- Individuals taking tests are informed of the reasons for the test and the conditions under which it will be used, how the information will be used and stored, and are given the opportunity to receive feedback on the test results.

Figure 5.5
IPD guide on
psychological testing
(*Source:* IPD, 1997)

in their booklet 'Psychometric Tests and Racial Equality'. Finally, tests should be *adapted for disabled candidates.*

The CIPD has produced a *Guide on Psychological Testing* and a summary is shown in Figure 5.5.

Interviewing the candidates

An interview has been the traditional method of selection for decades and yet research studies have shown, as indicated at the start of the chapter, that they are a poor predictor of future performance (Anderson and Shackleton, 1994). This is due to a number of factors, all centering around the faults of the interviewer. Graves and Karen (1992), for example, found that 29 interviewers from the same company used 13 different criteria weightings to make their decisions, which often lead to different conclusions.

Problems associated with interviewing

Difficulties with arriving at a consistent and objective decision on a candidate is hampered by a long list of irrational but understandable tendencies by interviewers who have the following.

- *Different views on the person they are looking for.* The person specification may be too vague or ambiguous so interviewers have different ideas on what would be the success factors in the position. One interviewer may place great importance on the candidate's previous experience, another may be influenced by a candidate's perceived inflexible ideas. In one research programme, a group of interviewers who were aware of the person specification and were in possession of the application forms, were shown a group of video-taped interviews and yet there was still a variation in the recommended candidate for the position. This was despite having identical information.

- *Decide intuitively.* Despite repeated calls for interviewers to base their decisions on the objective evidence which they have collected, there remains a constant temptation to make overall judgements based on intuition. The 'I have a gut-feel' school of interviewing still has a number of ardent supporters, who usually also subscribe to the 'I can spot them as soon as they come in the door' association!

- *Make decisions before the interview takes place or early on in the interview.* Studies show that the average length of time between a candidate entering the interview room and a decision being made is just under 4 minutes. This 'expectancy effect' arises from a study of the CV or application before the interview. All the subsequent information is recorded but adjusted to fit into the decision that the interviewer has already made.

- *Prefer candidates like themselves.* The so-called 'clone factor' indicates that interviewers give higher ratings on some traits to candidates who are similar to themselves, rather than matching the candidates against the person specification.

- *Continue to stereotype candidates.* Despite the illegality of judging candidates on the basis of their sex, ethnic origin, disability or marital status, interviewers, often unknowingly, will allow such considerations to cloud their judgements. This can extend to areas such as age, geographical origin, accent, height and even their attire.

- *Cannot take on board all the information provided.* The brain can only assimilate a certain amount of information. Each candidate provides a wealth of data and even 30 minutes of interview time can be transcribed into more than 10 pages of written text. A recommended interview period therefore should not extend beyond 1 hour individually or 4 hours in a day and certainly not beyond five or six candidates. Notes need to be compiled during the interview, and compared and agreed after each one.

- *Influence candidates' behaviour.* How an applicant behaves is partly dependent on how the interviewer behaves. Particular interest has been focused on non-verbal behaviours (signals such as nodding, smiling and eye-contact) during the interview. In one study it was found that where interviewers had already decided to reject the applicants, they talked less and were more cold and critical; the candidates in this trial reported that they were more uncomfortable and became more hesitant in their replies. However, where interviewers were warm, had good eye-contact and nodded their head more frequently, candidate became more relaxed, acted in a more friendly way themselves, became more talkative and generally were found to be more effective in creating a good impression.

■ *Raise their ratings if they feel pressurised to select.* After all the time, effort and cost involved in recruitment, there is considerable pressure on the interviewers to come up with a successful candidate. Knowing the delay that would be incurred if the position needed to be advertised again, interviewers may panic and allow the pressure to influence their decision. A candidate that is close to meeting the specification may be upgraded and candidates rejected for good reasons may be wrongly re-considered.

■ *Believe that they are good at interviewing.* Interviewing is not regarded in some circles as a skill that can be learnt and developed. Many line managers see it as an inherent managerial trait that they possess, chiefly because it is never pointed out to them that evidence indicates the contrary is true.

■ *Influence the candidates' responses to the offer.* The interviewer represents the organisation. The candidate will judge that organisation on how they are treated and how the interviewer has behaved to them. It has been shown that up to 50% of candidates change their minds about their likely acceptance of a potential job offer as a result of their experience in the interview, irrespective of the benefits and attractiveness of the post.

These are pretty serious criticisms of the interview process. They indicate that the whole process is so flawed that it ought not to be operated at all in such an important area as selection. There is an alternative view, however, which goes someway in explaining why the interview is still the most popular aid to selection decision-making. This view is that, partially flawed as it is, it has some distinct advantages and serious attempts can be made to overcome the flaws through training and specifically through utilising the more systematic and objective method of structured interviews which will be dealt with shortly.

The general *advantages* put forward in favour of interviews are:

- It is a relatively low-cost exercise, with additional expenses limited to the time of the participants and any travelling and accommodation expenses.
- No decision on selection should be taken without an interview of some sort being carried out. At the basic level, it is a pure courtesy, an introduction both to the organisation and the people involved.
- Used properly, valid judgements can be made on a number of items of behaviour, especially inter-personal behaviour. Sociability, verbal fluency, social confidence can all be competencies detailed in the job specification and measured effectively in the interview process. The interview can be viewed as a type of 'work sample' of these behaviours and should give some degree of prediction about future behaviour and performance.
- The interview is important in selling the job to the applicants and this is vital in certain high demand, low supply occupations, such as information technology or accounting. If the interview is handled positively and carefully, disappointed candidates will still feel good about the experience and the organisation.
- A degree of negotiation can and often should take place before an agreement is reached between the organisation and the selected candidate. The interview allows informal negotiation to take place on the nature of the job together with the terms and conditions.

Who carries out the interview?

There are three options for the interview format: *One-to-one interviews, paired interviews or panel interviews.* Each should be used in specific situations and avoided in others. The decision as to the appropriate format is made by reaching a balance between two contrasting objectives. Firstly, the need for informality which gives the opportunity for a frank exchange of views and information and, secondly, the need to include as many stakeholders involved as possible and work to a structured and objective agenda.

In a professionally handled *one-to-one interview*, the candidate is more likely to open up, respond to careful probing and give all the required information regarding their skills, experience, competencies and viewpoints. However, the interviewer will be unlikely to be able to deal with all the information successfully (have you tried listening to the answers, taking notes and thinking of the next question at the same time?). Another problem arising is that the decisions made will be based on one person's views which can be biased or wrongly based. Thirdly, there are serious questions to be answered in the area of equal opportunities where only having one interviewer greatly increases the chances of a discriminating viewpoint. In fact, it can be quite dangerous. A number of organisations have faced tribunals by unsuccessful applicants who have claimed that interviewers have made statements or asked questions which can be regarded as discriminatory in the fields of sex, race or disablement and, with only one interviewer, it becomes more difficult to refute.

One-to-one interviews, therefore, are appropriate in only a limited number of situations. For example, a candidate for a senior position can be invited to meet a number of potential peers who will each talk to the person separately and informally, comparing overall notes afterwards. This may result in a degree of fatigue for the applicant as the same questions are repeated but this may be regarded as part of the selection process, that is to see how the candidate handles the situation. Another situation is when a candidate may have a preliminary interview with, say, the human resources manager, as part of a wider short-listing process. The human resources manager will be entrusted to select a number of possible candidates who will progress to the final stage.

At the other extreme, a *panel interview*, which can consist of up to 10 interviewers, presents its own problems. Pure logistics is one, where simply finding a convenient time for all the participants can be difficult enough. If a candidate cannot make the required date, it is not uncommon for them to be ruled out of the equation as another date for the panel cannot be arranged. Another difficulty is the inevitable formality of a number of interviewers appearing to interrogate the applicant, moving rapidly from one questioner to another ('sorry, Counsellor Jones, but we must move on') and from one topic to another. Question slots have to be agreed beforehand which makes it difficult to enter into probing mode. The applicant will find it difficult to read the body language of all the interviewers, or to gauge how well the answers were received. It may also need some time after each interview for the panel to compare notes and reach a decision on each candidate, which prolongs the exercise.

So panel interviews are only used where it is considered essential for a number of stakeholders to be present and for a decision to be taken on the day when the interviews have been held. This is currently the chosen mantra within the public sector, especially in local authorities. For many such jobs, a head of department, one or more line managers, a member of human resources and a counsellor may be present. There may also be a clerk to take notes and an equal opportunity adviser to ensure procedures are followed. Internal equity and consultation is carried out and justice is seen to be done, despite the difficulties of getting agreement of a number of staff and who will be the successful candidate. Many of the applicants spend their lives in such an environment so they know what happens and are prepared for it. There is some evidence that the actual numbers are being reduced due to the continuing cutback of staff in the public domain. In certain departments of Beds County Council, for example, it has been agreed as policy that three people (no more, no less) will be present at each interview.

Given the difficulties with the other two forms, it is no surprise that the most common interviewing format is *a paired interview* where the line manager is supported by a member of the human resources department. They agree on the nature of the interview, which one will take the lead at particular points and will normally share in the note-taking role. A second interviewer allows probing to take place and for a merging of combined views of the outcome of the questioning.

Interviewing technique

Although interviewing is still seen generally as an art form, there are a number of essential ingredients which make up a successful interview. These can be divided into *preparation, operation and summation.*

Preparation includes the following elements:

- All the relevant documents, especially the application form and candidate's accompanying letter, should be read thoroughly.
- It should be firmly agreed between the interviewers the nature of the measurement of the candidate. It may be carried out by a points system based on how closely they meet the person specification or by an agreed system of elimination.
- The division of the interview should be agreed, with time divided between telling the candidate a little more about the organisation and the position, the questioning of the candidate and giving the candidate the opportunity to ask questions.
- The room allocated for the interview should be prepared. It is better for it to be informally set out, rather than interviewers

on one side of the desk and the candidate on the other. There should be no interruptions of any kind.

- The nature of the data recording must be agreed, the stationary printed and the recording roles assigned.

Operation covers a wide area and can be divided into a number of areas:

- opening the interview,
- listening,
- asking the right questions,
- structured interviews.

Opening the interview is important as it sets the tone of the interview process. Some informal questions concerning travel arrangements or knowledge of the organisation or area are often used to break the ice. It is important at an early stage to introduce the interviewers and to make it quite clear what will be happening during the interview and after it is over. It is normal for the lead interviewer to say a few words about the position, referring to documents already sent to the candidate. This allows the candidate to relax into the interview and a chance to observe the interviewers.

For the interviewers, one of the most important techniques is *listening*. It is easy to spot the inexperienced interviewer; they believe they should dominate the proceeding and do most of the talking. The reality is that, apart from words at the start to allow the candidate to relax into the interview, the vast majority of the interview should consist of the candidate talking. The more the candidate talks, the more complete the picture the interviewer can draw.

A sign of effective listening is that the interviewer asks relevant questions, which can probe the candidate, especially any implied points that are made. For example, a slight hesitation in answer to a question as to the relationship with a certain manager would be followed up carefully. Maintaining eye-contact and summarising what the candidate has said from time to time demonstrates to the candidate that what they are saying is being followed carefully and sympathetically.

Asking the right questions in the right way is a large subject area. There are a number of different styles and techniques that can be used. All of them depend on the nature of the information that you want to draw out from the candidate. They can take a number of forms:

1   If you want to find out some clear factual information or to check points, then *closed* questions are appropriate, those to

which the answer is either yes or no:

- Have you a clean driving licensee?
- Were you dismissed from that employment?
- Do you have a level A BPS qualification?

2   If you want candidates to expand on information they have given and generally open up more, then you ask *open* questions:

- Why did you want to leave that employment?
- What do you enjoy about customer service work?
- Which do you consider to be your major strengths in managing people?
- Tell me about the difficulties you faced when you became a supervisor?
- How did you cope with moving from a local authority to working in the private sector?
- When did you really discover that your career should be in training?

The more experienced you become in interviewing, the more is learnt about how to mix the majority of open questions with the occasional closed question. For example, when interviewing for a supervisory position, you would ask a number of open questions relating to the candidate's experience of supervision and their views on how it should be done well; you would intersperse these questions with some closed questions relating to how long they acted as a supervisor or whether they had disciplined an employee for poor workmanship/attitude/timekeeping.

3   If you want to get into the fine detail about a candidate's work history, behaviours or attitude, you would ask *probing* questions. For example, you have sensed a slight discrepancy between the starting date of one job and the leaving date of the previous job and that the manner of leaving may not have been too happy. You would probe this situation with questions such as:

- You seem to indicate that you were not entirely happy working at xxx. For how long were you looking to leave the employment?
- Did you have any indication that your manager found your work unsatisfactory? I should add that we may want to take up a reference with her.
- Did you finally leave the employment voluntarily?
- Was there any gap between leaving xxx and starting at yyyy?

Experienced interviewers often probe simply by asking candidates, when they pause at the end of explanation, to 'go on' or 'tell me more' or ask them ' was there any other reason?', leaving a pause for the candidate, which often results in either the fundamental truth of the situation or the candidate getting themselves caught up in the knots of their own deception.

4 If you want to find out how a candidate may behave in a given situation, then you would ask a *situational* or *hypothetical* question. Here you would set out a specific scenario, usually related to the work situation and ask the candidate what the options would be and how they would act. An example of this is set out in Figure 5.6.

The problem here is deciding what you are trying to find out. You may want to know the candidate's knowledge of how to deal with that specific situation; however, you may simply find out how quick thinking they are

---

An interview has been fixed for the position of campaigns manager for a small charity at a salary of £18,000. It is possible that a young graduate will be appointed to the position.

The situation agreed by the panel is as follows:

You have agreed to telephone round to the regional officers between 10.00 a.m. and 11.00 a.m. to discuss the agenda for a critical meeting in order to decide the response to a government initiative. They all work on a voluntary basis and have full-time jobs and this time for communication was arranged a fortnight ago. You have an appraisal meeting with the charity director at 11 a.m. that has been put off a couple of times and is very important to you. Just before 10.00 a.m., you get a call from the news desk of a national newspaper asking you to ring a particular journalist. This journalist has wasted your time on a couple of occasions in the past and is not a very pleasant character. The next moment, the charity director's secretary comes in to say that the director has to go out at 11.00 a.m., could the appraisal meeting take place now? What do you do?

The panel have decided that candidates will be judged by their views on the best course of action as matched against the panel's concerted view of the best course of action, that is:

Explain to the Director's secretary that you need to call the journalist and do not know how long this will take. Try to arrange another time for the appraisal. Call the journalist and deal with the issues raised. No matter how much difficulties there are with such people, keeping a good relationship with them is crucial and they can give you the publicity that can be vital to your organisation's development. As soon as that call is over, start ringing round to the regional officers, explaining the issues with the national newspaper and fixing alternative times to talk if possible (get somebody else to help if they are available). Use e-mail where appropriate. Your own appraisal will need to wait.

A scoring system has been devised against this answer with a maximum of 10, with marks deducted for a different set of priorities or communication faults.

Figure 5.6
A situational or hypothetical question

and their ability to come up with the 'right answer'. How they will act in practice may be entirely different. There is also the difficulty in deciding what is the 'right' answer and this needs to be clarified before the interview and the candidates' answers measured against this answer.

An alternative version to this type of questioning is to describe the situation as in Figure 5.5 and then ask the candidate how they reacted in a similar situation that they faced in the past. This is called *a Patterned Behaviour Description Interview (PBDI)*. The advantage here is that that you will be talking about a real situation. The problem, however, is that the candidate may not have faced such a situation or the situation they describe may not have the main elements you want to examine.

Criterion-based interview technique (CIT) is a similar version where candidates are asked to produce evidence of how they acted in situations where a specific competence is required. An example of its usage at the Ministry of Defence is shown in Case study 5.4.

Case study 5.4

CIT – Ministry of Defence

This is an extract from the interviewer's guidebook to help determine the level of competence of an applicant in the area of '*working effectively with others*'.

Firstly, here is a list of indicators against the competence:

Evidence for	Evidence against
Builds rapport with others and tries to resolve conflict with tack	Poor relationships with others
Remains calm and courteous when handling differences with others	Easily ruffled or abrasive when handling differences with others
Helps others with their work	Little knowledge of colleagues' work
Sensitive to others' needs	Insensitive to others' needs
Willing to cover for others	Keeps information to self
Shares information with people	Does not inform manager of problems/progress
Follows managers' instructions willingly	
Knows when to tackle directly or ask someone else	Poor judgment on when to ask for someone else's advice
Puts forward ideas	Puts forward few (if any) ideas

Here are the questions that will help you to judge the candidate's competence:

Opening question:
On your application form, you wrote about a time when you had to work in a group or team and what you did to keep up good relationships within the group. Can you tell me about another time when you had to work in a group or team? If candidates cannot think of another example, probe on the one they gave on the application form:

- What did you do to keep up co-operation and good relationships?
- What problems or difficulties did you face?
- How did you overcome these?

Follow-on questions:
Can you tell me about the occasion when you have had to help resolve conflict between people who were not co-operating with each other?

- What action did you take?
- What did you say?
- How did you react/respond?
- What was the outcome?

Give me an example of an occasion when you helped a colleague at work.

- What led up to the situation?
- What did they need?
- How could you tell?
- What help did you give?

Give me an example of a situation where you referred a work issue to your supervisor/manager

- What did you refer to him/her?
- What did you do?
- What was the response?
- What was the result?

Source: Ministry of Defence internal documentation.

---

5   Some interviewers use *Stress questions* as part of an interview. The intention here is to examine how candidates react to an

aggressive or disparaging interviewer or to particularly critical remarks. This is a controversial and risky strategy as the candidate, although dealing with the situation well, may be put off the organisation by being treated in this way. Only if the job is highly specialised, such as intelligence work or direct selling where selection methods tend to be somewhat unpredictable and this is recognised by candidates, could such a method be held to be acceptable.

Structured interviews

To be successful in the whole operation of interviewing, a planned structure is necessary. Referring again to the Anderson and Shackleton table of predictive success in selection at the start of this chapter, *Structured interviews* come very high on the table with a predictive rating of 0.62 and research in recent years backs up this high reliability (Cooper *et al.*, 2003). As explained by Palmer and Campion (1997):

> In the 80 year history of published research on employment interviewing, few conclusions have been more widely supported than the idea that structuring the interview enhances reliability and validity.
>
> Palmer and Campion (1997: p. 655)

Structured interviews take many forms but the essential features include:

- A sense of direction and purpose, that is a clear agreement on what the interview is trying to elicit.
- The interviewing process attempts to predict how candidates will perform in the work situation.
- The question format is laid down and agreed beforehand which are job analysis based.
- Controlled prompting and follow-up questions.
- No questions from candidates allowed during the interview.
- A thorough and consistent approach used with all the candidates in the same way.
- Interviewers are trained in the process to be used.
- Candidates are evaluated using the same scale.

Although it has proved to be highly successful, this approach has its critics. The strict following of a pre-planned process allows little ability to deviate or to follow up any areas that may be of interest to both the candidate and the interviewer. Occasionally it can appear stilted and artificial. Where mass recruitment takes place, interviewers may become weary and bored by having to follow an identical format. An example of structured interviews is given in Focus on research 5.1.

Focus on research 5.1

Structured interviews

This article analyses the development of the selection process of Beyer for sales representatives in Russia and Eastern Europe. The organisation had encountered a very high turnover rate for sales staff in these areas which had not improved with increased training or improved management. The conclusion was reached that there was a fundamental fault in the selection process. The organisation moved firstly into a greater use of assessment centres but it became clear that the cultural differences between countries was so great that mixing candidates at one centre was not effective. Nor could they be set up at the speed and flexibility that was required.

Structured interviews were then developed for each location, using teams of experienced local managers. A detailed job analysis and associated competencies were constructed and a four-part interview structure built up, consisting of questions on job experience and background, question sets focused on the required competencies, behavioural event discussion (past oriented) and situational role-play (future oriented). Standard evaluation forms were produced alongside this structure. The structured interviews took place for those candidates who pass the telephone and base-line interview screening process.

Under this setting, structured interviews take over 2 hours with a panel of three interviewers who have pre-determined roles, either in question asking, observation or note-taking. A detailed description of each part of the interview is set out in the article. The outcome for the organisation is not clear but early responses were very positive, especially from staff involved in the selection process.

Source: Engle (1998)

Summation, is the final stage of the interviewing process. This involves recording all the necessary data and closing the interview. Before an interview is closed, it is important that candidates have the opportunity *to ask questions*. Indeed, some interview processes allow candidates to ask questions at the start. In any case, it encourages the interview to be a two-way process, it indicates how interested the candidate is in the position and how much research they have carried out and allows a judgement to be made on how well organised the candidate is.

When questions from both sides are over, the interview is normally *closed* by a word of thanks for attending and a re-iteration of the next stage in the process. Sometimes, especially for manufacturing environments, a short tour of the premises is arranged.

Recording the interview data is vital. Not only this is essential so that decisions can be taken on the basis of objective measures but such information may be necessary as a defence against an action for discrimination in selection, which may be taken against the organisation at some time. A final use is for giving feedback to unsuccessful candidates.

Assessment centres

Assessment centres are not just used for selection, although this is their main purpose in practice. They can also be used for diagnosing the training and development needs of individuals, especially those in positions of authority: as a general tool to improvement, teamworking within a department; to assess the special needs of those employees who can be identified as potential high-performers. Their use has been growing for a number of reasons:

- In today's flatter organisations, mistakes made in management selection decisions are far more costly so it is vital to get them right at the start.
- Candidates that have taken part in them are more motivated, recognising the high level of time, effort and cost put into them.
- There is a benefit for the assessors who take part. ICI found that Training Managers as assessors made them far better at the day-to-day management process (Arkin, 1991).

Essentially, an assessment centre brings together a number of selection methods into a concentrated period which lasts 1 or 2 days. A programme can be made up of group exercises, presentations, role playing, personality tests, structured interviews and in-tray exercises all of which are scored by trained assessors.

Roberts (1997) has suggested the grid in Figure 5.7 for using various tests at an assessment center to probe for certain competencies:

The assessors are usually made up of experienced managers in the organisation, usually one or two ranks above the candidates involved in

Competency	Screen	Test	Interview	Exercise
Achievement	X			
Leadership				X
Creativity		X		
Resilience		X		
Flexibility			X	
Technical knowledge	X			
Judgement		X		
Decision-making		X	X	
Planning				X
Financial acumen				X

Figure 5.7
Techniques to test for various competencies (*Source*: Roberts, 1997)

the centre, plus some external assessors who are usually consultants. The internal assessors need to be thoroughly trained in the nature of the tests and how to assess the candidates. For example, observation of team-working will involve an assessment of positive and negative contributions, idea generation and leadership, all of which need to be objectively scored. Skills of assessing are made up of observing, recording, classifying, summarising and rating. The ratio of assessors to candidates at a centre is in the order of 1:2 so the staff utilisation costs are quite high.

The aim of the activity tests is to create situations that are as realistic as possible to the work place or where the candidate behaviour has an important bearing on the expected behaviour in the work place. The way that candidates interact with each other, persuade, negotiate and lead each other can actually be seen, rather than discussed from a theoretical viewpoint. The centres put considerable pressure on the candidates; they are stressful occasions, especially as the outcome is perceived as success or failures with little in between. Experienced assessment centre planners try to ensure that the candidates consider the selection process is carried out with them, and not done to them. Detailed feedback to the candidates is another essential requirement.

Development centres are less pressurised. Some are set up with complete confidentially for the participants who play a major part in planning and running the centre themselves. The outcome is a programme of training and development for each participant to help them to achieve agreed goals. (There is more on this subject in Chapter 10.)

Centres are expensive to set up and run. The costs include accommodation and travel, the tests and their interpretation, consultant fees and operating managers' time. They are not to be taken on lightly. An example of an assessment centre is detailed in the Meteor case study.

Choosing the successful candidate

The final decision on selecting the preferred candidate should follow the same process that applies to short-listing. Only the candidates who match the 'essential' aspects of the person specification should be considered. It is a poor decision to select 'the best on the day' when this person only reaches half of the necessary criteria. It is far better to start the process again than take a serious risk in a potentially hazardous investment. If there is more than one candidate who meets all the criteria, then the final decision can be made by a number of ways. Generally, the decision is given to the line manager who will have to motivate, develop and manage the person concerned. Much is talked about the necessary 'personal chemistry' that needs to exist between the line manager and the successful applicant but one must be wary of the potential discrimination aspects. The manager should justify the decision in terms of as much objective criteria as possible.

Sometimes other parties are brought into the decision-making process. At The Bodyshop and at Pret à Manger (see Case study 5.5), the existing unit staff are consulted about the candidates and have a serious input into the equation. For senior University posts, candidates are often asked to give a formal presentation to staff in the appropriate department or faculty who are then consulted, especially on the technical elements.

Case study 5.5

The Pret à Manger Academy

An unusual approach to selection has been adopted by Pret à Manger, the ethical and rapidly expanding sandwich chain with 118 shops and 2400 staff. Despite a staff turnover far less than their competitors' average (90% against 150%) it still leaves a great deal of recruitment to carry out each year: 55,000 applications for 1500 job were received in 2001.

To ensure it gets people with the right qualities, Pret uses what is perhaps the ultimate assessment centre: a job experience day. But, unlike the conventional assessment centre, would-be team members are assessed by their working colleagues who vote on whether a job is offered or not. When the team buys into a recruit, they take responsibility for getting them team oriented and up to speed.

Before their working day, candidates have to get through a competence-based interview, which aims to discover those that have an outgoing, positive attitude to life. Candidates passing this stage are then thrown in at the deep end, working as a paid employee in the shop from 6.30 a.m. until 2.30 p.m. A team member will be assigned to act as guide and mentor with the idea that candidates carry out as many different tasks as possible, working with all the shop staff. The shop manager carries out an informal interview but does not have a vote, although their view can have some sway. At 2.30 p.m., the manager gathers the team members' votes and informs the applicant. Unsuccessful candidates go away with £30, a free lunch and feedback on their performance.

All the team take a lot of pride in their role in the Pret experience and they appreciate how important is their responsibility in taking the decision. Since it is their decision, they want it to work out, so the team provides a great deal of help and encouragement to the new starter giving them a good induction into the organisation.

Source: Carrington (2002)

Obtaining references

The offer of employment should not be made, even informally, until references have been obtained.

Once a decision is reached on the chosen candidate, it is normal to make approaches to past employers to check the accuracy of information provided by the applicant and to ensure that there is no 'skeleton' lurking in the applicant's past that has not been revealed.

References are one of the most unsatisfactory aspects of human resources in practice. Most organisations make attempts to obtain them (99% according to a IRS poll (IRS, 1997)), but the actual results are woefully inadequate. Either the requested reference never arrives, or it provides a set of platitudes that can be unconvincing or it is incomplete, leaving out some key information that may affect the decision to offer employment. In certain circumstances effective references are vital, such as in jobs involving a high degree of security or where the work is with vulnerable people.

Cowan and Cowan (1989) set out many of the pitfalls in obtaining references, including hidden meanings (*A sociable and gregarious individual* means the candidate drinks too much) and explain how most of them can be overcome.

The legal situation is summed up by Howlings (1998):

'Unless specified contractually, employers are not obliged to give references but, if they are supplied, they must be true and accurate or the referee may be open to a charge of negligence. As long as the job offer is subject to the receipt of satisfactory references, an employer may withdraw an offer if the references are not satisfactory. An employer should avoid disclosing the contents of a poor reference to an employee in order to protect the confidentiality of the referee.'

Howlings (1998: p. 22)

For jobs where the security or personal risks are small, a simplified reference system is to obtain at interview the names and telephone numbers of the managers that the applicant worked for in previous employment (interestingly, by telling the applicant that these people will be approached for a reference sometimes draws the applicant to tell more details about why they left their employment). The reliability of certain crucial pieces of information can be verified by one short phone call and it is not wise to make an offer until such information is received. Despite recommendations about making offers of employment 'subject to satisfactory references' it is a very unpleasant process to actually withdraw an offer when a poor reference is received. The applicant may have already handed in their notice to their existing employer and the reference received may just be vindictive or out of date. It is far better to ensure the reference is obtained before the offer is actually made. Finally, except for school leavers, it is not worth considering references from the applicant's friends or colleague who are unlikely to be able to make an unbiased judgement.

Having said all this, references should be treated as just one part of the jigsaw. Just as with selection tests, a decision should not be based on the reference alone; a reference will always be a subjective and incomplete item, representing a period in time. Individuals change over time and younger ones will often blossom given a supportive, encouraging and developmental environment.

Offering the position

Once satisfactory references have been obtained, the offer of employment can be made to the successful candidate. This needs, of course, to be confirmed in writing but, because of the need to inform the candidate as soon as possible, especially if you aware that they are in the market for other positions, then a telephone call with the main details usually takes place as soon as possible. Should the candidate wish to negotiate any of the details, then this call allows such negotiations to proceed quickly.

The offer of employment should contain the following details:

- Job Title.
- Starting Date.
- Starting salary and any agreed details on salary progression and how it is determined, especially during the first year.
- Any help with re-location if appropriate.
- Company car level and arrangements for petrol, if appropriate.
- Details of confirmation of the offer (the candidate is usually asked to sign their agreement on one copy of the letter, returning it to the company in the envelope supplied).
- Details may also be supplied of other company benefits if not given beforehand. These can include medical and life assurance, staff discounts, parking arrangement and pension scheme.
- The candidate may be asked to bring with them on the first day their driving licence and any qualifications they have claimed for which the organisation have not yet obtained confirmation.

This offer will, when accepted, need to be followed up with a formal 'contract of employment' which needs to be given to the employee within two months of their starting employment.

Unsuccessful candidates need to be informed at this stage, usually by letter, although the candidate who is 'first reserve', should also be telephoned to be told of the decision. They will be informed that they are waiting for confirmation but, if the chosen candidate declines, they will be offered the position. This is more than just a courtesy as it keeps this candidate interested and positive towards the organisation. A further position may arise in the near future in any case.

Organisations are increasingly giving feedback to unsuccessful applicants. This is certainly carried out with internal applicants for whom the decision may be a difficult one to take. Some form of supportive counselling can be of considerable help here because they need to face their colleagues who will know they have not succeeded. An action plan can be drawn up with their line manager to allow them to work towards filling those gaps that caused them to be unsuccessful.

For external candidates, the issue is more difficult. It would be a logistical nightmare to give personal feedback to 200 or so applicants who may apply for one or more positions. However, it is not good practice to fob off an enquiry from a disappointed candidate who politely requests areas where they went wrong. For this reason, a number of high profile companies have, in recent years, instituted a policy of giving detailed feedback to all candidates at short list and to any others that make a positive enquiry. The feedback is constructed from the assessment process that is used in the selection process, is explained very carefully and truthfully and attempts to be as positive as possible. It is usually given verbally which emphasises the belief by the organisation that each candidate should be treated in a fair and individual way. However:

> 'Don't get drawn into detailed debate about the rights and wrongs of your decision. Make it clear that it was based firmly and fairly on the evidence presented during the selection process.'
>
> Hackett (1995: p. 76)

Evaluating the selection process

Evaluation takes two forms:

- Judging how successful the selection process has been.
- Examining the process to judge the effectiveness of each stage.

When can you tell that you have made the right selection decision? That depends on the position. For a post-room clerk or receptionist, you may be fairly sure within a few weeks. For a factory manager, you should have a good idea after a year is up and objectives are reached. At the extreme end, for the research director of a pharmaceutical company, it may be a question of 5–10 years before one or two successfully marketed drugs indicate a good level of success. However, a successfully completed recruitment exercise, one minute can change into a failure the next when the employee concerned abruptly decides to leave. It is impossible to distinguish between those factors that you can influence, such as the job design, the selection process and the way the successful candidate is managed and motivated, and the external factors over which you have no control, such as the way the economy moves, the market changes and the personal circumstances of the successful candidate changes. So recruitment is a long-term process where constant evaluation is necessary.

There are some hard facts that will give you some indication of success:

- How quickly was the position filled, measured from the date of the request to the starting date of the successful candidate.

- The average length of tenure of the person recruited.
- The proportion of employees recruited that were promoted within 5 years.
- The response cost per candidate in terms of advertising (that is, cost of advertising divided by number of responses).
- The proportion of candidates who met the minimum requirements specified.

None of these, on their own, will give you a complete answer. As with many management statistics, it is the comparison against previous years and similar companies that will be a better indicator of selection performance. An effective guide to the efficiency and candidate-friendly nature of recruitment can be gauged by carrying out a attitude survey of unsuccessful candidates.

Meteor case study

The assessment centre

Sarah stood up to introduce the assessment centre. In the room were 9 candidates for the two call-centre senior adviser posts, together with Gary Hands, the manager of the call-centre team and Helen Roads, a consultant psychologist that Sarah had brought into design and run the assessment centre. The 9 had been chosen from 120 applicants by having the required level of experience and through matching the preferred competencies mapped out by Gary and Sarah.

She knew it was going to be a hard 2 days for all the participants. The programme was as follows:

Day 1

9.00	Assemble and introductions
9.30	Work simulation test 1. Call-centre activity
11.00	Warm-up exercise
12.00	Battery of ability tests: verbal reasoning and analytical ability
13.00	Lunch
14.00	Teamwork exercise: outdoors
16.00	Review and feedback on exercises
17.00	Interview/personality questionnaire
19.00	Break
20.00	Interview/personality questionnaire feedback

Day 2

9.00	Negotiation exercise and feedback
11.00	Work simulation test 2. In-tray exercise and feedback
1.00	Lunch and finish

The programme had been designed by Helen, who had carried out similar work for three other call-centre operators. The ability and verbal reasoning tests were of Helen's own construction while the personality test used was the Myers–Briggs-Type Indicator and the ideal candidates were those who came out strongly on 'thinking and judging'. The work simulation tests consisted of a short call-centre activity simulation and an in-tray exercise. The simulation was set up to ensure that the candidates had a basic knowledge and understanding of call-centre operator competencies and candidates only needed to pass this activity. The in-tray exercises were specifically adapted for Meteor-style call-centre management situations and marks were awarded for skills in planning, time management, initiative, judgement and realism. The negotiating test had also been designed by Helen, and involved negotiations with employee representatives in changing work patterns, with candidates playing roles on different sides of the table.

The outdoor activity, involving the construction of a bridge over a stream with a limited assortment of materials and tools, was designed to test teamworking, leadership and completion skills. Sarah had brought in three additional managers to help with the interviews, which would be video-ed along with a number of other exercises to help in the final decision-taking process.

The introductions went well and the early tests went smoothly and to schedule. The problems started after lunch when the outdoor activity began amidst a torrential downpour. Not all the candidates had brought appropriate clothes and the protective garments provided were not totally proof against the extreme conditions. At one point, Sarah was going to announce the abortion of the exercise but the weather immediately abated and it was decided to complete it. However, extra time was allowed and all the candidates and observers needed more time than planned to shower and generally recover from the ordeal. This led to the programme being delayed by more than an hour and the evening sessions stretched almost to midnight. Of the three teams taking place, only one produced a reasonable result and, although this allowed interesting assessments of working under stress, the assessors realised that judgements had to be moderated in view of the harsh conditions.

Most of the candidates were clearly weary by the second day and one was close to exhaustion. Extra time was allowed for the exercises so, again, the programme became delayed and did not finish until around 3.00 p.m.

Having wound-up the assessment centre and thanked all the candidates for their contribution, Sarah, Helen and the Assessors met up to examine the test results. They agreed to eliminated five of the candidates whose scores overall were the lowest on either the practical tests or because their personality test indicated a profile that did not match the specification. They then spent the remainder of the afternoon and much of the early evening watching videos of the remaining four candidates in their interviews and performing in the group tests.

One candidate emerged as an agreed clear favourite but the second choice was more difficult. One of the female candidates, who scored highly on most of the tests, acted poorly on the outdoor activity and was not particularly strong on the negotiations. There were varying views as to her performance in the interview, some regarding her as unnecessarily critical and others regarding her personality as one that is very determined.

The other four came close to each other in the overall scoring but had weaknesses on certain tests (as shown on the scorecard). Sarah watched the discussion going backwards and forwards, knowing that the candidates had been promised a quick decision and the difficulties involved in getting the selection group together again. By 8.00 p.m., she knew time was rapidly running out.

Candidate	Max score	1	2	3	4	5	6	7	8	9
Work simulation 1 – call-centre	40	20	30	30	20	20	30	20	30	40
Ability tests	30	0	15	30	0	15	35	0	15	30
Team-working exercise	50	20	40	40	20	30	15	15	15	30
Personality test match	50	30	40	50	20	40	40	20	20	50
Negotiation exercise	40	30	20	30	20	30	25	20	30	10
Work simulation in-tray	40	20	25	30	20	30	40	25	30	20
Total	250	120	170	210	100	165	185	100	140	180

Summary

- Approaches to selection can be made either on the basis of a clearly defined pre-determined system or it can concentrate on the process, whereby the job is less clearly defined and can be moulded around the person selected.
- Short-listing can be carried out through exclusion or inclusion. Telephone and automatic screening are becoming much more common in recent years.
- Selection tests can be divided into ability, aptitude and personality and, to be effective, they must be valid and reliable. Strict guidelines have been produced on their correct use.
- The traditional interview has been shown to be unreliable and subjective. Structured interviews have a better record and numerous techniques have been developed to strengthen the process.
- Assessment centres involve a collection of tests and have a high validity as a selection process. However, they put pressure on the candidates and can be costly.

Student activities

1. Consider the Pret à Manger case and decide whether the organisation operates 'best practice' in its recruitment method.
2. Taking the Meteor case study, do you think an assessment centre is a fair method of making the final selection? What are the successes and problems associated in this particular case? Make your decision as to which candidates should be selected, justifying your decision.
3. Automatic telephone screening (Case study 5.2) helps to reduce the exclusion of those over 50. Has it any other advantages for minority groups?
4. Using the example of the testing for pub landlords in Case study 5.3, draw up a list of specialist positions where the use of tests may produce some interesting personality profiles.
5. Construct a structured interview for the position of student counsellor, using situational questions, patterned behavioural descriptions and criterion-based questions (see Case study 5.4).

6 Are employment references worth the paper they are written on?

References

Anderson, N., Shackleton, V. (1994) Informed choices. *Personnel Today*, 8 November, 33.

Arkin, A. (1991) Turning managers into assessors. *Personnel Management*, November, 49–51.

Butcher, S. (2004) Be tough and outgoing at the top. *EFinancial Careers*, 7 April.

Carrington, L. (2002) At the cutting edge. *People Management*, 16 May, 31.

Cooper, D., Robertson, I. (1995) *The Psychology of Personnel Selection*, Routledge.

Cooper, D., Robertson, I., Tinline, G. (2003) *Recruitment and Selection: A Framework for Success*. Thomson Learning.

Cowan, N., Cowan, R (1989) Are references worth the paper they are written on ? *Personnel Management*, December, 38–42.

Employers Forum for Age Newsline (1997) October, 1.

Engle, R. (1998) Multi-step, structured interviews to select sales representatives in Russia and Eastern Europe. *European Management Journal*, **16** (4): 476–484.

Fowler, A. (1997) How to select and use psychometric tests. *People Management*, 25 September, 45–46.

Graves, L., Karren, R. (1992) Reconsidering the employment interview. *Personnel Psychology*, **45**: 313–340.

Hackett, P. (1995) *The Selection Interview*. London, IPD.

Herriot, P. (1994) *Down from the Ivory Tower*. John Wiley and Sons.

Howlings, J. (1998) Law at work. *People Management*, 15 October, 22.

Iles, P. (2001) Employee resourcing In: Storey, J. (ed.). *Human Resource Management: A Critical Text*, 2nd edition. Thomson Learning.

IPD, (1997) *The IPD Guide on Psychological Testing*. IPD

Lord, W. (1994.) The evolution of a revolution. *Personnel Management*, February, 65.

Mullen, J. (1997) Starring roles. *People Management*, 29 May, 28–30.

Newell, S., Rice, C. (1999) Assessment, selection and evaluation. In: *Strategic Human Resourcing* (Leopard, J., Harris, L., Watson, T (eds). pp. 129–165.

Palmer, D., Campion, J. (1997). A review of structure in the selection interview. *Personnel Psychology*, **50**, 655–702.

People Management, 1998 28 May, 11 (anon).

Roberts, G. (1997) *Recruitment and Selection: A competency approach*. IPD.

Robertson, I. (2001) Undue diligence. *People Management*, 22 November, 42–43.

Sappal, P. (1998) The changing face of recruitment. *Human Resources*, March–April, 19–24.

Smethhurst, S. (2003) The road to sedition. *People Management*, 7 August, 30–31.

Taylor, S. (2002) *Employee Resourcing*, IPD.

Trompenaars, F., Williams, P. (2002) Model behaviour. *People Management*, 5 December, 31–34.

Further reading

For a critique of *selection testing for call-centre staff*, see:

Whitehead, M. (1999) Churning questions. *People Management*, 30 September, pp. 46–48.

For *Psychological Testing*, see:

Edenborough, R. (1999) *Using Psychometrics: A Practical Guide to Testing and Assessment*. Kogan Page.

Iles, P. (1999) *Managing Staff Selection and Assessment*, Open university Press.

Toplis, J., Dulewicz, V., Fletcher, C. (2004) *Psychological Testing*. CIPD.

Cooper, D., Robertson, I., Tinline, G. (2003) *Recruitment and Selection: A Framework for Success*. Thomson Learning.

For the process of *matching people and jobs*, see:

Beech, N., Kumra, S. (1997) *Never Mind the Quality, Find the Fit. A Survey And Analysis of Managerial Selection Methods*. Warwick working papers.

Edenborough, R. (1996) *Effective Interviewing*. Kogan Page.

Little, P. (1998) Selection of the fittest. *Management Review*, July–August, 43–47.

Leary-Joyce, J. (2004) *Becoming an Employee of Choice*. CIPD.

Web site

http://sol.brunel.ac.uk/~jarvis/bola/recruitment/
Recruitment and selection process from the Business Open Learning Archive (BOLA) Brunel University School of Business and Management.

Effective ways of working

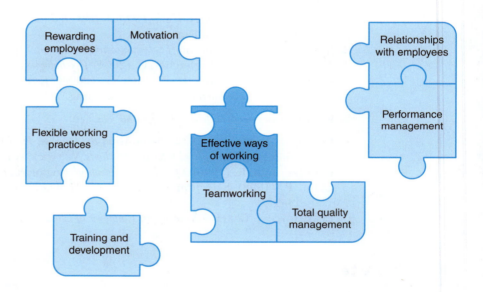

When you have read this chapter and carried out the activities, you will be able to:

- Understand the role of human resources (HR) in creating an effective working environment.
- Grasp the significance of the psychological contract in influencing high-employee performance.
- State the various motivation theories and their effect in practice.

- Distinguish between the different strands of flexible working practices – temporal, numerical, geographical, occupational and family-friendly.
- Analyse in what circumstances these practices contribute to organisational effectiveness.
- Demonstrate the value of an organisation where Total Quality Management (TQM) is practised.
- Explain the importance of developing the culture of team-working.

Introduction

We have seen in Chapter 1 that the competitive nature of the global economy combined with the changing social and demographic forces have led to organisations having to adapt their shape, structure, culture and ways of working. No longer can they expect a reliable and sub-servient market to allow them to grow and prosper in a steady and pre-dictable rate. One of the major responses to this situation is to place more emphasis on effective ways of working, especially those that lead to the most efficient use of HR. An initial analysis of high-performance organisations was set out in Chapter 1, and you may wish to refresh your memory here before reading this chapter.

Building on the concept of high performance, this chapter will examine the concept and operation of the psychological contract, including research into the state of the contract in practice. All forms of high-performance working depend upon employees being motiv-ated to work effectively so an examination of the three main strands of motivation theory follows. The chapter ends with a brief understand-ing of two other key aspects associated with high performance, namely TQM and team-working.

Motivating employees

Student activity 6.1

The contract that employers and employees enter into in the work-place contains many subtleties relating to behavioural expectations. Consider what are some of these expectations firstly from an employee's viewpoint and then from an employer's viewpoint.

Discussion of Student activity 6.1

You may have thought of a number of the expectations set out in Figure 6.1.

These expectations, none of which are expressed formally in the employment contract, sometimes lead to disappointments when they are not realised. Broken promises, poor communication and misunderstandings over what is expected can lead to mutual recrimination and a reduction in the degree of motivation from the employees. This, in turn, can lead to deteriorating performance and eventual termination of the employment by dismissal or mutual agreement. As an example, Bathmaker (1999) found the work bargain at a new university to be interpreted very differently by staff and management, especially when considered in an organisational context.

The '*psychological contract*', as the group of mutual expectations has been called (Sims, 1994), is crucial in helping to determine the base line for the way employees respond to the objective of working more effectively. Employers help to establish a positive contract by creating a culture where these expectations are discussed openly, where they have a strong degree of mutual agreement and where there is a genuine attempt by both sides to reach the desired goals. Although there is much discussion in the media and elsewhere that employees in the 2000s are less satisfied, feel less secure, are overworked and held in

What employees expect from their employer	What employers expect from their employees
To be treated fairly as a human being	To work hard for the organisation
To be provided with work that suits their ability	To be committed to the organisation values
To have opportunities for self development and promotion	To be loyal and dependable
For employer's promises to be kept	For employees to keep their promises
To know what is expected of them	To keep to the work standards set by management
To be rewarded equitably	To be prepared for change in the job they do
To have a friendly and safe working environment	To think about how they can improve the work they do

Figure 6.1
Expectations of employers and employees from each other

lower regard, the research evidence does not seem to support that view, as shown in Focus on research 6.1.

Focus on research 6.1

The state of the psychological contract

The Chartered Institute of Personnel and Development have carried out an annual research project for a number of years examining employee's view of the psychological contract, defined in terms of their judgement of fairness, trust and the delivery of their employment 'deal'. The report in 2001, carried out by Guest and Conway from Kings College, London, found that 91% of respondents feel secure in their jobs and the majority considered employment relations to be fair or good. Motivation levels were high, especially so in health workers and local government. Thirty-one per cent believed that the work picture had improved in the last year and only 24% considered it had got worse. Since the previous year, private sector workers are consistently more satisfied and positive while public sector workers are more dissatisfied and less positive, especially in respect to the work-life balance. Only a minority reported that management promises had been kept, especially in the area of involvement and consultation about change.

The report picked out the difficulties expressed by employees in the public sector in responding to all-too-frequent changes and the low levels of consultation. There is a strong viewpoint that satisfied customers will only result from having satisfied staff.

Source: Conway and Guest (2001)

An earlier model by Guest *et al.* (1996) indicated the link between the psychological contract and motivation as shown in Figure 6.2. Here it is indicated that the consequent level of motivation is influenced firstly and immediately by the level of perceived trust and sense of fairness in the organisation and by the way the deal is delivered and ultimately by factors such as the employee's own experience, expectations and the organisation's culture and Human Resources Management (HRM) Policy and practices. Motivation will join with high levels of commitment, a good feeling of satisfaction and well-being and a sense of being an important part of the organisation (organisational citizenship) to produce high levels of performance.

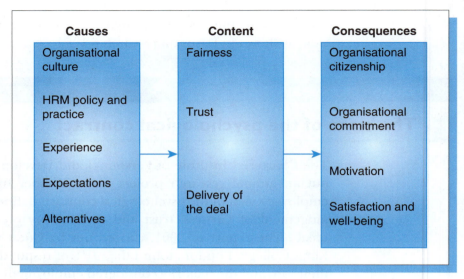

Causes	Content	Consequences
Organisational culture	Fairness	Organisational citizenship
HRM policy and practice	Trust	Organisational commitment
Experience		Motivation
Expectations		
Alternatives	Delivery of the deal	Satisfaction and well-being

Figure 6.2
Model of the psychological contract (*Source*: Guest *et al.*, 1996)

Motivation theory

Motivation theories can be divided into three main groups: *Instrumentality*, *Needs* (sometimes known as Content) and *Cognitive* theories.

Instrumentality theories emerged in the early 1900s and are based on the assumption that work has no outcomes other than economic ones. Employees, motivated only by money, need to be put in a situation where they have no choice but to work hard and efficiently. To achieve this in practice, work was grouped into large factory units, maximum specialisation was achieved through the limitation of the number of tasks an employee had to do and work was deliberately made repetitive with as limited amount of training time as possible. Set out by Taylor (1911), and implemented throughout the Ford factories, where much of the labour force had migrated to Detroit from their farming origins, it led to the wide application of work study techniques, incentive payments and the attitude that employees must be rigidly controlled in the most cost-effective way. This belief held sway for 50 or more years in the Western world and is still followed in some establishments today.

The difficulties arising from this theory is that it does not take into account the personal and social needs of employees or the rising level of intelligence and expectations. Subservient employees become more difficult to motivate and often take action to avoid the harsh controls. The rise of collective action (strikes, work to rules, etc.) or high levels of illness and absenteeism have been shown to be a direct result of instrumental controls.

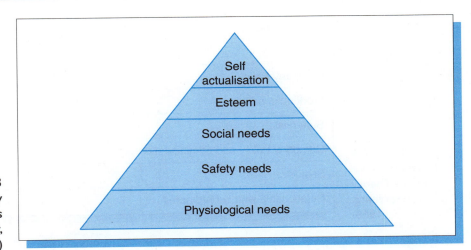

Figure 6.3
Maslow's Hierarchy
of Needs
(*Source*: Maslow,
1954)

Needs theories, on the other hand, emphasise that unsatisfied needs create tension and disequilibrium which leads to individuals striving to achieve a goal. Maslow (1954) developed a Hierarchy of Needs (Figure 6.3) from lower order basic needs (food and shelter) to higher order needs (social needs, self-esteem and self-actualisation). The higher order needs become motivators when the lower order needs have been met. Pay has generally been regarded in this theory as a lower order need which rarely motivates, although the implication is that basic pay must be set high enough to provide employees with the economic means to meet their basic living needs. It has also been argued that transparent benefits, such as the company car, can help to meet the need of self-esteem and that group incentive schemes can help to meet the need for 'love' through teams working together with mutual respect.

Herzberg's (1968) well-known two-factor theory distinguished between hygiene factors and satisfiers (see Figure 6.4). Hygiene factors (or dissatisfaction avoidance factors) include pay, company policy, method of supervision and administration, all of which he called extrinsic factors. They rarely in themselves motivate employees to work harder or better but can cause the employee to work less hard if they are not satisfied. *Satisfiers*, on the other hand, which include achievement, recognition and the nature of the work itself, are the major motivating force. The implications here are clearly that reward schemes based on performance are unlikely to motivate and can be the cause of considerable de-motivation. This belief is held strongly by employees in the many of the public services, including health and education, who find all their motivation from the intrinsic factors and strongly resent suggestions that they would be motivated by contingent pay.

Hygiene factors	Satisfiers
Pay	Achievement
Company Policy	Recognition
Working conditions	Advancement
Supervision	Responsibility
Company Policy and administration	Personal growth
Security	Advancement
Relationship with subordinates	

Figure 6.4
Herzberg's Two-Factor Theory
(*Source*: Herzberg, 1968)

Schoolteachers, for example, have been strongly opposed to compulsory schemes where additional payments are made based on some form of individual performance measure, although they ultimately accepted performance pay as a reflection of their ability and commitment in the early 2000s.

Cognitive theories assumes that individuals think their way through the situation and work out how they can benefit from particular courses of action. The leading cognitive theory is *Expectancy theory* expounded by Vroom (1964). Here, motivation is the product of three variables:

- *Instrumentality*, which is the degree of an employee's self-belief in their ability to achieve a goal.
- *Expectancy*, which is the degree to which they believe that, having achieved a goal, it will lead to a secondary action, namely a reward.
- *Valency*, which is the value they put on that reward.

Reversing the needs theories, Vroom believed that employees respond to attempts to motivate them on an individual basis in their own specific situation. They may not need additional pay or they may not value the particular reward. They may not trust the organisation to come up with the rewards or they may simply consider the targets or goals unobtainable. Any of these beliefs will reduce or eliminate entirely the degree of motivation. The implication for employers is that incentive schemes will not work with everybody, that considerable care has to be taken with the rewards to ensure there a reasonable degree of valence and that honesty and trust must prevail with both the level of targets and the application of the rewards.

Another influential theory has been put forward by Locke (1968) regarding the *effectiveness of goals*. He supports the view that goal setting is an important part of motivation but, to retain the necessary intensity and duration of commitment, the goals must be challenging, accepted by the employee, there must be an element of participation in the goal-setting process and the employee must get valued feedback on their performance.

The notion of fair play is never far away from reward considerations. *Equity theory* (Adams, 1963) detailed the main pointers to maintaining motivation through the concepts of *distributive justice*, where pay is seen to be fairly distributed in line with employee's worth and output, and *procedural justice*, where the methods of arriving at these judgements are seen to be fair. These methods include employee participation, accurate measurement, fair appraisal and appeals processes.

Summing up motivation

It is clear from many research projects that employees are motivated in different ways and that encouraging employees to work effectively is contingent upon the nature of the organisation. Knowledge workers may respond better to challenges for their small teams, together with freedom of action to influence the result. For manufacturing employees, motivation may arise from greater involvement in their workplace and shorter span challenges. Communication and effective feedback is crucial to the process in all cases, as is injecting a degree of stimulation, enjoyment and excitement into the way that employees are challenged.

Flexible working practices

It was emphasised in Chapter 1 that the willingness and ability of employees to work flexibly is a key to improving organisational performance. Flexible working has been traditionally described as part-time and temporary employment but it covers, in reality, a very much broader picture. As first modelled by Atkinson (1984), it includes all activities that operate to allow a quicker and more focused response to the needs of customers and clients. The subject therefore covers:

- *temporal flexibility*, fine-tuning the total hours of the labour force through part-time working, annualised hours, job sharing and zero-hours;
- *numerical flexibility*, by extending the use of temporary employees;

■ *occupational or functional flexibility*, by developing the skills and experience of employees so they can switch jobs to meet immediate needs and encouraging employees to look beyond their employment contract;

■ *geographical flexibility* through encouraging teleworking, home-working, outsourcing work and replacing face-to-face contact by call centres.

We will look at each of these in turn, but we will start by examining the strategy employed by organisations in relation to the concept of the 'Flexible Firm' put forward by Atkinson and Meager (1986).

The Flexible Firm

Although first put forward in the 1980s, the model of the 'Flexible Firm' is still a valuable tool to analyse the overall concept of flexibility (see Figure 6.5). The starting point is that employees are divided into two main groups. Firstly, there are the 'core' employees who tend to be full-time, permanent, career employees who carry out activities that are essential to the longer-term success of the organisation. Originally, these included managers, supervisors, plus other groups who possessed

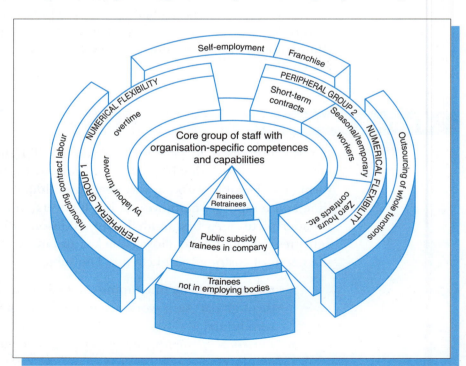

Figure 6.5
Core and peripheral workforces (*Source*: Atkinson and Meager (1986). Adopted by Professor John Purcell.)

specific, relevant and vital skills in the technical, sales, production, professional and administrative areas. These groups would be well paid, investment would be made in their training and development and they would have career paths charted for them. In return, they would be expected to be loyal and to have a full commitment to the organisation in terms of a willingness to working flexibly when necessary, such as through multi-skilling, shift working or re-locating. The success of their work would ensure that their organisation was differentiated from its competitors.

The other group of employees are those on the 'periphery' of the organisation. Divided into two sections, the first group are employees whose skills are more general, rather than specific to the organisation's success. They may be full-time on 'permanent' contracts but their job security is not well defined and their work activity could be re-engineered or outsourced without causing harm to the business. These employees will be paid according to internal equity and average market rates and there will some investment in training but not in long-term development. A high degree of flexibility is generally not expected from them as their work tends to be generalised. This group, however, can be the source to fill any vacancy that occurs in the core group through a competitive process.

The second periphery group are those with employees who enjoy even less security. They may be on short-term contracts or secondment or be under some form of Government traineeship, such as the New Deal. The group also includes those on part-time and job share, although it is interesting to note here that the legal situation has changed since the model was devised in that part-time and job-share employees now have identical rights as full-time employees under European Law. When it is necessary to change the labour input in these areas, the tap is turned on or off through the non-renewal of short-term contracts and non-replacement of trainees or part-time staff that leave. In the work they carry out, this group would be expected to work flexibly (this would be specified in their contract) and co-operation is likely to be high because many in this group would want to be considered for permanent employment. They are paid at the same rates as their periphery colleagues but there is little or no investment in training.

The final labour group are not employees at all. They include agency staff, sub-contractors, self-employed and those carrying out work that has been outsourced. This group is interesting in that they may have moved from any of the above groups. A skilled group of information technology (IT) staff may have moved from the core group to set up their own company and provide outsourced services. They have been made redundant from the first periphery group and now provide occasional services on a self-employed, low pay, high hours basis. This last group work on a performance basis with high flexibility to complete the contract on time and within the cost.

There is considerable evidence that the use of flexible working practices is spreading but scant evidence of strategic intent to become Flexible Firms. Reports by the Policy Studies Institute (Casey *et al.*, 1997), by the Department of Education and Employment (Rajan, 1997) and Labour Market Trends (2004) all confirm a growing use of most of the areas of flexibility. The practicalities of implementing flexibility have been greatly assisted in the last 15 years by the lack of opposition from weakened trade unions who have traditionally opposed much of numerical and occupational flexibility proposed. Pockets of resistance have still occurred such as the opposition to the use of part-time labour in the Post Office or to the use of annualised hours on some of the railway networks.

Implementation by employers seems, however, to take place on an incremental basis rather than through longer-term strategy (Hunter and MacInnes, 1991). It is part of a continuing process of change rather than a sudden volte-face from traditional employment methods. Areas such as outsourcing and use of part-time labour, have shown a steady growth while others, including annualised hours and job sharing have risen slowly from very low bases.

Temporal flexibility

Part-time working has shown a considerable increase since the second world war as shown in Figure 6.6.

The rise for females was pronounced by the 1960s as the growing respectability of the married woman's part-time job became established and rose to the plateau of around 45% by the 1990s compared to the gradual rise in men's part-time work to 8% for most of this period, with a

	1951	1971	1986	1997	2002
Male part-timers	139	584	843	982	1450
Male employees (%)	1.9	4.4	6.7	8.3	10.5
Female part-timers	417	2757	4108	4728	5700
Female employees (%)	6.0	33.6	47.1	44.3	44.5
Total part-timers	556	3341	4951	5710	7100
All employees (%)	2.7	15.5	23.6	25.0	26.9

Figure 6.6
Part-time workers 1951–2002 ('000s)
(*Source*: Labour Market Trends, 2003)

faster rise at the turn of the century up to 10%. Both figures have been influenced by the huge growth in full-time students, most of whom need to obtain a part-time job following the abolition of student grants.

Part-time work can be categorised as classical, supplementary or substitution. *Classical* part-time jobs are posts where the jobs are only required for a few hours per day such as school-meals staff. *Supplementary jobs* are those used to augment and improve the efficiency of the full-time operation such as where house-builders employ site negotiators at weekends, accounts staff may be employed for end-of-month accounting and sales staff for busy days in the week. *Substitution* part-time jobs are those where part-time employees replace full-time jobs. This has been prevalent in major retailing where part-time staff, who are easier to recruit, can be seen as just as committed and often more flexible than full-time staff. In America, United Parcel Service (UPS) had implemented a policy in 1998 to replace almost all of their full-time positions with part-time ones at a lower pay rate but a national strike by their 185,000 employees managed to achieve a reversal of this policy.

This area of employment has also been augmented by *portfolio workers* (Handy, 1994) who are those employees who have more than one part-time job. Examples can be a person with a morning office employment who also works occasional evenings and weekends for a banqueting company or an executive made redundant in their 50s, who combines consultancy with lecturing in the UK and Eastern Europe. Some employees have found the need to *downshift*, leaving successful, if stressful employment, to take up more satisfying but less remunerative part-time work. Another version of this is *V-time*, practiced by a few larger organisations such as Abbey National, where employees are allowed to reduce their hours for a limited time period for personal, family or self-development reasons. *Job shares* are a growing form of part-time work, normally operating at a routine level but with developing examples in the managerial field. *Zero-hours* arrangements are where employees have no fixed or contractual hours of work but are called in when required. These forms of contracts exist in catering, sporting activities, film and media work, and in some retailing (Cave, 1997).

Systems of flexible working are attractive to employees with caring responsibilities and the 2002 Employment Act gave the right to request shorter or more appropriate hours to employees with responsibility for children under 6 years old (18 years old if disabled). The employer may refuse the request on certain grounds, such as additional costs incurred, inability to re-organise work among existing staff or the detrimental effect on the ability to meet customer demand. If faced with a refusal, the employee may apply to a tribunal that the refusal was unreasonable. In practice, however, few such requests have been completely refused since the act was implemented, despite the additional burdens that changes in working hours can place on employers, especially ones with few staff.

Student activity 6.2

Draw up a list of the advantages and difficulties from an employer's viewpoint in employing part-time employees.

Discussion of Student activity 6.2

You may have thought of some of the following advantages:

- Part-time staff are usually easier to recruit than full-time staff so the quality of the applicants may be higher.
- In the event of absence or holidays, part-time staff will normally be able to fill in by working a few extra hours, so cover is easier to obtain. This is normally the case in a job share where the parties work together to ensure the job is covered.
- When a part-time member of staff works a few extra hours, the payment will generally not be at overtime rates as such rates are paid only when the full-time hours are exceeded.
- Employees who are working part-time because they are bringing up a family, may be available later on to switch to full-time work, which provides an efficient method of recruitment.
- In the case of zero-hours, employees are only used when they are strictly necessary, with no waste of expensive resources.

The *difficulties* may include:

- In the case of job shares, there will be double the amount of training, appraisal and records to maintain.
- It is usually easy to obtain part-timers for morning jobs, not so easy to fill gaps in afternoons or evenings.
- Managers can find part-timers more difficult to manage, especially if they depart in mid-afternoon, leaving as half-empty department.
- As most part-timers have caring responsibilities, they may be more likely to need time off, although there is no strong evidence of this.

A further variation on temporal flexibility is *annual hours*. Rather than employees being contracted for a fixed number of hours per week, say 38, they are contracted to work annual hours of, say, 1976. The actual weekly hours they will be asked to work could be seasonal, such as in food production or for the Christmas trade, where the hours may vary between 25 and 50 per week. Alternatively, they could be on a fixed rota of shifts averaging 32 hours a week, leaving a certain amount of 'reserve hours' which would be called upon in times of absence, machinery breakdown or any other difficulties. In both cases, the main aim of the system is to achieve greater flexibility in the use of available labour and to reduce or eliminate the amount of overtime that had been worked where the labour availability did not meet the business needs at that time.

An example of annual hours in an service environment is detailed in Case study 6.1. How the introduction of annual hours changed both the formal and informal methods of working is examined in Focus on research 6.2.

Case study 6.1

Annualised hours at the RAC

In the late 1990s, the RAC faced very fierce competition in their market place. This was not just from the traditional rival, the Automobile Association, but also from a string of small players that had seen niche opportunities and who could move faster than the traditionally organised, overweight duopoly. Moreover, they had recently become a demutualised company and needed to aim for better overall performance to match the expectations of their new masters.

Their prime objective was to move away from a standard 40-hour week for their patrol teams which did not match the seasonal variation in their work or the unpredictability of demand caused by weather and conditions. The large gaps in the service had to be supplemented by excessive (and expensive) overtime and by a network of independent garages contracted to meet unfulfilled attendance at breakdowns.

Negotiations with the TGWU produced a new system based on 1831 annualised hours on roster (net of holidays) and an agreed level of paid reserve hours – the choice is from 92 to 368, equating to average weekly hours of 42–48. This was accompanied by a higher basic salary. The hours for each patrol team is rostered a year in advance with hours reduced in the quieter summer months and extended during the winter with appropriate cover for weekends, keeping throughout the year within the Working Time Regulations. Patrols are notified monthly of the use of their reserve hours, based on detailed previous demand patterns plus a day's notice of 'red alert' days when really bad weather is forecast.

The scheme was launched with substantial communication with newsletters, meetings, an audiotape and feedback from patrols using an independent interviewer. This variety of hours did not suit every patrol team and 60 employees left within the first 2 months although the majority appear very satisfied.

With productivity rising by 8%, using fewer patrol than previously, and a big rise in on-the-spot completions, the scheme has proved successful, reinforced by a satisfying increase in the customer satisfaction index.

During 2000 and 2001, the scheme was extended to their three main call centres where staff had the choice of three levels of contracted hours – 991, 1304 or 1826, depending on whether they wanted to work full- or part-time and the nature of the shift pattern. The shortest contract covers fixed peak periods only while the other patterns are:

- Semi-flexible – earlies or lates (1304 or 1826 hours).
- Nights – 1826 hours varying between 9 PM and 7 AM across the year.
- Flexible – shift times varying during the year between 6 AM and 11.30 PM.

Staff on 1304 or 1826 hour contracts also sign up for a number of 'flexible hours' which management will allocate when they are needed. In quiet periods, call centre staff who have agreed flexible hours may be invited to leave early and half of the hours remaining not worked are then banked to be used at a busier time.

Source: IDS (2002)

Focus on research 6.2

Annualised hours and the 'knock' in a Yorkshire Chemicals Plant

Jason Hayes spent 6 weeks in an old, heavily unionised chemicals plant in West Yorkshire studying the effects of the introduction of annualised hours in response to the need to improve labour utilisation. It employed 75 men working on intensive and hazardous work. An agreement with the union in 1993 introduced multi-skilling, a reduction of the working week to 36 hours, a six-shift system and annualised hours.

Management was aware that, prior to annualised hours when an overtime culture prevailed, that overtime had been systematically created through planned absenteeism – called 'knocking'. This was where one person agreed to go sick while another covered for him and received overtime with premium payments. The following week, the roles would be reversed. This meant that they both received enhanced pay for working standard hours. This reflected, in the view of Hayes, 'purposeful behaviour' rather than 'negative withdrawal'. Until the changeover, the workforce had kept it within acknowledged limits of management toleration but the external forces of the early 1990s required such indulgences to cease if the business was to be kept open.

The outcome of the annualised hours system was that labour costs were reduced by £700,000 and absenteeism dropped substantially to half its previous level with the 'knock' almost entirely eliminated. Employees were not entirely happy with the new system or the way it was operated.

Source: Hayes (1997)

Numerical flexibility

Being able to vary the number of employees allows an organisation to respond quickly to its varying needs. This is most commonly achieved by either using *temporary staff* through an agency or by using a pool of specifically recruited temporary employees. The label 'temp' or 'casual' conveys an image of employees who are of no great importance to the organisation – unskilled, short-term and low status. Because this label is often incorrect, the term *'complementary employee'* is starting to take its place. These are often key employees taken on for short-term but crucial contracts and who make a sizeable contribution to their host company. In HR, for example, a small team of complementary managers may be employed to implement a major change programme which can involve important selection processes – for both promotion and redundancy.

An example of a partnership approach to managing temporary employees is shown in Case study 6.2.

Case study 6.2

Working partnership – Manpower and Xerox

In 1999, one of Xerox's strategic plans was to reduce the company's operational costs while maintaining a high level of customer service in the competitive photocopying market. To meet these objectives, Xerox wanted a strategic partner to assist in dealing with customer requests to fix faulty equipment across the UK. Xerox's key requirement was for a quality supplier of staffing solutions that could enhance their own internal capability with a fixed price, provide skilled staff and deliver a national solution with the ability to flex the workforce according to customer demand.

Manpower set up a new staffing infrastructure within Xerox, consisting of HR managers, support managers and a team of 100 skilled engineers nationwide, which had risen to 350 by 2004. Manpower managed the recruitment and training process for field engineers and schedulers, who were a mix of temporary and permanent employees. Xerox's call centre customer call routing system was integrated with a tracking and fulfilment system to schedule engineers to deliver the required work across different customer site.

The outcome of the partnership was a reduction of between 15% and 18% in staff and an improvement of 10% in productivity. As Sandy Menzies, Xerox's service partner and logistics manager explained:

> 'By partnering with Manpower, Xerox has been able to effectively transition its highly seasonal workload to a more flexible workforce, gaining both productivity and cost per fix benefits, whilst maintaining the high quality of performance to meet our customers' demands. But the biggest benefit is for our customers, who now see an engineer more quickly.'

Source: Stredwick and Ellis (2005)

Geographical flexibility

Teleworking

In today's new technological world, it is no longer necessary for staff to work from a specific office location. They can operate more flexibly by being a *teleworker* (*tele* is the Greek word for distance) and having a home base, using the organisation's facilities only on the specific occasions when this is essential. As office space represents a considerable cost, teleworking, as well as providing location flexibility, can also provide large cost savings in terms of office costs. For some project-based jobs, especially in IT, the person concerned could live in the Outer Hebrides (some do, of course) as long as their computer and telephone links are powerful, safe and effective.

The drive to increase teleworking has various starting points. In the case of Mobil Oil, the re-location of their head office from London to Milton Keynes in 1995 provided the situation where a number of key sales employees wanted to continue to work for the company but not to move house or travel long distances. It was also realised that proximity to the customer was probably more important a factor than proximity to the head office.

Student activity 6.3

Draw up a list of the issues you need to consider when setting up a formal teleworking operation and how you would deal with them.

Discussion of Student activity 6.3

You may have listed some of the following issues:

- How is the work of the teleworker controlled? Day-to-day supervision becomes far more difficult when that person is not around to be supervised. A system needs to be drawn up with regular checks on objectives, targets and reviews with specific meeting dates to allow more 'normal' feedback than is possible by e-mail.
- How do you avoid the teleworker being out of touch with developments and with colleagues? Teleworkers are actually quite capable of linking up with colleagues through e-mail and experience shows that a teleworkers' grapevine can be more imaginative than most.
- How should you pay teleworkers? Given the difficulty in supervision, teleworkers are much more likely to have a good proportion of their pay by way of performance reward, rather than paid for the hours they work. Crucial to this is the need

for clear and robust performance criteria and targets that are realistic and agreed.

■ How can you be certain that a teleworker will be successful in that mode of work? You cannot be certain, of course, although psychometric tests can now give a reasonable indication of how they may respond to the special demands of isolation and self-reliance.

■ Will teleworkers miss out on promotion? Given that most promotions, especially into management, entail the supervision of other staff and office-based administration, then teleworkers may not be the natural candidates for such positions. However, lateral moves and additional technical career development are alternatives to demonstrate confidence and support.

Case study 6.3 shows how Hertfordshire County Council (HCC) moved into teleworking for a number of strategic and technical reasons.

Case study 6.3

Teleworking and hot-desking at HCC

Workwise was an initiative in the mid-1990s by HCC to combine flexibility at work with a 'green' approach to travelling. With an increasing congested road networking where gridlock loomed each rush hour and difficulty in recruiting staff at all levels, the council hit on two major solutions. The first initiative was to encourage a culture of flexible working hours and locations which was piloted with their Trading Standards Office. This department and its staff covered the whole county and originally worked from one central office. Under the new scheme, staff worked mostly from home but came into office 'Oases' to file reports and other administrative duties. The council had over 500 individual sites, employing 26,000 staff. Within 20 of these sites an 'Oasis' was set up which had a drop-in office with telephone, PC, e-mail and intranet facilities. Trading standards staff, operating mostly in their own patch of the county, use whatever Oasis is convenient. They do not even need to bring standard reference books or policies with them as they are all available on the intranet. This produced an immediate saving of 10% in travelling costs, including employee's time and cost of getting into their office.

The second initiative was in the social services department where 4500 staff worked from five office sites. After substantial consultation, the plan was implemented to shut and sell three of these sites and open one purpose built one, which would include further Oasis areas with pleasant meeting rooms and coffee areas. Employees would have the choice of being home-, mobile- and office-based. Each group had the appropriate technology depending on their base. Those home-based would be wired-up, those mobile would have laptops; those office-based would have pedestal storage to ensure maximum advantage of storage space. This produced savings, improved the working and travelling conditions for the great majority of the department and ensured further funds were safeguarded to provide essential services to vulnerable people.

Source: Wustermann (1997)

Outsourcing

A further way that organisations can increase flexibility in the location where they carry out their work is through outsourcing, which means paying a third party to run the operations or entire function concerned. It has always been quite conventional for organisations to outsource their catering or security operation but recent developments have stretched this concept to cover many activities that may be considered at the core of a business. British Airways, for example, transferred 85% of its ground fleet services (415 employees) to outsource provider Ryder in 1997 under a 5-year deal. A year earlier, it had outsourced its flight documentation service to printing company Astron.

In the Institute of Management's guide on outsourcing, Mike Johnson (1997) lists four strategic reasons why organisations go down this route:

- *To improve business focus*. Outsourcing lets a company focus on broader issues while having operational details assumed by an outside expert. It avoids siphoning off huge amounts of management resources and attention on non-core activities.
- *To gain access to world-class capabilities*. Outsourcing providers, especially in the IT field, can bring extensive worldwide knowledge and experience, giving access to new technology and career opportunities to employees who may transfer to the provider. In addition, it brings competitive advantage to the organisation through an expanded skills base.
- *To benefit from accelerated re-engineering*. This lets the provider, especially one that has already re-engineered to world-class standards, take over the process.
- *To share risks*. A co-operative venture with a provider can halve the risks.

In addition, outsourcing can also offer a cheaper alternative where wage rates can be lower and efficiency higher through economies of scale, when the operations are carried out by an organisation concentrating on providing such services to a large number of customers.

Beginning at the end of the 1980s, the Conservative government introduced legislation to force local authorities to put their services out to tender through the process called Compulsory Competitive Tendering (CCT). Reports from the Audit Commission have indicated that authorities have achieved savings, sometimes in the order of 20%, without a loss in quality standards. Although less than half of the contracts have been won by external bodies, where the existing in-house organisation (usually called Direct Services Organisation) has won the contract, it has usually been at the price of fundamentally changing the way it has worked. Overtime has been reduced, numbers of employees reduced, incentives have been introduced and more flexible operations implemented. The Labour governments from 1997 onwards have continued to encourage a similar policy under the name of 'Best Value', although greater protection have been given to employees who transfer from the public sector to the private sector.

Student activity 6.4

What are the HR implications of outsourcing a service or operation?

Discussion of Student activity 6.4

You may have thought of the following points:

- Clear communication of the impending decision to outsource, and why it is being made, needs to be made to those employees involved at an early stage to prevent rumours spreading which may demotivate staff.
- When a final decision on who has won the outsourcing contract has been made, employees who currently work in the operations to be outsourced need to be counselled over the choices available to them. Current legislation (Transfer of Undertakings Protection of Employment Regulations – a complex act stemming from European legislation) ensures the right of employees transferred to retain identical terms

and conditions on transfer and for a period afterwards. They also retain all of their employment rights. Some employees may not wish to transfer and consideration has to be given as to opportunities available in other departments for such staff and under what conditions.

■ Some older staff may wish to take redundancy or retire at that point and they will need to be counselled over rights and financial details.

Call centres

A final aspect of geographical flexibility is the recent establishment of call centres. More than 300,000 employees (more than 1% of the working population) now work at 500 or more centres set up at locations which can be some distance from their parent company. London Electricity, for example, have their customer payment and services call centre in Sunderland, in north-east England and many other call centres are gathered around Leeds, in Yorkshire and in Scotland. The availability of labour and the lower pay rates are the main reasons for the location decisions.

Call centres operate on a mix of rigid systemisation (the fixed scripts for operators, the technology-driven call distribution system and the need to reach pre-determined call targets) and flexibly serving the customer (24-hour-a-day service, availability of all services through one operator). This systemisation can have HR implications as a number of surveys have shown (Armitage, 1997; Taylor and Bain, 1999). Absenteeism and sickness rates are higher than the average, as is reported stress levels. Staff turnover is very high with one company reporting that they expect their call centre staff to 'burn-out' after 12–20 months. Some of the offices resemble factory units with operators sitting in tiny pigpens or in long lines.

In terms of flexible working practices, call centres operate many of the features that have been detailed above. They employ a good proportion of part-time and temporary employees. Multi-skilling the operators to handle all calls is an important aspect of the training. There are even a few call centres where calls are transferred to operators working at home. Some companies have outsourced the whole operation to a call centre specialist.

An example of the difficulties involved in setting up a call centre is given in Case study 11.1 in Chapter 11 (Health and Safety) and in the Meteor Case study at the end of this chapter.

Occupational flexibility

There are two main strands in the development of occupational flexibility. *Horizontal flexibility* encourages employees to develop their skills beyond their initial specialism, becoming multi-skilled and able to handle a number of different aspects of work. Traditional demarcation lines between jobs, built up over 100 years or more of union rivalries and long apprenticeship schemes, are broken down. For example, in 3M PLC factory near Darlington, maintenance staff used to be either 'electrical' or 'mechanical' and this caused considerable inefficiency when machines needed attention as it was necessary to have one from each trade in attendance. When the two separate unions amalgamated in the 1980s, multi-skilling between the two trades began with an extensive training programme to fill all the skills and knowledge gaps. This situation has been replicated all over modern and traditional manufacturing.

Other examples of multi-skilling are as follows:

- An insurance company, who used to have separate administrative departments for dealing with selling policies, changing existing policies and handling claims, found that their clients, (mostly insurance brokers), resented having to deal with three different groups of staff. The company then re-engineered their administration into one based on geography, and multi-skilled their staff so that they could deal with queries and action required in all three administrative areas. Customer response was very positive to this change and most staff, though being uncertain at first to the need to go through an extended learning process, found the skills acquisition challenging and satisfying.

- A motor manufacturer found that their labour costs were too high where absence of key staff caused too much overtime to be worked. They completely re-organised the production line, developing 'cells' of workers who would all be trained in three or more jobs so that they could easily replace an employee absent. The training stretched to technical and assembly-based knowledge but was then extended further to basic maintenance and housekeeping tasks. This allowed much greater continuity of production and labour cost reduction. It also provides greater job satisfaction for the employee together with greater employability to counter the increased risks and insecurity within manufacturing.

The second aspect of functional flexibility is *vertical flexibility*. This refers to the acceptance and performance of tasks at a higher and lower level than in their existing job description and employment contract. In the motor industry case above, cleaners used to be employed to clear up the assembly areas periodically. Part of the flexibility agreement transferred the periodic cleaning and housekeeping duties to the cell. An interesting bi-product of this arrangement was that the assembly employees kept their areas far cleaner in the first place, knowing that they would have to clean up for themselves! A final aspect of this case was the transfer of certain supervisory responsibilities to the cell who, together with their team-leader, would decide on rest breaks, holiday rotas, overtime duties and movement within the cell. This is sometimes referred to as *empowerment*.

Other examples of empowerment programmes are:

- In a retail company, service staff were empowered to decide whether customers would be given replacements to items they considered faulty rather than refer it to their manager.
- In the Body Shop, employees are given the opportunity to decide on the staff that are employed at their branch.
- Supervisors at Rank Hovis were empowered to run budgets and negotiate terms with suppliers, rather than rely on standard national arrangements.

A more informal process in this area is that of expecting employees to 'work beyond contract'. This does not just mean working longer hours than specified but being part of a team and contributing their ideas so that planning ahead and solving problems are a natural part of every team member's brief.

Policies that support flexibility

Employees can be persuaded to change to work within the required flexible parameters through a number of policies. The *reward structure* can be altered to emphasise a pay for performance culture which is dealt within Chapter 9; employees can be supported towards *self-development and learning processes* as set out in Chapter 10. A third process is to introduce or extend *family-friendly policies*.

Family-friendly policies

Demographic forecasts show that the workforce of available full-time, permanent employees will begin a secular decline in the twenty-first century as the gradual reduction in the birth rate since the 1970s comes into full effect. This is likely to lead to a shortage of labour overall, especially in the service and public sectors. The only internal sources of labour available comprise the increasing proportion of women who enter the workplace, the majority still on a part-time or temporary basis and, to a smaller extent, semi-retired employees also working part-time.

To meet this expected shortage, employers themselves will need to demonstrate flexibility in meeting employees' needs. The government has encouraged this process by passing the Flexible Working Regulations (2002) which allows employees who have children under 6 years and have more than 6 months service, the right to raise with the employer the request to vary their hours and conditions so they can care for the child. The employer has the right to refuse the application but only for certain reasons and practice appears to indicate that refusals are relatively rare. Employers can also demonstrate their family-friendly credential by offering systems of work and benefits that are especially attractive to women and families under the general banner of a 'work-life balance'.

- *Flexible working hours.* Rather than forcing all employees to start and stop at the same time, employees can be offered a choice of hours, such as 10.00 AM to 6.00 PM or 8.00 AM to 4.00 PM, perhaps varying during the week to meet the employee's child-care or personal arrangements. Compressed working weeks into four and a half or 9-day fortnights (operated by Texaco, amongst others) also has attractions to families.

- *Flexitime.* Here the employee can choose each day their starting and stopping time within the core time constraints (usually 10.00 AM to 3.30 PM). Around 2.5 million employees worked under flexitime in 2002 mostly in London and other large cities where rush hour travel presented employment difficulties. In a number of schemes, employees can work under or over their contractual weekly or monthly hours, carrying forward the surplus or making up their shortfall in later months. They can convert some of their surplus into additional holidays. The system allows employees to manage their work and home commitments far better than if they were working fixed hours. If they have to make a regular visit to an ill relative, they can make up the hours at a later date.

- *Career breaks.* Employees may wish to take an extended break from work either to enlarge their maternity break beyond the statutory right to return to work or because they need to look after an elderly or ill relative. Around 15% of organisations have such a scheme with a small but significant (and highly grateful) take-up. In many of the schemes, contact with the employee is retained through a short period of work each year (often 2–3 weeks over holiday periods), which also helps to update the employee and keep them committed to the organisation. The arrangement helps to attract and retain qualified and experienced staff over a longer period of time. Most schemes have a 5-year limit to the break.

■ *Childcare provision.* The lack of suitable childcare is usually quoted as the largest barrier to returning to the labour force. Seventy-three per cent of women reported in one recent survey that it had affected their job or career prospects. Companies can make life easier for the 52% of women with children under five who now work in a number of ways. They can set up an in-house nursery or creche, or get together with a group of other employers in the area to do so, (this is expensive but there are some tax advantages) provide childcare vouchers or a child-care allowance, or be generally sympathetic in the workplace through time-off provisions. The latest available statistics show that developments are still slow. Only 3% of employers operate a workplace nursery or jointly fund one and another 2% provide childcare vouchers. Around 30% have a generally sympathetic approach through formal time-off provisions.

Summing up flexibility

One way to look at flexible practices is to examine the requirements of employers and employees and to identify the areas of overlaps. This is shown in Figure 6.7.

Some of the requirements match up well. Multi-skilling benefits both sides of the equation as does the move to provide more part-time employment. Both sides are moving towards the benefits of recognising the contribution rather than simply the time spent at work. Respondents to a 1993 survey (Watson and Fothergill) of part-time workers suggested that they had the 'best of both worlds'.

There is a less pleasant side seen by commentators, however, where the requirements are out of balance.

Flexibility may push more employees into the periphery where insecurity is enhanced; where wages become more dependent on performance and more variable between groups; where contracts become only transactional (only for what takes place) rather than relational (based

Objectives for Employers	Objectives for Employees
Temporal flexibility	
Matching employees' time to the market needs	*Matching work to personal and family needs*
Complex but efficient shift systems	Choice of working patterns – morning, afternoon, evening
Annualised hours	
Eliminating hours form the contract through 'working beyond contract' and zero hours	Keep hours to a level that allows family and personal responsibilities
Making greater use of available labour sources through temporary and part-time work	Greater demand for temporary and part-time/ job share work
Geographical/occupational flexibility	
Improving operational efficiency	*Providing greater involvement and work interest*
Increasing value of labour through multi-skilling	Opportunities for broadening skills and experience
Teleworking – saving in office space	Benefits in flexible hours and reduced travel costs
Outsourcing functions and workloads	Stability in the workplace
Call centres to replace face-to-face contact	
General objectives	
Reward for contribution made, not time at work	Reward for contribution made, not time at work

Figure 6.7
Flexibility requirements

on longer term relationships with trust and mutual obligations to the fore); and where the organisation has little long-term concern with most of the labour force. There is also some evidence that employees who choose to take advantage of the opportunities of flexible working lose out on the pay front, as shown in Focus on research 6.3.

Focus on research 6.3

Flexible working and the gender pay gap

The researchers interviewed 50 chartered accountants on their experience of flexible working and found that women who worked flexibly or part-time to combine their work with caring arrangements, damaged their career prospects and opportunities of well-paid promotions. This did not apply to men who, when they worked flexibly, did so at a much later stage when their career had progressed further and were therefore on a higher rate of pay when they worked flexibly. This has been contrary to the expected belief that the opportunity to work flexibly provides the means to reduce the gender gap, not reinforce it.

It is concluded that the attitudes to flexible working need to change in the professions so that those who work flexibly are not seen as 'time deviants' and that it is actively promoted for men to give them an opportunity to be active parents. Only then can the pay gap be reduced.

Source: Smithson *et al.* (2004)

Employees become more vulnerable, liable to forced changes and being asked to share in the risks of the enterprise. Outsourcing is seen as the least satisfying from an employee's viewpoint. Having taken employment with a known organisation, under agreed terms, and in an agreed location, the employee is asked (often without a reasonable alternative) to transfer to an unknown organisation, with terms that may alter in the medium term and often in a changed location.

Evans (1998) has recommended nine key ingredients for success in managing flexible workers:

- Provide clear sign posting concerning the options available on flexibility.
- Invest considerable time in getting the right fit between the needs of the organisation and the preferences of the employee.
- Be realistic about the relationship between skills, responsibilities and work patterns required and whether they can be accommodated through flexible working.
- Show respect for employee's other commitments and let them be involved in decisions that affect these commitments.
- Create a balanced team of age, experience and working patterns.
- Ensure responsibilities for service quality and delivery are shared by employees on conventional and flexible contracts.
- Be prepared to experiment with new ways of working.
- Adopt a flexible approach to training and development.
- Provide support for managers who look after flexible workers.

Total Quality Management

One of the main reasons to explain the decline in British manufacturing in the period 1950–1985, was the poor quality of the products as compared to those arriving from the Far East. Attention was increasingly given by the early 1980s to the systems of Japanese management and especially their ways of involving the workforce in ensuring high-quality production. This led to the adoption in many organisation firstly, of 'Quality Circles' followed by a more integrated system, called TQM.

Quality Circles are groups of volunteers from sections, usually between four and ten in number, who meet regularly to identify, analyse and solve job-related problems. They are supported through training in analytical methods and problem-solving techniques and make formal presentations to management on their proposals. The prime concern was in quality issues but it was recognised from an early stage that quality issues could not be separated to those of efficient use of labour, time and materials together with on-time production. By 1990, an ACAS Survey found that 27% of manufacturing organisations were utilising this technique. There has been evidence that involvement in Quality Circles has a positive effect upon attitudes and performance (Griffin, 1988) and led to incremental improvements in the manufacturing process but the 1990s saw a general decline in their use. Reasons for this included the difficulties involved for Supervisors in working with the circles and their voluntary nature, which meant that much of the workforce chose not to be involved or to contribute to the improvements.

An example of a successful Quality Circle initiative is given in Case study 6.4.

Case study 6.4

Who needs ashtrays?

Brittania Airways, the world's largest charter air company, bases its Engineering and Maintenance division in Manchester. Through its Quality Council, a group of Quality Teams were set up in 1990 to facilitate the development of continuous improvements by utilising the reservoir of staff ideas and experiences. One of those teams, 'Quality Street' Line Engineering was made up of 40 staff who met monthly and who began by learning to use the Britannia problem solving model.

Among the 50 items that they produced under their 'problem list', a priority item that was held to be within their total control was the investigation of the costs of continuing to include, service and repair ashtrays in all passenger seats, even though the 'smoking permitted' section of the aircraft represented a small proportion of the total seating. Their investigation discovered that the non-smoking ashtrays took more time to clean as they included difficult items such as chewing-gum. Moreover, over 500 ashtrays needed replacing each year at a cost of over £10,000, some stolen, some damaged. The major problem was that ashtrays were required on all seats on some charter flights while some flights were totally non-smoking.

The team closely investigated the processes involved including videoing the cleaning itself. A number of possible solutions were investigated but the best solution they concluded was to remove the ashtrays altogether. This would increase the cleaning costs in the smoking areas but it had the advantages of reducing weight in the aircraft and a substantial overall saving in cleaning time. Overall a savings of £13,500 a year would be made. After an effective presentation by the team, the Steering Committee, on behalf of the Quality Council, approved the solution and the team received congratulations from the Board.

Source: Teare *et al.* (1997)

TQM took the involvement process a stage further. Rather than being a bottom-up, voluntary, isolated process, TQM was introduced as a compulsory requirement, led from the Board. It became part of an employee's duty to become involved in problem-prevention and problem-solving initiatives; employees had to be in charge of their own quality, rather than their work being inspected further down the line; quality is designed into the product with the aid of cross-departmental teams; constant communication on quality performance is fed back to employees, especially in the process of how they compare with organisational aims and 'best practice'. It is system which relies on a high degree of trust between management and employees and it expects employees to be committed to organisational objectives. In the Focus on research 6.4 there is an analysis of the role of the personnel function in relation to TQM.

Focus on research 6.4

TQM and the personnel department

The authors examined 15 organisation, ranging in size from 100 to 10,500 employees, who were in the mainstream of TQM management, not just leaders or exemplars. Their sources included documentary information from published and internal reports and 150 interviews with a range of staff from different functions, including chief executives and trade union officials.

Their findings presented an optimistic portrait of the roles and opportunities of the personnel function which helped to increase their importance and credibility in the organisation. Their contributions included helping to adapt the culture of the organisation to one suited to TQM, the choice of the TQM system itself and an important facilitating role through communications and training. It also helped the department in its search for legitimacy by assisting in a process that was customer-focused – both internal and external. Finally, it assisted the ability of personnel to pose as a neutral – free from the typical conflicts which take place between departments such as production, design and marketing.

Source: Wilkinson and Marchington (1994)

Team-working

The growing importance of teams has been emphasised from a number of viewpoints. Teams are more effective in helping to solve problems and in achieving the required higher standards; the growing dependence on technology requires fewer employees in total but greater interdependence between them or systems will break down; the reduction of management and supervisory levels, called 'de-layering' has meant that teams need to work together with far less supervision; the creation of customer-focused teams, especially in the retailing and financial services areas, has arisen because of the need to provide an integrated service that meets the immediate needs of customers and tries to preserve their loyalty.

An effective, high performance team:

> 'invests much time and effort exploring, shaping and agreeing on a purpose that belongs to them, both collectively and individually. They are characterised by a deep sense of commitment to their growth and success.'
>
> Katzenbach and Smith (1993)

Such a team is often largely self-managed or self-directed, who are allocated an overall task with the required resources but with discretion over how the work is carried out. They may plan, schedule and distribute tasks themselves amongst their members. The team-leaders, where they exist, provide guidance, coaching and a degree of motivation, acting to represent the interests of the team to management and external interests. Well-matched teams with clear objectives have, in theory, much lower absence and turnover rates and new members find themselves in an effective learning environment.

Not all team-working settings provide the hoped for success as is shown in Focus on research 6.5.

Focus on research 6.5

Team-working

Kinnie and Purcell (1998) carried out research into team-working as part of the IPD-sponsored lean organisation project. They examined the introduction of teams in seven organisations, three small or medium sized and four large, all of whom introduced team-working in response to the conflicting demands of their customers, suppliers and competitors. Most required team members to be more flexible requiring a greater variety of tasks and a wider range of skills. There were also a number of examples of empowerment.

The research showed strong evidence of performance improvement in these organisations and most employees responded enthusiastically to the changes. However, there were clear signs of stress associated with the intensification of the work and this was quite strong in many of the team-leaders who found their new role difficult to assimilate. Where the scheme was most successful, the organisation had integrated other HR Policies with team-working. Close attention here was paid to recruitment, selection, training and rewards which all fitted in with the team-working ethos.

Source: Kinnie and Purcell (1998)

Meteor case study

Setting up a call centre

It had been a thoroughly dispiriting experience, Sarah admitted. Six months ago, she had being seconded at a weeks' notice to work with an small team and an external consultant to set up a call centre, which needed to be up and running within 3 months. This was for an associated company that dealt with IT equipment and servicing. It was located within a factory site where spare office facilities were available. The initial appointee to advise on human resource issues had suddenly left the team to join a competitor. When Sarah arrived, she had found that many of the basic HR decisions had been made, as had the internal call centre layout and technology.

It had been decided that the centre would be staffed exclusively on a full-time basis with standard shifts of 7 AM to 3 PM (day), 3 PM to 11 PM (back) and 11 PM to 7 AM (night). Night shifts would be on a permanent basis with days and back shifts alternating each week. Overtime shifts would be worked during the day on Saturday and Sunday. This system was going to be used because it reflected the existing factory arrangements as would other terms and conditions including holidays and sick pay. Employees had 4 weeks' intensive training to learn the basics of the business and to deal with customers. There would be 70 staff in total, based in teams in three departments, dealing with specific IT purchase areas, plus a fourth concentrating on the servicing operation. The payment system had a heavy loading onto incentives, with employees able to add up to 70% to their base salary. There were also team incentives, which could add a further 10%, plus some one off team non-cash prizes, such as vouchers and celebratory 'Events'.

The recruitment was far from easy with most applicants being young men whose IT experience was very limited. As time was short, the employment decision was based on an interview and short IT knowledge test with some references followed up afterwards. It was hoped to recruit a number of team leaders with experience of call centres but there were few applications so appointments were made based on age and experience.

The first few days after opening the centre were chaotic. The refurbishment of the office environment fell behind schedule and the time to test the technology was truncated so numerous technical faults occurred. The initial call rate was very high and a number of staff left in the first fortnight deciding that the pressure in the job was not for them. Others reported on leaving that they did not like the office arrangement with staff in long rows with little space of their own. Difficulties in recruiting the right calibre staff continued so many were thrown into the 'hot seat' with little preparation.

The first customer survey after 3 months of operation revealed the depth of the problem. Customers complained that either they were pressurised to buy IT equipment that did not really meet their specification or they were passed from one member of staff to another with long waits in between. There were strong complaints about staff who could not answer the questions or gave answers that the staff could not understand. There were numerous examples of the wrong equipment being sent or of servicing staff being completely unaware of the details of the servicing required.

In discussions with some of the staff who left, Sarah heard stories of pressure from their team leaders to meet their quotas or to be top of the league table together with the difficulties between one shift and another in communicating information. She decided that the whole operation needed a complete revamp.

Summary

- High-performance work places require the operation of a strong psychological contract so that employees are committed, involved and motivated.
- Motivation is a complex subject where no simple theory explains the efforts that employees put into a particular work situation.
- Flexibility in the work place has developed rapidly in recent years. It can be divided into temporal, numerical, occupational and geographical flexibility, each representing a system that attempts to utilise the skills, time and energy of the labour force to the benefit of the business.
- Recent developments include sophisticated systems, such as annual hours and flexible rostering, a rapid rise in the operation of call centres and extension to the concept of teleworking.
- Multi-skilling has been a crucial factor in retaining the competitiveness of manufacturing and has been extended in administrative and technical areas.
- TQM and team-working have led to a greater involvement of employees in quality and efficiency movements in the work place.

Student activities

1 Family-friendly benefits may be attractive to staff but have disadvantages to employers. Select three of the benefits detailed in this chapter, list the disadvantages that may accompany introducing the arrangement or benefit and consider how those disadvantages can be overcome.

2 In respect of the Meteor case study, put yourself in Sarah's position and carry out the following:

- Explain how you would put together a proposal for a series of changes, including how you would gather information and the objectives you would set.
- Suggest a series of proposals that may go into the report which would include the shift system, hours of work, the office lay-out, the pay system (you may want to look at Chapter 9 here) and other areas you consider relevant.

3 You have 50 points to allocate between the following aspects of a job:

- Physical working conditions
- Hours of Work
- Pay
- Relationships with your boss
- Relationships with colleagues
- Opportunity for promotion
- Benefits
- Convenience of location

Allocate those points, compare your results with your colleagues and draw conclusions on how this may affect motivation in the work place.

4 Annualised hours (see Case study 6.1 and Focus on research 6.2) appear to have considerable advantages for the employer. Read the article and book chapter on which these extracts are based and discuss the advantages and disadvantages for the employee.

5 With two other colleagues, carry out a TQM exercise on the process of revising for your examinations. Consider all the options, how the quality of the revision could be improved and how it could be evaluated.

6 Look at the article on which Focus on research 6.5 was based. What does this article tell us about the benefits of team-working?

References

Adams, J. (1963) Towards an understanding of inequity. *Journal of Abnormal and Social Psychology*, **67**: 442–436.

Atkinson, J. (1984) Manpower strategies for flexible organisations. *Personnel Management*, **August**: 28–31.

Atkinson, J., Meager, N. (1986) *New Forms of Work Organisation*. IMS Report 121.

Armitage, M. (1997) Give call centre staff a stake in their jobs. *Personnel Today*, **July 31**: 8.

Bathmaker, S. (1999) 'So, what's the deal?' The state of the psychological contract in a 'New' University. *Journal of Vocational Education and Training*, **51**(2): 265–281.

Cave, K. (1997) *Zero Hours Contracts*. University of Huddersfield.

Conway, N., Guest, D. (2001) *Public and Private Sector Perceptions of the Psychological Contract*, CIPD.

Evans, C. (1998) *Managing the Flexible Workforce*. Roffey Park Management Institute.

Griffin, R. (1988) Consequences of quality circles in an industrial setting. *Academy of Management Journal*, **31**: 338–358.

Guest, D., Conway, N., Briner, R. and Dickman, M. (1996) *The State of the Psychological Contract in Employment*, Issues in People Management, IPD.

Handy, C. (1994) *The Empty Raincoat*. Hutchinson.

Hayes, J. (1997) Annualised hours and the 'Knock'. The organisation of working time in a chemicals plant. *Work, Employment and Society*, **11**(1): 65–81.

Herzberg, F. (1968) 'One more time: how do you motivate employees?' *Harvard Business Review*, **January–February**: 53–62.

Hunter, L., MacInnis, S. (1991) Employers and labour flexibility: the evidence from case studies. *Employment Gazette*, **June**: 307–315.

IDS (2002) Study 721, January.

Johnson, M. (1997) *Outsourcing … In Brief*. Butterworth Heinemann.

Katzenbach, J., Smith, D. (1993) *The Magic of Teams*. Harvard Business School.

Kinnie, N., Purcell, J. (1998). *Getting Fit, Staying Fit: Developing Lean and Responsive Organisations*. Plymbridge Distributors (Summarised in 'Side Effects'. *People Management*, 30 **April**, pp. 34–36.

Labour Market Trends (2003) *Part Time Working Patterns*. March, 116.

Labour Market Trends (2004) *Work Life Balance Survey of Employers*. January, 11–12.

Locke, E. (1968) Towards a theory of task motivation and incentives. *Organisational Behavior and human Performance*. **3**, pp. 157–89.

Maslow, A. (1954) *Motivation and Personality*. Harper and Row.

Pemberton, A. (1991) The barriers to flexibility: flexible rostering on the railways. *Work, Employment and Society*, **5**(2): 241–257.

Sims, R. (1994) Human resource management's role in clarifying the psychological contract. *Human Resource Management*, **33**(3): 373–382.

Smithson, J., Lewis, S., Cooper, C., Dyer, J. (2004) Flexible working and the gender pay gap in the accounting profession. *Work, Employment and Society*, **18**(1): 115–131.

Stredwick, J., Ellis, S. (2005) *Flexible Working Practices*. CIPD.

Taylor, F. (1911) *Principles of Scientific Management*. Harper.

Taylor, P., Bain, P. (1999) 'An assembly line in the head': work and employee relations in the call centre. *Industrial Relations Journal*, **30**(2): 101–117.

Teare, R., Scheving, E., Atkinson, C., Westwood, C. (1997) *Teamworking and Quality Improvement*. Cassell.

Vroom, V. (1964) *Work and Motivation*. Wiley.

Wilkinson, A., Marchington, M. (1994) TQM: Instant pudding for the personnel function. *Human Resource Management Journal,* **5**(1): 33–49.

Wustermann, L. (1997) Moving up a gear – workwise at Hertfordshire County Council. *Flexible Working,* **September**: 18–22.

Further reading

Flexibility

- For a case study of *integrated flexibility at Autoglass in Bedfordshire,* see Jones, C., Stredwick, J. (1998) Cracking service. *People Management,* 3 September, pp. 50–53.
- Clutterbuck, D. (2003) *Managing the Work-life Balance,* CIPD.
- Holbeche, L. (1998) *Motivating People in Lean Organisations.* Butterworth Heinmann.
- Thompson, P., Warhurst, C. (eds) (1999) *Workplace of the Future.* MacMillan Business.
- Nickson, D. and Siddons, S. (2003) *Remote Working: Linking People and Organisations.* Butterworth Heinemann.

Team-working

- For a detailed *analysis of how to operate team-working,* see Belbin, M. (2003) *Management Teams: Why they Succeed or Fail.* Butterworth Heinemann.
- For the *American experience of team-working,* see Meyer, C. (1994) How the right measures help teams excel. *Harvard Business Review,* **May/June**: 95–103.
- For a study of *Virtual Teams* (those that are composed of members scattered around the world), see Gignac, F. (2004) *Building Successful Virtual Teams.* Artech House Publishers.
- Hardingham, A. (1998) *Working in Teams.* IPD.

Web sites

http://www.smartbiz.com/sbs/cats/perf.htm
Smart Business web site: American site with comprehensive list of articles and topics on improving performance in working life.

http://www.eto.org.uk
European Teleworking web site. Information about all aspects of teleworking, teletrade and telecooperation.

Relationships with employees

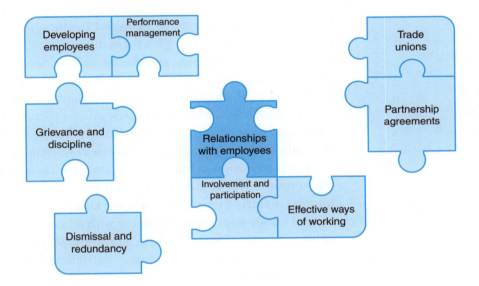

Objectives

When you have read this chapter and carried out the activities, you will be able to:

■ Identify the issues involved in the choices that organisations make in their relationships with their employees.

■ Explain what is meant by the terms 'unitarism' and 'pluralism'.

■ Describe the various actions that employers can take to encourage participation and involvement.

■ Outline the essential features of a grievance, disciplinary and redundancy procedure.

■ Appreciate the role of human resources in effectively handling procedures.

Introduction

An organisation will not operate effectively unless it has a stable and relatively harmonious relationship with its employees. Conflict and disaffection will lead, almost inevitably, to high staff turnover, poor attendance, lack of involvement and other indicators of poor performance. In this chapter, we will be looking at the employment relationship from a number of viewpoints. Firstly from a *workplace negotiating* viewpoint. Here, the relationship is determined by an agreement on terms and conditions reached through a formal process of negotiations by representatives of management and the workforce. Secondly, from an *involvement and participation* viewpoint. This examines how the relationship is affected by the effectiveness and influence of the 'employee voice'. Finally, from *a legal and procedural* viewpoint specifically related to grievance, discipline, dismissal and redundancy, where an examination will be made of the approaches to individual sources of conflict.

These three approaches are not mutually exclusive. A heavily unionised environment has as much opportunity to make considerable progress towards involving employees and working towards partnerships as does a small family controlled company with a history of enlightened paternalism. Whatever system of bargaining is in place, even where none exists, the edicts of the law remain extremely influential in the nature of relationships.

Workplace negotiating

Trade unions

In Chapter 1, we saw that the post-war development of the human resources (HR) function was very centred around the role of negotiator and facilitator in a growing union environment. Trade union membership grew from around 6 million in the early post-war years to a peak of over 12 million in 1979. However, for the next 20 years, there was a consistent and precipitate decline to a figure of around 7.7 million in 2003. This reduction in what is called *union penetration*, has been caused by the combination of 18 years of hostile Conservative Party legislation and major changes in the labour market away from manufacturing and public service (which are the main areas of union membership), to the service sector, which has generally smaller working units, more female and part-time employees. These changes have produced a more difficult environment in which to recruit members, despite the generally buoyant economy and a rise in the numbers employed.

There are currently approximately 220 trade unions in the UK but the membership of the four largest unions represented 40% of all union members (see Figure 7.1). These four and a further 13 unions with more than 100,000 membership, dominate the Trade Union Congress (TUC), which acts as the collective voice of the trade union movement. The TUC is very much a political body that acts as a pressure group to influence government policy and legislation and to work towards improving public opinion towards trade unions.

UNISON: The Public Service Union	1,272,700 members
Transport and General Workers Union	848,809
Amalgamated Engineering and Electrical Union	728,508
GMB (formally General, Municipal and Boilermakers Union)	689,276
Total of all other 219 unions	4,200,375
Total of all unions	**7,739,668**

Figure 7.1 Union membership in 2002. (*Source:* Certification Office Annual Report, 2003)

Within the workplace, trade unions are represented by two groups of officials. There are shop stewards, who are elected by the members in that workplace to look after their interests. In most organisations, the stop stewards spend only part of their time on union business, carrying out their normal work for the rest of their time. In a handful of large organisations where union membership is high, however, an agreement may be reached with management that the chair of the shop stewards of one union may act in a full-time capacity, being provided with an office and even secretarial help. The second group are full-time union officials, employed by the union to look after all the members in their locality. They come into the workplace rarely and only by invitation but their presence can be vital at crucial times during major negotiations or to head off disputes that are simmering.

The role of management

In the post-war years, national bargaining was an important feature of industrial relations where agreements reached between employer's organisations and trade unions set the pattern for subsequent deals made locally. Today, there has been a strong move toward negotiations being de-centralised to each individual unit or local groups of units (Carr, 1999). The main driving force behind this change is to place pay and conditions in its localised context, just as each unit has responsibility for other operating issues, such as investment and marketing.

There are a number of strategies for management to consider in the field of the employment relationship:

■ *Should they adopt a unitary or pluralist approach?* A *unitary* approach emphasises that the organisation and its employees have a common goal and that all employees benefit from the successes the organisation can achieve. The outlook is that higher productivity produces increased profits which allows increased pay and investment to yield more jobs, all of which is a virtuous circle. Therefore, there is a stress on harmonious relationships and team working. Where conflict takes place, it is based on misunderstanding rather than differing interests and it is up to management to communicate and persuade more effectively. A *pluralist* approach, on the other hand recognises that:

> 'organisations contain a variety of sectional groups who legitimately seek to express divergent views. The resulting conflict is inevitable and the task of managers is to establish a series of structures and procedures in which conflict is institutionalised and a negotiated order is established.'
>
> Redman and Wilkinson (2001: p. 194)

Employees, for example, want increased pay and shorter hours but management will regard this as a way to erode profits. Supervisors will want their earnings to be higher than the employees they supervise but large amounts of overtime for these employees could erode this differential.

■ *Should unions be recognised?* There are two influences here. Firstly, the decision may reflect the positioning on the unitarist–pluralist spectrum. A pluralist approach will understand the genuine need for groups to have representation in the form of unions and will see them as a way to carry out disciplined bargaining over the inevitable conflicts. A unitary approach, however, will veer towards the view that unions may be irrelevant, that they interfere with the broad process of management, confuse the joint goals and produce exaggerated employee expectations that cannot be met. There are also a number of practical considerations that influence the decision, especially the wishes of the employees. Industrial or public organisations in large units find it difficult to fend off union penetration forever.

■ The second influence is legislation. In 1999, the Employment Relations Act gave unions the right to apply to the Central Arbitration Committee (CAC) to organise recognition ballots when their membership has reached at least 10% in the proposed bargaining unit. The CAC has a key role in guiding the two parties to reach an agreement within tight deadlines and, if this is not possible, taking decisions on the size and nature of the bargaining unit and whether a ballot should take place. If there is clear evidence that union membership is greater than 50%, then the employer must accept recognition. If it is less than 50%, a ballot must take place and, if the result shows that the union is supported by a majority of those voting and at least 40% of those in the bargaining unit, then the CAC will declare the union recognised.

■ This legislation has also made it difficult for organisations to attempt de-recognition which had been a small but influential movement in the 1990s. The Workplace Employee Relations Survey (WERS3) recorded 3% of organisations over 5 years old had de-recognised all unions (Cully *et al.*, 1999).

■ In the 3 years after the union recognition clauses in the 1999 Employment Relations Act came into effect, there were approximately 1100 union recognition agreements, which brought 200,000 more union members into the negotiating process. Only about 20% of such agreements went through the statutory route. Most were voluntary agreements influenced by the impending recognition legislation where employers wanted to be certain that the agreements reached were with a single union of their choosing. Those employers who tried to fight off recognition found this approach fraught with difficulty. This was mostly because the CAC has tended to side with the union applicants on issues such as size of bargaining units (Younson, 2002). However, the effects of the legislation can be viewed at best as marginal, mainly because the number of cases handled by CAC has been comparatively small, covering relatively low numbers of employees and these have been concentrated in sectors of the economy where unions have a presence (Wood *et al.*, 2002).

■ For these reasons, the continuing apparent successful operation of the recognition procedures has not led, as we have seen, to a general increase in union membership. This is still 'treading water' and unions have had little success, with certain notable exceptions, in gaining members in sectors of the economy in which they have traditionally been weak, namely services, retailing and hospitality where employment has grown substantially in recent years (Stevens, 2003).

■ *What form of bargaining should take place.* Once unions had been recognised, there are a number of forms of bargaining that can take place. There is *sole recognition rights*, which is granted to one union to represent all the employees on the site. For example, Nissan granted the AEEU the sole rights to negotiated on behalf of employees at their Sunderland plant and it is common in Germany and Japan. This makes the negotiation process easy to organise and avoids the possibility of inter-union conflict but it means that some employees who decide to join a different union will not be fully represented. An alternative is to have *single table negotiations* where unions sit on a joint committee and management will negotiate only with that joint committee. This encourages co-operation between the unions and presents a relatively single negotiating process but often needs facilitation and mediation to keep the differing union groups together.

Guest (1995) analyses four approaches that management can adopt (see Figure 7.2).

Figure 7.2 Guest model of approaches to industrial relations and HRM. (*Source:* Guest, 1995)

Industrial relations	HRM	Description
High	High	New realism
High	Low	Traditional collectivism
Low	High	Individualised HRM
Low	Low	Black hole – no group relationships

■ *New realism.* In this option, management attempts to take forward major transformational initiatives to improve productivity, quality or customer relations, but, at the same time, to forge a new relationship with the unions. This will help to bring them to the party and get them to be wholly committed to the initiatives, and to persuade their members to come along with them. Guest found only a small number of examples, mostly connected to entrenched unions in industries where changes were vital for survival, such as in vehicle manufacture.

- *Traditional collectivism.* Here, management accepts wholly the pluralist approach and does its best to live within this situation, helped by the recent more restrictive legislation. Guest found this approach prevailed within the public sector and in non-competitive or declining industries, such as railways and coal. An example of organisations in the National Health Service (NHS) is shown in Focus on research 7.1.

Focus on research 7.1

Local pay bargaining in the NHS

In the mid-1990s, the Conservative government began an initiative to de-centralise pay bargaining in the NHS and allow varying terms and conditions of employment to be negotiated which would aim to reflect the varying labour market conditions. This research investigated how this local bargaining was progressing in practice. It was based on questionnaires sent to over 100 NHS Trusts in two NHS Regions, which produced a 44% response rate, together with a number of follow-up in-depth interviews.

The findings were that there was a continued commitment to pluralism and a rejection of the unitarist HR management (HRM) approach. This conformed to Guest's 'Traditional Collectivism' approach. There was some change taking place but it was incremental and involved a shift towards greater consultation within a traditional industrial relations environment. Trusts recorded increases in the degree of bargaining (91%) and of consultation (68%) but many local representatives were hostile to any fundamental changes, having worked within the national pay framework for a long time. There was some evidence that they also had some problems in handling local bargaining, lacking experience in this area.

There were only modest attempts made to reduce the number of bargaining groups and a continuing trend towards a flexible single-table bargaining strategy. The trusts were making much more information available but within the traditional framework and no evidence of attempts to undermine the union's position by direct employee communication approaches. Most trusts (70%) were aiming to move towards a simplified grading system and harmonisation of terms and conditions but only a handful were considering going for personal contracts.

Source: Carr (1999)

■ *Individualised HRM.* A more radical approach is taken here with a clearly unitary approach, where the policy may extend to de-recognition and encouraging employees to accept individual contracts, whose terms will emphasise individual performance. Bargaining is abandoned but communication and involvement is supported and encouraged. Evidence is strong here in American controlled organisations and a number of new start-ups. Research into the nature of such approaches, as demonstrated in the move to personalised contracts, is shown in *Focus on research 7.2.*

■ *Black hole.* Guest found evidence in much of the quickly growing or changing service industries that industrial relations was not considered as of any importance. Their competitive advantage was based on cost and flexibility and many employees (and much of the work) will be temporary or outsourced. In their strong unitary approach, unions were totally ignored.

Focus on research 7.2

Personal contracts

A longitudinal study of over 1000 East Anglian organisations was carried out between 1991 and 1996 to investigate the nature and practice of individualised contracts and to investigate whether such contracts represented a genuine process of negotiation. If so, it would represent a move towards the empowering the individual who would be able to secure the terms and conditions that reflected their own individual preferences and needs.

Information was gathered from 1800 questionnaires in three batches (response rate of 30%) supplemented by telephone interviews and an analysis of documentation. Their overall findings were that management's motivation to replace collective agreements with personal contracts was to introduce a more managerialist culture and ethos into the organisation in order to establish more of a command structure between managers and the employees they manage. This was especially true in the public sector where managers gave strong support to the move, which was associated with the introduction of individual appraisal and performance-related pay. There was little evidence that such contracts were aimed to assist the empowerment process or that they did in practice.

One of the detailed cases involved a dock where union de-recognition and personal contracts were threatened unless the unions agreed to substantially reduced manning levels and improvements in labour flexibility.

Source: Welch and Leighton (1996)

Third parties

The Advisory, Conciliation and Arbitration Service (ACAS) is an unusual body in that it is entirely funded by the government but acts as an independent agency with the sole purpose of promoting and improving industrial relations. If it is invited by both the parties, it will attempt to solve a difficult situation through conciliation, mediation or arbitration. *Conciliation* is where ACAS will keep the two sides talking and assist them to reach their own agreement. An example of how their intervention through the conciliation process can help solve problems is shown in Case study 7.1.

Case study 7.1

ACAS Conciliation

In 1998, a dispute between the North East Bus Company and the TGWU over the introduction of split shift working had led to three separate days of strike action among the 100 drivers at the Durham depot. It was set to escalate, with picketing extended to the local bus station and prospects of drivers from other bus depots and companies becoming involved. ACAS were invited in to try to help the parties reach an agreement. Two days of conciliation brought movement from both parties. The company moved on the question of future guarantees for the drivers and the union on the numbers of drivers that may be involved. With another day of strike action looming, the parties agreed on a new deal which was accepted by the members by a 2:1 majority.

Source: ACAS (1999)

In *mediation,* an ACAS official will listen to the arguments from both sides and then make recommendations as to how the difference may be resolved. The parties are free to accept or reject these recommendations. *Arbitration* is where both sides agree in advance to abide by the recommendations of the arbiter who will take a decision after hearing both sides. The subjects may include pay increases, shift working or allowances. A recent development has been '*pendulum arbitration*' where the arbiter is bound to accept the arguments in full of one side or the other and cannot decide on a compromise between the two sides. The intention behind this system (which is often associated with no-strike bargaining) is to encourage realistic negotiation from both sides, who will be fearful of losing a decision where compromise is not possible.

Role of the government

From the early days of the nineteenth century, government legislation has been in place, principally taking the side of the employer and making it difficult for unions to operate effectively. Determined action for their just cause over the years has currently produced a legal framework which gives unions immunity in most circumstances from damage they may cause by taking concerted action, as long as they follow certain procedures. They need to have ballots before action is implemented, action must only be in their place of work (secondary action is illegal), picketing is strictly limited and there can be no attempts to stop employers from using non-union suppliers. Other legislative controls include the outlawing of the closed shop (employees can join, or not join, any union of their choice) and the requirement for full-time officials to be re-elected periodically. Most of the legislation governing these controls over trade union activity were brought in the Conservative government between 1979 and 1992, following a decade of disruptive industrial warfare, where days lost through strike action reached 30 million by 1979. The legislation could be judged to be very successful in that days lost have reduced to an average of around 500,000 per annum in recent years, a rate that is one of the lowest in Europe. In 2003, for example, the number of strikes fell to only 133. Most of the disputes are in the public sector, especially in the transport and postal sectors.

The arrival of the Labour government in 1997 brought some change of direction with, alongside the recognition procedures already mentioned, the introduced of the National Minimum Wage in 1999, an initiative that has been in place in parts of Europe for two decades or more.

It was originally set at £3.60 per hour (less for younger employees) and there has already been some limited evidence of its effect upon closing the gap between male and female pay (Denny and Ward, 1999). It has been increased since that time (see Chapter 9 for more details).

Negotiating and bargaining

Negotiations are defined as:

> 'The coming together of two parties to confer with a view to making a jointly acceptable agreement.'
>
> Gennard and Judge (2002: p. 297)

Negotiating is not synonymous with bargaining. Negotiations can take place in grievances and discipline situations relating to single employees, but bargaining normally involves the exchanging of 'shopping lists' between the parties and trading in items in order to reach agreement. Formal bargaining normally takes place only once a year over the annual pay review but separate bargaining can occur over issues that arise during the year or over longer-term changes in working patterns or processes.

Student activity 7.1

Consider what subjects could be included in the bargaining process?

Response to Student activity 7.1

You may have included in your list any of the following issues:

- Basic pay, including differentials between skilled, non-skilled employees.
- Allowances for the exercise of skills or relating to special working situations, such as travelling or working under difficult or dangerous circumstances (confined space, heights).
- Bonus rates and the operation of the bonus scheme.
- Sick pay and pension schemes.
- Overtime rates and allocation.
- Issues of equal treatment for pay, conditions, promotion and relationships.

- Redundancy arrangements.
- Performance management schemes.
- Flexibility issues, including between jobs and locations.
- Rights to maternity or paternity pay.
- Improved benefits for holidays, paid time off, career breaks and other family friendly areas.

Much of bargaining is associated with ritual, including the presentation of claims and counter-claims and much debate over historical circumstances, promises and half-promises. However, successful bargaining arises from a well-planned and executed management campaign where the union side is supported and encouraged to work within the agreed systems and procedures. Clear establishment of aims, carrying out extensive research into the market place, competitors' rates and the external labour environment, welding a tightly controlled negotiating team, each with specific responsibilities and handling the informal contacts with the other side, all are aspects considered important by experienced negotiators.

Involvement and participation

There are few who would dispute the fact that employees who are *involved* (in the broader sense of the word) in their work, in their department goals and in the organisation's long-term aims, are more likely to be committed to that organisation and to working well and effectively. A further step is to say that the involvement is linked to the degree that the employee (singly or as part of a group) *participates* in the decision-making processes of the organisation. Research by Millward *et al.* (2000) has found that employee perceptions of the extent to which they are provided with information by their managers and the degree to which the manager provides the chance to comment and respond are closely associated with levels of job satisfaction, organisational commitment and performance.

Involvement and participation can take many successful forms. The IPD, in its position paper 'Employee Relations in the 21st Century' (IPD, 1997), argue that partnership is essentially about particular processes of management, rather than structures. Moreover, it is not whether employees are members of unions or not that influences the success of the process, it is the actual management practices themselves and the degree of conviction with which they are operated by management (Guest and Conway, 1997). Encouragement towards involvement and participation can take place *individually* through the introduction of

certain techniques and mechanisms, such as attitude surveys, team brief-
ings and employee recognition schemes, or through *collective* approaches,
such as works councils or a more innovative initiative demonstrated in
the recent growth of 'partnership deals'. The process of effective communication underpins both systems.

In April 2005, the Regulations on Information and Consultation, came
into effect, arising out of the European Union (EU) Directive on this
subject. This requires employers with more than 50 employees to inform
and consult employee representatives about employment prospects and
decisions likely to lead to substantial changes in work organisation or
contractual relations. Too often, employees get to learn of such major
changes affecting them through the press or television and the aim is to
avoid this situation and to improve employee consultation in general.

Individual approaches

Attitude surveys are increasingly used today to seek the views of employees. They can be annual events, such as those operated by British
Telecom, where a questionnaire is sent to an employee's home and
returned to an external body, such as MORI. Alternatively, they can be
used to gauge the degree of employee support for ideas such as flexible benefits before the organisation commits themselves. *Focus groups*,
which are a representative sample of employees, can also be set up to
provide a balanced opinion on new or existing issues. Carrying out a
survey every year will indicate the trend in morale and employee satisfaction. Whichever system is used, it is essential that a report on the
findings is published to the employees with a considered action plan,
where employees have indicated that action is necessary. An additional
benefit of attitude surveys is that employees involved in these processes
believe that the organisation has taken some effort to gauge employee
views and this, in itself, can go some way to raise the general level of
satisfaction.

Employee Recognition schemes. In the past, these were called 'suggestion
schemes' and had a somewhat dowdy image with little real support or
enthusiasm from employees. The success of major Japanese manufacturing companies in world markets in the 1970s and 1980s, however,
forced their competitors to examine carefully their system of '*Kaizen*'
especially in the light of a report in 1988 that Japanese employees produced 100 times as many suggestions as their American counterparts
(NASS, 1988). '*Kaizen*', and the various western alternatives, such as
Quality Circles and QED, place obligations on each employee to get

involved in their local area at work and to come up with proposals for improvement. Employees are trained in how to analyse and solve problems and how to present them to management. When proposals are accepted and implemented (and the small, incremental proposals are as welcome as the grand design) then employees receive a proportion of the cost savings. In Vauxhall Motors' scheme, for example, a number of proposals have led to employees receiving in excess of £3000 (Stredwick, 1997).

Briefing groups (sometimes called team briefing) are a form of communication which attempts to provide information in a systematic and timely way to all employees, so that they have the opportunity to remain involved with the progress of the organisation. Information is cascaded through the levels of the structure over a short period (half a day if possible) from a prepared script but with opportunities provided for questions to be asked and replies given. With briefing size groups of 6–20 (average of 12), a unit of 1248 could, in theory, cascade the information very quickly as shown in Figure 7.3.

Financial involvement. A number of companies encourage their employees to identify with the organisation's success through share savings and option schemes by providing shares at discounted prices and through profit-sharing and profit-related pay schemes. This policy stems from the unitarist approach, presented in a positive-sum terms, in which both employees and the enterprise seek to enhance company wealth from which both parties benefit (Hyman, 2000). Around 2000 such schemes operated involving 1.3 million employees in 2001. By their nature, they can only operate in the private sector although attempts

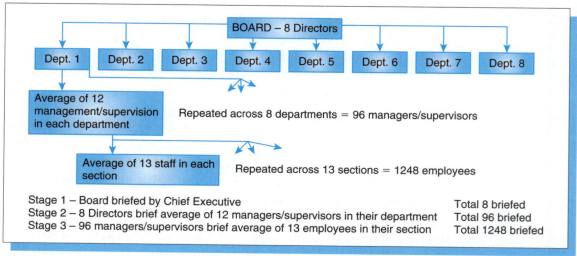

Figure 7.3
Briefing group operation

have been made to create 'notional' shares as a means of delivering bonuses to more senior staff in some public sector enterprises. The schemes tend to be highly regarded when share prices are rising but fall into disrepute at times when the stock market drops, such as the period between 1999 and 2003. In fact, some senior commentators question the wisdom of such schemes:

> 'Should we really be encouraging lower-paid employees to have a large amount of their investments in shares, because the equities market is so volatile.'
>
> Vicky Wright, partner in Ernst and Young,
> quoted in Smethurst (2003: p. 33)

Certainly the share-owning employees of Marconi and Telewest, who saw their share become worthless in the early 2000s, agree with these sentiments.

A more long-term sustainable system operates at the John Lewis Partnership, which is actually owned by the employees, its partners. They operate the most innovative of financial participation schemes with substantial annual bonuses being paid to all partners, dependent upon the level of profits, linked closely to other types of employee participation (Stredwick, 1997).

Collective approaches

Works councils

An encouragement for employees to participate in decision-making processes through their representatives was the European Works Council Directive, which was issued by the EU in 1994 and which became law in the UK in December 1999, covering around 300 organisations in practice (DTI, 1999). Organisations with more than 1000 employees in any one EU member state or more than 150 employees in each of two or more states, are obliged to set up a pan-European works council which will include employee representatives. At the meetings of the council, management must provide information and be consulted on the organisation's progress and prospects in a number of laid-down areas including employment, economic and financial performance. Some organisations, including United Biscuits, set up councils with enthusiasm before the requirement came into effect as detailed in Case study 7.2.

Although opposition to the introduction of the councils was strong from the Institute of directors and the Confederation of British Industry, there is some evidence that the hostility is demonstrated less in practice. Research by Southampton University (Overall, 1999) found that companies saw some positive features about the councils including a comprehensive way of getting management views across to employees, hearing the employee voice, exchanging information and getting employees involved in the business. Negative viewpoints were expressed about the bureaucracy and expense involved, the risk of fostering transnational unionism and the unnecessary duplication in employee relations.

Case study 7.2

United Biscuits European Consultative Council

The council comprises 20 representatives from its European operations including 13 from the UK. Members are nominated by their unions or their local works council and up to four full-time officials are eligible to attend in addition to the worker representatives. It takes place annually and is chaired by the Human Resources Director and attended by the Chief Executive, focusing on its financial performance, its strategic direction, jobs and employment policy and on the broad commercial factors which affect the operations of the company. It cannot deal with issues that are the preserve of national or local negotiating processes.

Partnership agreements can be seen as representing the progressive thinking on collective relationships. In return for formal recognition and bargaining rights, together with elements of job security, unions agree to a commitment to work together to make the business more successful and to encourage their members to take a full part in the involvement processes. The attraction to the unions is that it is one of the few viable paths to a position where they might be valued by employers while retaining an independent workers' voice (Guest, 2001). Joint initiatives on quality and productivity improvements, staff skills developments, flexibility, all supported by an effective communication and representation process are important aspects of a successful partnership deal. They can also be part of the process of saving the company from bankruptcy, such as the case of MD Foods (Arkin,

1998). There is evidence that employers are taking a less overall hostile view of unions and moving towards agreements of this type (Milne, 1999).

A 1998 report on partnerships by the Involvement and Participation Association shows evidence that organisations performance is better, there is a better psychological contract and much higher level of trust between employees. However, the voluntary nature of the agreement can be questioned:

> 'To a large extent these approaches to partnership understate the role of employee voice and leave open the question of assent or acquiescence. Reference to external threats has often achieved considerable change in employee relations – particularly so in those sectors where they are a potent danger.'
>
> Beardwell (1998: p. 36)

An example of a recent partnership agreement is shown in Case study 7.3.

Case study 7.3

Partnership agreement between Tesco PLC and USDAW

The starting point for the agreement was the realisation that the polarised and inflexible structures of Tesco's employee relations were at odds with the organisational culture. Innovation and flexibility had been critical to the firm's success in overtaking the competition in recent years. The deal was brokered at Cranfield School of Management in 1997 through a series of workshops between top management and USDAW officials. Union membership penetration was over 50%, totalling some 85,000 members which is the largest single cohort of union members in the entire private sector. Tesco had recognised that the union adds value to the organisation and to the employees in legitimising change, representing staff views and providing expertise on health and safety.

The agreement brought about consultative staff forums at each of the 586 UK stores with members elected by all store employees which meet quarterly. They do not have to be union members though there are reserved places for a union representative and the store manager. The Store Forums will send representatives (which must be USDAW members) to three regional forums who will, in turn, elect a national forum with responsibility for the annual review of terms and conditions and for discussing major business issues. An important aspect is that USDAW is recognised as an independent countervailing force to the might of Tesco who are able to make considered challenges when appropriate.

The deal extends the negotiating agenda beyond pay to issues, such as training, career planning and job security while providing information on customer research, HR statistics and company performance. There were four 'pillars for partnership':

Pillar	Comments
Individual representation	Union channels co-existing with new staff forums. Union and company structures to be aligned. Tesco to assist in training for advocacy, health and safety
Consultation and communication	All employees involved. Procedures speeded up.
Commitment to common values	Union to act as conscience, highlighting any failure by the company to live up to its declared values
Understanding and promoting the business	Co-operative approach to embracing change

The agreement represents an unprecedented attempt to reconcile strategic HR imperitivies with established, but reformed, industrial relations institutions and procedures.

Source: Allen (1998)

Not all partnership agreements work out successfully. In March 1999, Centrica's retail division entered into an agreement with Unison to share information, involve the union and 'maximise employment security'. The aim was to help to stem the large losses in that division and staff co-operated even to the extent of accepting pay cuts. However, just 4 months later, the decision was taken to close all of the former gas retail showrooms with the loss of 1500 jobs (Overell, 1999). There is also the risk that partnership becomes a device for management to incorporate unions, a new form of flexibility deal where 'responsible' trade unionism means that unions can never endorse industrial action. A summary of the advantages and disadvantages are set out in Figure 7.4.

Advantages	Disadvantages
Moves unions away from adversarial agenda. Encourages ethical business through tolerance and mutual respect for differing positions.	Hostage to fortune: relations may break down irreparably if commercial pressure forces a rupture of partnership agreement.
Commits both employees and unions to the success of the business.	Promotes trade unionism by the back door: unions are perhaps only interested because of current weakness.
Meshes with the spirit of employment legislation.	Forces disclosure of more information. Hindrance to swift managerial decision-taking.
Can build reputation for progressive employment practices.	Social partnership is unlikely to link directly to business success.

Figure 7.4
Partnership agreements (*Source*: Adapted from Overall, 1999)

Dealing with individual sources of conflict – grievance, discipline and dismissal

Just as a procedure for conflict resolution between management and the workforce is essential, every organisation also needs to have a system in place to deal with areas of disagreement that arise between the individual and the organisation. Where the individual is aggrieved due to an action, or a lack of action, by management, then this can lead to a formal *grievance* process. Where the organisation is dissatisfied with the actions, or lack of action, of an employee, then this can lead to a formal *disciplinary* process and, ultimately, if serious enough, to *dismissal* taking place.

Most minor grievances and disciplinary matters can be dealt with in the day to day informal contact between employees and management. A small request here, a word of advice there, an informal discussion on the shop floor or in the office can solve 90% of problems from both sides. However, to find a solution to this 10% which cannot be settled in this way needs a formal procedure that provides an agreed system and approach within which both sides can work towards a solution. Procedures for grievance and discipline are in place in 92% of establishments and they exist at almost the same level in companies employing less than 50 staff (Cully *et al.*, 1998). Having said this, there are specific skills that relate to successfully running a grievance or disciplinary session, and there is strong evidence that insufficient training for managers and supervisors takes place in this area (Hook *et al.*, 1996).

In 2004, the regulations relating to *grievance and disciplinary procedures* arising out of the 2002 Employment Act were brought into effect.

These regulations set out minimum standards that must be followed and, if it transpires at an employment tribunal that employers have not done so, then compensation for the applicant can rise by up to 50%. The regulations are essentially setting out good practice contained in ACAS Code of Practice. It is unlikely that these procedures will become contractually binding but the main aim of the regulations are to assist in the resolution of workplace disputes and thereby reduce the number of cases for unfair dismissal (Gaymer, 2004).

Grievances

There are numerous incidents or situations that can lead to an employee holding a grievance. They can be extremely serious, such as a sexual assault or a severe safety hazard. They may be less serious in totality but of serious concern to the employee, such as a new shift rota, a failure to consider for promotion, a critical appraisal report, a lack of opportunity for overtime or too much pressure of work.

A grievance is like an infection. Unless it is dealt with quickly and efficiently, it will fester and may spread quickly causing unnecessary pain and suffering (lower productivity, reduced co-operation and commitment). A procedure, then, will aim to ensure that the employee's case is heard quickly, that the employee concerned will have a fair hearing with the opportunity for full discussion to take place and that a response from management will follow without too long a gap. The procedure should make clear to whom the grievance should be addressed, who should accompany the employee if they require somebody to help them in the process, and specific time limits for the meeting to be held and the decision given, plus the stages of any appeal. Figure 7.7 shows a typical progression. It is always wise for a clear record to be made of the grievance and the outcome.

Discipline

An inevitable consequence of employing people is that there must be a set of rules laid down which, to a large extent, regulates their behaviour. The original meaning of discipline was associated with learning and study – to be a disciple – but now its associations are closer to punishment and penalties. It may be regarded as the exercise of management's legitimate prerogative of control. This is unfortunate in many ways because the concept of self-discipline and working within a mutually agreed code of behaviour are essential features of an effective workplace today. Indeed, it could be regarded as a failure on management's part whenever a disciplinary session takes place. Perhaps it is a failure in selection, or to explain the rules at induction or a failure in sufficiently understanding or influencing the behaviour of the employee in their performance in the workplace. A better approach is to regard any issue of friction that may lead to discipline as that of problem to be solved and that punishment is only one solution that should only be used as a last resort.

Up until 1972, employers had almost unlimited powers to discipline and dismiss employees as long as the required notice was given. Since the introduction of the legal concept of Unfair Dismissal in that year, constraints have been imposed and clear guidelines set down. If they are not followed at any time during the disciplinary procedure, then the dismissed employee has the opportunity to make a claim at an Industrial Tribunal. If successful, then the sanction against the employer is to have to pay compensation or, occasionally, to be forced to take the employee back on.

A discussion of discipline has three parts. Firstly, the *common rules* in place which, if broken in some way, lead to disciplinary action. Secondly, the *disciplinary procedure* and external guidance that is given on how it should be formulated. Thirdly, issues that arise as to *operating the procedure* in practice.

Rules

In the museum in Sunderland, there are old photographs of shipyards in the late nineteenth century with workers gathered under lists of rules written large onto the shipyard walls. They make interesting reading including the various financial penalties for, amongst other heinous crimes, spitting, lateness, and losing employer's tools. Lateness is still an offence, of course, but rules in most organisations are now published in a 'employee handbook' or similar and financial penalties are far more subtle.

Rules can be categorised under a number of headings:

■ *Safety rules.* These are a vital part of the employer's duty of care to protect employees. They cover the operation of plant and equipment, wearing of safety gear and limiting access to areas of work, tools and machinery unless trained or qualified.

■ *Performance rules.* These relate to many aspects of an individual's performance including attendance, timekeeping, flexibility on hours, working practices and location, levels of performance, willingness to work overtime, the requirement to take part in bonus schemes or raise suggestions for improvements.

■ *Behaviour rules.* Included here are rules that concern the relationship with customers and fellow employees, from the need to be courteous and responsive to customers, to wear certain regulation uniform and to take part in team processes.

■ *Rules evolved through custom and practice.* Not all rules are written down. Rule books would be far too long if they had to include every conceivable situation so common sense assumes that, for example, certain violent behaviour would be not allowed. Nor do written rules apply if they are not implemented by management. For example, the rules may clearly indicate that employees may not take out of the premises any materials belonging to the organisation. In practice, employees may have been taking small quantities of certain low-grade materials for their own use with the knowledge of management so the original rule is regarded, at law, as being amended to take this custom into account.

Disciplinary procedure

A starting point here is the long-standing ACAS Code of Practice (1977, revised in 1998). A summary of the main points are set out in Figure 7.5 which also contains some additional explanatory comments.

Operating the disciplinary procedure

The objectives of the procedure are three-fold. Firstly, it is to point out to the employee the error of his or her ways. It is important to clearly establish that a gap exists between the level of performance or behaviour required from the employee and that which has been observed and to obtain the employee's acceptance of that gap. So if the employee is accused of poor attendance, then their record has to be matched against standards that have been laid down and the records of their colleagues. The same applies with performance levels where any accusation needs to be backed up with a clear record of how the performance is below that required. The employee will have the right to question the facts put before them and, if they produce evidence that throws doubt on the original facts, then further investigations need to

Disciplinary procedures should:

1. *Be in writing.*   This is to aid communication of the procedure and to ensure that it is applied consistently.
2. *Specify to whom they apply.*
3. *Provide for matters to be dealt with quickly.*
4. *Indicate the disciplinary actions that may be taken.*   These include warnings, dismissal, and any other sanction.
5. *Specify the levels of management which have the authority to take the various forms of disciplinary action, ensuring that immediate superiors do not normally have the power to dismiss without reference to senior management.*   In a small organisation which has few levels of management, this is difficult to implement in practice.
6. *Provide for individuals to be informed of the complaints against them and to be given the opportunity to state their case before decisions are reached.*   This is a key aspect of natural justice. Difficulties arise over the whether the accused employee should have the right to question witnesses, as in a court of law. Internal procedures are not courts of law, there are no independent judges or juries and witnesses may not be prepared to come forward if they have to face a form of cross-examination. Organisations take differing practical viewpoints in this area.
7. *Give individuals the right to be accompanied by a trade union representative or fellow employee of their choice.*
8. *Ensure that, except for cases of gross misconduct, no employees are dismissed for a first breach of discipline.*   Gross misconduct is explained under the section on dismissals.
9. *Ensure that disciplinary action is not taken until the case has been carefully investigated.*   This is another important aspect of natural justice and one that tribunals take very seriously. In the case of a serious offence, the employee may be suspended with pay while the investigation takes place.
10. *Ensure that individuals are given an explanation for any penalty imposed.*   Which clearly tells them what they have done wrong and how long any penalty, such as a warning, will apply for.
11. *Provide for the right of appeal and specify the procedure to be followed.*   The appeal will need to be made to a person in higher authority who has not been involved in the earlier decision.

Figure 7.5
Essential features of a disciplinary procedure (Source: ACAS 1977, revised 1998)

take place. The employee should be encouraged to explain the reasons for their failings. Some may be acceptable, such as severe family illness leading to temporary poor attendance and will indicate areas where help can be provided.

Next, the objective is to set the employee on the path of improvement. As Honey (1996) puts it:

'... changes in behaviour, particularly if the behaviour in questions has become habitual, requires more effort than a quiet word. Persuading the problem person invariably involves getting them to accept the need for change. Increased awareness and intellectual acceptance, while useful, are rarely enough. This is because behaviours have been acquired through practice, sometimes over many years, and further practice is required to unlearn a problem behaviour and replace it with something better.'

Honey (1996: p. 20)

A positive approach can involve an action plan with the employee working with their supervisor or manager to improve performance, timekeeping or any other weakness. As with any other action plan, it will need its own objectives which are time based. Solutions that arise from the employee themselves are more likely to be successful. Help from the organisation may be needed. Where performance has deteriorated, then training or guided experience can be expedited; problems with caring for an aged relative can be helped through temporary changes in the hours worked; difficulties with relationships can be rectified by providing help through counselling.

The final objective is to come to a decision on a fair sanction for the offence committed. Figure 7.6 clarifies the difference between a misdemeanour and gross misconduct.

Misdemeanours	Timekeeping not up to required standard Attendance not up to required standard Performance not up to required standard Inappropriate attitude to management, fellow employees, customers or suppliers
Gross misconduct examples	Fighting Working under the influence of drink or drugs Providing confidential information to competitors Theft Fraud, such as claiming false expenses Sexual harassment Causing a severe safety hazard, such as smoking where prohibited Refusing to obey a reasonable instruction

Figure 7.6
Misdemeanours and
gross misconduct

In the case of proven gross misconduct, the employee has clearly indicated that they have gone beyond the bounds of the contract and the employer has the right to instantly dismiss the employee. With misdemeanours, which are lesser offences, there is no right of dismissal for a first offence so warnings are the appropriate penalty.

That is not to say that a warning is necessary in every case. Fowler (1996) suggests when informal reprimands may be more appropriate. This very much depends on the nature and severity of the offence, the reasons given by the employee and their willingness to remedy the situation. Agreement about the offence, an action plan and an enthusiastic willingness to improve the situation should lead to no more than a mild rebuke and an agreement to review the situation over the next few weeks and months.

Procedures have a number of stages. An example of typical grievance and disciplinary procedural stages is set out in the example in Figure 7.7.

	Grievance procedure	Disciplinary procedure
Stage 1	Employee raises grievance informally with immediate supervisor.	Manager raises issue informally with employee. The issue is settled with a mild rebuke or advice or an Oral Warning, the latter being recorded.
Stage 2	If employee is not satisfied, a meeting is convened between the employee and manager with the supervisor present.	If the issue is more serious, such as persistent absenteeism, or if the less serious issue continues to arise, a meeting is convened with the employee and his representative/colleague. The manager will normally have another member of management present, such as HR officer. If proven, the outcome can be a First Written Warning, which is recorded.
Stage 3	If the employee is still not satisfied, they can take the grievance to the level of a director who, with the manager present, will listen to the issue and take the final decision within seven working days.	If the issue is still one of a misdemeanour but no improvement has taken place since the last warning, a further meeting will be convened by the manager with the employee and his representative/colleague. If proven, the outcome can be a Final Written Warning which makes it clear that the employee will be dismissed if the offence is repeated.
Stage 4		If the issue is not of **gross misconduct** or if there has been no improvement since the Final Written warning was given within the agreed elapsed time, then a further meeting will be convened. A senior member of management may be present together with the parties at the previous meeting. If the offence is proven, then the employee may be dismissed. The employee has the right of appeal.
Stage 5		At the appeal, which will take place within 3 days, a Director of the organisation will listen to all the evidence and decide either to uphold the dismissal or to change the natural of sanction to a further Written Warning, demotion and/or suspension. This decision is taken within a further two working days.

Figure 7.7
Grievance and disciplinary procedure stages

Dismissal

We have already discussed some of the legal aspects of the process that leads to dismissal. In order to defend a case at a tribunal, the employer needs not only to have a good reason for dismissing the employee but must also show that they followed the correct procedure in a fair and consistent way. It is only logical to do this in any case if they want their organisation to be regarded as a good employer and to have committed and hard-working employees.

There are a number of other elements that need to be considered. These are *the process of an employee claiming unfair dismissal*, including the operation of tribunals, the concepts of *constructive dismissal, admissible and inadmissible reasons for dismissal* and a brief examination of *common reasons for dismissal* and *recent legal developments*.

Employment law is a very complex area that is constantly changing so students are encouraged to follow regular legal reports as shown in the section on further reading.

Claiming unfair dismissal

The qualifying employment period for claiming unfair dismissal was reduced to 1 year in June 1999 and applies to both full-time and part-time staff. It is only employees that can claim but clarifying the definition of an employee has taken up much time in the courts. As with much of employment law, it is not what is written down that is conclusive, but what actually happens within the employment relationship. Sales agents, for example, whose contract shows them to be self-employed, have made successful claims to be classified at employees when they have demonstrated the extensive degree of control by the employers, their inability to refuse any work or to be able to work for anyone other employer while they were under contract.

Employees need to make a claim within 3 months of losing their jobs and they do this by completing a form ET1 setting out their case, available from ACAS or from consumer bodies, such as Citizen Advice Bureaus. A copy of this claim is then sent to the employer to respond. The next stage is that a Conciliation Officer from ACAS will try to get the parties to consider settling the case before it goes to the tribunal. The Officer will communicate with both parties and help them to consider alternatives, including a cash settlement, re-instatement of the employee or the claim being dropped altogether. In 2003, of the 45,261 claims received, 21,974 were settled and 12,124 withdrawn leaving only 8973 actually going to the tribunal while 2190 had other outcomes (ACAS 2004).

Tribunals, which can last for a day or as long as a month or more in the most complex cases, normally consist of three people: a legally qualified independent Chair, and one representative each taken from a list of nominated individuals by employers' bodies and trade unions, all of whom have experience of industry or commerce. The tribunal therefore represents a fair balance of opinion although the members of the tribunals act as individuals, not representing their constituency. The process of the tribunal is less formal than a normal court of law.

In England and Wales, witnesses sit in for all the proceedings whereas they are precluded from doing so in a normal court until they have given evidence. The normal rules of evidence apply but the tribunal members take much more initiative in directing the questions, acting more as investigators than would a judge, who, as a generalisation, leaves it to the prosecution and defence to bring out all the important elements in their case. The difference is because many individuals take their own case to a tribunal and are faced by corporate lawyers, which can be very daunting. Having listened to the evidence from both sides, the tribunal will give its written decision a short time afterwards.

Another difference to a court of law is that the organisation does not have to prove their case beyond reasonable doubt, just on the balance of probabilities. Tribunals are not allowed to replace a decision with their own view. They will only interfere with the decision if it is outside of the range of reasonable decisions that could have been taken in the circumstances. For example, take the case of an employee who has been accused of fraud where the evidence is strong but not sufficient to ensure a conviction in a court of law. The organisation have investigated thoroughly, have followed all the right procedures and have come to the conclusion that the employee actually carried out the fraud and have dismissed the employee. A tribunal, would be unlikely to allow the claim to be successful as long as they are satisfied that the procedures are fair, that all the evidence was considered carefully and that management have a strong conviction of the guilt of the employee.

The decision by the tribunal will set out whether or not the employee was unfairly dismissed and, if so, the nature of the compensation, although often the tribunal will allow the sides to try to settle their own deal first and only if they cannot do so will they work out the compensation to be paid. Very occasionally, when the dismissal is patently unfair, they will order re-instatement. If the employers refuse, then additional compensation will be ordered. From October 1999, the maximum compensation was raised from around £12,000 to £50,000 and has been increased in line with inflation since that date.

If either of the parties choose to appeal against the decision, they do so to the Employment Appeals Tribunal. From there, further appeals can go to the Court of Appeal and thence to the House of Lords. Finally, an appeal can be made to the European Court of Justice (ECJ) in Luxembourg. Cases that reach that level are ones of major principle, tantamount to a change in the law. For example, Miss Marshall, who was forced to retire at age 60, took her claim all the way to the ECJ and eventually won the right to equal treatment, causing the British Government to change the law and equalise retirement ages. She then went on to claim compensation for being forced to retire early but this had a limit of around £10,000 at that time. So she followed the same route all the way back to Luxembourg and, again, won her case. This meant that unlimited compensation applied to all cases relating to sex discrimination throughout Europe.

Constructive dismissal

An employee will sometimes face a situation where the actions by the employer makes it difficult for them to continue at work. This may be because they have been insulted or bullied by the employer in front of their colleagues, sexually harassed, or treated in a totally cavalier fashion, such as bonuses being withdrawn for no reason. The claim by the employee will be based on the concept that the employer has indicated by their actions that they no longer wish to be bound by the mutual contract of employment, even though it may not be intentional. Two examples are given in Spotlight on the law 7.1.

Spotlight on the law 7.1

Constructive dismissal

Hilton International Hotels (UK) Ltd. versus Protopapa *1990 IRLR 316*

Mr Protopapa, who was in a position of authority in the hotel, had taken time off work for a dentist appointment without prior permission. As a consequence, he was reprimanded in the presence of his subordinates in what he claimed to be a humiliating fashion. The tribunal described it as 'officious and insensitive'. He resigned and was successful in his claim for constructive dismissal. By their actions, the employers had repudiated the contract, carrying out an action that went to the heart of the contract.

Source: Pritchard (1995)

Goodwin versus Cabletel UK Ltd EAT *1997 IRLR 665*

Mr Goodwin was a construction manager for CUK who were engaged in setting up a cable television network in South Wales. As part of his duties, Goodwin had to ensure that the employer's subcontractors complied with the relevant statutory health and safety requirements. He found one subcontractor, CC Ltd., especially lacking, which included an incident when roads were excavated without any traffic control. Goodwin recommended that no more work be given to CC Ltd. CUK disagreed with Goodwin and asked him to act in a more conciliatory fashion.

At a subsequent meeting between the parties, CC Ltd. severely criticised Goodwin who felt that he had received no support from CUK at what he felt to be a humiliating and intimidating experience. A few weeks later, Goodwin was removed from all dealings with CC Ltd. and transferred into the position of assistant construction manager. He resigned and claimed constructive dismissal because of the apparent demotion and lack of support over health and safety matters.

The tribunal rejected his claim, finding that Goodwin had not responded to the justified advice given to him concerning his approach on health and safety. The employer's action had not gone to the heart of the contract as the change of job title was not a demotion. EAT, however, indicated that employees with health and safety responsibilities must be afforded some protection in the way they carry out their duties and this had not been considered by the tribunal. They allowed the appeal and the case was referred to a new tribunal to consider whether the manner in which the employee approached the health and safety problems took him outside of the scope of health and safety activities.

Source: IDS (1998)

Admissible reasons for dismissal

Apart from redundancy, there are four circumstances in which dismissals may be regarded as fair at law. They are:

- *The employee's capability.* This covers the area of poor performance or the lack, or loss of a necessary qualification.
- *An employee's misconduct.* These include the remainder of the misdemeanours and all of the acts of gross misconduct set out in Figure 7.6.
- *A statutory restriction*, such as the lack of a work permit or security clearance in parts of the public sector.

■   *Some other substantial reason.* This covers other areas such as pressure from a customer, or the inability to work with other members of the department or making false statements on an application form.

The first two reasons cover the vast bulk of cases although some of the most interesting cases are to be found under some other substantial reason.

Three common reasons for dismissal

Two further cases are set out which indicate some of the issues involved under three of the most common reasons for dismissal. Dismissal for poor attendance (Spotlight on the law 7.2), refusal to obey a reasonable instruction (Spotlight on the law 7.3).

Spotlight on the law 7.2

Post Office versus Wilson EAT

Wilson started working as a postman in 1995. In the Post Office, there was a lengthy procedure applying to frequent/extended absences from work due to medical conditions which was agreed with the unions. It involved three stages; the outcome of each could be an informal warning, a formal warning and dismissal, respectively.

Wilson's employment was beset with absences and injuries. In February 1997, he received a first stage informal warning and this was followed by a formal warning in June 1997 following an absence for 1 day for an upset stomach and 2 days absence for a chest infection. The warning stated that, if during any 6 months period in the following 12 months, he was absent on two separate occasions or for a total of 10 days absence, it could lead to dismissal. In October 1997, Wilson was absent for 10 days as a result of a neck injury sustained while playing football for the Post Office team. At the subsequent third stage, his case was considered and the decision was made to terminate his employment, a decision that was upheld at appeal. The procedures had been followed carefully, including giving Wilson all the rights of union representation. Wilson subsequently applied to a tribunal for unfair dismissal.

Source: IDS Brief 641 (July 1999)

Spotlight on the law 7.3

Farrant versus The Woodruffe School 1998 ICR 184

Farrent was employed as a laboratory assistant. In his original contract letter, it indicated that he would spend the majority of his time in the laboratories but would also spend some time in the Craft, Design and Technology (CDT) area. In November 1993, the head teacher decided that there was insufficient technical support in the CDT area and, as there were no funds to recruit a new technician, he advised Farrent that he would be moved into the CDT area on a full-time basis. Farrent made it clear that he did not want to go, stating he was relying on his original contract as a laboratory technician. After further discussions, he was warned that, if he refused to move, it would be regarded as a refusal to accept a reasonable and lawful instruction and he would be dismissed. He still refused and was subsequently given 1 month's notice of termination. It was made clear that, if he changed his mind during that month that the notice would be rescinded. No change of mind took place and Farrant's dismissal took effect. He made a claim at the tribunal.

Source: IDS Brief 607, p. 14

There are a number of *inadmissible reasons* that have emerged as the law has developed in the last 20 years. They include dismissals relating to pregnancy or maternity, refusing to work on a Sunday, dismissals relating to trade union membership or activity, those related to reasonable actions taken by the employee as a health and safety representative, a pension representative or a representative for consultations on redundancy or business transfer. In each of these cases, a dismissal made solely or predominately on the basis of these reasons would be held to be automatically unfair.

Redundancy and its implications

One of the least pleasant activities within HRM is handling a redundancy situation. In parts of Europe there are tight controls on management's prerogative to declare redundancies but these limits are only lightly applied in the UK, so a redundancy situation is much more common. It is one of the almost inevitable consequences of change within the organisation and presents difficulties from the moment that rumours start circulating and has an effect for many months, sometimes years, after the actual redundancies take place. The situation is not helped by the numerous euphemisms that have arisen in recent years including 'downsizing', 'right-sizing' and 'letting employees go'. Creating redundancies is a sharp reminder of how HR can be seen as a cost that must be reduced, rather than an asset that attracts investment. If handled badly, the motivation and trust of the workforce can be irreparably damaged creating long-term problems in productivity and commitment. These difficulties can be ameliorated if the appropriate policies are in place and the events are handled with tact, honesty, diplomacy and sensitivity.

Redundancies can occur arising from a number of causes:

- The organisation, or part of it, can be sold, merged or taken over. The new owners will have seen opportunities for extracting higher returns through cost saving, closing certain operating sections due to duplication or poor performance, re-structuring central services (especially head offices) and generally to stamp their mark on the new organisation.
- The organisation may be part of a business that is going through a structural decline. UK shipbuilding, coal and steel industries all had massive redundancy programmes in the 1970s and 1980s as they had to face up to a declining demand and international competition.
- A recession, even if short-lived, can bring the chill wind of sharply reduced demand and a demonstrated over-manned situation, which will need to be remedied.
- Advances in technology can have an especially major effect on process and assembly industries where, for example, a robotised paint shop can reduced the number of employees involved by a factor of four or more.
- A major efficiency drive using techniques, such as business process re-engineering, or benchmarking, can show that benefits can accrue through a reduction in manpower.

Legislation has an influence in three main areas related to redundancy. In setting out the requirement for *consultation with the workforce*, in defining the parameters for *selection for redundancy* and laying out the way *minimum redundancy payments* must be calculated. There is also a clear legislative definition of redundancy (Employment Rights Act, Section 139(1)) which can be summarised as a cessation or reduction or a major change in part or all of the business activities which leads to a reduction or change in the requirements for employees. This is

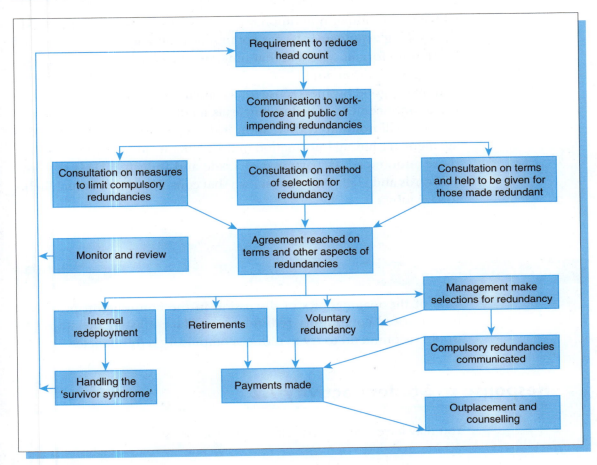

Figure 7.8
Process of redundancy

drawn very broadly and tribunals have very rarely challenged the right of employers to declare redundancies. The process of redundancy is shown in Figure 7.8.

Consultation with the workforce has to take place in some form in every redundancy situation. However, specific timings apply where:

- 100 or more employees are to be made redundant in which case consultation must commence at least 90 days before the first dismissal.
- 20–99 employees are to be made redundant in which case consultation must commence at least 30 days before the first dismissal.

Consultation takes the form of announcing the redundancies and giving the details of reasons for the redundancies, the timings, selection procedures and form of payments. Discussions are then entered into with either union or non-union representatives (or both depending on the existing arrangements) for communication and representation. If there is no formal system at that time, one must be set up to deal with this legal requirement.

It makes good business sense for as much openness as possible, once the announcement of redundancies is made. At this most difficult of times, it will not help the situation if the workforce believe that management are hiding information or are acting from other motives than those announced. Department of Trade and Industry (DTI) research (Edwards and Hall, 1999) has shown that consultation very much helps to save jobs.

Student activity 7.2

One of the major topics of discussion in the consultation process is how to avoid compulsory redundancies. Make a list of the steps you would recommend to try to reduce compulsory redundancies.

Response to Student activity 7.2

You may have considered some of the following:

Immediate actions

- Eliminating all overtime.
- Ceasing the use of agency staff.
- Freezing recruitment.
- Offering full-time employees part-time work, possible in the form of job-shares.
- Offering early retirement on terms that may be attractive, especially to long-serving employees.
- Accepting employees who volunteer to be made redundant.

Longer-term solutions

- Relying on natural wastage (i.e. employees leaving voluntarily) to reduce numbers.
- Business solutions such as bringing back into the business work that had been subcontracted outside and finding

alternative business that potentially redundant employees could carry out.

- Retraining employees who could slot into some positions that will continue but may be difficult to fill, such as in Information Technology.
- Putting employees onto short-time working; that is, 30 hours a week instead of 37. This has been operated for some time at Fords at Dagenham in the late 1990s.

There are advantages and difficulties for each of these solutions. Short-time working, for example, is a costly solution as a form of allowance is normally payable for each normal working day that the employee is not actually working. Productivity and morale tends to fall under short-time working as employees do not feel under pressure to produce at a high rate which as they may consider that this will simply make the redundancy situation worse. Freezing all overtime and recruitment may not be appropriate where there is a key vacancy or where an important contract has a vital delivery date. Early retirement is another costly solution if it involves adding years of service or enhancing retirement pay, although these costs may be borne by the pension fund.

Selection for redundancy

Another important aspect of the consultation process is the basis on which decisions are taken as to which employees are to be made redundant. Redundancy is covered by unfair dismissal legislation, so such decisions have to be based on procedures that are fair in themselves and are carried out fairly and transparently. A system for selection must be set out and it must be capable of being defended at a tribunal as being appropriate in the circumstances. This is far from easy and there are no simple solutions that fit all situations.

Common methods which can be used including the following:

- *Selecting those employees who volunteer.* This would seem an obvious solution but is not always that simple. A number of employees may volunteer who consider that they can obtain an alternative position relatively easily. This may be because they are in the age group 24–36, with good experience and possessing skills in short supply. These are precisely the employees that you want to keep! The dilemma presents itself as to whether you refuse to accept such volunteers and make others compulsorily redundant, which would cause considerable unrest, or whether you accept the volunteers and lose some good employees that will affect your capacity to perform in a competitive environment. From a business viewpoint, you may adopt the former viewpoint but the HR view should veer towards the latter. The culture of equity and good employee relations is not encouraged when jobs are taken away from some employees, when others are willing to leave the organisation in their place.

■ *Last in–first out.* This used to be the standard method universally applied, especially in a unionised environment. It is certainly transparent and can be regarded as fair in that long service is rewarded. In practice, however:

> 'it means that those who are selected for redundancy are those who . . . may be keen, enthusiastic employees who will have much to offer the organisation in the future. This may result in a stagnating, ageing work force who lack the skills and versatility required for future business success.'
>
> Foot and Hook (1999: p. 406)

■ *Performance measurement.* By using comparative measures of employee performance, the organisation can make redundant those employees who they judge are not up to the mark. This can be seen as a fairer system overall and one that benefits the longer-term future of the organisation. The measures that can be used include attendance, timekeeping, speed and accuracy in their job, whether the person has been disciplined for any reason and the general attitude of the employees to their work and authority. A score sheet (such as in Figure 7.9) can be produced which combines these measures and those with the lowest overall scores are made redundant.

These measures are fraught with difficulty, however. Can you give a low score to an employee whose attendance is poor due to being treated for cancer? Should a single parent be penalised on their timekeeping because of their home responsibilities? When it comes to trying to judge attitude, the problems are almost insurmountable. Such decisions must be taken primarily by the employee's manager or supervisor and objectivity can always be questioned.

■ *Skills and competencies.* A final version is to score employees on the type and quality of skills or competencies they possess.

Measure	Description	Employee 1	Employee 2
Attendance	15 points maximum with 3 points lost for each absence	12	9
Timekeeping	10 points maximum with 2 points lost for each lateness	6	8
Quantity of work	15 points for high, 10 for average, 5 for below average	15	10
Quality of work	15 points for very accurate, 10 for average, 5 for below	10	10
Warnings	10 points for clear, 5 lost for each warning	10	5
General attitude	Ranked on scale of 0–15	12	10
	Maximum = 80	**65**	**52**

Figure 7.9
Example of performance measurement system relating to redundancy selection

Those skills and competencies that are highly valued or are in short supply are scored highly. This system allows the organisation to retain those skills and competencies that it needs for future development. The problems of measurement also arise with this selection system. How do you distinguish between the skills and competencies acquired in the past and the way they are currently utilised?

Despite the difficulties involved, the latter two methods are growing in use and has been accepted by tribunals as long as the scheme is operated fairly and transparently and not simply put in place to construct a list of 'trouble-makers' that the organisation wants to dispense with. It was established at an early stage of the implementation of the legislation that employers do not need to prove the accuracy of the individual marks on their scoring system, only that the method of selection was fair and appeared to be applied reasonably in general. This has always seemed an unusual viewpoint to take as it limits the individual's right to question in detail the basis upon which they have lost their job. The only exception to this is where there are strong indications that discrimination has played a major role in the decision (see Spotlight on the law 7.4).

Spotlight on the law 7.4

British Sugar PLC versus Kirker **1998 IRLR 624**

Kirker had worked for the company for 20 years and was partially sighted. In the assessment for redundancy, he received a score of zero for both performance and potential and was selected to be made redundant. At the subsequent tribunal, it was decided that the scoring had not in any way been applied objectively and his low scores did not reflect the true situation. The employer's attitude towards Kirker's disability coloured their judgement of him in the selection process. He had been treated less favourably as a result of the employer's prejudice and was awarded compensation of £100,000, a decision subsequently upheld by the Employment Appeal Tribunal.

Source: IDS Brief 623, p. 10

Redundancy pay

The final intervention by legislation relates to the payments due under redundancy. Employees are entitled to the minimum of a week's pay for each year of service, although service over the age of 41 is paid at the rate of one and a half week's pay and service between the age of 18–21 inclusive is paid at the rate of half a week's pay. A maximum figure applies to the week's pay (around £260 in 2003), which is increased each year and entitlement only starts when employees have completed 2 years' service.

These sums are not especially large and many organisations choose to enhance them by increasing (or ignoring totally) the maximum week's pay restriction or by increasing the entitlement to, say, 2 weeks pay for each year of service. They take this decision both on the grounds of showing a degree of generosity towards the employees who are losing their jobs through no fault of their own and also because it may encourage a higher level of volunteers and thereby reduce the number of compulsory redundancies.

Helping employees obtain alternative employment

An important role for HR is to help those employees who have been made redundant to obtain a suitable alternative position. This can be achieved *internally*, through matching up suitable internal vacancies (perhaps replacing key positions where the incumbent has volunteered for redundancy, against candidates selected for redundancy. This can be a complex process and needs to be handled carefully and sensitively to avoid exacerbating an already difficult situation. Employees who accept alternative positions have the right of a 4-week trial period. If they take the reasonable decision that the position is not suitable for them at the end of that period, they retain the right to redundancy payments.

Student activity 7.3

What help can human resources give to help employees get alternative work externally?

Response to Student activity 7.3

You may have listed the following actions:

- Circulate all the major local employers telling them about the redundancies and listing the numbers and skills available (see Case study 7.4).
- Organise an 'open day' for local employers to attend who may be interested in taking on some of those made redundant. This may be held on site or at the local job centre.
- Giving paid time off for employees to look for employment and attend interviews (this is a statutory right although the maximum time has been defined only as 'reasonable').
- Helping employees to draw up curriculum vitae (CVs) and preparing them for job search and interviews.
- Working with an outplacement agency who will provide professional job search services on an individual or group basis. This will include help in coming to terms with the redundancy situation, career counselling and planning, a job-hunting strategy and office support. More important, the agency can provide continuing independent support for some months after the event. For supervisors and managers, the current average time to obtain an alternative position is around 4–6 months so such help can be particularly vital.

Case study 7.4

Helping redundant employees at the AA

When the AA decided to close 143 shops in 1998 and extend their call centre operations, 900 staff were made redundant throughout the country. In a bid to support these employees, the AA published advertisements in national newspapers and People Management, which aimed to interest the insurance industry looking for skilled and experienced staff. There was substantial interest from all quarters, not just in insurance and the placement level was very high, making it a very successful operation.

Source: Prickett (1998)

The role of HR in redundancy

Firstly, policies and procedures should be in place to deal with potential redundancies. These should include the way redundancies are announced, the consultation process, commitment to ways to reduce the impact of redundancies, the selection procedures for compulsory redundancies, an appeals process and a commitment to help with obtaining alternative employment.

It is not enough to have procedures in place. Managers will need to be trained in the selection process so that it is carried out in a fair and consistent way. The process will need to be carefully monitored and the results communicated in an efficient but sympathetic way by HR.

HR also need to ensure that the redundancy payments made are appropriate, which will involve influential discussions with the Chief Executive and, in a unionised environment, bargaining with the unions. Checking and communicating the actual payments is another important role. Finally, the involvement with helping those made redundant to obtain alternative positions is vital to help diffuse some of the bitterness that many will feel against the organisation. As Richard Baker, Human Resources Director at Hoechst Rousel, puts it:

'People need to be treated as if they are valued and handled in a humane a way as possible. They never forget the way they are treated when they are made redundant and neither do the friends and colleagues who remain behind.'

Summerfield (1996: p. 31)

Meteor case study

Moving head office

The merger between Meteor and Landline Holdings had been announced the previous month and it had become clear quite soon that two separate head offices would not continue. Meteor's offices, however, were not large enough to accommodate further expansion and was, in any case, coming to the end of its lease. The Board had decided to move to a new site 40 miles in a state-of-the-art business park, a move that would take effect in 6 months time. As soon as the announcement to staff had been made, Sarah was seconded back to head office to help David Martin prepare for the move and its consequent effect upon the employees. It was made clear that there would be no compulsory redundancies and that all Meteor and Landline staff would be invited to apply for a position in the combined head office. Details of re-location and redundancy packages would be given within 1 month.

The first decision David and Sarah faced was both legal and ethical. Who could be forced to re-locate as part of their contract? In other words, if there was an appropriate clause in their contracts entitling the company to re-locate them and they decided they did not want to move, they would not be entitled to any redundancy payment. This applied to 50 of the senior executives, managers and sales personnel, 47 of them male and three female. The ethical issue here, however, was that it may appear unfair if a manager feels unable to move, due to family or other constraints and therefore receives no payment, while one of their staff in the same position receives a generous sum of redundancy. There were two further complications with this issue. Firstly, they were aware that some recent tribunal decisions had appeared to indicate that forcing a woman to re-locate could be held to be discriminatory, especially where there were caring responsibilities. Secondly, the company had not actually implemented this clause previously as re-location came up only rarely and usually took place alongside an offer and acceptance of promotion. On balance, in the interests of an equitable situation, they decided to recommend the same legal situation to all staff – the alternatives would be re-location or redundancy – despite the cost involved.

Looking at the situation from a geographical viewpoint, some staff could re-locate without moving home and a special bus service would be laid on for the first year after the move. A decision, however, had to be made as to whether staff in this position should be offered the full package, including house move. There did not seem to be an imperative to do so, but the complications and apparent inequity of offering it to some staff and not others again influenced the decision to offer the full package to everybody.

The package was a generous one, covering all the costs of buying and selling, stamp duty, removal costs and a settling-in allowance of 5% of the value of the property. For those who did not own houses, a package of 6 months subsidised rent was offered plus a fixed settling-in sum. The generosity was based on the viewpoint that the cost of having to recruit and train key staff was very high so it was important that as many moved as possible. Bridging loans were also offered for up to 3 months for staff with more than 5 years service.

It was agreed that the redundancy package to be offered would be around the industry average so staff would receive the legal minimum plus a supplement of 40%. Given the fact that few staff had more than 10 years service, the costs involved would not be very high.

The complete information was communicated in a series of meetings across the offices during one long day with a printed summary given to each employee. A dedicated help line was made available to give a full calculation of entitlement together with any necessary financial advice. Outplacement help was also made available through a local consultancy that specialised in this area.

In the event, far more employees chose to accept redundancy rather than move and the costs to the organisation finished up 25% above those budgeted. Although the opportunity was provided to make saving in the overlapping services of the two organisations, the move became much more complex as it included a larger than expected recruitment programme, as well as all the complicated decisions arising from creating a joint head office structure. Sarah was not sure that they had made all the right decisions.

Summary

- Union membership has declined substantially since its high point in the late 1970s due to government legislation, the decline in manufacturing and the move towards a more flexible workforce.
- There has been a growing tendency for organisations to move towards a unitary viewpoint in their relations with their employees. This has shown itself in a greater emphasis on encouraging employee involvement and participation, through team briefing, recognition schemes and works councils.
- The growing number of partnership agreements indicate the willingness of employers and trade unions to work closer together to obtain common aims.
- Policies regarding discipline, grievances and redundancies need to be formal, fair, reasonable and communicated effectively if they are to remain inside the law.

■ Constructive dismissal takes place when the employer's actions indicate that they repudiate the contract, although this may not be intentional.

■ A fair employer will take a number of actions to try to avoid compulsory redundancy, which includes freezing all recruitment, eliminating overtime and offering voluntary retirement.

Student activities

1　Consider Spotlight on the law 7.2 and decide:
   ■ What was the basis upon which Wilson had been dismissed out of the four admissible reasons?
   ■ Do you think he was successful in his claim?
   ■ What is the basis of a good attendance management scheme?

2　Consider Spotlight on the law 7.3 and decide:
   ■ Did the school have the right to insist on Farrant moving?
   ■ Do you think he was successful in his claim?
   ■ How would you have handled the situation?

3　Consider the redundancy scheme set out in Figure 7.9. Make a list of the difficulties that could be raised by employees, the problems that could be faced in practice and how you would sell the scheme to the employees.

4　Read the article by Carr on local bargaining (Focus on research 7.1). Why do you think local representatives are opposed to changes in the bargaining stance? How would you convince them that changes are necessary?

5　In the Meteor case study, how reasonable do you think were the terms of the redundancy package? Look up the tribunal cases referring to re-location and equal opportunity. Do you think that the high costs of the redundancy package outweigh the risks of a tribunal claim?

References

ACAS (1997) *Code of Practice on Disciplinary Practice and Procedures in Employment*. ACAS.

Cully, M., *et al.* (1999) *The 1998 Workplace Employee Relations Survey – First Findings*. ACAS/ESRC/DTI/PSI.

ACAS (2004). *Annual Report 2004.*

Allen, M. (1998) All-inclusive. *People Management,* 11 June, 36–42.

Arkin, A. (1998) Cream of the crop. *People Management,* 12 November, 34–37.

Beardwell, I. (1998) Voices on. *People Management,* 28 May, 32–36.

Carr, F. (1999) Local bargaining in the NHS: new approaches to employee relations. *Industrial Relations Journal,* **30**(3): 197–211.

Cully, M. *et al.* (1998) *The Workplace Employee Relations Survey.*

Denny, C., Ward, L. (1999) Pay gap between sexes narrow. *Guardian,* 15 October, p. 2.

DTI (1999) *European Works Council Directive: Implementing Regulations.* DTI.

Edwards, P., Hall, M. (1999) Remission: possible. *People Management,* 15 July, 44–46.

Foot, M., Hook, C. (1999) *Introducing Human Resource Management.* Longmans.

Fowler, A. (1996) *The Disciplinary Interview.* CIPD.

Gaymer, J. (2004) Making a molehill out of a mountain. *People Management,* 26 February, p. 17.

Gennard, J., Judge, G. (2002) *Employee Relations.* CIPD.

Guest, D. (1995) Human resource management, trade unions and industrial relations. In: Storey, J (ed.). *Human Resource Management – a Critical Text.* Routledge; pp. 110–141.

Guest, D., Conway, N. (1997) *Employee Motivation and the Psychological Contract.* IPD.

Guest, D. (2001) *Industrial Relations and Human Resource Management.* In: Storey, J. (ed.). *Human Resource Management: A Critical Text,* 2nd edn. Thomson Learning.

Honey, P. (1996) *Problem People and How to Manage Them.* IPD.

Hook, C., Rollinson, D., Foot, M., Handley, J. (1996) Supervisor and manager styles in handling discipline and grievance. *Personnel Review,* **25**(3), 20–34.

Hyman, J. (2000) Financial participation schemes. In: White, G., Drucker, J. (eds). *Reward Management: a Critical Text.* Routledge.

IDS (1998) *IDS Brief 605,* January, pp. 8–9.

IPD (1997) *Employee Relations into the 21st Century: an IPD Position Paper.* IPD.

Milne, S. (1999) Team mates. *The Guardian,* 15 September, p. 19.

Millward, N., Bryson, A., Forth, J. (2000) *All Change at Work: British Employment Relations 1980–1998 as Portrayed by the Workplace Industrial Relations Survey series.* Routledge.

NASS (1988) *Participation and Cost Saving in US and Japanese Participation Schemes.* National Association of Suggestion Schemes and Japan Human Relations Association.

Overell, S. (1998) British managers warm to European works councils. *People Management,* 19 February, p. 10.

Overall, S. (1999) An unsocial agreement. *Personnel Today,* 26 August, 18–19.

Prickett, R. (1998) The AA puts recruitment into reverse. *People Management,* 17 September, p. 13.

Pritchard, G. (1995) *Constructive Dismissal.* Central Law Publishing; p. 21.

Redman, T., Wilkinson, A. (2001) *Contemporary Human Resource Management,* Financial Times Prentice Hall.

Smethurst, S. (2003) A Slice of the Cake. *People Management,* 6 February, pp. 32–34.

Stevens, R. (2003) Union recognition still rising. *Partnership @ work web site*, 18 February.

Stredwick, J. (1997) *Cases in Reward Management*. Kogan Page.

Summerfield, J. (1996) Lean firms cannot afford to be mean. *People Management*, 25 January, 30–32.

Welch, R., Leighton, P. (1996) Individualising Employee Relations: the Myth of the Personal Contract. *Personnel Review*, **25**(5), 37–50.

Wood, S., Moore, S., Willman, P. (2002) Third time lucky for statutory union recognition in the UK? *Industrial Relations Journal*, **33**(3): 215–233.

Younson, F. (2002) Employers face scoring own goal. *People Management*, 7 March, p. 19.

Further reading

ACAS publishes a number of short advisory booklets on the following subjects:

- Employee communication and consultation
- Employment policies
- Redundancy handling
- Supervision

Other publications include:
ACAS (1997) *Discipline at Work: The ACAS Advisory Handbook*. ACAS.

For details of bargaining processes, read:
Blyton, P., Turnbull, P. (2004) *The Dynamics of Employee Relations*, 3rd edition, Palgrave Macmillan.

Salamon, M. (1998) *Industrial Relations: Theory and Practice*. Prentice Hall.

For details of the complex legislation on union recognition, see:
Younson, F. (2000) How to handle a union recognition claim. *People Management*, 20 July, 44–46.

For a detailed analysis of *partnerships*, read:
Claydon, T. (1998) Problematising partnership: the prospects for a co-operative bargaining agenda. In: Sparrow, P., Marchington, M. (eds). *Human Resource Management: the New Agenda*. Pitman Publishing.

Reilly, P. (2002) *Partnership under Pressure*. IES Report 383.

For *retention policies*, read:
Bevan, S., Barber, L., Robinson, D. (1997) *Keeping the Best: A Practical Guide to Retaining Key Employees*. Institute of Employment Studies Report no. 337.

For *information and consultation*, read:
Beaumont, P. and Hunter, L. (2003) *Information and Consultation: from Compliance to Performance*. CIPD.

For a guide to carrying out *Employee Attitude Surveys*, see:
Walters, M. (1996) Employee Attitude and Opinion Surveys. IPD.

For a detailed study on *partnerships*, see:
Stuart, M. and Martinez-Lucio, M. (2005) *Partnership and Modernisation in Employment Relations.*

The CIPD publishes a guide on redundancy (2003).

For an example of an *employee recognition scheme* at Vauxhall Motors and an examination of the John Lewis Partnership employee involvement scheme see:
Stredwick, J. (1997) *Cases in Reward Management.* Kogan Page.

A comprehensive coverage of *employment law* is given in:
Lewis, D. (2004) *Essentials of Employment Law,* 8th edn. CIPD (this is updated annually).

You will find ongoing updates in:
Incomes Data Briefs, published fortnightly by Incomes Data Services.
Industrial Relations Law Bulletin, published fortnightly by Industrial Relations Services.

Web sites

http://www.acas.org.uk
The ACAS web site which includes their publication lists, some of which are available to download at no charge.

http://www.tuc.org.uk
The TUC web site giving information on union activities and viewpoints on legislation.

http://www.incomesdata.co.uk
Incomes Data Services web site including many articles from IDS reports, Studies and Briefs

CHAPTER 8

Performance management

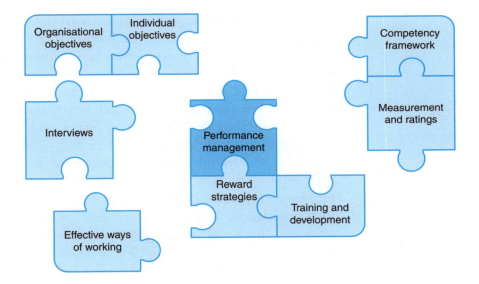

When you have studied this chapter, you should be able to:

- Understand the critical nature of the performance management process and the role of human resources in influencing the associated systems and operations.
- State the meaning of performance appraisal and performance management and to distinguish between the two.
- Carefully consider the appropriate measurement methods in given situations and be conscious of their shortcomings.

■ Put forward reasoned proposals on how to set up and operate a basic performance management system.

Introduction

To all intents and purposes, an organisation is judged by its performance. In the private sector, performance is measured principally by its profits and the growth in value of its shares; in the public sector, measures are more controversial but sets of various performance indicators in health, education and other public services give a general overall view of how well the organisation is performing in comparison to its peers.

Organisations can perform well or poorly due to external forces, such as the state of competition in the marketplace, long-term weather patterns, legal restrictions or the level of interest rates and taxation. However, the majority of economists and commentators agree that the biggest influence on organisational performance is the quality of the labour force at all levels of the business. Teams of highly skilled, trained and motivated employees will nearly always overcome most of the difficulties created by external forces while a poorly motivated, untrained and unskilled labour force will nearly always fail to take advantage of favourable external opportunities.

Given this situation, it could be argued that the most important role for human resources (HR) is to raise the performance of employees in the organisation. To do this, employees' performance has to be managed and this is not an easy job. As long ago as 300 AD, the Chinese philosopher, Sin Yu, was complaining about the unfair treatment dealt by senior mandarins in the Civil Service under their current performance management scheme:

> 'The Imperial Rater of nine grades seldom rates men according to their merits but always according to his likes and dislikes.'
>
> Swan (1991: p. 16)

Times have changed little since then with Peters and Waterman (1982) claiming that managers often took 6 months or more to get over their appraisal. Many practitioners are still very wary of working to a scheme, which attempts to measure the unmeasurable, communicate performance to the inattentive and make extra payments to the ungrateful.

There are strong signs in recent years, however, that a new approach is spreading which focuses much more on the whole performance management system and much less on appraisal as a single activity. *Appraisal* can too often be regarded as a once a year ritual (a rain dance, it is said, where the participants intone the right phrases, make the right movements and the money will fall from the heavens) whereas *performance management* is a total company system, built into all HR activities – recruitment, training, reward and relations. The appraisal process all too often looks backwards, looking for excuses and blame, while performance management is more concerned with looking to the future, to improvements, challenges and opportunities. And whereas appraisal is a diaried event, performance management is a continuous process, integrated totally with the way the organisation is run.

The purpose of performance management

There are two main purposes driving performance management, as set out in Figure 8.1. Firstly, the Operational reasons, which serve to lead and control. As organisations exist in an increasingly competitive environment, it becomes more and more important for employees to have clear guidance and direction towards the organisation's aims and objectives. The performance management system sets out to communicate the link between an organisation's mission and strategic direction and the required employee performance.

The process can also be used as a form of strict control over employees. Going back over 150 years, Robert Owen, in one of the first factory

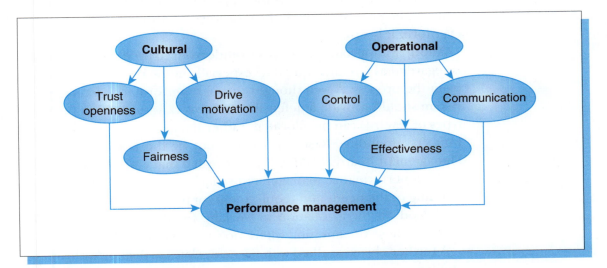

Figure 8.1
Performance management input model

settings, used a 'silent monitor': a piece of wood mounted over a machine with one of four colours to denote the daily performance of the operator. A similar process is in place in call centres today with typical control measures including the automatic measurement of call length against prescribed time, calls waiting to be answered, the abandoned call rate, the time taken to 'wrap up' and call availability. On top of this, calls are often recorded and remote monitoring takes place where managers check that the scripts are adhered to and customers are dealt with according to the rules (Boxell and Purcell, 2003). Whatever the system in force, employees working under a set of published performance targets and achievements will feel the control that is exercised over them.

Performance management also acts as a measure of the effectiveness or efficiency of the workforce, particularly where there are external or inter-unit comparisons. The strongest and the weaker performers can be readily identified; the strongest can be used as role models or utilised in training and the weaker employees helped to improve through coaching, training or discipline.

On the *cultural* side, the system can feature as part of the overall drive to build a more open relationship with employees. Organisation plans can be shared, appraisal discussions can be frank within a realistic context and means of improving performance can be encouraged and openly evaluated.

Moreover, because employees always have a higher motivation towards goals with which they agree or have had some input, the performance management system provides the opportunity for employees to have a voice in the process through the individual performance plan, in whatever form it is agreed.

Another important purpose is to endeavour to produce a system that is regarded as fair and equitable, especially in the rewards that emerge from the process. A well thought through performance management system should provide a defensible framework within which the many types of rewards can be allocated, rather than on the basis of personal whim or prejudice. Research carried out by the Local Government Management Board (LGMB, 1993) revealed that employees who work under a performance management scheme have an enhanced understanding of the needs and requirements of their job and have a higher 'feel-good' factor in relation to working for their organisation compared to those organisation where no such scheme is in place.

A further objective allied with fairness relates to dealing with areas of employee performance, which produce major concerns. Employees will not take kindly to criticism if they are unaware of the standards expected of them. It is certainly not possible to engage in disciplinary proceedings on performance that will be regarded as fair without having such standards in place.

All these reasons support the notion that an effective scheme embeds a culture for employees to focus on performance improvement, learning and development. An effective scheme will also add to the level of trust between employees and management as indicated by a research study summarised in Focus on research 8.1.

Focus on research 8.1

Performance management and level of trust

The researchers carried out a longitudinal survey of employee views of the trust for top management and their perceptions of the performance management scheme in a small, non-union, plastics manufacturing company in the American Midwest. A base line survey at the start of the programme was followed by two subsequent surveys between which time a new performance management scheme had been introduced. The major improvements were the inclusion of self-appraisal and an insistence that the discussions between an employee and their manager were centred on the specific behaviours and outcomes expected of the employees.

The results of the later survey showed that there was greater acceptance of the new scheme as one that was fairer and of more value. At the same time, the level of trust of senior management had risen, including the increased perception of management integrity.

Source: Mayer and Davis (1999)

What should the process be called?

Throughout this book, the word 'appraisal' has been kept at a distance. It has a degree of distaste to the writer being associated in the dictionary with the judging and valuing of objects, not people. It has a clear sense of being one way with the outcome being a label 'success' or 'failure'. There are some better names available.

Sainsburys call their process the 'Personal management Agenda', which sets in train the objective of performance improvement of all employees. Glaxo Wellcome encourage all their employees to develop their own 'Personal Fact file', which leads to the implementation of relevant personal development plans (PDPs). Many universities, including Luton, call their process by the more neutral name of 'Career Review'. A number of other organisations are starting to include the expression 'Employee Contribution' in the title of their scheme.

Focus on research 8.2

CIPD survey on performance management

A survey carried out by the CIPD in 2005 based on returns from 562 personnel practitioners found the following:

- 69% operated formal processes of performance management with a further 15% intending to introduce practices in the next 2 years.
- 85% of organisations operating performance management systems used objective setting, 68% used PDPs and 31% used competence assessment.
- 20% incorporated some form of subordinate feedback (180 degree) while 11% went further down this track by using 360 degree feedback.
- In terms of effectiveness, 75% considered that their objective setting system was either 'very effective' or 'mostly effective' while the figure for PDPs was 59%.
- Although 75% of respondents considered that it motivated individuals, 60% considered that it was bureaucratic and time consuming.
- 56% were proposing to make changes to their performance management system over the next 12 months.

Source: Armstrong and Baron (2005)

Stages in the performance management framework

Figure 8.2 (Armstrong, 2001) shows the various stages of the performance management framework and the key HR roles have been highlighted:

1 Establishing a performance agreement with each employee/ each team from which objectives and/or competency plans

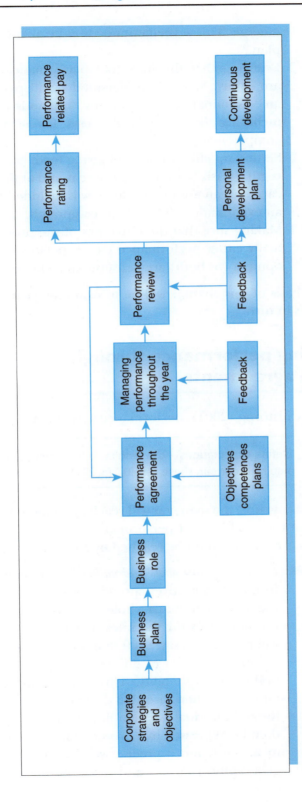

Figure 8.2
The performance management framework (*Source:* Armstrong, 1996a)

emerge. This agreement needs to be aligned with the business plan.

2 Ensuring that the ways that performance can be measured are robust, fair and understood by all parties. This includes an examination of various methods of measurement, including *Behaviourally Anchored Rating Scales* (BARS) and competencies.

3 Setting up effective ways of giving feedback to employees on a regular basis both during the year and at the year end. How to carry out an appraisal interview is included here together with an examination of 360 degree appraisal.

4 Making sure that the outcomes of the process, which are normally either performance pay or personal training and development (or both) are delivered in a fair and equitable way.

The basis of this chapter will be to examine each of these important stages in turn.

Stage 1: Raising performance through performance agreements

For Armstrong (2001), performance agreements:

> 'Define expectations – the results to be achieved and the competences required to attain these results.' (p. 237)

In other words, the manager will reach agreement with each employee on the required level of performance, and how it is to be measured. This agreement should be reached by a series of stages:

- *Ensure corporate goals and values are shared.* An employees' performance objectives should always be aligned with those of the organisation as a whole. This is best explained in terms of the objectives for the sales department. The corporate goal will be sales of, say, £100 million made up of a defined product mix (i.e. a set of different company products) that gave optimum profitability. This will be divided into divisional targets and then cascaded down eventually to the sales targets for an individual sales employee, say £500,000. The target will then be expressed in a product mix form and may be refined in an even more precise way in terms of monthly targets, geographical targets and new/existing customers. It is very important that the sales employee knows and understands how this target was reached and how it fits in with the corporate goals. If they were to sell in excess of £500,000 this may appear to be exceeding their target and be praiseworthy; but if this sales figure was made up of the wrong product mix it, it could affect the company's ability to make sufficient profit from the sales. The same principle applies in all employees' activities. They need to know what the company is trying to achieve and the part they have to play in the whole corporate plan. The role of HR is to ensure that the corporate goals and values (dealt with in Chapter 1) are widely disseminated and explained.

- *Agree an individual performance plan.* The plan for each employee needs to include a number of key features:
  - It must be integrated with the plan for the department.
  - It must go towards helping the individual to improve his or her own performance.
  - It must address any areas of concern regarding past performance.
  - It must clarify how the performance is to be measured.
- *Agree on how the performance is to be monitored, measured and evaluated.* The most important part of this process is choosing the most appropriate form of measurement out of the many available, both quantitative and qualitative, which will be discussed in the next section. The role of the manager, the employee and any third parties will need to be agreed as will the timing of meetings, both formal and informal, during the period in question.
- *Agree on help and assistance to achieve the targets set out in the plan.* Training and development will be important here and this can include internal and external courses, mentoring and coaching, periods of secondment to another department or role, work shadowing of senior colleagues and attendance at crucial meetings. Other resources need to be agreed, including staffing and budgetary issues.
- *Agree on the nature of the rewards available.* The plan will need to be quite clear on how the individual's pay will be influenced by the outcomes from the plan, whether promotion or any other career development issues are affected and in what way. Motivation towards achieving a successful outcome to the plan is dependent to a large extent upon how valuable are the rewards to the employee, including both extrinsic and intrinsic types of rewards.

Stage 2: Measuring performance

Inputs or outputs – objectives or competences?

Standards need to be developed in order to be able to measure performance. There are two main methods that are currently used for developing
the standards against which the employees' performance is measured.

The firstly method is by *establishing targets* for employees. These can
be quantified outputs or improvement targets or one-off targets relating to a particular project. They can also be standing targets dealing
with the day-to-day operations of the job. The second method is *to determine the level of competence* that the individual must achieve. Competencies will be dealt with in more detail in Chapter 10 but the main link
with performance is that they can be set out as required organisational
behaviours for which the employee should aim.

Both methods inevitably use some form of *rating scale*. With targets,
it may seem straightforward in that a target is either achieved or not
achieved. In reality, there are numerous situations where targets are
nearly achieved or not achieved due to certain extraneous factors. It is,
therefore, normal for the outcome of the exercise to be some form of
rating. With competencies, rather than measuring employees as competent or not competent, a rating scale is normally utilised, ranging
from 'not competent' through 'developing competence' and 'partly
competent' to 'fully competent'.

There is considerable controversy concerning the benefits and difficulties arising from both of these measures. In this section, a detailed
analysis will be given of each of these methods. The final part will
discuss and compare their benefits and the difficulties involved.

Establishing targets

There is a strong body of research which supports the theory that the
setting of goals leads to the overall performance improvement of the
employees concerned. Locke (1968) and Locke *et al.* (1989) provided
evidence that virtually any type of action that is able to be measured
and controlled can be improved as long as the goal is accepted by the
individual and the goal relates to the performance criteria being used.
Moreover, realistic, hard, specific goals produce better performance
than easy goals or no goals at all.

Goals and targets improve performance through four main mechanisms. They direct the attention of the employee to what needs to be

achieved, they mobilise the effort put in by the employee, they increase the persistence of the employee in their desire to reach the goal and get them to think carefully about the right strategies they need to employ to achieve the targets. A final point from Locke's research was that commitment to a goal can be considerably improved if employees participate in the goal-setting process.

These theories were integrated into an early form of target setting called 'Management by Objectives' (Humble, 1972) which was very influential in the UK in the 1970s. Under this system, the organisational targets were cascaded down the hierarchy so each manager had a set of targets to achieve. For a period of a few years, this method of management was seen as a panacea to the ills of British industry, but the system failed to produce the expected success. This was due to a number of external factors, specifically the appalling industrial relations of that period and the two oil crises of that decade which made any form of target setting extremely challenging.

To achieve the best results from an objectives-based system, there are a number of essential requirements:

- *Ensure that the targets set are in the SMART mode.* This acronym helps to set out the key features of a successful set of targets:
  - Firstly, they should be *specific* and *stretching*. *Specific* means that they are transparent and not open to dispute. To set *stretching* targets supports further aspects of Goal theory, which states that motivation and performance are higher when goals are difficult but accepted, support is given to achieve them and feedback is regular and valued.
  - Secondly, targets should be *measurable,* so that all sides can agree when they are achieved (or not). Measurable targets also make interim feedback so much easier.
  - Thirdly, targets should be *agreed* and *achievable.* If employees disagree with the targets because they find them too difficult to achieve, then they may well set out to prove this by determining to fail.
  - Fourthly, targets should be *realistic* and *relevant,* which makes them more attractive to all the parties.
  - Finally, they should be *time-related,* so that it is clear at what point they should be achieved.
- *Review the targets at regular intervals.* The external environment is constantly changing and the targets need to be adjusted to meet those changes. This is not to say that changes should be made each week or month but there can be no sacrosanct

target that will last for years. Organisational life is just not like that these days.

■ *Setting the right number of targets.* The right number of targets is difficult to judge. If an individual has a large number of targets, say 25 or 30, then the process of monitoring and measuring these targets would be insuperably complex. If there is only one target, then too much is at stake on this one target from the employee's viewpoint. Many organisations reach a compromise and provide for employees to have a minimum and maximum number of specific targets – usually from around 4–10. At Faberge's Seacroft site, employees have three main targets while, for AstraZeneca, employees can choose in the range of 3–7 (IDS, 2003).

The way that targets are set out can be in a number of forms. Sales employees will have a schedule, which will set out the target volume of sales and the ideal breakdown between products. Production employees will have a schedule of product throughput. Accounts employees will have a target of invoices to be issued or payments to be processed. The timing in a target may be of vital importance. In contracting, for example, if projects are late, then penalties are often incurred. Employees responsible for some part of a major project will themselves have very important deadlines as a target because, if they are late, then it can have a severe knock-on effect upon other parts of the project. At the time of writing, the many contractors involved in the new Wembley Stadium all have very clear time targets throughout their organisations as the fate of many sporting events rests on whether they meet their deadlines or not. On a less weighty note, the targets for a computer programmer may be to complete and test a new programme by Christmas or a HR manager's target may be to complete the recruitment for a new site by a specific date.

Figures 8.3 and 8.4 show two actual forms of target setting showing the difference approaches from two organisations in the public sector.

Targets can be also set for teams. The credit control department may have a target to reduce average payment time to a certain level (say, 20 days) within 6 months. The design team may have a target to produce a new product design within 6 months. An engineering department may have a target of a new factory layout designed, planned and implemented to be ready for operation at the end of the summer factory closure.

A more recent development has been the concept of the 'Balanced Scorecard' and an example of how this operates at Sainsburys is shown in Case study 8.1.

Figure 8.3
Performance targets
used in the
registration service
scheme
(*Source*: IDS Study
607 (August 1996,
pp. 23–24))

	Target
1	Ensure that a minimum of 79% of all visitors who come to register a birth or death or to give notice of intention to marry are seen within 30 minutes of arrival
2	Ensure that all responses to written requests for certificates and other information are despatched within 24 hours
3	Ensure that 95% of telephone calls are answered within five rings
4	Ensure that a minimum of 5000 historical records are entered on to the database each quarter
5	At least one customer-oriented quality suggestion to be provided at each monthly team meeting

Figure 8.3
Performance targets
used in the
registration service
scheme
(*Source*: IDS Study
607 (August 1996,
pp. 23–24))

Figure 8.4
Example of Technical
Objective, Dartford
Council
(*Source*: Internal
Dartford Council
documentation)

Target: SD4   *Directorship*: Development and Leisure

Target Title: Service Delivery
Target Description: CDM Regulations

1 Address requirements of Construction (Design and Management) Regulations 1994 (CDM) authority-wide in liaison with Drainage and Corporate Property by 1 July.

2 Prepare draft procedure documents for discussion by 1 April.

3 Prepare draft documents for Notification to Health and Safety Executive, Safety Plan format and Procedure Notes by 1 April.

Case study 8.1

Balanced Scorecard at Sainsburys

Sainsburys adopted the 'Steering Wheel' in the early 2000s as a method of measuring how well the organisation was performing and to communicate this in a direct but powerful way to employees. It was also linked to an individual's own performance. As shown in Figure 8.5, the performance measures are divided into four sectors, customers, finance, people and operations, as originally set out by Kaplan and Norton (1996). Within each sector, specific measurable objectives are defined with outcome communicated within the organisation on a regular basis. There are two development reviews, October for the half year and March for the full year, when the organisational performance is matched up with the individual's performance and a discussion takes place with

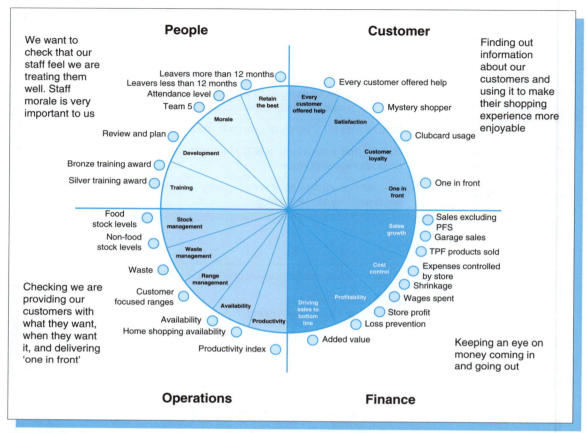

Figure 8.5
Balanced Scorecard at Sainsburys

the employee. Ratings are applied against the achievement of targets and the improvements in behaviours over the period and a 'pen sketch' results, dividing employees into six categories ranging from 'top' through 'strong', 'acceptable' to 'low'.

Linking the performance management scheme to the Balanced Scorecard is seen as essential to ensure each employee understands how their actions and achievements gell into the total organisational picture.

Competence-based systems

The competency movement has gathered strength in recent years, chiefly as a reaction to what is seen as the rigid, quantifiable, data-obsessed objectives methods. Encouraging the employee to adopt the behaviours required by the organisation and following the behaviours exhibited by high performers in the post are seen as a more coherent and broader approach to achieving improved employee performance.

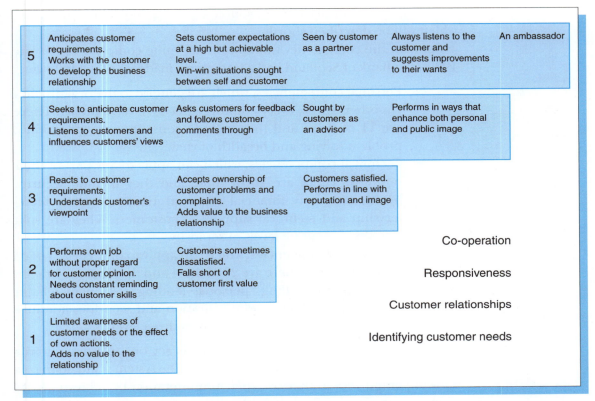

5	Anticipates customer requirements. Works with the customer to develop the business relationship	Sets customer expectations at a high but achievable level. Win-win situations sought between self and customer	Seen by customer as a partner	Always listens to the customer and suggests improvements to their wants	An ambassador
4	Seeks to anticipate customer requirements. Listens to customers and influences customers' views	Asks customers for feedback and follows customer comments through	Sought by customers as an advisor	Performs in ways that enhance both personal and public image	
3	Reacts to customer requirements. Understands customer's viewpoint	Accepts ownership of customer problems and complaints. Adds value to the business relationship	Customers satisfied. Performs in line with reputation and image		
2	Performs own job without proper regard for customer opinion. Needs constant reminding about customer skills	Customers sometimes dissatisfied. Falls short of customer first value		Co-operation	
				Responsiveness	
1	Limited awareness of customer needs or the effect of own actions. Adds no value to the relationship			Customer relationships	
				Identifying customer needs	

Figure 8.6
'The customer comes first' measurement grid

In Chapter 4, an example of drawing up a person specification around the required competencies was explained. It is a natural progression to measure employees' performance against those preferred competencies. The competencies, and the preferred behaviour that measures them, need to be drawn up.

Figure 8.6 shows an extract from the competency measures used in a telecommunication company. They developed a framework centred around their set of values, namely:

- The Customer comes first
- Total commitment to quality
- Teamwork makes a winning team
- Development of employee empowerment and responsibility
- Communication is open and honest.

The extract shown in Figure 8.6 relates to the value 'The customer comes first' and it shows the five levels, or ratings, that have been constructed against which employees can be judged. The judgements on the ratings are usually made by the employee's manager, although some organisations have a more sophisticated judgement process, involving a number of different sources, such as 360 degree appraisal, which will be described shortly.

Some of the competency frameworks are quite complex. In the late 1990s, the Bank of Scotland had a framework made up of the following:

- Personal competencies, which are generic to the organisation (in other words, every employee needs to have them). There are 11 of these and they include commitment, adaptability, problem solving and breadth of view.
- Technical competencies, which can apply to any part of their business. There are 26 of these and they include security, health and safety, financial administration, committee secretaryship and technical support to customers. They are split into three separate levels of seniority.
- Technical competencies, which can apply to only certain parts of the business. There are 20 of these and they include branch cash handling/telling, personal lending/risk management support, term deposit administration and securities administration. They, also, are divided into three levels.

Employees have a PDP where a pathway is set out to work towards achieving a number of these competencies. The system is linked to pay, allowing employees to increase their remuneration by achieving additional competencies (IDS, 1997b).

Timing of measurement

For each scheme, it is normal for there to be at least one main scheduled meeting when the manager will discuss the employee's performance with them in detail. Many organisations will incorporate two or more such meetings into their scheme as a year is seen to be too distant a time for discussion on such an important subject. At the Scottish Prison service, scheduled meetings take place twice a year while, for Microsoft, informal one-to-one meetings are encouraged much more often (IDS, 2003).

Which system is best? Target setting or competencies?

In terms of objectivity, it would appear that the target-setting approach wins hands-down. Targets are agreed and there should be a clear system of how they can be measured so there should be no argument or need to make judgements. Either the three-monthly sales target was met or the employee failed to meet it. Either the materials were sourced by the purchasing department and in place in the factory on time or they were late. But, as indicated earlier, it is seldom this easy. Here are a few situations that can cast cloud over the objectivity accolade:

- *Moving the goalposts.* The annual target for sales (part of the overall company business plan) is set in the light of a poor economic situation where sales are difficult to come by. As a sales representative, you work hard and, 6 months into the year, you are ahead of budget. As pay is partly determined by whether you are ahead of the target, you are feeling confident and pleased. The Board then announce a revised business plan on the basis that the economic situation is picking up. The sales target is then increased by 15%. From a position of being ahead of target, you are now only just up to the new target. The Board will argue that, if they do not increase the target, they will fall behind their competitors or give more pay to the sales force than they deserve in the light of the economic circumstances. You do not believe this is a fair move from your viewpoint.

- *Taking the goalposts away.* One of your major targets is to produce a revised working plan for the warehouse, which will involve increasing the number of shifts and introducing annual hours. This has to be completed within 6 months. After 3 months, you have worked hard and spent a lot of time on this project, with a revised system in draft form. The company then decide to sell the warehouse as part of a general re-structuring. You will get no credit for the work you have done.

- *Changing the rules of the game.* You run the credit control department and you are jointly charged with a systems analyst to introduce a new computerised system. Halfway through the period, the systems analyst leaves the company and a new one is assigned to the project. He has different views on a number of points (some of which are quite sensible) but these are not resolved in time to meet the deadline. You have failed on this target.

There are other criticisms of a system based solely on objectives/targets:

- *Are the objectives evenly matched?* It is all too easy for some employees to be seen as having 'soft' objectives, ones that are too easy to achieve, while others are set objectives that are too stretching. This may not occur too often in large departments, such as sales, where targets are similar (even so, difficulties can occur here). However, when employees all have different jobs, such as in an administrative setting, it is almost impossible to ensure that the objectives are of equal difficulty. The outcome is that some average employees with these soft objectives are considered high performers by the outcome of the scheme and, contrary-wise, some top performers come out with only average performance.

■ *Too narrow focused.* The individual may be tempted to put all their efforts into achieving their own objectives and treat the rest of their work as less important. After all, if they are to be measured on those specific objectives, this is a strong temptation. The outcome is that their work becomes unbalanced, important routine work can be neglected and unexpected problems may not be tackled with the required enthusiasm.

■ *Do they work against teambuilding?* An individual employee, focused on their objectives, will also be tempted to neglect other members of the team or other teams in the organisation. It is not uncommon for the employee to indicate 'I am sorry but I cannot help – I am too busy working on my objectives – I have a deadline'. This can have a severe effect upon both the short-term achievements, which can only happen when employees work together as a team (getting a contract completed on time, getting an complex order despatched to a customer) and upon the long-term culture of the organisation where team-working may be a required value.

■ *Is everything measurable?* Not all jobs have easily measurable objectives. Take HR, for example. Although examples can be given of reduced absence rates, recruitment on time, policy documents produced, training courses completed and reports that need to be completed, such as on exit interviews or comparative pay rates, it does not take too long before one may be scratching about for further significant objectives that go to the heart of one person's job. Much of HR activity relates to overall employee performance, attitudes, relationships and competencies, which are not too easy to measure, especially on the individual level.

In other occupations, considerable care has to be taken with what is measured. In the police force, you cannot measure on the basis of number of arrests. If you use the measure of clear-up rates, then you run the risk of repeating the scandal in one force in the mid-1990s who were found to have colluded with burglars to get them to admit to very high number of burglaries that they did not commit (in return for lower charges and sentences) so that the clear-up rate improved greatly.

(Incidentally, it was only when the number of identical burglaries continued and the real villains were apprehended by the police force in the next county that the fiddle came to light!) A final pause for thought: Would you like your operation to be carried out by a surgeon who is measured by the number of operations carried out?

Given these difficulties, should we not concentrate our energy on an effective competency framework? There are, unfortunately, difficulties here as well.

Rating problems

Even when systems are in place to assist managers to rate on a consistent basis (such as set out in Figure 8.6) managers may not keep to the straight and narrow:

- *Halo and horns effect.* Managers may rate employees on the basis of their personal relationships rather than by an objective measure of their competencies and abilities. Friendships may be regarded as too important to be spoilt by the harsh realities of a poor rating. On the other hand, a good performance can be ignored if an employee does not meet with the manager's overall approval.
- *Difficulty in damming people.* Even without personal prejudice, a good majority of managers do find it difficult to give their employees a bad rating. Having to face employees at an appraisal interview and justify their criticisms can be an experience that managers do not want to go through. It is much easier to simply give an average rating on the scale and hope the employee will improve anyway. This problem can also lead to *rating drift*, where managers are happy to raise the rating of their employees but never reduce the ratings, even when it is justified. Marshall and Wood (2000) describe a moribund system in the US Navy where a large proportion of the officers gave inflated ratings for their crew to secure promotion for their junior officers, to avoid potential conflicts with poor performing staff and to minimise the risk of being seen as a poor manager.
- *Recency error.* When coming to a decision on a rating on an annual appraisal, a manager may be too influenced by an event that happened a few days or weeks ago that are fresh in their minds. Let us take the example of an employee whose performance with customers had been far from satisfactory for most of the year. In the month before the appraisal, there

was a major achievement resulting in a letter of thanks from a customer. From the manager's viewpoint, it would be difficult and de-motivating to dwell on their generally unsatisfactory customer care competence and more tempting to concentrate on their recent success. However, this would result in putting the total rating out of balance.

- *Clone error.* A manager may regard the way they act and their methods of working to be the best practice. It is all too easy for employees who take a different approach to be rated lower, despite evidence that the differing methods work just as well.
- *Do competencies relate to performance?* There is much debate in academic circles as to the answer to this question. Is performance all about achievement of goals or can behaviour itself be regarded as a type of performance. An American psychologist, Campbell, for example, considered that:

'Performance is … defined as synonymous with behaviour.… By definition, it includes only those actions or behaviours that are relevant to the organisation's goals and that can be measured in terms of the individual's proficiency (that is, level of contribution).'

Campbell *et al.* (1993: p. 40)

In practice, however, there may be occasions where the two may not operate in tandem. Take the example of a credit control administrator. One major part of the job involves chasing up old debt by telephone. One of the competencies of the job would be 'customer relations'. The administrator may be have a very high rating with customer relations in that she builds up a rapport with the customer, treats them with respect and understanding and has good listening skills amongst other measures. But her job is to collect the overdue debt and, if her competence is too customer oriented, there runs the risk that the debt will not be paid.

There are also numerous examples of athletes who are extremely competent at their chosen expertise at a world-class performance level but who never manage to produce the results on the international stage.

Variations on rating systems

As the rating element of performance management is the most difficult area to get right, a number of variations have been produced to try to ensure that the system is fair, robust and more sophisticated.

	Points
Behavioural patterns	50 max
Consistently seeks to help others Tolerant and supportive of colleagues Contributes ideas and takes full part in group meetings Listens to colleagues Willing to change own plans to fit in	40
Keeps colleagues in the picture about own activities Mixes willingly enough	30
Is not aware of what colleagues are doing Inclined to alter arrangements to suit self	20
Always criticising others Lets everyone else do the more unpopular jobs	10
Never goes out of the way to help or co-operate	0

Figure 8.7
Example of BARS: teamwork dimension. (*Source*: Fletcher, 1997: p. 23)

Under BARS (Behavioural Anchored Rating Scales), a scale is established which reflects the dimensions expressed by employees' behaviour. An example of a scale is set out in Figure 8.7. The scale is normally drawn up in three stages. Firstly, examples of behaviour reflecting effective and ineffective job performance are obtained from people who are held to be expert about the job to be rated, which is then checked by a second group on the relevance of the behavioural examples within the dimension chosen (in this example, teamwork is the dimension). The experts then place each example of behaviour onto the scale. If the experts place the behaviour at different points on the scale, then this example is usually deleted because a high level of clarity and consensus is required. The advantage of the scheme is that the ratings are anchored against carefully agreed observed behavioural patterns. However, it does take considerable time and effort to draw up. Getting experts to agree upon the scale can be difficult, given the ultimately subjective nature of behaviour.

With *Behavioural Observation Scales (BOS)*, the end result is the same, with a series of performance dimensions linked to behavioural descriptions, but each example is given a separate rating and the overall rating is an average of the ratings. Extracting three examples from Figure 8.7, would give:

1 Consistently seeks to help others
Almost always   *1*   *2*   *3*   *4*   *5*   *Almost never*

2 Willing to change own plans to fit in
Almost always   *1*   *2*   *3*   *4*   *5*   *Almost never*

3 Volunteers for fair shares of unpopular work
Almost always   *1*   *2*   *3*   *4*   *5*   *Almost never*

Drawing a conclusion

In deciding on which system to use, objectives or competencies, organisations will be aware that both methods have clear advantages and benefits. It is no surprise, then to find that organisations are deciding to incorporate both sets of measurement in their performance management framework. Individuals have their job description or profile, which sets out their day-to-day responsibilities and accountabilities; they will also agree certain objectives for the period in question and they will also be measured against the competencies that apply to their job as part of the competence framework. By having both methods of measurement, the advantages of both are combined. On the other hand, it can lead to a performance management system that is complicated and difficult to grasp, especially for new employees.

Stage 3: Providing feedback

The third stage in the performance management process is to provide effective feedback to employees. There are two parts related to this process: firstly, deciding on what basis the feedback should be based and, secondly, how it should be carried out.

Feedback can be based on the traditional method of an assessment made by the employee's manager, augmented by a degree of self-assessment, and then given in a one-to-one meeting, commonly called the *appraisal* interview. In recent years, however, 360 degree appraisal has become increasingly popular where feedback is produced by a number of sources, including colleagues, subordinates, internal and external customers and then fed back to the employee. This normally takes place normally through a third party. We will look at both systems in turn.

Traditional appraisal interview

Moderating process

Most organisation, although delegating the rating process to the line managers, will build in a system of moderation whereby the results are considered as a whole by the next level of management. The HR department, as a disinterested third party, will often assist in tricky umpiring decisions.

Documentation

Every scheme has to have some type of form, which will record an individual's performance as related to the way they are measured. A major drawback for many schemes is that these forms are sometimes lengthy and complicated; it is not unknown for some long-established schemes to have as many as 10 pages to be completed. Although they are designed to be comprehensive and give support to the process, the parties concerned, especially the managers who may have to complete them for up to 20 employees, often baulk at having to fill them in.

The forms should therefore be as simple and short as is consistent with the nature of the scheme with all superfluous information or sections ruthlessly extracted. The emphasis should always be on the form being a working document, to be constantly updated and the basis of a number of informal meetings during the period concerned. It should not simply, when completed, be sent to the HR department for filing, although they may need a copy if decisions on pay are related to the individual's performance.

An example of the documentation for one rating scale for competencies is in Figure 8.8. In this banking example, negative and positive indicators are given with clear instructions on a marking key to assist in the rating process.

A simpler version, used by a local council catering division and called a 'job chat' is shown in Figure 8.9.

The performance review interview

Under most performance management systems, a time is set aside for the employee and manager to have an extended discussion, which reviews the past period and agrees plans for the next period. The period in question is usually a year but some organisations have decided that the process is so important that it needs to take place twice or four times a year. It is not an easy job to carry out. According to Longenecker and Gioia (1988) in their American study, less than 20% of appraisal interviews were carried out effectively.

In carrying out the interview, there are many similarities with the selection interviewing guidelines set out in Chapter 5. The same principles apply of careful preparation, effective listening and questioning, together with efficient note-taking and following up. The major differences relate to dealing with areas of unsatisfactory performance and handling areas of disagreement. More important is the fact that the interview is with an employee where there is a continuing relationship

Managers and Appointed Staff competencies Sheet 1

Name of Member of Staff:
Branch/Department:

Period _____ to _____ 19 _____

Marking Key: (Please mark the appropriate box like this ▨)

1 **Frequently fails** to display the appropriate qualities and attitudes.
2 **Occasionally fails** to display the appropriate qualities and attitudes.
3 **Generally displays** the appropriate qualities and attitudes to a satisfactory level.
4 **Occasionally displays** above average qualities and attitudes.
5 **Frequently displays** the appropriate qualities and attitudes to a high level.
6 **Consistently displays** the appropriate qualities and attitudes to the highest level.

Voluntary Self Appraisal: The appropriate mark 1 to 6 may be inserted in each self appraisal box.

Competency	Negative indicators	Marking	Positive indicators
Strategic Awareness – The extent to which the appraisee is aware of the Bank's competitive situation, is able to recognise business opportunities and threats and can relate these wider issues to own area of responsibility	• Out of touch with strategic events and their results • Infrequently identifies competitive opportunities and threats • Sees own work in isolation from the wider context	1 2 3 4 5 6 Self Appraisal Mark	• Clearly aware of strategic events occurring outside and inside the Group • Identifies competitive opportunities and threats • Sees how own work fits into the wider context
Initiative – The extent to which the appraisee will promote proactively and take personal responsibility for the achievement of goals and changes which are beneficial to the Group	• Takes a rigid and narrow view of own responsibilities • Conforms to established ways of doing things without identifying improvements • Tends to resist change or gives little help to those initiating change	1 2 3 4 5 6 Self Appraisal Mark	• Expands own responsibilities to seek business opportunities • Identifies ways of improving the way work is done • Takes the action needed to ensure that changes happen
Decisiveness – The readiness to take decisions and render judgements even though they may be difficult and/or unpopular	• Reluctant to take decisions; will disown decisions • Unable to explain or justify decisions • Gives way too easily when pressurised or dogmatically supports decisions that cannot be defended	1 2 3 4 5 6 Self Appraisal Mark	• Makes decisions and takes responsibility for their results • Easily explains and justifies decisions • Reviews a decision if new information makes this essential
Technical knowledge and experience – The degree to which the appraisee demonstrates breadth and depth of technical knowledge and experience in the performance of his/her duties	• Shows little evidence of technical expertise in performance • Content to rely on basic knowledge, makes little effort to keep abreast of technical developments • Unable to apply technical knowledge and experience in practical situations	1 2 3 4 5 6 Self Appraisal Mark	• Possesses a high level of technical expertise and experience relevant to present duties • Keeps abreast of relevant technical development • Applies technical knowledge and experience to enhance job performance

Initials	
Reporting Manager	Appraisee

Figure 8.8
Competency rating scales at a clearing bank (extract)

SHIRE COUNTY CATERING

JOB CHAT SUMMARY FORM – Example

DATE OF JOB CHAT: _____

EMPLOYEES NAME: *Jane Smith**   SCHOOL: *ABC Primary*
JOB TITLE: *Head of Kitchen*   SCHOOL NUMBER: *40006*
LENGTH OF SERVICE: *3 years*   NAME OF INTER VIEWER: *Teresa Brown*
NO. OF HOURS PER WEEK: *25*   POSITION: *Contract Supervisor*

JOB STANDARDS:

(PLEASE TICK)	MEETS OR EXCEEDS STANDARDS	ROOM FOR IMPROVEMENT
SKILLS AND KNOWLEDGE TO ACHIEVE DUTIES		/
MANAGES WORK SCHEDULE	/	
QUALITY OF WORK	/	

COMMENTS:

Jane is a new Head of Kitchen, been in post 4 months. She lacks confidence to try out new ideas. Manages existing work schedule, but would like to develop the menu range. Very good relationship with staff.

TRAINING AND DEVELOPMENT:

DEVELOPMENT AREAS IDENTIFIED: *Requires confidence building*
                                  Needs to broaden knowledge on SCC standards

TRAINING AND DEVELOPMENT NEEDS FOR NEXT 12 MONTHS:- *attend Practical skills course (M)*
      (INDICATE HIGH, MEDIUM OR LOW PRIORITY) *Visit 2 other school sites (H)*

CAREER PROGRESSION:- *Happy at present*

COMMENTS:

Jane felt she could have had more support moving from G.A. to H. of K. position. Perhaps a weekly visit from the Contract Supervisor for the first month.

SIGNATURE OF EMPLOYEE: *Jane Smith*

SIGNATURE OF INTERVIEWER: *T. Brown*

*Not a real employee

Figure 8.9
'Job chat' summary form

and where comments, statements and decisions made can have an enduring effect upon that relationship. So it is even more important that the interview is handled well.

Before the interview

As a basis for the interview, it is customary for both parties to complete one part of the documentation. For the manager, the form will ask for an examination of the employee's performance against the agreed measures and to point out any important areas of success and failure. This will include ratings, where appropriate. The employee will be asked their views on the same subjects with an opportunity for comments on factors that may have influenced their performance over that period. Employees are usually asked to assess and rate (where appropriate) their own performance. Both parties may be asked to consider any necessary training, development and support plus consideration of general career development.

The interview itself

The purpose of the interview is often forgotten. It is sometimes seen as a combat, where the contestants, armed with their data, examples, accusations and excuses, fight to the finish to try to win their point of view. This is all too prevalent where pay increases are largely determined by the outcome of the interview. At the other extreme, it can be seen as something of an embarrassment, where both sides have a tentative discussion but neither wants to risk their current placid relationship by drawing out any unpleasant truths. In the IPD research (Armstrong and Baron, 1998), 31% of individual employees reported that they did not get useful feedback from their interview and 38% were not motivated by the meeting. Over a quarter reported dissatisfaction with the way their manager carried out the meeting. From the other side of the table, 20% of managers reported they were not comfortable when conducting the meetings.

It is important from the outset to agree what the meeting is for and what will be the satisfactory outcomes. These can be summed up as:

- Agreement on the level of performance achieved.
- Agreement on the factors that influenced this level of performance.
- Outline agreement on the challenges/targets for the next period.
- Agreement on what support needs to be arranged for the employee.

In Figure 8.8, this is set out in diagram form with some of the major elements skills emphasised. Here, it is vital to get the employee to recognise their own strengths and weaknesses. The self-assessment form and a review of the agreed action at the time of the last review are good starting points. However, it is the quality of the questioning and listening skills that are essential to draw out a full understanding and agreement of the difficult areas. Questions here could include:

1 Do you think you could handle this situation any better when you face it again?
2 In your involvement with this project, would you have done it any differently with the benefit of hindsight?
3 The figures for Smith and Jones appear to be rather better than yours; are there any reasons for this?
4 This was clearly a difficult area for you; what help would you need for the next period?

Where differences of opinion exist, specifically on the performance ratings, then time must be given for effective feedback and discussion. The feedback from the manager must be first and foremost based on the facts of the situation, accurately described, not an arbitrary judgement. It should be related to specific behaviour, not impressionistic generalisations. It should be on the basis of presenting the problem and trying to ensure that this problem is solved on a joint basis. It should also be recognised by the manager that a long list of problem areas is truly demoralising for the employee, so only the major two or three difficulties should be detailed or it will result in the employee becoming over-defensive and putting up the shutters. The manager should also accept some of the reasons put forward by the employee, even if they appear doubtful, so that it is clear to the employee that their case has been listened to and not simply shot down in flames.

The interview should not be limited to areas of difficulty. Where the employee has made a substantial contribution or a major improvement, this should be fed back in congratulatory mode. To reinforce this positive feedback, suggestions should be considered as to how this could be followed up. For example, the employee may be asked to coach an inexperienced colleague in this area or to take some part in a training exercise. It is particularly helpful to express appreciation where tasks have not come easily and where the employee has put in considerable effort in their own time.

The interview should be completed by an agreed summary of the conclusions reached and an action plan for the future, which includes the major changes in the employee's responsibilities, the additional areas of help they will be given (training, time and resources) and a time span for implementation. This should be confirmed on the review form and signed by both parties with each having a copy.

This prescriptive approach is rarely followed by organisations with the result that most managers and subordinates dislike the appraisal interview, especially when it contains negative features in the feedback (Lawler, 1990) and few employees concede that they gain much benefit at all from the interview (Bradley and Ashkanasy, 2001). This has disappointed most human research practitioners and researchers, who have looked for a more radical method of operating a performance management system, such as 360 degree appraisal.

360 degree appraisal

Traditional appraisal schemes suffer from one major problem. If there is a difference of opinion as to the employee's performance that cannot be resolved between the manager and the employee, then the basis of the whole performance management process is undermined. Let us take a simple example where a switchboard operator is rated as below average on the measure of 'co-operation'. The manager puts forward examples on which her rating is based but, despite a long discussion, the employee regards these as isolated and atypical examples. The switchboard operator is convinced that the manager's opinion is wrong because nobody has complained to them. She is upset by the rating and convinced that it is unfair. The rest of the interview takes place under an atmosphere of resentment and resignation.

In this example, the manager will have to make the judgement as to co-operation largely based on information that comes from third parties because the manager's own experience of the employee's co-operative behaviour may well be very limited. This is not unusual. Many employees provide a service for other departments and external customers and their managers only have a rough snapshot of how they are actually performing. They may base their opinion of anecdotal evidence, good and bad, gathered from a limited number of sources in an unsystematic way.

This is where 360 degree appraisal comes in. Through obtaining information from a variety of sources, a more all-round version of an employee's performance can be gathered together and the information, because it comes from a number of sources, is more convincing to all parties. A second influence has been more subtle. Organisations are starting to talk about being 'feedback-rich', which has been part of the cultural change from being a 'command and control' structure to

Command and control	Support and enable
Set clear targets	Agree clear targets, working parameters
Give instructions	Consult
Check work	Discuss performance
Identify deviations	Jointly identify difficulties
Correct deviations	Coach and guide to solving deviations
Give criticisms	Provide balanced feedback
Organise	Encourage self-management
Plan schedules	Create an environment where employees are motivated
Task review	People review

Figure 8.10 Cultural approaches to performance management (*Source*: France, 1997)

one that is based on 'support and enable' concepts. Figure 8.10 shows the typical skill sets required for effective performance management under the two different cultures.

It is now commonplace for organisations to carry out customer care surveys (to see where strengths and weaknesses of the whole company operations lie from a customer's viewpoint) and employee attitude surveys (to identify how well employees are managed and valued). It is just one more short step, therefore, to carry out a survey of an individual's performance as seen by a wider strand of customers.

Is this the right name?

The name-tag has been fixed to this system because of the familiarity of the word 'appraisal', but organisations who dislike the association of the word 'appraisal' have changed the title to Team feedback, 360 degree review or multi-level assessment.

How does it work?

There are many versions currently operating and there are aspects that are much debated but the general process is as follows:

■ *Is it carried out for all employees?* Most organisations start the process at the top. Rhone-Poulenc, a French water company, centred their first system on their 60 senior managers before it was spread further down the organisation (Jacobs and Floyd, 1995). By starting at the top, it sends a message to the rest of the organisation that there is serious intent behind the initiative.

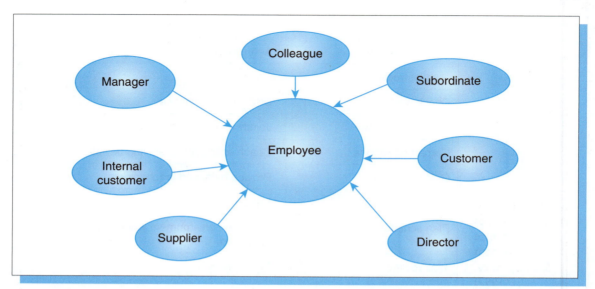

Figure 8.11
Sources of feedback

- *Agreement on the sources of feedback.* It is useful to have as many sources of feedback as possible but the cost of processing is quite high, so a balance has to be reached. Between six and nine sources is the norm (see Figure 8.11). The method of selection can vary between the employee concerned selecting their own sources, having their sources selected for them or a compromise whereby the employee selects the required number from a list of 25 or so sources prepared by those organising the scheme. The list should always include the immediate manager, and representatives from subordinates, peers and customers. In WH Smith's first scheme, there were eight sources for each manager (Thatcher, 1996).

- *Should the scheme be voluntary or compulsory?* It is generally voluntary because this accentuates the culture of openness and responsibility. In reality, it is likely that there will be internal pressures brought to bear on those who do not volunteer, especially if the scheme starts to obtain good results.

- *What form do the reports take?* They vary only slightly from the conventional performance management documentation but, in the interests of objectivity and ease of processing, most simply ask for ratings, rather than individual comments. An exception to this, a peer assessment by Eastern Group, which asks for specific examples, is given in Figure 8.12. The forms

EASTERN GROUP p/c

NAME OF PERSON BEING ASSESSED

Peer Assessment

MIDDLE MANAGEMENT COMPETENCIES

Try to complete this form as honestly as you can. If you wish, you can use the spaces below each category to provide further evidence to support your assessment

The three columns should be interpreted as follows:

ALREADY A STRENGTH – refers to an area in which you feel the person being assessed is already competent and has no strong development need.
NOT A PRIORITY DEVELOPMENT NEED – refers to an area which, although perhaps not a strength, is not – given the nature of his/her job or its current demands – a particular priority for development.
IDENTIFIED DEVELOPMENT NEED – refers to an area in which, in your view, the person is not particularly strong and needs to develop significantly.

1. MANAGING CHANGE	ALREADY A STRENGTH	NOT A PRIORITY DEVELOPMENT NEED	IDENTIFIED DEVELOPMENT NEED
Communicates openly, clearly and often with those affected by and involved in change so that all are aware of the reasons for change, its aim and progress			
Agrees a course of action to achieve new or changed long-term goals			
Agrees intermediate goals, performance measures and contingencies			
Allocates resources effectively to achieve goals			

Can you think of any specific examples of behaviour in support of the assessment you have made within this competency area?

Figure 8.12
Example of competences at Eastern Group

are generally completed on an anonymous basis although this is limited by the method of choice of the respondents.

■ *How is the feedback given?* This is an area that differs most from the conventional process. The information from the respondents needs to be processed anonymously to give some average scores. This processing can be carried out by the HR department or by a third party which is normally a specialised consultancy. Feedback is then given by that third party to the employee. Some of the information provided in this way can be quite disturbing, so it needs to be handled by a trained facilitator who will then proceed to help the employee develop their own PDP. This was the arrangement arrived at by Northumbrian water when they introduced the scheme in 1993 (Dugdill, 1994). A summarised version of the report may be given to the employee's manager so that an interview can be carried out after a reasonable delay to allow the employee to take on board the information and the consequent behaviour changes that may be required.

A more informal process of 360 degree feedback has been used at the Department for Environment, Food and Rural Affairs, called the 'Pairing for performance' scheme. Here, 12 managers have been each 'paired' with a volunteer member of their staff and the 'buddy', as they are called, provides detailed feedback on the performance of the manager at meetings, visits, telephone call and e-mails in a candid, but constructive way. This helps them to reflect on their performance, their preparation, outlook and communication skills. In the public sector, such feedback culture is not common but it has helped both sides to identify and operate better (Allen, 2004).

How AstraZeneca have introduced a form of 360 degree feedback is shown in Case study 8.2.

Case study 8.2

360 degree feedback at AstraZeneca

360 degree feedback was introduced in the late 1990s in the Zeneca division, arising from a decision to encourage self-development at every level in the organisation. The company had always believed that people development was critical for business success but it realised that the culture needed to alter to one that was much more feedback-rich

to ensure that feedback was an integral part of every personal develop-ment and management training programme.

It was launched in 1996, following a successful pilot programme with 10 senior managers in the pharmaceutical business team. One thou-sand managers attended three workshops over the period of a year, bringing to the second workshop feedback from at least four colleagues and subordinates from which they had worked out a PDP. The process was totally open, the feedback givers identified themselves and the workshop participants were encouraged to explore generally issues aris-ing from the process as well as those affecting their own programme.

This open, informal and unsophisticated approach proved so popular that it was expanded to most managers, supervisors and technical staff. Feedback is now obtained on one sheet of paper, based on behaviours derived from Zeneca's key competency framework. It is collated by the team facilitator, who is trained in the process, brings in other feedback from additional stakeholders and then the information is shared with the individual and the team. The individuals themselves declare to the team the actions they will work on. No central records are kept because the HR department regard it as a personal development issue and because pay is not dependent on any improvement outcomes. A greater empha-sis is now made on face-to-face feedback, rather than form filling and this has helped to develop a greater degree of trust and openness.

Source: Chivers and Darling (1999)

Advantages of 360 degree schemes

- The quality of the feedback is high, emanating from a number of sources. Those providing the information are quite likely to be part of the process and to know how crucial it is to be absolutely honest – not to be unpleasantly vindictive and not to simply give neutral responses if they are not appropriate.
- All the experience to date is that employees are more likely to change their behaviour on receiving the results from a collec-tion of sources. They change because they cannot argue with the findings.
- As managers find the traditional appraisal interview difficult to undertake (managers, apparently, prefer dental appoint-ments to playing 'God' in the appraisal interview according to Edwards (1989)) and we have seen how difficult the process is to get right, then 360 degree appraisal will allow such discus-sions to be carried out on a more even basis.

■ It is a strong indication to employees that the performance management is being taken seriously and encourages a feed-back-rich culture to develop with employees at all levels sharing advice on 'How did I do?' or 'Tell me how to improve'.

■ Even skeptical academics seem to find that it works, as shown in Focus on research 8.2.

Disadvantages

■ A report from Ashridge Research (Handy *et al.*, 1998) indicated that 50% of the 45 companies operating such a scheme found that the process was time consuming and expensive.

■ If it works well and is extended to most groups of employees, then the demands on the sources will be very large. A single source may have to provide as many as six or eight feedbacks, which could lead to feedback 'overload'.

■ There are some questions that the sources of feedback may find difficult to answer, especially those related to the employee's achievement of their objectives.

■ It is more difficult (but not impossible) to link employee's pay to the process. The sources of the feedback may be more reticent with their information if they know that criticism can lead to a reduced pay increase.

Research into manager's views of upward appraisal is detailed in Focus on research 8.3.

Focus on research 8.3

360 degree feedback at the Open University

During the late 1990s, the Open University initiated a 360 degree programme, which was competency based. Those managers choosing to take part received training on the aims of the programme, detailed feedback from their colleagues on their ratings on competencies, tuition on learning styles as well as one-to-one assistance with the design and implementation of their PDP. Using both interviews and questionnaires, the views of the 200 managers who took part in the 360 degree systems was compared with a similar sample of managers who participated in the traditional appraisal system.

The results indicated a widespread satisfaction with 360 degree feedback with significantly higher mean scores from participants in areas such as:

- Appraisals help my career development.
- I get regular feedback on performance.
- I am satisfied with the quality and relevance of training.
- The best uses are made of my skills.

Many examples were given of managers addressing weaknesses highlighted by 360 degree process, making progress in areas of personal development and receiving positive feedback from colleagues as a result. Moreover, the positive experience from the scheme led to more favourable assessments of the organisation as a whole.

It was considered that participants appreciated the organisational commitment to developing managers, enjoyed the opportunity for careful diagnosis and tailored, more meaningful training and heightened their awareness of the organisation's strategic intent.

Source: Mabey (2001)

An American research project found that the performance of managers improved after the introduction of a 360 degree system, especially where the subordinates ratings were lower than those of the self-ratings by the managers (Smithers *et al.*, 1995).

360 degree feedback is used by 14% of UK organisations (Armstrong and Baron, 2005).

Stage 4: The outcomes from the performance management process

There are two major outcomes, which follow from an effective performance management system: Rewards and Development.

Rewards

We will be looking much more closely at the financial rewards that are based on an employee's performance in Chapter 9. However, the intrinsic rewards of being recognised and congratulated for the good work that has been carried out are a very powerful and effective motivator, as Hertzburg (1968) first pointed out. There are also *negative* rewards in that performance data can be the basis of disciplinary proceedings or an important part of the criteria for choosing employees to be made redundant.

Development

Development can take two forms. The first is career development, where performance data can influence, often decisively, promotion decisions. The second is a PDP for the employee to help those areas where performance is weak. In other words, the performance management system acts as a training needs analysis. There has been a substantial increase in the use of PDPs over the last 20 years (Armstrong and Barron, 1998) as organisations recognise the need to continually follow up the performance management process and support the employee's development on a permanent basis.

Can the two outcomes clash?

There is considerable debate currently on the issue of whether to mix the planned outcomes of a performance management system. Foot and Hook (1999), for example, are quite adamant that:

> 'It is difficult, if not impossible, to devise a scheme that will appraise successfully all ... areas and there is a grave danger that the scheme will be rejected if it fails to live up to all that is claimed for it.'
>
> Foot and Hook (1999: p. 229)

There is always the danger that an employee will be unwilling to admit to development needs if this could lead to a lower rating and a consequent smaller salary increase. Without an honest and open discussion, many development needs may not come out into the open and this could affect the future performance of the employee.

On the other hand, it would be unusual, to put it mildly, if all the information gained from an effective system does not affect decisions on pay. Given that most organisations now operate a pay system that rewards higher performance in some way, it could be regarded as rather irrational to give the same pay increase to two employees, having identified that one employee performs considerably better than another, or to base pay increases decisions on a totally different system.

Operational issues

There are some final issues to clarify in respect of initiating and implementing a performance management scheme.

The need to consult

It is clear that the performance management is central to the way an organisation and its employees operates, so it is vital that all concerned understand the underpinning objectives of the scheme and how it should work in practice. Opportunities should therefore be provided for consultation with all stakeholders (managers, employees, unions and staff representatives) before a new scheme is launched. Meetings, focus groups and attitude surveys are all ways that this consultation could be carried out.

Training for participants

It is not sufficient to simply send round the organisation a printed guide to operating the scheme. Training for participants is essential. Nor is not just managers who need training for it is a joint process between managers and their staff. Some organisations have developed joint workshops for departments who role-play appraisal interviews, often with managers and departmental staff reversing their positions.

Teams or individuals

In the IPD report, Armstrong and Baron (1998) pointed out a general lack of interest in performance management for teams. This was remarkable, especially in the light of the attention currently given in most organisations to improving the quality of teamwork. If the performance management system is to reflect organisational priorities, it is important to consider ways that teamworking can be incorporated into a performance management framework. This can be through team targets, joint team appraisal interviews or applying teamworking as a core competence.

Student activity 8.1

Consider the roles that can be played by the HR department in the performance management process.

Discussion of Student activity 8.1

In your answer, you may have produced some of the following actions:

- Evaluating the current scheme and reporting on its strengths and weaknesses.
- Working with the Board to identify an outline performance management framework where vital business objectives can be cascaded through the organisation and key competencies developed.
- Designing an outline scheme and carrying out a full consultation process with all of the stakeholder groups.
- Agreeing a final approved scheme including revisions arising from the consultation and producing an information pack to all involved.
- Setting up a training programme for participants.
- Designing and producing the necessary paperwork.
- Coaching management in operating the scheme effectively.
- Monitoring the scheme's progress in terms of timing and quality of outcome.
- Acting in an overall moderating role, where decisions on pay are made arising out of the scheme to ensure consistency and fairness.
- Assisting in implementation of decisions on development and promotion.
- Evaluating the overall progress of the scheme.

Conclusion

Apart from the success of 360 degree feedback, it has been a theme of this chapter that performance management is difficult to devise, impossible to operate without severe problems, and normally received badly or, at best, indifferently, by employees. This would be too gloomy a prognosis overall. In fact, commentators such as Redman (2001) are far more optimistic, reporting from a major study in the health service (Redman *et al.*, 2000) that employees value the appraisal system and would hate it to be discarded. He quotes evidence that employers who have used appraisal for longer periods report fewer problems.

Without some system of performance management, it is highly unlikely, in all but the smallest organisations, that the performance of employees is going to improve or that employees will be given the opportunity to develop and progress. Certainly, some secure platform on which to base pay increases is vital. Although the problems are persistent and endemic, they are not completely unsurmountable.

Meteor case study

It was time for Sarah's own performance review meeting. She remembered, with horror, the appraisal interview in her previous organisation, where she was faced with a completed set of subjective ratings, a fixed 30 minute slot and an old-style manager who opened up the session with the comment 'we haven't a lot of time so I hope we don't have the same old irrelevant arguments as we've had in the past'. She co-operated by withdrawing from real discussions, accepting faint praise where it was due, closing her mind to the unjust criticism and identifying her own agenda for self-improvement, part of which was to move to a new company!

The meeting had been prefaced by a series of informal discussions during the year where progress on a number of projects was reviewed and developmental issues addressed openly. So Sarah did not expect too many surprises from the review meeting nor, as it turned out, did she receive any. By agreement, the meeting with Scott took place on a Saturday morning at a local training centre they had often used, so there could be no interruptions or time restraints. Sarah had completed her self-assessment the week before and given it to David. The scheme combined a set of objectives with a focus on key competencies attached to her role and she believed that she had achieved five of the six objectives and had made progress in improving her skills and competencies with one or two exceptions.

The meeting opened with a discussion of the overall progress of the department over the year – its influence and a review of its major initiatives. Scott gave Sarah a report of the department's ratings, based on a recent internal management service survey, which indicated satisfaction in most areas, except in achieving results on time. He indicated his pleasure at the success in the recruitment and selection areas, where the teams that Sarah had helped recruit appeared to be gelling well and bringing in excellent results. The introduction of assessment centres had been seen as especially successful by the managers participating. In terms of competencies, her communications skills were highly praised, both in writing reports, briefing documents and policies and also in giving presentations (David reported that her talk to senior management on the assessment centre outcomes had been highly commended). She was a valued member of the team and showed strong co-operation and innovative abilities.

Scott then raised the issue of completing projects on time, mentioning a degree of surprise and disappointment over the overrun of the project to revise the performance management system itself. Sarah was herself disappointed at this, explaining that much of this was due to the dispute in the managers' focus group between the majority who wanted to extend the 360 degree feedback and a vociferous minority who were strongly against such a move. As co-ordinator of the project, she did not feel able to over-rule the minority so a further set of meetings were arranged over several weeks where progress was achieved, although it was slow. She realised that this did not obtain the right result.

Scott then led into a detailed discussion on her influencing skills, getting her to talk frankly about how she dealt with opposition and dispute. She agreed that she did not find it easy to handle, taking some of it as a personal criticism and leading to a tendency to retreat into submission. Scott presented the view that some managers considered her not sufficiently tough or decisive enough on occasions. It was agreed that she needed to develop her skills in this area, and she was asked to talk to training colleagues about courses in this area. He would do the same, with a view to her attending an external course within the next 3 months plus a follow-up after a further 6 months. It was also fixed for her to spend a couple of days in the next few months work shadowing a consultant (an ex-colleague of Scott) to observe the skills exercised in this area.

They went on to spend time agreeing her overall ratings and then Scott listened to her feedback on their own relationship. Sarah had not felt comfortable in this part of the session in the previous year but she had gained some confidence in the relaxed atmosphere and raised two issues which had annoyed her, namely the lack of inclusion in an crucial departmental strategy meeting and the continuous urgency attached to certain issues by Scott. The first was settled by explanation of the special circumstances of which she was unaware and the second was integrated with the issue of decisiveness discussed earlier. The review ended with a planning session for the next 12 months, a discussion of the possible future long-term promotion plans and the likely salary implications of this review. Scott made it clear that her performance and level of commitment was very strong and he was gratified to see the good progress. But future progress up the HR ladder did require development in the areas discussed.

Sarah left the meeting feeling pleased, if rather drained by the intense, yet relaxed discussions. She realised that her good work was recognised, that she was making progress and was content that the criticisms of her were made in a constructive, positive and supportive way.

Summary

- An organisation is judged by its performance, so setting, measuring and monitoring employee performance are substantial HR activities.
- A performance management scheme can be a major aid to change management, both in operating and cultural terms.
- There are four stages to performance management, namely, entering into a performance agreement with the employee, designing robust measures of performance, ensuring effective feedback to the employee takes place and agreeing the outcomes of the process in developmental and/or reward terms.
- Measures can be based on either objectives or competencies or a combination of both.
- Performance normally has to be rated in some way, and this presents considerable difficulties to be overcome.
- Feedback can be on the basis of top-down or 360 degrees, which is feedback from different sources.

Student activities

1 Moving the goalposts, taking the goalposts away and changing the rules of the game can all present difficulties. Take each of these situations in turn and present arguments from the viewpoint of both the organisation and the individual employee as to how they should be resolved fairly and efficiently.

2 Imagine yourself to be a manager at Sainsburys (Case study 8.1) at the meeting where the scheme is being explained. Make a list of questions that you would want to ask to satisfy yourself that the scheme is fair and worthwhile.

3 In the Meteor case study, what were the key aspects of the meeting that left Sarah satisfied and enthusiastic?

4 Set up a debate between yourself and three other colleagues with two of you arguing in favour of your pay being affected by the performance management scheme and the other two arguing that it should only be used to help your personal development.

5 Consider the advantages and difficulties of using the Natwest competence form from the viewpoint of the manager and the person being appraised.

6 Read the article on which Focus on research 8.3 is based and give your views on what difficulties could be faced by introducing 360 degree feedback at a University.

References

Allen, D. (2004) Two's company, *People Management*, 15 January, 41–42.

Armstrong, M. (2001) *Human Resource Management Practice*. Kogan Page.

Armstrong, M. (2002) *Employee Reward*. CIPD.

Armstrong, M. and Baron, A. (1998) *Performance Management – The New Realities*. CIPD.

Armstrong, M. and Baron, A. (2005) *Managing Performance*. CIPD.

Boxell, P. and Purcell, J. (2003) *Strategy and Human Resource Management*. Palgrave.

Bradley, L. and Ashkanasy, N. (2001) Formal performance appraisal interviews – can they really be objective and are they useful anyway? *Asia Pacific Journal of Human Resources*, **39**(2): 83–97.

Campbell, J., McCloy, R., Oppler, S. and Sager, C. (1993) A theory of performance. In: Schmitt, N., Borman, W.C. and Associates (eds). *Personnel Selection in Organisations*. Jossey-Bass.

Chivers, W. and Darling, P. (1999) *360 Degree Feedback and Organizational Culture*. CIPD.

Dugdill, G. (1994) Wide angle view. *Personnel Today*, 27 September, 31–32.

Edwards, M. (1989) Making performance appraisals meaningful and fair. *Business*, July–September, 17–26.

Fletcher, C. (1997) *Appraisal: Routes to Improved Performance*. IPD.

Foot, M. and Hook, C. (1999) *Introducing Human Resource Management*. Longman.

France, S. (1997) *360 Degree Appraisal*. Industrial Society.

Handy, L., Devine, M. and Heath, L. (1998) *360 degree feedback: unguided missile or powerful weapon?* Ashridge Management College Occasional Paper.

Hertzberg, F. (1968) One more time: how do you motivate your employees? *Harvard Business Review*, January–February, 109–120.

Humble, J. (1972) *Management by Objectives*. Management Publications.

IDS (1997a) Shell International. *IDS Study 626*, May, 16–18.

IDS (1997b) Rewarding competencies at the Bank of Scotland. *Pay and Benefits Bulletin* 422, April, 2–7.

IDS (2003) Performance management. *IDS Study 748*, April.

Jacobs, R. and Floyd, M. (1995) A bumper crop of insights. *People Management*, 9 February, 23–25.

Kaplan, R. and Norton, D. (1996) *The Balanced Scorecard: Translating Strategy into Action*. Harvard Business School Press.

Lawler, E. (1990) *Strategic Pay*. Jossey-Bass.

LGMB (1993) *People and Performance*. Local Government Management Board.

Locke, E. and Latham, G. (1990) *A Theory of Goal Setting and Performance*. Prentice Hall.

Longenecker, C. and Gioia, S. (1988) Neglected at the top: executives talk about executive appraisal. *Sloan Management Review*, **29**(2): 42–48.

Mabey, C. (2001) Closing the circle: participant views of a 360 degree feed-back programme. *Human Resource Management Journal*, **11**(1): 41–53.

Marshall, V. and Wood, R. (2000) The dynamics of effective performance appraisal: an integrated model. *Asia Pacific Journal of Human Resources*, **38**(3): 62–89.

Mayer, R. and Davis, J. (1999) The effects of the performance appraisal system on trust for management. *Journal of Applied Psychology*, **84**(1): 123–136.

Megginson, D. and Casserly, T. (1996) Mbracing Mpowerment. *People Management*, 24 October, 42–44.

Peters, T. and Waterman, R. (1982) *In Search of Excellence*. Harper and Row.

Redman, T. (2001) *Performance Appraisal*. In: Redman, T. and Wilkinson, A. (eds) *Contemporary Human Resource Management*. Financial Times.

Redman, T., Snape, E., Thompson, D. and Ka-ching Yan, F. (2000) Performance Appraisal in the National Health Service: a trust hospital study. *Human Resource Management Journal*, **10**(1): 1–16.

Smithers, J. *et al.* (1995) 360 degree appraisal – does it work? *Personnel Psychology*, **48**(1):1–34.

Swan, W. (1991) *How to do a Superior Performance Appraisal*. John Wiley.

Thatcher, M. (1996) Allowing everyone to have their say. *People Management*, 21 March, 28–30.

Further reading

Strebler, M. (2004) *Tackling Poor Performance*. IES Report 406.

For a detailed discussion of the role of competencies in performance management and a large number of examples, see Chapter 5 of Williams, R. (1998) *Performance Management: Perspectives on Employee Performance*. Thomson Business Press.

A more detailed discussion on the major issues around performance management is set out in Chapter 3 of Armstrong, M. and Baron, A. (2005) *Managing Performance*. CIPD.

A practical guide to carrying out the appraisal is given in Gillen, T. (1998) *The Appraisal Discussion*. IPD; Moon, P. (1997) *Appraising Your Staff*. Kogan Page.

A variety of approaches to performance management systems is given in Hartle, F. (1997) *Transforming the Performance Management Process*. Kogan Page.

For a summary and discussion of American PM systems, see Lawler, E. and McDermott, M. (2003) 'Current Performance Management Practices', *WorldatWork Journal*, Spring, 49–60.

Web sites

http://www.pmn.net/index.html
The website of the Performance Management network.

http://www.pmassoc.com/links.html
A list of performance management links compiled by Performance Management Associates Inc.

CHAPTER 9

Rewarding employees

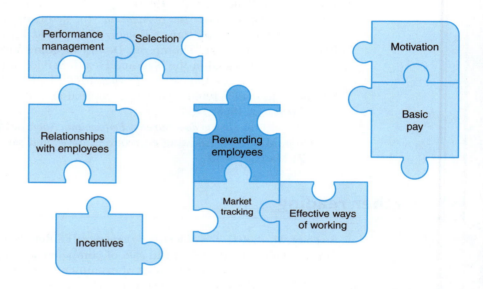

Objectives

When you have studied this chapter, you should be able to:

- Understand the importance of using reward in a strategic role.
- Identify the elements that make up the employee reward package.
- Distinguish between the different types of job evaluation and how and when they should be used.
- Appreciate the difference between conventional pay systems and broad-banded pay systems.
- Evaluate the main methods of paying for performance in an individual and team setting.

Payment systems have changed out of all recognition over the last 20 years. In the 1970s, when trade unions were at their zenith, pay itself was regarded as an outcome of the industrial relations process where a compromise was reached between the conflicting demands of the two antagonists. Today, organisations, with varying degrees of success, attempt to harness the powerful forces of pay as a motivator to encourage employees to work in ways that lead to the achievement of organisational objectives. There are many more forms of incentive payments, many varieties of recognition awards and the number of employee benefits has greatly expanded. Pay is also a vital element in the recruitment process and we have seen in Chapter 8 that it is one of the major outcomes arising from the performance management (PM) process.

In recent years, the expression 'reward' has started to replace 'pay' in the human resources vocabulary. It indicates a much broader approach, including elements of non-cash awards and presupposes that employees need to actually achieve something to receive their wages or salaries, unlike the more mechanistic attachment that pay indicates. Most of the developments in reward come from America and it is surprising that they still refer to the subject as 'compensation' with its connotation to the belief that work is unpleasant and should be avoided.

In this chapter we will be examining the important components of designing a total reward system which is made up of the following sections:

■ Determining the *strategic elements of reward* and how they link with other aspects of human resource.
■ Summarising the *component parts of the reward package.*
■ Designing *basic pay structures* through job evaluation systems, market tracking and competence approaches.
■ Deciding which aspects of *pay for performance* schemes should be implemented and under which conditions.
■ Constructing a *benefits package* which fits the needs of both the organisation and the employees.

Strategic elements of reward

You will recall from Chapter 1 that human resource strategy must be aligned with the business and policy objectives of the organisation. Reward strategy should clearly play its part in this alignment process.

'There is no doubt reward should play an important role in supporting changing organisational values, business strategies and work cultures.

> An effective reward strategy, although often overlooked, can be critical in effectively harnessing the forces of change and moving the organisation forward.'
>
> Flannery et al. (1996: pp. 20–21)

Figure 9.1 indicates a number of areas where major changes have taken place and these can be grouped into a number of strategic areas although many of them are inter-linking:

Past	Present
Pay regarded as an expense	Reward systems seen as an investment to achieve competitive advantage
Pay policies based on government control or national agreements	Reward determined by the organisation to meet its global, national or local conditions
Fixed pay scales in a rigid job evaluation structure	Reward utilised flexibly within a broad-banded salary structure
Pay seen as compensation for having to be at work	Rewards given for employees achieving the desired results
Pay to compensate for reluctant acceptance of change	Rewards to encourage positive acceptance of cultural changes
Payments made for length of service	Rewards given for performance, skills and competence
Pay differentials compressed	Wide variations in reward from board room to home improvement centre
Incentives based on narrow measures of production or sales	Performance-based systems based on broad measures of unit or organisational success
Paying for attendance	Rewarding employees for ideas, initiative and innovation
Fixed benefits without choice	Flexible benefit programmes to suit individual requirements
Equity sharing limited to directors	Share options for all employees

Figure 9.1
Changing nature of pay and rewards

Achieving competitive advantage

This can take a number of forms. The reward structure can be set at the top of the market range at all levels of the organisation to encourage the best people to join. This is the policy adopted by the UK pharmaceutical company GSK PLC, and most leading consultancies and merchant bankers. Although pay becomes a major expense, this is outweighed by the benefits obtained from employing the best talents available. In the case of GSK, by employing, amongst others, very high-quality research and development staff, the flow of successful long-term pharmaceutical products is ensured. Employee retention under such a strategy generally remains high, saving on recruitment costs. Another example is computer companies that have adopted the strategy of paying high-performance premiums to their staff for on-time project completion, leading to customer satisfaction and repeat business. Finally, schemes covering groups of employees, such as gainsharing, encourage employees to have a broad understanding of what the organisation is trying to achieve, and the associated commitment and involvement process helps the teams to work together to try to reach these objectives to the benefit of the organisation, its customers and all the employees.

Emphasise performance

The global marketplace and the increasing competition has ensured that organisations cannot rely on past performance or on employees having their own performance agendas. The proportion of contingent pay (pay that depends upon the achievement of results by the individual or teams) has risen compared to automatically paid basic pay. This is to encourage employees to 'share the risks' of a business. In the John Lewis Partnership, for example, all the employees are partners and receive an annual bonus depending upon the performance of the business. In 1988, this bonus was 24% of salary (almost £5000 on a salary of £20,000) but this had fallen to 8% by 1993 and only rose above 20% again in 1998. It has continued to oscillate in the early 2000s. In many companies, the guaranteed annual increase has vanished, being replaced by an increase based on individual performance. This has been the case for most financial institutions, including the Nationwide Building Society.

In BP Amoco 1999 Annual Report, the aim of their reward philosophy is explained as:

> 'to provide a competitive reward for delivering on-target performance while superior rewards can be earned for delivering outstanding results.'

Encourage flexibility in working practices

The increased movement towards a greater use of flexibility has led to the introduction of rewards for employees increasing their breadth of skills and competencies. SKF have introduced skills-based pay and the Rover group are extending its use while the Bank of Scotland and Triplex Safety Glass award-pay increases when employees achieve an increased set of competencies which allow them to carry out a wider range of jobs.

Oil the wheels of change

Organisations that make major cultural changes use rewards to help embed those changes. For example when, in 1994, GPT Telecommunications engaged in a number of human resource changes in response to the rapid marketplace, they introduced performance-related pay (PRP) to support their greater emphasis on customer-related objectives and higher-quality performance.

Support key competencies

Rewards can be used to encourage specific competencies. Vauxhall Motors developed an extensive recognition scheme to reward employees who demonstrate innovation and creativity. Some of these payments exceeded £2000 and were seen as vital to the company to compete on the level of productivity and quality in a world-wide marketplace.

Encourage local decision taking

As part of a centrally negotiated process, pay decisions used to be made at the headquarters but the need to respond to local conditions has led both to decisions on pay being delegated to localised units. Increasingly this is being taken a stage further by delegating individual pay decisions to local managers as part of the generally increase in local empowerment. Managers then have to justify such decisions in the light of their budgetary restrictions, local performance and market rate indicators.

An example of a company aligning its reward strategy with their organisation's business plan is shown in Case study 9.1 and research evidence of the changing nature of reward strategy is shown in Focus on research 9.1

Case study 9.1

BOC Gases's reward strategy

In 1997, a reorganisation of compressed gas supply business led to an improved financial information system. This, in turn, made possible the identification and measurement of profitability right down to individual functions and post-holders. Up until that time, the company's pay mechanisms had been built up over time with extra elements being added on as required but without obsolete elements being jettisoned. This meant that the variable element of the pay bill comprised an array of sometimes obscure payments, incentives and bonuses that were only partly understood by managers and employees and there was no mechanism for reflecting profitability or individual contribution in the variable pay system. The range of payments between high and average performers was small, there was no account of contribution by teams of employees and it was clear that the reward system had a short-term focus.

The new scheme was designed to include the following elements:

- A significant element of the incentive pay would be the achievement of profit targets. For example, for sales representatives, 70% of their incentive pay would be based on their own territory profit (not their volume of sales) and 30% on their area team's profit.
- There was no upper limit on what the individual might be paid.
- Under-achievement of profit targets would attract no payment.
- Employees would have extensive feedback as to their own and their team's performance and likely incentive pay outcomes.

By basing incentives on robust measures of profitability, it meant that employees would be focused on a collection of behaviours, including building up customer relationships, rather than just selling volume.

An evaluation a year later found that employees had a good understanding and acceptance of the scheme and that profits were above forecast. More important, managers reported that there was a discernible improvement in the profit orientation among employees.

Source: Corkerton and Bevan (1998)

Reward strategy

This research was based on 900 questionnaires (30% response rate) received form IPD members. Questions were asked about the reward strategy within their organisation on a five-point Lickert scale. The findings included the following responses:

- 63% supported/strongly supported a philosophy of using merit pay in various forms including PRP.
- 54% supported/strongly supported paying for good customer service and quality.
- 52% supported/strongly supported paying for innovation and creativity.
- 48% supported/strongly supported paying for productivity gains.
- 26% supported/strongly supported a strategy of employees sharing the risks with the organisation.

Interesting features of the findings were the high degree of support for paying for customer service, quality, innovation and creativity, and the lower proportion that supported paying for productivity gains. Support for all these strategies was greater in the private sector than the public sector, in large rather than small organisations and in expanding rather than static or declining organisations. The findings included a degree of scepticism as a proportion of respondents indicated that the actual practice of reward policy differed somewhat to the strategy in place.

Source: Poole and Jenkins (1998)

The influence of motivation theory

We have seen from Chapter 6 that conclusions on *motivation* are difficult to reach. There is no doubt that money motivates in many ways for many people much of the time but certainly not everybody all of the time. Even more perplexing, money can motivate up to a certain level but this differs greatly between individuals. To add further confusion, much of the research basis of Herzburg and Maslow have been disputed in recent years with results leading to varying conclusions.

For this reason, the reward area remains, in practice, an area of conflicting policies. Much of the private sector has adopted the expectancy and goal-setting approach, and aims to motivate the majority of its employees through pay for performance schemes based on the achievement of goals. In the public and voluntary sectors, on the other hand, the picture is very mixed with needs theories mostly to the fore and much concentration on the intrinsic satisfaction related to the job.

Component parts of the reward package

There are a numerous elements in the reward package and they are set out in Figure 9.2.

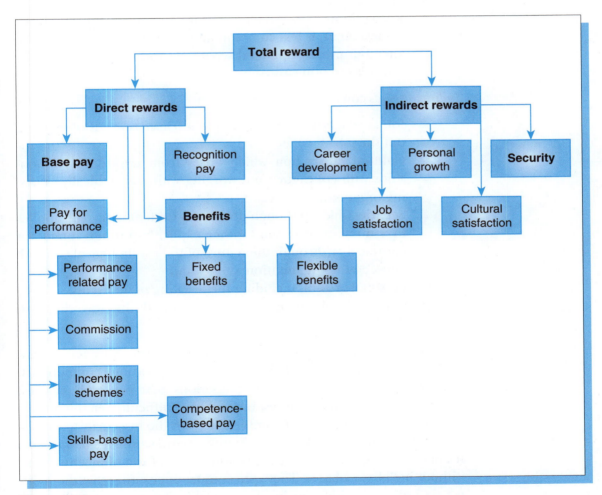

Figure 9.2
Components of the reward package

Direct rewards consist of the following:

- Basic Pay which is the hourly wage or weekly/monthly salary which is guaranteed to be paid.
- Pay for performance which is the pay that can vary depending on the performance of the individual, group or organisation as a whole. Adopting skills and competencies come into this group.
- Benefits which relate to a wide range of 'extras' from company cars, private health insurance and share options to sick pay, pensions and holidays. Most are fixed and there is a strong movement towards harmonising most benefits throughout an organisation rather than separate schemes for different groups of employees.
- Recognition pay, which are special awards for employee achievement, is less common and is associated with performance but usually operated separately and where many of the rewards are non-cash.

Indirect rewards consist of the following:

- Job satisfaction consisting of the intrinsic rewards of carrying out the job.
- Cultural satisfaction which arises from rewarding relationships with colleagues and working within an ethically satisfying organisation or sector.
- Security which, although not greatly evident today, still applies in a number of settings either explicitly through long-term contracts or through the nature of the psychological contract between the organisation and its staff.
- Personal growth, including the learning of new skills.
- Career development opportunities and the way they are developed.

Reward is not just about pay, although this is the major part, and organisations need to develop a balance between the various components. For example, there are some organisations that pay high salaries, based on performance bonuses, but still have difficulty retaining their staff, many of whom are not comfortable with the insecurity and pressure that this brings. Other organisations, perhaps still a small minority, maintain high staff performance without any form of incentive and without high-base salaries. They concentrate on ensuring that the indirect rewards are of high quality. Later in this chapter, there will be an examination of different aspects of performance pay and benefits.

Indirect rewards will be looked at in Chapter 11 that deals with training and development.

Designing basic pay structures

The major part of most employees' reward is their basic remuneration. As Frans Poels puts it:

> 'A systematic framework is required to manage differences in (basic) pay in such a way that they support the objectives of the organisation and result in fair remuneration for the individuals.'
>
> Poels (1997: p. 9)

For individuals, the sense of fairness about their basic pay is related to three key facts. These are, firstly, the objective value they put on the nature of the job and the way they perform it; secondly, their perception of how this compares with other jobs in the organisation, especially those jobs and employees with which they are familiar; thirdly, how their pay compares with their perception of the 'market rate' for their job.

In small organisations, the salary structure is informal with the Chief Executive (CE), who will know each employee, deciding the basic pay on an individual basis. The CE will be able to meet Poels' requirements and record it on one sheet of paper. However, when the organisation stretches beyond 60 or 80 employees this becomes increasingly difficult. The CE will find the individual judgement of comparing of one individual's worth against another, their comparable performance and the market rates for their jobs a complex process. Moreover, if mistakes are made, they can be costly. If remuneration is increased too much, it is almost impossible to reduce it subsequently (certainly without complaint) and if it is not increased sufficiently, then the individual may decide to look elsewhere. When the organisation expands beyond 150 or 200 employees the task becomes practically impossible.

This is where two remuneration processes enter. *Job evaluation* attempts to ensure that the internal pay relativities are objectively set and *market tracking* compares the appropriate rates with the marketplace. When the necessary preparation has been carried out on both these processes, a remuneration structure can be put together to try to satisfy the requirements for both the organisation and the individual.

Job evaluation

The usual end result of a job evaluation exercise is to produce a hierarchy of jobs in the organisation through valuing them all against a clear set of objective criteria. Objective is the key word here because individual perception of job worth is so variable. Let us take the case of the computer programmer. Outside of people working in this skills area, there is a strong perception that it is a far from demanding position filled by people often with few qualifications, where the job holders spend much of their time sending e-mails to their colleagues, playing computer games and only working hard when it gets close to the deadlines. Is this correct? It depends entirely on how you value job worth. Many research scientists will look back on a number of years working on research projects which came to nothing and which appeared to add little or no value to the organisation. Yet these positions will be regarded as having a high job value.

The crucial starting point for job evaluation, therefore, is to decide on the criteria for measuring the value of jobs which can be *analytical* or *non-analytical*. Having agreed on this, the long and complex process of actually carrying out the evaluation can take place and, finally, it can be put together into a hierarchy of jobs. It has to be remembered throughout the process that it is the jobs that are being examined, not the performance of the person carrying out the job.

Non-analytical schemes

These are schemes which look at the job as a whole and do not examine their component parts. The evaluation process is normally carried out by a small group of executives working confidentially with their own knowledge of the jobs. They are only suitable for small- or medium-sized organisations. It has to be said that these methods generally have a distinct lack of objectivity and are operated because they are cheap, quick and informal. They consist of the following:

- *Job ranking.* This is where jobs are simply ranked in order by the evaluation team. They may consider aspects of the jobs, such as responsibility or skills, but no agreed weight is given to these factors.
- *Paired comparison.* This takes ranking a stage further. In this process, all the jobs to be evaluated are compared on a one by one basis (see Figure 9.3) The job with a higher worth gets

Job titles	Estimator	Senior Purchasing Officer	Receptionist	Finance Manager	Training officer	Purchasing Clerk	QS	Senior Site Secretary	Marketing Manager	Administrator	Commercial Manager	Accounts Manager	Accounts Clerk	Planner	Personnel Assistant	Total score	Ranking position
Estimator		0	2	0	1	2	1	2	0	2	0	0	2	1	2	15	4
Senior Purchasing Officer	2		2	0	2	2	2	2	1	2	0	0	2	2	2	21	3
Receptionist	0	0		0	0	1	0	1	0	1	0	0	2	0	0	5	7
Finance Manager	2	2	2		2	2	2	2	1	2	1	1	2	2	2	25	1
Training Officer	1	0	2	0		2	1	2	0	2	0	0	2	1	1	14	5
Purchasing Clerk	0	0	1	0	0		0	0	0	1	0	0	1	0	0	3	9
Quantity Surveyor	1	0	2	0	1	2		2	0	2	0	0	2	1	2	15	4
Senior Site Secretary	0	0	1	0	0	1	0		0	1	0	0	1	0	0	4	8
Marketing Manager	2	1	2	1	2	2	2	2		2	1	1	2	2	2	24	2
Administrator	0	0	1	0	0	1	0	1	0		0	0	1	0	0	4	8
Commercial Manager	2	2	2	1	2	2	2	2	1	2		1	2	2	2	25	1
Accounts Manager	2	2	2	1	2	2	2	2	1	2	1		2	2	2	25	1
Accounts Clerk	0	0	1	0	0	1	0	1	0	1	0	0		0	0	4	8
Planner	1	0	2	0	1	2	1	2	0	2	0	0	2		2	15	4
Personnel Asst.	0	0	2	0	1	2	0	2	0	0	2	0	2	0		11	6

Points scored according to 'value' to Laing Limited.
Jobs valued > = 2 Points
Jobs valued < = 0 Points
Jobs equal value = 1 Point

Figure 9.3
Example of paired comparison job evaluation scheme

two points and, if they are considered equal, both get one point. The total points awarded under this system are added for each job to get a ranking of the jobs. This is certainly an easier process in the sense that comparing two jobs is more straightforward than trying to put a whole collection in order. However, it takes more time and there is a limit of the number of jobs that can be compared with this process. As pointed out by Armstrong and Baron (1995), to evaluate 50 jobs involves 1225 individual comparisons.

■ *Job classification.* This is the process where each job is classified into a grade by reference to a prepared set of grading classifications. The number of grades is usually limited to between four and eight and are described in terms of factors, such as experience required, quantity of non-routine tasks and elements of supervision required or which are part of the job. Each job is taken in turn and agreement reached as to which grade the job appears to fit into best. Again, this is a reasonably simple process on the surface but can lead to considerable dispute amongst the team making the decision because many jobs will not naturally fit into any grade, having elements of one and not the other. Decisions, in the end, will often be by compromise or due to internal political factors rather than any form of objectivity. Figure 9.4 shows an extract from a typical office classification scheme.

Rank Descriptions
Rank 0 – Director
This rank covers all grades of Director (Chairman, Managing Director, Functional Directors, Non-Executive Directors, Vice Presidents, etc.). Entries should be made to this grade for all Directors with the legal responsibility of that title. It should not include those with the courtesy title 'Director' (e.g. Account Director) unless they have responsibilities for general company policy outside their functions, possibly as part of an executive management team, commonly found in foreign organisations without UK-based Directors.
Rank 1 – Senior Management or Senior Specialist
This rank covers the heads of major functions reporting to the Rank 0. In smaller organisations the Rank 0 appointment may well cover the duties of the Rank 1 and, consequently, there may be no incumbent in the Rank 1. The duty of these staff is the day-to-day running of an important major function in the organisation. Some policy formulation will be a normal part of their responsibilities.

Figure 9.4
Job classification scheme

In addition, this rank covers very senior and highly qualified specialists who may have no function or department to manage. An example is Legal Adviser.

Rank 2 – Senior Middle Manager

The majority of entries into this rank will be for heads of main departments normally reporting to a Rank 1 Senior Manager, but in smaller organisations, or for less important departments, reporting to a Director. Alternatively, they may be the deputy to the Senior Manager.

In addition, some important specialists whose effort is more directed to an individual technical or administrative skill, rather than the management of people, could be covered by this rank. Examples of such jobs are a Scientific Specialist, Pensions Manager, Consultant, etc. A Specialist Sales Manager may well be ranked at this level, although he may not control any Regional or Area Representatives.

Rank 3 – Junior Middle Management

The heads of less important departments are likely to be graded at this rank, as well as many specialists such as Senior Engineers, Project Leaders, Senior Systems Analysts. In the sales field, a Regional Manager controlling several Area Managers (Rank 4) would be graded Rank 3 unless the company equated his responsibility to other Rank 2 holders in the company.

Most people at this rank will have Supervisors or Section Leaders reporting to them.

Rank 4 – Junior Management

This is the lowest level of management and is one rank above the first-line supervisory positions at Rank 5. Many holders of this rank would be managing a section and could be qualified or part-qualified professionally. Examples are Production Section Manager, Engineer, Accountant (not equated to Rank 3).

Office Managers would normally be at this rank except in smaller organisations where they would be graded as Office Supervisors at Rank 5.

Many Specialists would appear in this rank such as Senior Programmer, Health and Safety Officer, Buyer, Sales Area Manager (controlling a number of Representatives) or a Senior Representative.

Rank 5 – Supervisor and Senior Technician

This is primarily a rank for supervisory staff, either in the office or on the shop floor (e.g. Foreman). It also includes Senior Technicians or Specialists, such as Sales Representative, Programmer, Draughtsman, Work Study Officer, Nurse, Assistant (often newly joined graduates) Engineer, Senior Secretary, etc.

Rank 6 – Senior Clerical and Technician

This rank covers all those staff with minor supervisory roles (e.g. Section Leader, Chargehands, Senior Telephonist, etc.), Technicians and very junior Trainee Managers (e.g. Assistant Personnel Officer, etc.). It covers tasks in the office of a senior clerical nature which require experience and a limited degree of initiative such as Secretary, Senior Sales Clerk, etc. Technical jobs at this rank would include Computer (not VDU) Operator, Buying Assistant, Progress Chaser and Laboratory Technician.

Figure 9.4
(*continued*)

Rank 7 – Skilled Operative and Specialist Clerical Grade

This rank includes all staff working under close supervision but classified by experience, training and ability as fully skilled. This would include Welders, Fitters, HGV Drivers, Craftsmen, Skilled Production Operatives and Shop Floor Inspectors.

Within the office this rank would cover clerical duties of a specialist nature or those requiring skills above general clerical workers. This would include such activities as Sales Ledger Clerk, Credit Control Clerk, Shorthand Typist, Word Processing Operator, Shipping Clerk, Production Control Clerk, Telephone Sales, etc.

Rank 8 – Semi-Skilled Grade

This rank covers all those whose skills are better than unskilled or completely inexperienced, and lower than fully skilled or very experienced. They would be doing routine tasks under supervision, using their knowledge, experience and aptitudes.

This grade covers all Semi-Skilled Operatives, General Drivers, General Clerks, Telephonists, Typists, Laboratory Assistants, Handymen, etc.

Rank 9 – Unskilled Grade and Juniors

This rank covers all unskilled staff doing routine, simple tasks. It also includes all staff paid on age scales that is 16, 17 and 18 year olds whether they are working in the office, on the drawing board, in an apprenticeship or working on the production line.

The unskilled heading includes jobs like Filing Clerk, Junior Clerk, Unskilled Storeman/Packer, Labourer, Cleaner, Canteen Assistant, etc.

Figure 9.4
(*continued*)

Analytical schemes

Analytical schemes, on the other hand, can have a much greater transparency, objectivity and rationality if they are carried out in an open and consistent basis. In Armstrong and Baron's survey of job evaluation in the UK (1995), 35% of companies concerned had a form of factor–point system. The basis of an analytical schemes is that each job is evaluated against a grid of factors and points, a simple example of which is set out in Figure 9.5.

In designing this grid, there are three decisions that need to be taken:

- ■ *What factors to use.* In this example, only six factors have been selected. Armstrong and Baron (1995) list 31 factors in common use but only five to 10 factors are normally selected in the interest of simplicity and comprehension. It is important, therefore, that consideration is given to factors which are relevant and vital to the set of jobs being evaluated and to skills which are important.

Factors	Levels				
	1	2	3	4	5
Experience level required	100	200	300	400	500
Complexity of post	80	160	240	320	400
Staff supervised	80	160	240	320	400
Responsibility	100	180	260	340	420
Innovation required	50	100	150	200	250
Financial accountability	60	120	180	260	400

Figure 9.5
Job evaluation
factor point grid

- *How many levels.* Evaluating is an attempt to discriminate between jobs so a definition is required for each level for each factor to enable the evaluators to place the position into the right slot and attribute the correct points. The more the levels, the more difficult it becomes to discern the correct level so it is not common for the levels to exceed six.
- *What points to allocate at each level for each factor.* Some factors are more important than others and this varies in different organisations depending on the cultural emphasis on aspects, such as financial prudence, communication or teamworking. There may even be an agreement, as in the example for financial accountability, that the points awarded should rise by unequal amounts.

There are more sophisticated factor–points schemes available that have been developed by consultancies. By far the most widely used is the Hay Guide Chart-Profile, operated by over 7000 organisations throughout the world. This has eight factors gathered into three groups, know-how, problem solving and accountability, and is used principally for management and supervision grades. Although there are substantial purchase and training costs in utilising this scheme (and other similar proprietorial schemes), there are no design and validation costs, and information on market tracking is included in the package.

Carrying out a job evaluation

Having agreed on the nature and content of the scheme, there are a number of stages involved in competing a full evaluation. *A job evaluation committee* needs to be put together which should consist of representatives of both managers and the employees who are being evaluated.

It is essential that the scheme is seen as one that is fair and participative, especially when it comes to convincing the employees that the results are based on robust evidence. It is all the more convincing when the committee is made up of equal numbers from management and employee representatives and ensures that the committee needs to work very closely together to avoid intransigent split votes. Each job to be evaluated needs a thorough and *comprehensive job description* on which the rating can be made. In some processes, a detailed questionnaire is sent to the manager and the job holders to elucidate areas of responsibility so the decision on rating can be made easier.

The first jobs to be evaluated are called '*benchmark*' *jobs* because subsequent rating decisions are made in comparison to those key jobs. These should be the jobs which have the largest number of job holders. It is customary for the manager and a job holder to be interviewed regarding their views on the points to be allocated to ensure procedural justice. When the benchmark jobs have been agreed, the remainder of the jobs can be evaluated. When the process is complete (this can take 6 months to a year to evaluate 100 or more jobs), a '*sore-thumb*' discussion takes place to ensure that the full picture is reviewed and no job has been clearly wrongly evaluated. The final act is to *publish the results* of the evaluation, usually in the form of a straight hierarchical list of jobs and points, and provide the opportunity for employees to *appeal* if they believe the overall rating is wrong.

Factor–points evaluations, if carried out with full consultation and with a well-designed and operated scheme are clearly superior to non-analytical schemes. They are based on more objective data and the organisation has demonstrated the importance it attaches to producing a fair salary structure. However, they are very time consuming and a typical evaluation can take up two or three staff full time for 6 months or a year. Moreover, the data can never be completely objective, needing individual judgements to be made in selecting the criteria and awarding points.

Market tracking

Before using the job evaluation scheme to produce a salary structure, the relationship of the organisation's pay compared with the market-place needs to be examined. The level of pay in an organisation can be influenced by a number of factors:

- *How much the organisation can afford to pay?* All too often in union negotiations is the argument used that the organisation simply cannot afford a high settlement and, one has to say, it usually cuts little ice with the world-weary union representatives who have just seen the latest executive car replacements come through the gates. However, there is always a good deal of truth in this assertion in the public sector where pay increases are mostly funded directly or indirectly by the government so there is usually a fixed pot for pay increases. For other organisations that faced sectorial hard times, such as housebuilding in the early 1990s, farming in the last 20 years and much of manufacturing in the early 2000s, higher-pay increases may simply serve to bring forward bankruptcy. For other organisations, there are deeper issues to consider. If a company gets a reputation as a poor payer, then it will not attract quality applications and many good employees will leave to go elsewhere. Cost saving through low-pay increases may appear to be good accountancy but rarely makes good human resource practice. The question that needs to be answered is how to get higher performances from employees that will more than pay for the higher-pay increases. That is another reason why many companies are moving towards extensive pay for performance schemes, often with fewer employees on board. The size of the organisation is sometimes an influence. Larger private organisations who wish to build a reputation will often pay more than small- or medium-sized organisations in the same industry.

- *Government legislation.* It has a part to play through the Equal Pay Act (see Chapter 3) and the National Minimum Wage (NMW). The NMW was implemented in April 1999 with a minimum figure of £3.00 an hour for employees aged 18–21 years and £3–60 an hour for all other employees. This has been increased each year subsequently at a rate higher than inflation so by 2004 it had reached £4.80 for employees 22 years and over.

- *Shortage of key skills.* It can have the effect of increasing pay rates. This applied at the end of the 1980s in the construction industry where very rapid pay rises occurred for bricklayers and other skilled trades, and have gradually increased throughout the 1990s in information technology (IT) staff with a massive rise since 1998 due to the need to cope with the problems that seemed likely to occur with the arrival of the Millennium, although the shortages turned into a glut a few years later.

■ *Geographical location.* It can have a strong influence with rates of pay for a secretarial position in Central London as much as 30% on more higher than a comparable job in, say, Stevenage or Chelmsford. Similarly, pay in the South East tends to be higher than the North East or Scotland.

■ *Macro-economics.* These are especially the state of the economy and the level of unemployment, will have an effect on both the demand and supply of labour, thereby affecting pay rates. At a time of high unemployment, usually associated with low demand for labour, employers are likely to pay low-pay increases and there are circumstances where it is possible to recruit new staff at lower rates. The situation is, of course, more complex than this as it is far from easy to lower union-agreed rates, nor is it seen as equitable to have staff doing the same job on different rates of pay. Another important element is the rise in the cost of living as measured in the UK by the Retail Prices index. Employees would consider that a pay rise less than the cost of living was equivalent to a reduction in real pay.

Being aware and informed of the actual market pay rates is an essential prerequisite of formulating an effective pay policy. The sources of such information can include published national surveys, such as those by the Reward Group, management consultants, examining current job advertisements and being part of a pay club whose members exchange information. It must always be borne in mind that there are serious difficulties in precise matching of jobs and defining precise pay rates (e.g. whether to include bonuses or not) so defining a 'market rate' for a job is almost impossible.

Equal pay

All pay structures need to be compatible with the Equal Pay Act (1970) and the Equal Value Regulations (1983). This means that men and women must be paid under the same arrangements if they are carrying out like work, work that is rated the same under a job evaluation scheme or jobs that have the same value. In any job evaluation exercise, care must be taken that: factors are not weighted in favour of men (such as ability to lift weights), women are represented on the job evaluation committee and there is not a 'sink' grade at the bottom of the structure that contains jobs that are all filled by females. More details of this Act are given in Chapter 3.

Salary structures – conventional and broad banded

Having obtained a hierarchy of jobs through a job evaluation exercise, obtained market data on these jobs and decided on the market positioning aspect, the last stage is to produce a salary structure.

Figure 9.6 shows the outcome of a completed administrative job evaluation scheme. The division of the jobs into grades has been carried out in what is inevitably a subjective way because some jobs on the borderline could easily be on one or the other side of the grade line. These decisions are taken locally and often for political and cost-related factors linked to the individuals carrying out the job.

Grade	Minimum points	Maximum points	Minimum salary (£)	Maximum salary (£)
1	250	499	7000	8999
2	500	749	9000	10,999
3	750	999	11,000	12,999
4	1000	1249	13,000	14,999
5	1250	1499	15,000	17,999
6	1500	1749	18,000	21,999
7	1750	1999	22,000	25,999
8	2000	2249	26,000	29,999
9	2250	2499	30,000	34,999
10	Over 2500		35,000	40,000

Figure 9.6
Job evaluated salary structure

Under a traditional salary structure, employees would be appointed at or towards the bottom of the salary range for the grade and would move up the grade through *increments*, usually paid on an annual basis. The number of increments related to a particular job could range from 3 to 7 or 8. They would only move from one grade to another through promotion or if their job changes sufficiently to warrant the re-grading. The decision on re-grading is taken by a committee, which will consider the case put forward by the employee and their manager, taking into account the equity of the situation and any subsequent effects upon the salary structure. It is also possible to have pay grades that overlap but this means that one employee may be in a position that is in a higher grade but receiving lower pay than an employee in a lower grade. This is shown in Figure 9.7.

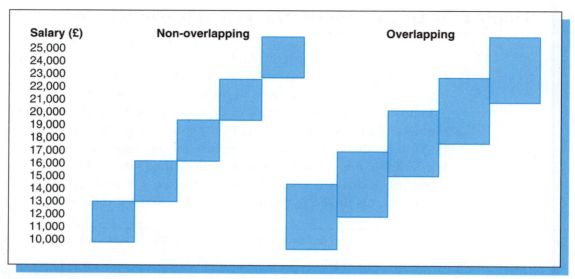

Figure 9.7
Overlapping and non-overlapping salary grades

Criticisms of formal job evaluation schemes

In the past, it has been common to create at least 5 and sometimes as many as 20 grades in a formal scheme. The aim has been to create equity by highlighting the differences between the sets of jobs and giving greater rewards to those whose jobs are rated higher than others. The structure is seen to motivate by encouraging employees to bid for promotion to a higher job through a permanent, fair and transparent system. A higher job, a higher grade, a bigger salary, nothing could be simpler or fairer. The first major grading system like this was set up by the American Government in 1923 and operated, with some amendments, for 60 years.

Today, the external environment has changed considerably. The salary structure has to reflect the required culture of the organisation and the traditional job evaluation-based structure may not always be appropriate:

> 'Formal job evaluation schemes do indeed work well in stable, hierarchical organisations. But it has to be recognised that job evaluation methodologies which emphasise place in hierarchy, numbers of people supervised or resources directly controlled, without taking into account technical expertise or complex decision-making, have little to contribute.'
>
> Armstrong and Murlis (1994: p. 110)

Increasingly in a business environment where organisations want to respond flexibly to global developments and customer requirements, the rigidity of a traditional scheme has too many disadvantages. Promotions are now far fewer as organisations have de-layered, reducing greatly the number of management and supervisory positions. Employees need to be far more flexible, willing to change their roles and learn more skills to meet the needs of the quickly changing national and international marketplace. The stiff, hierarchical grading structure is far less likely to match the quick-moving, responsive culture required in both manufacturing and service industries.

A further criticism of the multi-grade system is that it can encourage the employee to adopt a rigid approach to the job:

'My job has been described closely, it has been fixed at a particular grade therefore that is the job I am paid for. I am not prepared to do anything new or extra outside of the job description unless I am paid more for it.'

In this situation, employees would apply for re-grading which, in itself, tends to be an adversarial contest. If the employee wins, it can well upset other colleagues and lead to further claims. This can lead to grade drift which causes salary drift and headaches for the remuneration specialist. If the employee loses then the extra work will only be carried out grudgingly, it at all. Too often, employees think of themselves, or describe others, in terms of their grades. In research the author was carrying out in a large engineering company, the question was asked what job a particular employee did. 'Oh, she's a grade 4' was the reply as if that explained everything! In this respect, the system has a de-humanising aspect.

An alternative approach is to implement a scheme which is based on the broad-banding concept.

How broad-banding works

When the job evaluation has been completed, the artificial divisions, which normally distinguish between grades, are ignored. What normally happens is that a set of generic titles, such as Manager, Supervisor, Operative, Clerk, are gathered into one large band. This allows all of the employees in an organisation to fit into a salary structure, which may have as few as 5 broad-bands.

Being broad, there is a large difference between the top of the band and the bottom. Sometimes the top of the band can be 250% higher than the bottom (i.e. a range for the 'managers' band from £16,000 to £40,000) This is shown in Figure 9.8.

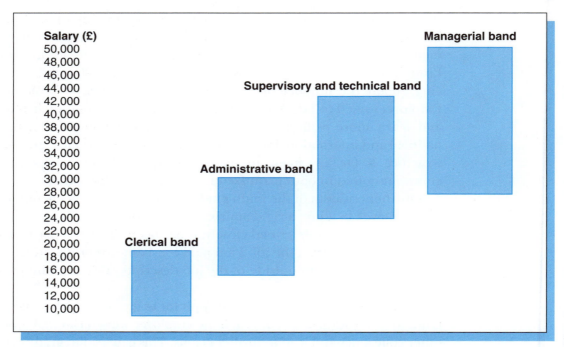

Figure 9.8
Broad-banded salary structure

Moving up the band is the key to the whole concept. First of all, the decision process is in the hands of the departmental manager to act within guidelines and in line with their budget. This replaces the formalised and Personnel-controlled re-grading process. The criteria for authorising movement falls into four main areas:

■ A *competence* approach where clear guidelines are laid down on the acquisition of important competencies. Measuring them is not easy and will be a mix of subjective analysis, the attainment of NVQs or equivalent, or through third-party judgments, such as in 360° appraisal.

■ An informal system of *job development* where employees move from a probational role through experienced employee to expert performer with guidelines on how long that should usually take.

■ An *Enlarging experience* approach, where employees move between jobs and between departments, gaining extra skills and generally becoming more useful and knowledgeable employees.

■ By *performance*, where the outcomes of the PM scheme indicates a movement up the band due to enhanced and proven performance.

Benefits and difficulties of a broad-banded structure

Advocates of the scheme put forward the following advantages (Armstrong and Brown 2001):

■ Employees have a much greater incentive to achieve results for the organisation. If they become more competent, have a higher performance or enlarge their skills and experience, then they can be paid more. This encourages the type of values that organisations want to promote. They do not have to wait to apply for grading or a promotion.

■ Given the lack of managerial and supervisory jobs, employees can still make progress with the organisation. By employees improving and being motivated to improve, the job of the overstretched manager becomes easier.

■ The system is far more flexible. New jobs and processes can be introduced easily without worrying about employees' narrowly defined jobs.

■ By putting the decisions in the hands of the manager they will act realistically and responsibly towards their staff and their total salary bill.

However, there are a number of disadvantages to such systems. It can be seen that broad-banding is not much more than the type of salary structure in a small informal organisation that has not yet found the necessity for job evaluation (In fact, broad-banding can be so flexible that there is actually no need for job evaluation). This informality can lead to all the accusations of subjectivity and favouritism that led to job evaluated wage structures in the first place. Unless the criteria for salary progress are robust, really understood and operated fairly, then the system will not be seen as fair itself.

There can also be a tendency for it to be expensive. Under narrow grades, employees came to the top of their grade and realise they may have to stay there unless promoted. Under broad bands, most employees see an almost unlimited opportunity to make continuing progress and managers may find difficulty in holding salary increases back, particularly if employees meet the criteria. Employees may also be demotivated if they meet the criteria but the manager's budget restrictions stop the increase. Under traditional job evaluation schemes, budget restrictions could not stop a re-grading.

Making sure that managers act in a consistent fashion across the whole salary structure is not easy. Personnel's role here is crucial in acting as an auditor, an advisor, mentor and informal adjudicator. Without such fall back, the wage structure is likely to fall into chaos.

As Milkovich and Newman explain:

> 'Flexibility is one side of the coin; chaos and favouritism is the other. Broad-banding presumes that managers will manage employees' pay to accomplish the organisation's objectives (and not their own) and treat employees fairly. Historically, this is not the first time greater flexibility has been shifted to managers and leaders. Indeed, the rationale underlying the use of grades and ranges was to reduce the former inconsistencies and favouritism that were destructive to employee relations in the 1920s and 1930s. The challenge today is to take advantage of flexibility without increasing labour costs or leaving the organisation vulnerable to charges of favouritism and inconsistency.'
>
> Milkovich and Newman (1996: p. 285–6)

Paying for performance

The traditional job evaluated pay system with incremental movement is based on a collectivist approach where employees are all treated the same, regardless of their performance. It is assumed that employees become increasingly knowledgeable and competent in their job as time goes by, that is why they receive increments. It is a simple scheme rewarding employees for their service and loyalty.

This picture is fading fast as society changes. As the capitalist, free-enterprise society now dominates most of the world's economies, employees have come to accept, expect and mostly approve of pay systems which differentiate between different levels of performance. As Brown (2001) explains:

> '…we are witnessing a rapid growth in the incidence of bonus schemes and variable pay as companies attempt to obtain more variability in their total pay costs and endeavour to create a stronger "line of sight" between what employees do and are rewarded for, and the strategic goals and performance of the organisation.'
>
> Brown (2001: p. 137)

There are many forms of performance pay schemes. The original individual piecework systems promulgated by Taylor (1911) operated for 50 years or so and have a modicum of apparent fairness but have fallen into disrepute since the mid-1960s for a number of reasons. Constant arguments can occur over piecework rates and allowances, especially when new materials, processes or machinery are introduced; rates of pay may fluctuate through no fault of the operator due to lack of work or poor materials; individual piecework encourages the employee to only work for themselves rather than be part of a co-operating team; a costly set of rate-fixers and work study engineers to maintain the system; workers may be encouraged to cut corners in health and safety to boost their income.

Today, piecework is only in evidence in the remnant of the textile and other traditional industries, although it still also is operated in some industries where employees work at home. It has mostly been replaced by *group incentives schemes* which operate in a department or unit wide environment. They can take the form of production targets only or, increasingly, a broader set of targets including quality, on-time production and accident levels. The objective is to encourage employees to understand the basis of the targets and to aim to achieve them, working co-operatively as a team. This has been taken further in America through a system called *Gainsharing*, where a unit shares the cost-savings achieved through higher productivity, waste-saving and quality improvement, in the form of quarterly bonuses. One of the crucial aspects of the system is that employees have full information on the objective-setting process, are informed of the current performance on a regular basis and are encouraged to participate in problem solving and innovation committees to aid the achievement of the objectives. An example of gainsharing is given in Case study 9.2.

Case study 9.2

Gainsharing at Southern California Edison (SCE)

In 1994, deregulation of the electricity industry led to increased competition and SCE needed to change its compensation policies to meet the more commercial realities of the marketplace. As part of the major revisions, an old salary-grade system, with 3200 job titles for 9000 employees, was abandoned and revised with a broad-banded system which has only 170 titles. Another large change was the introduction of a gainsharing arrangement. Employees were invited to sacrifice 5% of their basic salaries in return for up to 10% gainshare if the organisation met its savings and profits targets.

100% of employees agreed to this proposal and most joined in the process of generating ideas to save money. As a small example, employees agreed to wash their own overalls. The outcome was that the scheme generated an estimated $96 million and $40 million was paid out to employees. More important, the scheme played its part in getting employees focused on what was important in working cost-effectively and being involved in designing effective working methods.

Source: Lambs (1996)

In the retailing and sales environment it is common to pay a *Commission*, which a small percentage of the price of the goods sold, to the employees concerned. In a few industries, such as double glazing and computers, some sales staff are employed on a commission-only basis.

Another version of payments come under the general title of Employee Recognition schemes which have developed in recent years. Jarvis Hotels, for example, make instant payments of between £25 and £100 in vouchers to staff if they are spotted showing excellence in their jobs in areas, such as customer service, productivity or attitude (Robinson, 1998).

The most common, and controversial, system of performance pay in the UK, however, is PRP and, due to its importance, we will devote a separate section on this subject.

PRP

A number of recent surveys have shown that PRP is operating formally in 40–60% of organisations surveyed (Cannell and Wood, 1992; IPD/IMS, 1992; IPD, 1998). Despite a considerable degree of scepticism surrounding these outcomes, the majority of organisations believe that there should be pay distinctions between those individuals that perform well and those that do not. This view appears to be shared by the majority of employees, as indicated by research by Thompson (1993) and Marsden and Richardson (1994). Focus on research 9.2 looks at a survey of PRP of managers in the health service.

PRP in the National Health Service

This research was based on 114 questionnaires (53% return) from managers covered by a PRP scheme in six National Health Service (NHS) trusts, together with structured interviews with Senior Management. Managers' views were obtained through a 30 question, five-point Likert scale covering questions in the areas of motivation, system of PM and effects on personal relationships.

It was found that more managers agreed that the scheme motivated them than disagreed with the statement, although it was not considered that they worked harder or that that it allowed them to be given credit and recognition that they deserved, or that it was the financial rewards that drove them on. Overall, it was the process of objective setting, in which most of them took part, the regular discussion of their performance, the challenging but fair nature of the objectives and the way that the scheme allowed them a certain freedom to achieve their objectives that influenced their positive view on the scheme. Not all agreed with the total fairness of the judgements made, most agreeing that the process was inevitably subjective. Concerning the allocation of pay rewards, there was understanding of the context in which they worked. As one respondent stated:

'I cannot see how PRP can possibly be applied fairly in a cash limited environment like the NHS. If all the assessments … were to add up to a figure that a Trust could not afford, what then? We all fall back into old habits … And limit pay increases to a flat 1.5% with all the pain, cynicism and loss of credibility that would surely follow.' (p. 356)

Source: Dowling and Richardson (1997)

Schemes can either use the outcomes of a performance review to add a bonus payment on top of a annual increase relating to cost of living. Increasingly, however, the automatic cost of living rise is being replaced by rises linked entirely to performance.

You will recall from Chapter 8 that the process of PM underpins any payments arising from the employee's performance. An essential set of requirements for any PRP scheme includes an agreed set of targets (either objectives or developing competencies or both), an effective and robust method of measuring the performance against the targets and regular feedback to the employee. The outcome of a review at the end of the period (usually a year) is normally a performance rating. This can be fairly simple, such as the rating from one to five in Figure 9.9 or a more complex calculation as in Figure 9.10.

The figure for the pay increase is pre-determined, based on the budget available for increased labour costs.

Performance description	Rating	Pay increase (%)
Excellent performance, all targets greatly exceeded	5	8
Superior performance, majority of targets met or exceeded	4	6
Normal performance, good proportion of targets met although a few missed	3	4
Below average performance with a number of key targets missed and weaknesses shown	2	2
Very weak performance with few if any targets met and disciplinary action to be considered	1	0

Figure 9.9
Conversion of ratings into a pay increase

There are six objectives for the employee to achieve with the following weightings:-

Objective 1	Weighting 30%	Objective 4	Weighting 10%
Objective 2	Weighting 20%	Objective 5	Weighting 10%
Objective 3	Weighting 20%	Objective 6	Weighting 10%

At the end of the period, a decision is reached that the level of performance on the objective is:

Objective	Achievement level (%)	Rating (%)	Outcome (points)
1	80	30	24
2	100	20	20
3	90	20	18
4	50	10	5
5	100	10	10
6	60	10	6
		Total points	83

Conversion to salary increase

Points	Salary increase (%)
0–50	0
50–69	2
70–89	4
90–99	6
99–100	8

In this example, the employee would receive a pay increase of 4%

Figure 9.10
Conversion of ratings into a pay increase in a complex scheme

In both of these examples, the schemes are set up as an *incentive*, to demonstrate to the workforce that there are opportunities to achieve a higher-pay increase than average through working harder and smarter to meet the agreed targets. They can also act as a *reward* to those employees who perform above average.

The arguments in favour of PRP schemes include:

- It is fair to distinguish between the high performer and those that are only average or below average.
- Making payments to high performers reinforces the message that the organisation recognises and encourages high performance, and establishes a clear culture throughout the organisation.
- The process of setting objectives clarifies what an employee need to achieve and thereby focuses their attention and effort.
- By being focused, employees act in a flexible way to achieve the required results rather than simply carrying out their job as defined by their job description. They become facilitators and problem-solvers, and circumvent bureaucratic barriers.
- The opportunity for differential earnings is a recruitment aid, attracting ambitious, results-oriented applicants.
- Achieving results and obtaining good pay increases is a positive force for raising morale in the organisation.

There are, however, just as many criticisms of PRP:

- In an influential Harvard Business School article, Kohn (1993) attacked performance pay schemes for a number of reasons. He asserted that there was no hard evidence that they were effective motivators, that they discouraged employees from risk-taking as their objectives where so circumscribed, that they undermined interest and motivation in the job itself, that they punished employees when they failed, thereby de-motivating them, as much as rewarded those that succeeded, and they ruptured relationships between employees. His final criticism was that rewards took away from managers the right approach to managing:

> 'Managers often use incentive schemes as a substitute for giving workers what they need to do a good job. Treating workers well – providing useful feedback, social support and the room for self-determination – is the essence of good management. On the other

hand, dangling a bonus in front of employees and waiting for the result requires much less effort.'

Kohn (1993: p. 59)

■ The problems have already been set out in Chapter 8 relating to the effectiveness of the PM process, including the danger of concentrating on just a few objectives, ignoring the needs of the team and the difficulties in actually defining meaningful objectives.

■ It is not clear how good a motivator it is. In most schemes, including the example shown in Case studies 9.1 and 9.2, the pay difference between the average performer and the high performer is only, at most, 3 or 4%. On an average salary of, say £20,000, this represents an after-tax monthly difference of only £35 or so. Most evaluations find that employees do not regard PRP in financial terms as an effective motivator.

■ Managers may be tempted to pick out their favourites to award them higher PRP than the rest of the staff creating a considerable sense of cynicism and unfairness.

■ Managers, on the other hand, may not want to go through the hassle of differentiation and the difficulties it causes and may put all staff on the same level which produces, ultimately, the same effect. Distributive justice, as it is called, has not been done or seen to be done.

■ Individual PRP can work against team working. If individuals are assessed entirely on their own performance, they will want to shine, to claim all achievements as their own, rather than a team's.

Making it work

Helen Murlis (1993) has set out a series of key criteria for the successful implementation of a PRP scheme, including the following:

■ Top management 'ownership' of the concept and commitment to its introduction as an integral part of the organisation's strategy and to be personally involved with implementation' to walk as it talks.

■ The system to be strategically integrated with the organisational objectives and its human resource, and pay strategy and policies which include a clear and shared vision of the anisation's future.

■ A robust PM scheme on which pay increases are based, introduced in phases from the top downward at a pace that ensures employees understand what is happening and why.

■ The PM scheme should be integrated with the way that employees are managed, rather than an additional paper exercise, and which includes regular reviews during the year and no surprises at the annual review date.

■ The review should encourage honest, positive and fair management of poor performance with time and resources to put the situation right.

■ Rewards should be capable of being 'significant' for the market sector and to be easy to understand and be publicly defensible.

■ Avoiding using PRP to compensate for recruitment problems, market pressure, inability to promote, taking on significant additional responsibilities and other issues which risk confusing the messages implicit in the system.

■ Substantial training and communication for all concerned to ensure it is thoroughly understood.

■ Regular reviews and flexible adaptation of the scheme as lessons are learnt and to respond to employee feedback, reflecting the way an organisation needs to constantly develop and change.

Skills-based and competence-based pay

There has been a growing emphasis, especially in manufacturing organisations, to support initiatives that increase the level of skills and competencies in the workforce. Encouraging production employees to learn a variety of jobs on their team, or to learn maintenance skills, has become an essential part of the jigsaw of improving productivity and quality. This encouragement sometimes takes the form of *skills-based pay*, where the acquiring of a set of specific skill levels earn the employee a higher rate of pay. These skills can be linked to NVQs or to a specific skill set devised by the organisation. Rhone-Poulenc Agriculture employees can obtain an NVQ and a pay increase of up to £4000 a year through their comprehensive multi-skilling scheme leading to technician status. British Home Stores, on the other hand, started down the NVQ route in 1994 for their retail employees but then switched to their own training and development package called Spotlight on Success which consisted of 18 job-related skill sets (IDS, 1996).

Competency-based pay has many similarities in that employees are encouraged to develop a set of competencies which, when obtained, leads to the opportunity of higher pay. Abbey Life introduced such a scheme in 1994 (Competency, 1994) and pay progression operates only on the basis of competency and performance criteria.

Benefits

The final part of the reward jigsaw is the selection of benefits payable to employees. The total cost of benefits are high, adding up to as much as 20% of the pay bill when pension are included. The collection of benefits available are generally haphazard, having grown without a strategic basis or direction. It is often because of the perceived need to be competitive in the marketplace that they are introduced or extended. Rarely are they withdrawn, although this is not unknown, and usually some form of compensation may be offered if this occurs. They can be divided into three main groupings:

Personal security. This is the welfare section where the employer is prepared to subsidise the employee when they have specific health or associated needs. Sick pay, Life Assurance, Private health Insurance, Prolonged Disability schemes and Pensions all come under this heading. They operate because employers wish to be regarded as kind and generous (as they may well be). However, the generosity of a sick pay scheme may be an organisation's undoing as too many employees find that they may be just as well off on the sick as at work.

Job-related benefits. Some jobs have 'perquisites' (perks) the most common being the company car. The UK have the most generous company car policy in the world with cars being issued even when the jobs are almost entirely office or factory based. Other benefits include re-location allowances and protective clothing allowances.

Family friendly benefits are also developing in these times of acute awareness of the need to accommodate employees with caring responsibilities. Creches, Child-care vouchers, compassionate leave, maternity and paternity leave plus special working hour arrangements are all regarded as welcome benefits to those hard-pressed by conflicting demands of home and work.

Meteor case study

Designing a reward structure

Another year has gone by and Sarah had achieved the promotion to the position of human resources manager at head office with specific responsibility for compensation and benefits. On appointment, she had attended a three day course on Reward Management run by the CIPD and had joined a small group of fellow specialists in her immediate locality who met every 2 months to talk informally about reward developments and market rates.

Her first major assignment was to examine the reward structure that had been in place at the corporate headquarters for over 10 years. This structure served 700 employees, half of whom were management and administrative staff and the others were a mixture of sales and service staff for the telecommunications business. The base rate was set through a Hay job evaluation scheme and consisted of 15 grades from filing clerks on grade 1 to executive managers on grade 15. There was no performance pay scheme and the only variable element in the pay was an annual Christmas bonus decided by the CE which had given an average of 3% of salary over the last 3 years.

An examination was necessary for a number of reasons. Pay drift had become a matter of concern, adding nearly 2% to salaries over the previous 18 months. It was difficult to see why this had accelerated recently but it was partly self-perpetuating as increases won through revised job grading by one group of employees was swiftly followed by a similar claim by a group in the next door department. Another concern was that this grade drift had started to cause the pay rates to move beyond the median rate in the locality that they had previously occupied. To try to draw the annual salary costs back to compensate for the salary drift, the annual pay increase awarded in the previous year had been low but this had caused discontentment and a sense of unfairness amongst the staff. A final cause of concern was the growing unwillingness of staff to take on new duties without a major discussion arising about their grading. As many such changes had come about and were being planned for the next 12 months as the nature of the business altered, it was considered essential that a major new initiative took place.

Sarah began by talking to all of the Senior Management concerning the current difficulties and the possible options. She also commissioned a specific short Attitude Survey through MORI regarding employees' views on pay and benefits. Finally, she set up a series of Focus Groups with the staff to try to obtain a balance of their views.

She found that there was a clear consensus for change in most areas. Neither managers nor staff had a great commitment to the Hay scheme, recognising that it was being used for political purposes and for sectional gains. The large number of re-grading claims and the time they took to sort out merely served to divide staff rather than giving a sense of fairness on pay issues. Staff were also generally satisfied with their current pay level but that there was a strong view that there should be some sort of pay arrangement that differentiated between good, average and poor employees.

Having cleared her tactics with Senior Management, Sarah sent out a communication briefing to staff which set out her findings on employees' current pay attitudes. Rather than come up with a new pay system to implement, Sarah offered two alternatives for staff to consider and discuss in their management teams. The first was the complete abolition of the job evaluation scheme and the introduction of a loose, broad-banded pay structure with only four bands. Movement within the band would be based entirely on the employees' performance as judged by their line manager. The second alternative retained the vestiges of the grading structure but the number of grades would be reduced to seven and the movement within those grades would occur through a combination of performance and the achievement of competencies.

After widespread debate within the teams, a majority view (although not voted on) emerged in favour of the second option. Sarah then set about designing a detailed scheme using a competency framework she had 'borrowed' from one of her colleagues in the local group who had a similar head office unit. It needed to be adapted to fit the revised Mission statement and values recently issued by the board but the overall match was good and considerable savings were made in this way by not using expensive specialist consultants. The existing jobs would need to be re-evaluated and place in the reduced number of grades and this would be achieved by redefining jobs against the overall competency framework. With only seven grades, there would be less opportunity for arguments at the borders.

Establishing how employees would achieve competencies was carried out through the services of a specialist who worked in the Business school at the University. The most complicated process was establishing the method of converting an individual's performance and level of competence into a rating scale. For this, she spent time with each head of department agreeing the nature of the vital performance indicators and how they could be balanced from one department to another. She knew that managers would take the decisions on both areas and that she would have to act as umpire to make sure departments were neither too generous or strict in their overall judgements.

After a series of short training courses for the managers and supervisors, the scheme was launched at the time of the pay increase. It had been agreed that the pay increase would be at an acceptable level and that employees who came out of the re-grading exercise as being over-paid would be 'red-circled', in other words, their pay would stay the same until annual pay increases brought their pay into line. There was general approval from staff of the overall pay increase but Sarah knew that the real test of the scheme would come towards the end of the year when employees could see the direction that their own pay and jobs were going.

At the same time, Sarah persuaded the Board, through her HR Director, to replace the arbitrary annual bonus with a Gainsharing Plan. A number of site targets were set which related to overall labour costs, customer complaints, on-time delivery, employee innovation and a selection of departmental specialist targets which added value to the organisation. Achievement of these targets would lead to a percentage bonus on a sliding scale from 1% to a maximum of 10%. Tying this in with profits was a challenging process as she knew that profit sharing rarely motivated a head office environment. The final version was complicated and needed a great deal of selling. Moreover, it would be difficult to get employees involved until they saw that it actually produced the required results. A monthly meeting of a group of interested employees representing all the departments plus a monthly information sheet would be the vehicles to gain employee commitment.

Summary

- Reward strategies should be aligned to the corporate strategy to ensure that they motivate employees to achieve the required objectives and adopt the preferred skills, competencies and behaviours.

- In recent years, there has been a sharp shift from payment employees according to their job and length of service to paying people for their achievements and competencies.

- Salary structures are being developed using broad-banding techniques that are beginning to replace traditional job evaluation techniques.

- There are a wide variety of performance pay systems for various employment situations. Performance related pay, the best known, remains controversial with critics equally balanced between those who view it as subjective, divisive and too complicated to operate and those who see no alternative to a system that differentiates between those employees who perform well and those that do not.

- Payment systems should aim to be fair, equitable and cost-effective.
- Benefits make up a sizeable part of the pay bill and serve a number of functions, including personal security and supporting family friendly policies.

Student activities

1 As a human resources manager, you have been asked to carry out a local survey to find the 'market rate' for a Marketing Assistant. Detail how you would plan and implement this project, list the difficulties you would encounter and how you may overcome them.

2 Look up cases involving 'red-circling' which relate to job evaluation and equal pay claims. Examine the legal implications of the red-circling that took place in the Meteor case study.

3 In the Meteor case study, what would be the outcomes of the new pay system that would make employees very unhappy with the new system?

4 Discuss with two of your colleagues which benefits are the most important ones to offer, putting them in a league table of importance. Justify your decisions.

5 Look up the article that is the basis for Focus on research 9.1. Why do you think that some of the respondents consider that their reward strategy does not operate in practice?

6 In the article that is the basis for Focus on research 9.2, examine the views of the respondents on the appraisal process. How well does it appear to operate overall and what are the greatest difficulties?

7 BOC's new reward system appears to be working well, according to the article. Make a list of all the aspects of the scheme that could go wrong and what the company might do about them.

8 In Case study 9.2, what would happen if business turned down and the company made little or no gains over a pay period?

References

Armstrong, M., Baron, A. (1995) *The Job Evaluation Handbook*. IPD.
Armstrong, M., Brown, D. (2001) New Dimensions in Pay Management. CIPD.
Armstrong, M., Murlis, H. (1994) *Reward Management*, Kogan Page.

Brown, D. (2001) *Reward Strategies.* CIPD.

Cannell, M., Wood, S. (1992) Incentive Pay. IPD.

Corkerton, S., Bevan, S. (1998) Paying hard to get. *People Management,* August 13, 40–42.

Competency (1994). Abbey life – Helping managers to use competencies, 1, 3, p. 2.

Dowling, B., Richardson, R. (1997) Evaluating performance related pay for managers in the health service. *International Journal of Human Resource Management,* 8(3): 348–366.

Flannery, T., Hofrichter, D., Platten, P. (1996) *People, Performance and Pay.* The Free Press.

Gomez-Mejia, L., Balkin, D. (1992) *Compensation, Organisational Strategy and Firm Performance.* Southwestern Publishing.

IDS (1996) *Skills-based Pay.* Study 610. IDS.

IPD (1998) *Performance Pay Survey.* London, IPD.

IPD/IMS (1992) *Performance Management in the UK: An Analysis of the Issues.* IPD.

Kohn, A. (1993) Why incentive plans cannot work. *Harvard Business Review,* September/October, 54–63.

Lambs, J. (1996) Leading organisational change. *Personnel Journal,* July, 61.

Marsden, D., Richardson, R. (1994) Performance for pay? The effects of merit pay on motivation in a public service. *British Journal of Industrial Relations,* 32(2): 243–262.

Milkovich, G., Newman, J. (1996) *Compensation.* Irwin.

Poels, F. (1997) *Job Evaluation and Remuneration Strategies.* Kogan Page.

Poole, M., Jenkins, G. (1998) Human resource management and the theory of rewards: evidence from a National Survey. *British Journal of Industrial Relations,* 36(2): 227–247.

Robinson, J. (1998) Hotel pays out on the spot to staff. *Personnel Today,* 23 April, 2.

Thompson, M. (1993) *Pay and Performance – the Employee Experience.* Report No. 258. Institute of Manpower Studies.

Further reading

For publications covering the whole of reward issues, see:

Holman, G., Thorpe, R. (eds) (1999) *Strategic Reward Systems.* Financial Times Management.

Kerr, S. (1997) *Ultimate Rewards.* Harvard Business Review Books.

Murlis, H. (ed.) (1996) *Pay at the Crossroads.* IPD.

Wilson, T. (1994) *Innovative Reward Systems for the Creative Workplace,* McGraw Hill.

White, G., Druker, J. (2000) *Reward Management, a Critical Text.* Routledge.

For publications covering specific areas of rewards see:

Bevan, S., Thompson, M. (1992) *Merit Pay, Performance Appraisal and Attitudes to Women's Work.* Institute of Manpower Studies. Report 258. IMS.

Brown, D., Armstrong, M. (1999) *Paying for Contribution,* 1999 (Excellent detail on PRP).

Gunnigle, Turner, D'Art (1998) Counterpoising collectivism: performance related pay in Greenfield sites. *British Journal of Industrial Relations*, 36(4) 565–579.

Gross, S. (1995) *Compensation for Teams.* Amacom.

IPD (1997) *Guide to Broad Banding.* IPD.

Jorgensen, K. (1996) *Pay for Results.* Merrit.

Pritchard, D., Murlis, H. (1992) *Jobs, Roles and People – the New World of Job Evaluation*, Nicolas, Brealey.

Reilly, P. (2004) *New Reward I: Team, Skill and Competency based Pay.* IES Report 403.

Thompson, M. (1995) *Team Working and Pay.* Institute of Manpower Studies Report 281. IMS.

For an article showing the links between culture change and incentive pay, see:

Ashton, C. (1999) Merit pointers. *Personnel Today*, 1 April, 61–62.

Income Data Services and Industrial Relations Services have numerous articles and reports on Pay Issues.

Web site

http://www.streetwisemotivation.com
American site on motivating and rewarding employees.

Learning and development — theory and practice

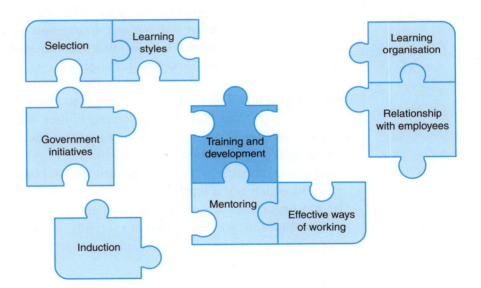

When you have read this chapter and carried out the activities, you will be able to:

- Explain a number of different approaches organisations take to training and development.
- Understand the component parts of the learning cycle.

■ Analyse the various techniques of training.
■ Identify the importance of training arrangements such as action learning, induction and sales training.
■ Assess the role of government in initiating development in learning and training.

Introduction

As we saw in Chapter 8, there is a strong argument that the most important role in human resources is to help employees to improve their performance and, by so doing, improve the performance of the organisation. To improve, employees need a combination of the will to improve (motivation) and the encouragement to acquire job-related knowledge, skills and attitudes (KSAs). We have dealt with motivation in Chapter 6 and this chapter will cover how the second part can be achieved, by looking firstly at *the way people learn*, followed by an examination of a selection of *training and development techniques*. Finally, we will look at the *government initiatives* that are intended to help the learning process, including Investors in People.

Storey and Sisson (1993) refer to the 'virtuous circle' of development, whereby a high investment can lead to a more effective utilisation of high technology, higher skill levels, higher wages and lower unit labour costs, leading ultimately to competitive advantage. On the other hand, a large swathe of business and industry relies on badly applied 'on-the-job' training, with little opportunity for planned personal development which often leads to the opposite effect, namely lower wages, higher unit costs and an inferior competitive stance overall.

The Bennett and Leduchowicz (1983) model seeks to plot why organisations train and the predominant ways in which they carry out their training (see Figure 10.1).

The vertical axis shows the contrast between maintaining the existing organisational and employee work patterns (as with the old apprenticeship schemes) and simply responding to situations to, at the other end of the spectrum, using training to support initiatives in fundamental changes to the organisation and its practices. The horizontal axis indicates how the training takes place from a traditional tutor led programme to one that may be less structured but intervenes in the workplace through such methods as mentoring, action learning and team building.

■ The *Caretaker* approach keeps training on its traditional path to support what is in place without rocking the boat.

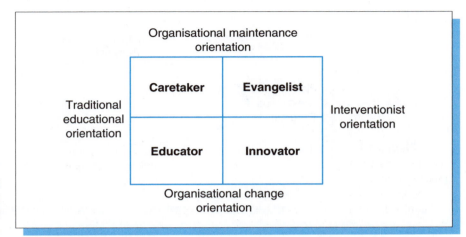

Figure 10.1
Bennett and
Leduchowicz model
(*Source*: Bennett and
Leduchowicz, 1983)

- The *Educators* use traditional means but see their role as assisting in organisation change. This is the least likely to be successful in practice.
- An *Evangelist* still want to maintain the status quo but will use all the more progressive methods of training to support this viewpoint.
- *Innovators* also use such methods but utilise them to support major organisational change.

Learning needs to take place not just at the start of employment life or on commencing a new job but throughout a person's career right up to their retirement day. Some people would argue that learning to live with retirement is one of the most difficult learning processes and many large organisations even run courses on this subject for their impending retirees!

How people learn

Learning has taken place, as defined by Honey and Mumford, when someone:

'Knows something they did not know earlier, and can show it and is able to do something which they were not able to do before.'

Honey and Mumford (1992)

We all know that people learn in different ways but models can be useful which show a comprehensive approach to the learning process.

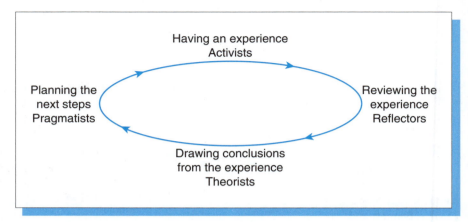

Having an experience
Activists

Planning the
next steps
Pragmatists

Reviewing the
experience
Reflectors

Drawing conclusions
from the experience
Theorists

Figure 10.2
The learning cycle
(*Source*: Kolb, 1984
and Honey and
Mumford, 1992)

Kolb's (1995) learning cycle (see Figure 10.2) is the most well known and is based on the concept that learning starts from having a concrete experience. The learner then moves on to review that experience by observation and reflection, draws conclusions from that experience, often with the use of abstract concepts, and finally plans the next step by testing the concepts.

Let us take an example of a learning cycle with which you may be familiar. Mary, a student, joins with two others in sharing a flat. They make no formal arrangement at first on buying basic essentials, such as bread, milk and potatoes, leaving it to chance as to when they need them.

■ *Stage 1.* Mary experiences for the third week running that they are out of essentials and she has to go out and buy them.
■ *Stage 2.* She reflects on this situation, considering that it is not fair and equitable or an efficient way of running the flat.
■ *Stage 3.* She concludes that some formal system will need to be introduced whereby one person is responsible and collects money from the other two on a regular basis to reimburse her.
■ *Stage 4.* She sits down with the other two students and obtains their agreement and together they plan how it is to be operated.

Kolb's original work was carried out in the 1970s and it has been adapted and developed by Honey and Mumford, who have created a Learning Style analysis based on the learning cycle. They realised that some people are stronger at one stage then another and have put titles to people who prefer each of the four stages, which can be identified by why of a learning styles questionnaire:

■ *Activists.* Some very active people look at life as a continuous set of new experiences from which to intuitively learn. They approach each new experience with enthusiasm and tend to act first and consider the consequences later. They often lead in discussions but do not necessarily produce logically thought-out ideas or proposals.

- *Reflectors.* Others may prefer to have fewer experiences but will reflect carefully on those experiences, collecting data and bringing in to discussions a range of other people's experiences. They are good at listening and may not take it upon themselves to lead discussions.

- *Theorists.* A third group are those that can think through problems, and create sound and logical theories to explain what they see. They prefer everything to fit together and may not be happy to proceed unless every 't' has been crossed.

- *Pragmatists* are those that like agreements to be reached so they can be put into action. They are down to earth, can be good negotiators and realise that agreements often leave small details to be sorted out later.

An understanding of learning styles can be advantageous to the individual to assist them in fine-tuning their own style to gain the greatest advantage from it, perhaps in making it more balanced and rounded. It can also help in relationships between staff. An example here can be the greater understanding that can be achieved between an 'Activist manager' and their 'Theorist' subordinate when they are considering a current incentive scheme that appears to be failing. The manager will want to move quickly on from that scheme and introduce a new idea that he has just thought up, whereas the subordinate will want to take more time in trying to put the experience of the failed scheme into a theoretical context, so that the same mistakes are not made a second time. If they are aware of their learning styles, they will have a better appreciation of each other's viewpoint and be more likely to reach a compromise on a course of action.

Honey and Mumford's four groupings are not mutually exclusive. In fact, the great majority of individuals emerge from the questionnaire with a combination of two. For example, the Reflector–Theorist will both consider all aspects of the experience and come up with theories and explanations to give a comprehensive and well thought through analysis of the learning experience. On the other hand, the Activist–Pragmatist will be good at coming up with ideas and to get them agreed and put into practice so the learning process takes place quickly.

There are a number of theories that attempt to explain the learning process itself which Marchington and Wilkinson (2002) place into four groups:

■ *Learning by association.* The experiments by Pavlov and others with animals show that learning takes place through association with food and praise and this can be applied to human learning through immediate feedback and recognition. For example, the immediate praise (and, perhaps, some criticism) of a student's presentation after the event will lead to a reinforcement of how to carry out a good presentation. Taking association a stage further, much of customer-care training will aim to build into the minds of the trainees immediate positive responses to customer needs, so that trainees will learn to give the appropriate response and even anticipate what customers want.

■ *Cognitive learning.* This is what most of us understand as conventional learning when we sit down and think our way through a situation or theory, learning in the process. An easy example here is learning a new computer programme from an instruction manual (badly written, of course!) where the combination of using logical thought with the pleasure of gaining insight act as a powerful reinforcer of learning.

■ *Cybernetics.* This approach regards learning as an 'information-processing system in which a signal containing information is passed along a communication channel subject to interference from a variety of sources' (Collin, 2001). Learning a language through programmed learning will come into this category with the interference being personal problems of the trainees that can impair their learning.

■ The final category is *social learning theory* which used to be known as 'sitting by Nellie' or picking the job up by imitation. The advantage of this form is that the social processes are learnt at the same time but it is by no means systematic and, in practice, the trainee learns to imitate the wrong ways as well as the correct ways of the job.

The learning organisation

Research in the late 1980s introduced the notion of the learning organisation. This concept involves regarding the organisation as a living organism existing in its environment that needs to have good feedback mechanisms and the ability to adapt to changing circumstances by taking timely action (Moorby, 1996). A definition by Wick and Leon (1995) is an organisation that 'continually improves by rapidly creating and refining the capabilities required for future success'.

In practice, it has a very broad interpretation but is generally regarded as having some or all of the following features:

- The ability to approach problem-solving in a systematic way by encouraging employees to learn statistical and questioning techniques.
- A willingness to search for new ideas and to use them, especially when they come from employees through a 'kaizen' scheme or similar.
- A desire to openly evaluate past successes and failures and to learn from both.
- To continually look outside the organisation for 'best practice' and analysing if and how it can be transferred to the organisation successfully.
- To establish a culture where employees can question existing rules and procedures and to take part in decision-making processes from which they can learn.
- The acceptance that mistakes will be made and that this is part of the learning process.
- A recognition that learning is open to all employees, not just managers or supervisors and that self-development is as important as development planned by management.
- To implement systems that can be accessed by a wide group of users, not just experts.

Organisations that subscribe to these tenets will aim to create a labour force that that is eager to learn, to questions, to experiment, to take part in decisions and to take responsibility for its actions. It can be seen at once that this conflicts with a culture that is hierarchically based, where management takes decision and where employees carry out the work as directed. Moving to a learning organisation will normally need major cultural shifts as well as the adoption of the some of the features listed above. An example of such a move is given in the *Meteor case study* at the end of the chapter.

In practice, the change is not an easy one to achieve. As Harrison (2002) has pointed out it requires a 'skillful balance between formal systems and informal features … and presupposes a sophisticated approach to the knowledge process that does not fit easily with the lack of expertise and awareness that research indicates actually prevails in the field' (p. 388).

Training aims and objectives

The fundamental aim of training is to help the organisation to meet its organisational objectives by increasing the value of its major resource, namely, its employees. Armstrong (2001) sets out three specific training objectives:

- To develop the competences of employees and improve their performance.
- To help people grow within the organisation in order that, as far as possible, its future needs for human resources can be met from within the organisation.
- To reduce the learning time for employees starting in new jobs on appointment, transfer or promotion, and ensure that they become fully competent as quickly and economically as possible.

There needs to be a systematic approach to training, which means that training must be directed towards specific ends. It is all too common for employees to be sent on training courses as a result of an attractive brochure arriving on a manager's desk without considering the real needs of the employee or the implications of the training. A systematic approach is best explained through an analysis of the training cycle.

The four-stage training cycle

The training cycle (see Figure 10.3) has similar stages to the learning cycle with which it has more than a passing resemblance.

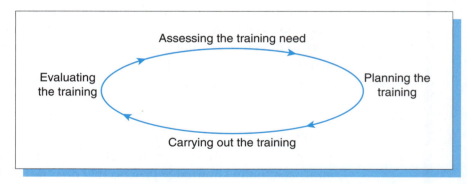

Assessing the training need

Evaluating the training

Planning the training

Carrying out the training

Figure 10.3
The training cycle

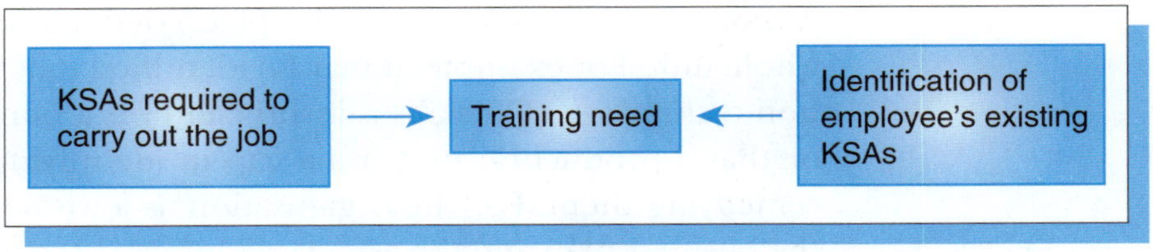

Figure 10.4
Identification of
training needs

Stage 1 Assessing training needs

A training need arises due to the identified gap between the required knowledge, skills and experience for the individual carrying out the work and that actually possessed by the employee concerned (see Figure 10.4). This identification of training needs process can take place in a number of ways:

- When an employee starts a *new job*, an analysis will be carried out which examines the job requirements (through the job description and specification – see Chapter 4) and matches that against the employee's existing profile. No candidate is ever perfect so there will always be a number of gaps to fill, especially if it is an internal transfer or promotion or if the new employee is specifically taken on as a trainee.
- Through the *annual appraisal* process (see Chapter 8) where the employee and their manager sit down together and draw up a list of areas where training can help the employee to perform better, after agreeing on the existing job requirements and the employee's actual performance level.
- Where a *specific incident* occurs which demonstrates a major gap. For example, a number of customer complaints close together will indicate customer-care training is required for the employee concerned. If a member of staff takes up a grievance against a manager's attitude or actions, then this could indicate that the manager concerned needs some form of training on handling staff. If there is a 'near miss' reported which lays the blame on a pilot, then it is vital that re-training of that pilot takes place.
- A *development centre* (see Chapter 5) will throw up a selection of needs, especially those relating to inter-personal skills, such as group problem-solving or running meetings.
- *Exit interviews* may also show training needs, in that employees leaving the organisation may make it clear that one of the reasons they are leaving is because they were not adequately prepared for the work they were doing.

A training needs analysis can also be carried out for a department or a whole unit. For example, it may be identified that the level of information technology (IT) skills is insufficient for a purchasing department or that a production unit has a gap in identifying quality errors and remedying them. For the organisation as a whole, an examination of the business plan and the associated human resources plan may immediately bring training needs to light. An example here was the identification by Pearl Assurance of the need for a new approach for sales training. Bringing together a collection of individual training needs may show that areas of required training can be common across many employees, sections or units. Training needs arise specifically when a major change programme occurs in the organisation.

Having carried out the analysis, the next stage is to negotiate a *training plan*. It is very rarely the case that all the training needs identified can be met within the budget, so negotiation needs to take place to decide on priorities across departments, roles and individuals. Prioritising through need is a better system than the arbitrary allocation of funds on the basis of adding, say, 5% onto last year's budget for each department (Reid and Barrington, 1997).

Stage 2 Planning and carrying out the training

There is no distinct cutting-off point between planning and implementing the training. Inherent within the planning process is the decision on a number of issues:

- Should the training take place on-the-job or off-the-job?
- Should it be held in the company or outsourced to a training provider?
- Which techniques should be used?

On-the-job training is appropriate where immediacy and realism are essential. Its advantages is that it provides instant entry into the job, the trainees work, learn and develop expertise at the same time, they can see the results of their actions and they can usually be effectively supervised while they are learning. They also learn the social aspects of the job, the informal culture and the small details that are often omitted from training manuals or job descriptions.

The disadvantages all centre on the quality of the supervisor responsible for the trainee and the way the information is passed to the trainee. All too often, the information is passed on in a haphazard way by an overworked supervisor who is untrained in instruction techniques. Worse still, the instruction may be completely delegated to an experienced fellow-employee who may then instruct them on all the short-cuts and bad habits that have developed over the years. The environment is an important aspect here in that the trainee may be put off and distracted by the noise or apparent confusion of a totally new experience and find it difficult to cope with learning to work with new people, as well as a new job. Trainees are bound to make mistakes and this can be expensive in an on-the-job situation; in fact, because of such potential costs, the trainees are often held back for an extended period from doing the important work.

Off-the-job training, which takes place usually in a training school or appropriate facilities away from the immediate workplace, has the advantage of allowing the trainee to concentrate on learning the new job without distraction and for the training to be delivered systematically by skilled and experienced trainers. It can also help to give an immediate good first impression for a new employee. Trainees can make mistakes without the fear of an immediate cost to the organisation and tests can be set up for each stage to ensure that the job has been learnt thoroughly before being released into the real working situation.

The disadvantages are that it is difficult to re-create a situation that is close to a real-life one without a high investment cost, such as the training carried out by airlines who, understandably, spend millions of pounds in creating simulated flying conditions. When trainees transfer onto the job, they may come across situations not covered in training or find the work to be far more complex than it was set out in the training school.

Outsourcing the training is an alternative chosen when the training skills required are not present within the organisation. This applies with managerial, professional and technical training where the specialist training organisation has built up a reputation for running special courses. They may run these courses in their own premises, or within the company or in convenient hired premises, such as hotels or conference centres. The advantage is that experts should provide high-quality training and expose employees to situations that they have not experienced. Trainees may also learn from their fellow delegates how operations are carried out differently in other organisations. Until the arrival of mobile phones, there used to be the advantage that the trainees would be able to concentrate totally on the training without fear of interruption!

The disadvantages include the fact that the cost is usually higher, that the specialist organisation may not be aware of the organisation's specific requirements and that they do not normally follow up the trainees to see how effective the training has been in practice.

Stage 3 Styles and techniques of training

Many of the styles and techniques to be described can apply only to off-the-job situations but some can also apply to on-the-job training. Another way to divide the techniques is between those that have considerably active learning ingredients, such as action learning, computer-based learning or working with case studies, and those that are essential passive, such as demonstrations, lectures and videos. A final division is between those techniques that can apply to individual training, such as mentoring and those which apply to groups, large or small, such as role-play or workshops. Figure 10.5 will indicate which category each technique falls into.

Technique	Comments	On- or off-the-job or both	Active or passive	Individual or group
Job instruction	Trainer must be trained, have a clear plan and build up an effective and encouraging relationship with the training. Applies principally to basic jobs, such as assembly or hairdressing or some retail counter work.	Both	Mostly passive	Individual or small groups
Computerised training	This allows the trainee to work through the programme at their own pace with immediate feedback. It can cover simple skills such as learning about spreadsheets to highly complex processes such as pilot simulations. It is particularly effective for the essential basics of language learning.	Off-the-job	Active	Individual
Planned sequence of experience (job rotation)	Often operated within a department to ensure the employees to know all the department's work, the training needs to be well-planned and co-ordinated, with mutual support given to each other by the employees within the department. There must also be clear learning objectives.	On-the-job	Active	Individual
Lectures and demonstrations	Lectures to large numbers will need an inspired speaker and an attentive, motivated audience. That is why it mostly fails! It is theoretically efficient in passing on information but research shows that only 20% or less sticks. Visual aids are important and follow-up/practice is essential for this activity to be of any value. Demonstrations	Off-the-job	Passive	Small or large groups

Figure 10.5
Techniques of training

	can be more effective if small groups are involved, if questions are allowed and the opportunity to repeat difficult sequences are allowed.			
Role-play	One of the most attractive forms of training where individuals adopt a role set out for them and act out the scenario as a group. In so acting, they remember much of what they have done, it can be highly relevant and practical to the subject of the training and is generally great fun. The difficulties arise if the end result of the role-play is not as planned or if any of the 'actors' do not take the activity seriously enough. A further version of role-reversal, which can be used, say, with appraisal training where the manager and the appraisee change roles, can be highly effective in helping with inter-personal skills.	Off-the-job	Active	Small groups
Group discussion	Success emerges from the way a discussion is handled, to ensure it is led well, keeps to the point, involves a wide number of participants and is effectively summarised.	Off-the-job	Mostly Actively	Small groups
Video	A straight video, well produced, can be a useful vehicle for imparting knowledge and demonstrating skills but it needs to be reinforced through questions or practice.	Off-the-job	Passive	Small or large groups
Distance learning	By using specially prepared materials which involve the trainee listening to tapes, carrying out exercises and responding to questions, the trainee can work at their own pace and learn the subject in a systematic way. The only major disadvantage, if the materials are well prepared, is the isolation of the trainee where a high degree of self-motivation is required.	Off-the-job	Passive and active	Individual
Project work or case study	If the project/case study chosen is stimulating and realistic, the trainee(s) will learn in-depth the subject in question and will increase their investigative and creative skills. It can also be utilised for discussion and advocacy skills can be developed.	Off-the-job mostly	Active	Individual or small group

Figure 10.5   (*continued*).

In addition to these techniques, there are a number of specialised training schemes, such as mentoring and action learning that will be examined towards the end of the chapter.

In terms of carrying out the training, it is important to ensure that the employees concerned are fully aware of the objectives before they start and that they have the necessary information regarding the training itself. Nothing puts trainees off more than poor administration so it is vital that all the necessary preparation is made in respect of materials, exercises, workbooks, cases and technology.

Stage 4 Evaluating the training

The last part of the cycle is vital to the whole process. Unless there can be reasonable proof that the training actually added value, then it becomes easy to dismiss it as a waste of time and money. There are two forms of evaluation, subjective and objective. *Subjective evaluation* can be made by the trainer, who will be aware whether or not the training went well. It will also emerge from the trainees who should be asked for their opinions at various stages through the programme, both verbally and in written 'happy sheets'. A final evaluation by the trainees should move towards the *objective viewpoint*, having to answer questions such as: 'How has this training benefited you in the workplace?', or 'name a number of areas where you will put into effect improvements that have arisen from what you have learnt during this training.'

Other objective measures can be involved in observing improved performance (productivity, quality, customer relations) and any measures considered robust by the organisation. These will be balanced with subjective measures from the trainee's manager and internal customers. Some training, such as graduate training programmes, take some time to bear fruit, so a final evaluation may take place a year or two after the training is completed.

Specialised training arrangements

Induction

Induction is often considered as an early part of the training process. Once an applicant accepts a position, then they can be passed on to the training department who take over from that point. Recently, induction has been seen more as the final but vital part of the selection process. The selection job is not complete until the applicant is safely introduced into the organisation and helped to overcome the difficulties and pressures of those first few days and weeks.

For most positions, an induction of 1–2 days is allowed to provide the basic information to the new recruit and to introduce them to the important aspects of working in the organisation.

Student activity 10.1

Make a list of all the activities and information that you would include in an induction programme for a trainee in a small engineering company.

Discussion of Student activity 10.1

Some of the points you may have written down (in no particular order) are shown in Figure 10.6.

Activities	Information
Basic Safety training, including protective clothing and emergency procedures	Safety rules and regulations
Tour of the premises, including toilets, canteen and first aid provisions	Map of premises – departments
Introduction to colleagues, management (maybe shop steward)	Up to date organisation chart
Brief outline of company history, mission statement, set of values, system of communication	Any relevant documents
Outline of products and what they do (including demonstration) plus brief summary of customers and suppliers	Copy of main product brochures
Introduction to company handbook, including benefits, procedures on holidays and sickness and company rules, disciplinary procedures, payment of wages	Copy of employee handbook
Introduction to work of department and the role of trainee. System of performance management	Copy of any working procedures and details of practices regarding breaks, clocking, use of materials, etc. Performance management scheme
Introduction to any social activities	Details of clubs, outings

Figure 10.6
Induction programme

This can be converted into a short programme, led by the human resources officer, but bringing in other friendly faces, including the safety officer, training officer and the works manager. It is not unknown in a small organisation for the owner or Chief Executive to want to personally meet each new person on the first day. They are, after all, a considerable investment and should represent a priority. A balance needs to be drawn between ensuring that the trainee has all the information required as soon as possible and flooding them with too much information and causing them confusion and a degree of disorientation.

Team building

In Chapter 6, we examined the role of team building in developing a more effective organisation. Teams rarely flourish naturally; like tender plants, they need constant attention and encouragement. Team building training has many forms, but the essential feature of most is for the team to go through some testing experiences together which then forge them into a unit with common successful experiences and a '*combat d'esprit*'. If that sounds like the army, that is because most team training originated from US or UK armed forces research into the subject.

The most quickly growing area here is outdoor training where teams are set challenges, often, but not always, in a competitive situation. Having successfully completed the challenge, the teams then reflect upon the process, teasing out learning points. These centre around what makes teams successful, including effective team leadership, the ability to jointly solve problems while under a degree of stress, to listen very carefully (especially when it is getting dark, the wind is howling, the flood water is rising and the centre is across the river!). Such training is also important in developing personal competencies, such as time management, planning, delegation and evaluation and to retain a degree of confidence under adversity.

The experience is not always successful. Sometimes fundamental flaws in the teams rise to the service under stressful conditions and there are some team members, even in the best teams, where the physical challenges are simply not appropriate. Having said this, the author's own limited experience in two organisations was that the activity was an unqualified success with the teams concerned improving their performance by more than 20% over the next 12 months and still talking about it 5 years later. Evidence shown in Focus on research 10.1 would support the positive outcomes of outdoor training.

Organisational change and outdoor management education

McEvoy studied the responses of two groups of employees with similar demographic attributes in one organisation. One group were measured before they undertook outdoor training (control group) and the other group after the outdoor training had taken place. Thirty follow-up interviews were undertaken 2 months after the training and a second set 3 years later. McEvoy found that outdoor management education positively influenced participant knowledge, organisational commitment and self-esteem together with the intention to implement what they had learnt. The improvement in these areas were immediate and were retained at the end of the 3-year period, as measured by such indicators as reduced sickness and better implementation of Total Quality Management Schemes.

Source: McEvoy (1997)

Mentoring

For new employees, and those that are less experienced, it is valuable to have a figure to turn to who will support their career development. A mentor will not have a hierarchical responsibility over the protégé and will often be far removed in the organisation chart. They will certainly be older and will gain satisfaction through observing the successful progress of their protégés. Their main role is to provide a cultural map of the organisation, to help them through bottlenecks in their careers, to develop their own self-development skills and generally to give advice and encouragement when this is required. The mentoring role will normally be between 2 and 5 years with meetings very much on an *ad hoc* basis. An example of a mentoring scheme is shown in Case study 10.1.

Mentoring in Castle Care Nursing Homes

At the Castle Care Village Group of nursing homes, they believe that if it is worth investing in finding the right people, it's worth taking time to make sure they stay, which is why mentoring has been introduced. Each new member of staff is allocated a mentor from day 1 with the organisation, chosen from existing staff who have the attributes of patience and adaptability as well as strengths in skills and knowledge. An attempt is made to match the 20 strong mentor team (out of 180 staff) with the new staff member in terms of personality and experience. They provide a vital support for new staff in the 6-week training course, helping them to identify gaps in basic skills and answering questions and dealing with any day-to-day anxieties. They also check off regularly what has been learnt and how it can be implemented in practice. If basic literacy, numeracy and IT support is required, mentors support their attendance at a twice-weekly course provided by Hull College, giving discrete guidance in what could be regarded as an embarrassing weakness.

Mentors attend a specific training course and a regular refresher conference each year at the University of Hull. Before the scheme began, many new staff did not last even the induction course (a regulatory requirement) but the support and encouragement given by mentors has meant that those who leave within the first 6 months are now a very small minority. The enthusiasm for the job from the mentors rubs off on the trainees and provides a firm foundation for excellent service provided for the vulnerable clients.

Source: Learning and Skills Council 2004 (web site lse.gov.uk/guide2/mentoring)

Action learning

Revens (1989) developed a process of training through problem-solving, essentially for managers, and gave it a new name. He recognised that most people enjoy a continuing set of challenges that they would not face if they simply worked on the same job for long periods of time. His theories, which he tested at the National Coal Board in the period after the Second World War, were centred round the concept that we are motivated to learn *something*, not just motivated to learn, and that learning is deepest when it involves the whole person, using both mind and body. He set out to use the experience, growth and prior learning of colleagues in an active way to solve real problems. In the process, by sharing their hopes, aspirations, successes and errors, each participant learned about themselves, about working together and all about the subjects in question which broadened their whole experience. An example of action learning in Westinghouse Brakes is shown in Case study 10.2.

Case study 10.2

Action learning in Westinghouse Brakes

Westinghouse, a major manufacturer of brakes and door control systems to the rail industry, works closely with its 400 or so suppliers to ensure that there is a simplified supply chain. Around 40% of its costs are in the bought-in materials and there is a constant struggle to balance cost control with quality products in a highly competitive environment.

Since 1995, the company has moved from a position of conflict over price/quality with its suppliers to one of a win/win situation through a programme called 'IMPACT' (Improved Manufacturing Performance through Active Change and Training). On a series of 6 monthly weekends, a dozen participants from different companies meet up to work on a project concerned with Westinghouse's manufacturing processes, sharing ideas and getting practical experience. Their results, which are tested on site, are presented to senior management. The benefits were two-fold. It provided an opportunity for joint problem-solving, which led to a closer working relationship and greater learning about mutual objectives. It also led to successful cost analysis. For example, the replacement of a bespoke component by a standard component reduced the delivery time from 20 weeks to 8 days and saved over £150,000.

The programme was initiated by Phil Brittain, head of company improvement, which includes personnel and training. He had been acutely aware of the need for training and development to underpin all improvement activities which would lead to an increased return to the business. By providing a vehicle for both sides to learn, it has led to substantial benefits for both the suppliers involved and the company and was an Award Finalist in the 1997 National Training Awards.

Source: Evans (1997)

Continuous (or continuing) Professional Development

It is increasingly recognised that professional expertise is not simply learnt at the outset of a career but needs to be constantly refined and updated. Nor should professional learning be restricted to management or supervision but to all employees who wish to journey up the ladder to one or other professional qualification.

The Chartered Institute of Personnel and Development (CIPD), along with other such bodies in professions such as accounting, law and medicine, has set up a regulatory system to encourage its members to continue to learn throughout their careers. This is to make sure that they remain up to date, are aware of the power of learning and contribute towards the high standard of the profession. The encouragement takes the form of advice of recording their learning experiences through such devices as a learning log or diary, as well as actually experiencing the learning itself through courses, conferences, action learning, mentoring and the other specialist learning systems dealt with in this chapter. Upgrading within the institute is dependent upon evidence of such learning (Megginson and Whitaker, 2004).

Sales training

This has been traditionally regarded as a specialised area, carried out by experienced sale personnel where the training is directed towards ensuring the trainees meet their specific targets. Subjects include product and technical knowledge, prospecting, handling objections and closing the sales. There are a number of reasons, however, why sales training has been the subject of wider analysis and interest in recent years:

- Selling is so vital to the company's prosperity that generous resources are usually allocated to the activity. This has led to many of the post-war training innovations being developed in this area, including role-play analysis, the use of videos and telephone simulations, which have then been transferred and utilised in other training areas.

- Opinion has moved from the view that salesmen are born, not made, to the view that potential, which can be identified in psychometric testing, is the key and that focused, structured training and support can lead to long-term success in the sales field. Again, the research carried out, especially in America, has been one of the elements that has encouraged the more general use of psychometric testing.

- The ethical aspects of selling (or mis-selling) have come to light with major UK scandals in the 1980s and 1990s concerning pensions and endowment mortgages where the skill of the sales agent has convinced the customer to buy an expensive product that is poor value to them. Arising from a tougher regulatory environment has been the requirements of sales personnel in a number of areas to be accredited through attending approved courses, which have a more balanced ethical framework. An example of Pearl Assurance is given in Case study 10.3.

■ The increased attention by organisations on satisfying customers (internally and externally) has led to the greater adoption of sales training techniques for all staff, called 'customer care'. Employees in all parts of the organisation are encouraged to find out what the customer wants, to meet those needs and to aim to provide a continuing service – all standard features of sales training. Alongside this has been the encouragement of other sales training features such as encouraging self-belief, working towards goals and using persistence and determination to see the work through to successful conclusion.

Case study 10.3

Selling expertise at Pearl assurance

In 1995, Pearl Assurance was on the brink of disaster. Industry watchdogs had just fined the company for failing to comply with regulations and were threatening to close it down unless things rapidly improved. However, 2 years later, sales had recovered and sales staff turnover reduced from 28% to 12%. The improvements were brought about by re-structuring the jobs to make the selling less complex, improved selection procedures, including a psychometric testing and an assessment centre. Finally, by huge improvements in the training process.

For every team of 12 sales people, two training and competence managers (TCMs) have been assigned, who are responsible for individual team member's skills and the quality of the advice they give. To be able to sell financial products, each member of the team has to pass the financial planning certificate, which involves a 7–12 week off-the-job training programme, depending on their level of experience. The training, however, does not end there. On their first 10 visits to customers, they are accompanied by their TCM who has to be satisfied that they demonstrate the acquired skills in a 'live' situation. Subsequently, they will be observed once a week for the next 10 weeks. The company has estimated that every recruit that fails the certificate costs them £30,000 in recruitment and training costs.

The overall success was shown by Pearl being voted one of the 100 most attractive firms to work for in *Britain's Best Employers*, published by the Corporate Research Foundation.

Source: Arkin (1997)

Adult learning

Associated with much of the thinking behind the learning organisation, a number of larger organisations have developed initiatives to encourage the labour force to return to the learning process that they may have last seen at school. Such schemes, often called 'Gateways to Learning', provide personal development and training of the employee's choice outside of working hours and generally unrelated to the work the employee is carrying out. A fund is set up, either as a personal sum for each employee or a general fund to which the employee applies run jointly by the company and their unions or employee representatives. The training can include learning a language, a manual skill or simply a leisure pursuit (IRS, 1995). An example of the use of individual learning accounts is given in Case study 10.4.

Case study 10.4

Individual learning accounts at Liverpool, Victoria

In October 1997, a pilot individual learning accounts scheme was set up jointly funded by the company and the local TEC. In return for an investment of £25, employees are entitled to up to £300 of training at Bournemouth and Poole College and an hour's career advice with Dorset Careers. On successful completion of the chosen course, the employee receives a £50 bonus. Within 6 months, 40 employees out of a total labour force of 1500 had enrolled on the programme, taking up course ranging from computer skills to management courses. The Training Manager, Tony Miller, saw the advantage to the employees of being given the back-up they need to take control over their own learning and the help to overcome fears about returning to education. It also enhanced the range of skills within the organisation. One employee had used the account to successfully develop her career from being a customer adviser to a training officer. This example has been featured in a DfEE video on lifelong learning launched in 1998.

Source: Prickett (1998)

Such schemes provide an opportunity for employees to develop the learning process, to gain greater self-esteem and confidence, to make use of competencies that can be transferred back into the workplace and to support a culture of partnership.

Management development

Managers have special training needs arising from their specific responsibilities in respect of, amongst others, controlling, motivating, appraising and disciplining their staff whilst planning, innovating and setting the boundaries of their department. Specialist skills required include setting targets, delegation, time management and problem- solving.

These needs can be met through structured self-development, which means learning through experiences on the job, perhaps with the aid of a mentor, or through a formal system of longer-term training, that may involve attendance on qualification courses, such as a Masters in Business Administration (MBA). Alongside such formal training, a planned system of work experience may be established, such as existed at traditional clearing banks where managers were moved on to another branch with new challenges every 3–4 years. The UK does not have a good record on investment in management training, according to a report by the DTI and the University of London (*People Management*, 2004). The average annual investment per person was only £1085 compared to over £2000 per person in Germany. However, there are some good examples of initiating training that is at the heart of business development, as shown in the Dixons' Case study 10.5.

Case study 10.5

Management development at Dixons Group

By carefully studying the characteristics of high achievers out of Dixons' middle managers, seven 'stretch' factors were identified which were made central to both the selection of potential managers and to their development programme. These factors were:

- passionately driving Dixons' future,
- broad and innovative long-term thinking,
- simplifying business complexity,
- driving and using partnerships to benefit Dixons,
- creating 'joined-up' teams,
- building Dixons' learning and development capability,
- demonstrating learning agility.

By using these factors and other assessment centre techniques, 20 managers were chosen in 2003 to engage in a 15-month programme containing six modules – leadership, personal effectiveness, organisational performance, financial performance, business transformation and e-business. Group members are expected to support and challenge each other over the period and take part in a 'live' business project. One of the main objectives of the programme is to ensure there is a steady flow of well-trained and confident managers so that for each senior appointment made externally, there will be four made internally. This stimulates a high retention rate and a huge saving in recruitment costs.

Source: Upton (2004)

Knowledge management

A more recent concept is that of 'intellectual capital', which represents the greater part of intangible assets within organisations. It is created and held by knowledge workers, that is those that are not involved directly in manual, sales or administration operations. The knowledge refers primarily to patents and organisational competencies but also to the corporate culture, the 'way things are done around here', how it developed and why it is successful, which can define key competitive advantage. Capturing this knowledge, disseminating it throughout the organisation, building on it and then taking incremental steps towards advancing the knowledge level and depth has been promoted as an essential feature of developing employees. It has also been recognised that losing this knowledge through large-scale redundancies, early retirement of long-service employees or groups of employees moving to a competitor or setting up a business in competition can be disastrous in the longer term in reducing the value of those knowledge-based intangible assets.

In terms of developing employees, the challenge is in the effective dissemination of both the *explicit* knowledge, that which can be easily written down, such as company policies and procedures, but also the *tacit* knowledge, which takes the form of subjective insights, intuitions and hunches (Taylor, 2002). This can include knowledge on building relationships and networks, solving real problems and developing innovatory ideas. Encouraging the exchange of tacit knowledge is a subtle process but organising secondments, exchanges and informal networking opportunities can provide effective methods.

Government initiatives to help learning and development

There is a long history of government interventions in the UK to try to improve the level of vocational training, especially in view of the low overall investment compared to the rest of Europe. The two key problems that initiatives have aimed to address are the skills shortages, especially those that relate to high-organisational performance and high levels of unemployment, especially among young people. In the 1960s and 1970s, Industrial Training Boards were set up which levied the pay-rolls of each company by between 1% and 2.5%. The funds created were then distributed back to the companies if they carried out training in an approved way. The aim was to discourage companies from simply poaching their required skilled employees rather than carrying out the training themselves. Unfortunately, the system became bogged down in the bureaucracy of making claims and no real evidence emerged that there had been a measurable increase in the quantity or quality of training, especially in the smaller- and medium-sized organisations. By the early 1980s, most had been abolished by the Conservative government who laid more stress on the way that a competitive market place would force organisations to improve their training.

Their own initiatives in the early 1980s tended towards measures that would have an immediate effect upon reducing unemployment, such as the Youth Opportunity Scheme (1980) and the Youth Training Scheme (1983), both of which provided free or subsidised young people to organisations that agreed to carry out an approved training scheme. As youth unemployment declined in the late 1980s and 1990s, chiefly due to demographic changes, the government switched their attention to a broader spectrum. A National Vocational Education and Training framework was devised which continues to have an overriding vision of 'lifelong learning' for every citizen, rooted in both and economic and social theory. People need to be constantly learning and developing skills and competencies to ensure they can contribute in the workplace. It is also vital that no group is socially excluded or marginalised so they cannot contribute to society, thus drifting into crime or benefit dependency.

The government initiatives can be divided into those that provide the organisational framework, such as the creation of Learning and Skills Councils and which also aim to create training innovation; those that provide a training framework, such as the drive towards National Vocational Qualifications (NVQs); those that are directed at getting all young people to enter into vocational training, such as youth training and modern apprenticeships (MA); and finally those that encourage organisations to aspire to training excellence through the Investors in People standard.

The National Learning and Skills Council was set up in 2001 with a budget of £6 billion and responsibility for the funding, planning, delivery and quality assurance of all post-16 education and training (except higher education). With its 47 local Learning and Skills Councils, it is required to encourage all 16–19-year olds to partake some form of education and training and achieve at least a Level 2 NVQ, together with raising the standards in teaching and training, increasing the demand for learning by adults and ensuring that all such education and training is directed towards improving economic performance. It has a strong representation of employers and trade unions on its local councils and its remit covers around 6 million people. It aims to achieve its goals through MA, Investors in People and the New Deal, amongst other initiatives.

National Vocational Qualifications

In 1986, the National Council for Vocational Qualifications was set up to rationalise and reform vocational qualifications. Lead bodies, principally of employers and unions, have been set up for every industry who have laid down agreed performance standards against which trainees can be judged. Assessment is not by examination but by assessment in the workplace. A system of independent assessment and verification moderates and confirms the process. Five levels of the awards have been established which reflect increasingly demanding competence requirements. These range from:

Level 1.   Occupational competence in performing a wide range of work activities that are routine and predictable.
to:
Level 5.   Competence at a professional level with mastery of a range of relevant knowledge and the ability to apply it in situations that may be unpredictable. It is likely to be accompanied with personal autonomy together with responsibility for the work of others and the allocation of resources.

The qualification is independent of any specific course and trainees can obtain the qualification through a variety of ways including open learning. There is no restriction by age or occupation and levels do not need to be tackled in chronological order. The emphasis is on the outcome of work tackled, not on the trainee's knowledge, although it is recognised that underpinning knowledge and understanding is an essential ingredient to the learning process.

NVQs got off to a slow start but began to take off in the 1990s. By 1998, 2.4 million employees had been awarded an NVQ, with 400,000 awarded in 1996, an increase of 33% over the previous year. 43% of employers offer the opportunity to obtain an NVQ (Finn, 1998).

Qualifications at Levels 1 and 2 have been generally agreed to be very successful. They are relevant to the trainee and their situation, provide a clear aim for the trainee to head for and the success in achieving the NVQ reinforce the learning process. Another pointer in their success is the way that practical achievement is accompanied by the requirement for basic literacy and numerical skills, so the NVQ provides the medium for those skills to be developed almost without the trainee being aware of their development. A good example of a comprehensive approach is that of INA Bearing Company where all 200 operators are working towards an NVQ Level 2 in performing management operations, alongside initiatives in team building and a Kaizen (idea generating) scheme (Roberts, 2003).

At Level 3 and beyond, the qualifications are more debatable and no more so than in the management standards. Here the problem is the way that the trainee can demonstrate his or her own competence. With bricklaying, assembling and hairdressing, the finished result can be observed as well as the way the trainee has gone about the task. This is not the case for management standards, such as problem solving or time management, where observation presents organisational problems. Moreover, for the majority of cases, the trainee has to try to prove their competence through paper-based solutions, using a portfolio of support materials for each unit, some of which may be acceptable to the assessor and some not. The drop-out rate on such NVQs is very high indeed – more than 60% on average – with many trainees being put off by the bureaucracy involved and disappointed by the lack of emphasis on the training that actually takes place. It becomes, it is said, a 'paper-chase'.

A further criticism of the NVQ approach is that it is conservative process in that trainees have to demonstrate they can carry out existing methods and processes rather than using training to develop new approaches and methods. Some organisations, such as ASDA and British Home Stores, having started down the NVQ route, have abandoned them because they failed to focus on business needs.

National training targets

These were set for the first time in 1991 and have been revised every few years since. Although some were based on traditional academic achievement, such as GCSEs, some of the targets were couched in NVQ terms, such as the target for 28% of the workforce to have a vocational, professional, management or academic qualification at NVQ Level 4 or above. They have tended, as with most government targets, to be aspirational, with few being actually reached. For example, the target for 2002 was that 85% of 19–21-year olds should have achieved at least a NVQ Level 2 but the actual outcome was closer to 80%. In recent years, the targets have become more shorter term and the targets set for 2004 are set out in Figure 10.7.

Figure 10.7
Example of government-set national training targets
(*Source*: www.lsc.gov.uk, 2004)

	19-year olds at NVQ Level 2	21-year olds at NVQ Level 3	Economically active adults at NVQ Level 3
Target for 2004 (%)	85	55	52
Actual 2000 (%)	75	51	47
Actual 1995 (%)	67	45	39

Modern apprenticeships (MA)

Traditional apprenticeships, whose origin go back hundreds of years, had developed into a very rigid and limited vehicle for training young people in practical skills by the 1960s. They had a fixed entry point at 16, were time rather than standards-based, and had a limited content related to the specific craft skill. The skills involved were usually those of the particular union of skilled workers who jealously guarded the ownership of those skills and limited entry, so the training was often narrow. For example, an electrical apprentice would not learn any mechanical skills because there were two different unions involved. This reduced the value and relevance of the training and, together with the overall reduction in numbers of employees in manufacturing, led to a major decline in traditional apprenticeships since the 1970s.

MA, announced in 1993, are promoted by Learning and Skills Councils in co-operation with local employers and are available in over 80 sectors. Apprentices work towards achieving an NVQ Level 3 and encouragement is given towards a multi-skilling approach. Literacy, numeracy, problem-solving and people-relationship skills are important features of the training schedule. There is no time limit and training outcomes must be achieved in the shortest and most realistic times. Moreover, although they are normally commenced at 16 or 17, they can, in theory, be commenced at any age through the development called 'accelerated modern apprenticeship'. For example, a number of workers in their 30s started an apprenticeship in Swan Hunter shipyard in 2002, while the Eden Project in Cornwall launched an apprenticeship scheme in 2004 with 40 employees over 25. Although the image of MAs are improving, it is recognised by the Learning and Skills Councils that they are still seen as low-paid and a second-best option, while some employers see them as bureaucratic and inflexible.

National Traineeships

These are a development of the Youth Training Scheme which attempts to ensure that all young school-leavers enter into some form of training which leads to a qualification. Under this scheme, which has similarities with MA, the trainee works under a formal training scheme towards NVQs at Levels 1 and 2, under quality standards designed by the industry.

New deal

The latest in a long string in initiatives associated with reducing unemployment is the *New Deal*, originally established in 1997 to help every person 18–25 to gain employment or training. The first part of the programme is the 'gateway', which is a period of intensive training to prepare the trainee for gainful employment before they actually seek work. It includes basic numeracy and literacy skills training, careers advice and how to deal with inter-personal situations, such as job interviews. The gateway length of time varies depending on the existing skills of the trainee. When employment is obtained with an employer who has signed up to the scheme (and who obtains a subsidy), training must continue either with that employer or with a third party. Due to the improved economic situation since the scheme was announced which has led to a large natural reduction in youth unemployment, the scheme has been opened up to all people who have been unemployed for 12 months.

Investors in people

This is a national standard established in 1993 and based on the practical experiences of successful organisations in developing people to meet the business goals that have been set and communicated. The standard is based on four criteria that must be met by aspiring organisations:

- A public commitment from the top to develop all employees with a business plan which includes information on how employees will contribute to its success.
- Regular reviews of the training and development needs of all employees built into a performance management system.
- Full evidence that the training and development takes place, starting with induction and carrying on throughout their career with the organisation.
- An evaluation system is in place to judge the success of the training against the needs of the individual and the organisation.

The scheme is administered by the Learning and Skills Councils with national supervision from Investors in People, UK. When organisations have met the standards, they receive the recognition for a period of 3 years at which time they need to prepare a portfolio to demonstrate that they still meet the criteria. Research carried out by Cranfield University indicates that IIP is associated with overall benefits for the organisations concerned (see Focus on research 10.2).

Focus on research 10.2

Investors in people

Cranfield University conducted research in 1996 for Investors in People, UK comparing the experiences of 62 organisations that had achieved IIP within the last 3 years (once-recognised) and those that had been recognised for the second time (re-recognised). The research was carried out by means of telephone interviews and drawing together case studies. The findings that re-recognised organisations were more likely to have experienced a reduction in staff turnover, they were more likely to fill vacancies quicker, with better quality recruits and to believe that IIP had a positive effect on the company's image in the labour market. In the latter case, the figures were 92% for re-recognised organisations compared with 44% for once recognised. Overall, it indicated that the longer the organisation was an Investor in People then the more likely that it saw the benefits, supporting the view that training and development are long-term investments.

Source: Alberga (1997)

Meteor case study

Moving towards a learning organisation

At Sarah's third annual performance meeting, one of the major tasks given to her for the next year was to research the concept of a learning organisation, and recommend whether a move in that direction would be appropriate for her site and what form it would take. This was to be achieved within 6 months. This was not one of her areas of expertise so the project was a learning experience for herself.

She researched the issue in three ways; she obtained a list of books and articles from the CIPD library service and delved into a selection; she booked herself onto a 2-day training course with a specialist consultancy; finally, she visited three organisations that had attempted to move in this direction – one who had spoken on the training course and two through networking in her local CIPD branch.

She felt this was a thorough approach but it left her somewhat confused and perplexed. The books and articles tended to be far from clear with many varying viewpoints and muzzy objectives, while the three organisations she visited had very different approaches. Some put more emphasis on every individual being involved in drawing up a learning plan with strong support and intervention. One of the organisations, however, was happy to leave it very much up to the individual and their managers to decide how much they would 'buy into' the concept.

She found that the most impressive organisation was Mattocks, a hospitality organisation of medium-sized hotels, that had a large number of outlets and employed many staff joining them with no qualifications. They had managed to combine the culture of rigid hygiene and quality standards with considerable unit flexibility in areas such as staffing systems, learning and development. They had moved away from centralised direction because it led to over-control and bureaucracy and did nothing to motivate staff in the outlets. They had introduced a new approach to learning after experimenting at three separate units that had been keen to take part and then comparing results. The framework agreed upon consisted of the following:

- A voluntary approach, where employees signed up to a learning contract when they felt ready to do so.
- The learning contract would involve developing a learning plan for an appropriate time period from 6 months to 5 years, supported by their line manager and a mentor working within the same unit. The employee would be expected to take part in 'innovation teams', which are small leaderless groups who meet up after hours to discuss ways the work of the unit can be improved. It is expected that at least 40% of any ideas would be implemented, with members of the groups taking the initiative in putting them into effect successfully. This would help to develop a number of their analytical and inter-personal skills.
- An individual learning account of up to £1000 to be spent at a number of specified training establishments. The employee would have the choice of both the location and the course but it would be linked to the training plan.

Sarah believed that this framework could be transferred successfully to her site but she knew there would be some difficulties. Up until now, the training had been quite prescriptive, partly due to the need to build up the skills of the labour force in order to meet the production requirements. This had been achieved successfully, led by a dynamic Training Manager who led from the front and had a small team of loyal and competent instructors. She was not sure how they would respond to the idea that employees had the choice on whether or not to join a training programme or that the programme would be very much self-designed.

Scott had been very supportive when she had described her enthusiasm for Mattocks' system and encouraged her to float the ideas with the training staff. As she expected, their initial response was very guarded. They appeared unconvinced that her ideas would add value to their training structure which, they believed, continued to serve the company well. A major concern, not unexpectedly, was the transfer of much of their control over the training operations and the programmes, with its budgetary implications. They also appeared dismissive of the vague concepts behind the learning organisation. Sarah knew she would have a hard job on her hands to put forward proposals that could be found acceptable, not just to the training staff but to managers as a whole.

Summary

- It is important to appreciate that people learn in different ways and have preferred learning styles in order to produce an effective learning environment.
- A learning organisation seeks to encourage employees to search for new ideas, solve problems, question existing methods and look for best practice from a variety of sources. The organisation, on its part, will accept that mistakes will be made.
- The four-part training cycle consists of assessing the training needs, planning the training, carrying it out followed by evaluation.
- Training techniques need to be chosen to meet the specific needs of the learning situation.
- Mentoring and action learning are techniques which support the development process.
- Government initiatives to encourage training include the setting of national targets, supporting the development of NVQs, together with starting up MA and Investors in People.

Student activities

1 Obtain a copy of Honey and Mumford's Learning Style Analysis and identify which grouping indicates your preferred style. Discuss with two of your colleagues how will this knowledge influence your approach to your studies.

2 Taking Sarah's position in the Meteor case study, draw up the proposal she will need to make to convince the managers of the benefits of working towards a learning organisation.

3 Specify which techniques of training are best suited to the following:
   - Learning to drive a car.
   - Students needing a basic understanding of the business cycle.
   - Teaching teenagers about personal relationships.
   - Getting to grips with Powerpoint (or equivalent).
   - Induction for a graduate in a large blue-chip organisation.

4 Read the McEvoy article on outdoor learning and draw up a list of the benefits and difficulties involved in organising and carrying out such a programme for 20 final year students.

5 Read the Evans article on action learning and suggest ways that the idea could be instituted in (a) a supermarket chain, (b) a bank and (c) a government department of your choice.

6 Having read the Alberga article on IIP, talk to two people who have had experience as employees of IIP and compare their views of the effectiveness of the accreditation.

References

Alberga, T. (1997) Time for a check-up. *People Management*, 6 February, 30–32.

Arkin, A. (1997) Assurer foundation. *People Management*, 11 September, 40–41.

Armstrong, M. (2001) *A Handbook of Human Resource Management Practice*, 8th edition, Kogan Page.

Bennett, R., Leduchowicz, T. (1983) What makes for an effective trainer? *Journal of European Industrial Training*, **7**(2): 31.

Collin, A. (2001) Learning and development. In: Beardwell, I., Holden, L. (eds). *Human Resource Management – A Contemporary Approach*. FT prentice Hall.

Ernst, Young (1996). *The Evaluation of Modern Apprenticeship Prototypes*. DfEE.

Evans, J. (1997) An arresting development. *People Management*, 6 November, 40–42.

Finn, W. (1998) Qualified success. *Personnel Today*, 25 April, 24–26.

Kolb, D. (1984) *Experiential Learning*. Prentice Hall.

Harrison, R. (2002) *Learning and Development*. CIPD.

Honey, P., Mumford, A. (1992) *The Manual of Learning Styles*. Peter Honey Publications.

IRS (1995) EDAP challenges anti-learning culture. *Employee Development Bulletin No. 68*, August, 2.

Labour Market Quarterly Review (1999) The new national learning targets for England for 2002. August, 10.

Marchington, M., Wilkinson, A. (2002) *People Management and Development*. CIPD.

McEvoy, G. (1997) Organisation change and outdoor management education. *Human Resource Management*, **36**(2): 235–250.

Megginson, D., Whitaker, V. (2004) *Continuous Professional Development*, CIPD.

Moorby, E. (1996) *How to Succeed in Employee Development*. McGraw-Hill.

Oppinions (1999) Sigma's mentoring scheme at Bass encourages a culture of self-managed learning. *Newsletter of Oxford Psychologists Press*, July, 5.

People Management (2004) UK Near the bottom of the training pile. 3 June, 8.

Prickett, R. (1998) Insurance firm claims ILA pilot scheme is a success. *People Management*, 5 February, 15.

Reid, M., Barrington, H. (1997) *Training Interventions*. IPD.

Revens, R. (1989) *Action Learning*. Blond and Briggs.

Roberts, Z. (2003) Learning leads the way. *People Management*, 6 November, 34–35.

Storey, J., Sisson, K. (1993) *Managing Human Resources and Industrial Relations*. Open University Press.

Taylor, S. (2002) *People Resourcing*. CIPD.

Upton, R. (2004) Electric avenues. *People Management*, 22 April, 42–43.

Wick, C., Leon, L. (1995) From ideas to action: creating a learning organisation. *Human Resource Management*, **34**(2): 299–311.

Green Paper (1998) *The Learning Age – A Renaissance for a New Britain*. HMSO.

Further reading

Strategy

Mayo, A. (1998) *Creating a Training and Development Strategy*. IPD.

Pont, T. (1995) *Investing in Training and Development*. Kogan Page.

Learning and personal development

Sloman, M. (2003) *Training in the Age of the Learner*. CIPD.

Marquardt, M. (1999) *Action Learning in Action*. Oxford Psychologists Press.

Scott, A. (1997) *Learning Centres*. Kogan Page.

Tamkin, P., Barber, L., Hirsh, W. (1995) *Personal Development Plans: Case Studies of Practice*. Report no. 280. Institute of Employment Studies.

For a further example of a company-wide adult learning programme see:

Hougham, J., Thomas, J., Sisson, K. (1991) Ford's Employment Development and Assistance Programme (EDAP): a roundtable discussion' *Human Resource Management Journal*, **I**(3): 77–91.

For a discussion on in-company training programmes see:

Martin, G. and Pate, J. (2001) 'Company-based education programmes: what is the pay off for employers?, *Human Resource Management Journal* **11**(4): 55–73.

Beaumont, P. and Bee, R. (2003) *Learning Needs, Analysis and Evaluation*. CIPD.

Induction Mentoring

Clutterbuck, D. (2004) *Everybody Needs a Mentor*. IPD

Fowler, A. (1999) *Induction*. IPD.

Development centres

Jackson, C., Yeates, J. (1993) *Development Centres: Assessing or Developing People*. Report no. 261. Institute of Employment Studies.

Training evaluation

Bramley, P. (2003) *Evaluating Training*. IPD.

Spilsbury, M. (1995) *Measuring the Effectiveness of Training*. Report no. 282. Institute of Employment Studies.

Investors in people

McLuskey, M. (1997) *Introducing Investors in People*. Kogan Page.

Web sites

http://www.lsc.gov.uk
Learning and Skills Council web site

http://www.iipuk.co.uk/iipuk/index2.html
The Investors in People web site.

http://www.newdeal.gov.uk
More information on the New Deal.

www.CIPD.co.uk
The CIPD produces an annual report on Training and Development.

Health, safety and welfare

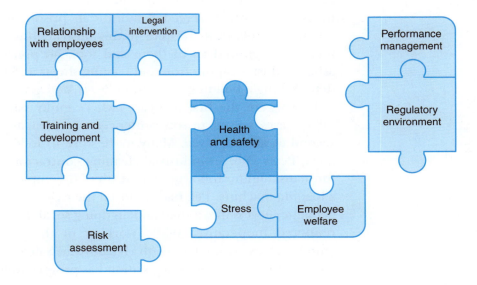

Objectives

When you have read this chapter and carried out the activities, you will be able to:

- Understand the importance to the organisation of a sound and pro-active approach to health, safety and welfare.
- State the main legislative interventions and their principal components.
- Design a health and safety policy.

■ Draft a proposal for a risk assessment exercise.

■ Identify the elements of an effective employee assistance programme.

■ Appreciate the effect of stress on employees and how it can be alleviated.

Introduction

In December 1994, Peter Kite was jailed for 3 years. He owned a small outdoor activity company and was found guilty of manslaughter as a result of the death of four teenagers under his control on a canoe outing off the Dorset coast (Whitfield, 1995). Two years later, Roy Hill, a demolition worker, served 3 months in prison for grossly violating asbestos regulations. Despite having instructions on safety requirements, he ignored all of them and took no precautions to prevent asbestos dust escaping from old roofing sheets and pipe lagging when demolishing a building in Bristol (*People Management*, 1996).

These were the first two cases where guilty parties in health and safety cases served prison sentences, the first as an employer, the second as an employee. Many more were to follow. For example, in 2004, Peter Pell, an industrial cleaning contractor, was sent to prison for manslaughter following the death of his employee who was driving a loading machine. Pell had removed the cage to allow the machine to get better access into a shed and, in doing so, all the safety devices were rendered inoperative. While working in the confined space, the employee was crushed to death (Health and Safety Practitioner, 2004).

Over the last 150 years, legislation has progressively imposed greater obligations on all parties in the workplace to try to prevent unnecessary suffering arising from accidents and unsafe working conditions and to provide adequate opportunities for compensation where they do occur. The severity of the sentences in all three cases cited above demonstrates that the courts continue to interpret the law in an increasingly strict fashion and that the penalties for wrong-doing are becoming harsher.

The number of fatal accidents in the workplace has shown a steady decline in the last 10 years (see Figure 11.1), which continues the pattern during the twentieth century. Although much of this reduction has been due to improved safety operations, the sharp decline in mining and manufacturing has also played its part. Mining, for example, has declined from 900,000 employees in 1926 to less than 10,000 in 2005. It is significant that the number of deaths in services industries makes up over half the total and over 100 of the total deaths are members of the

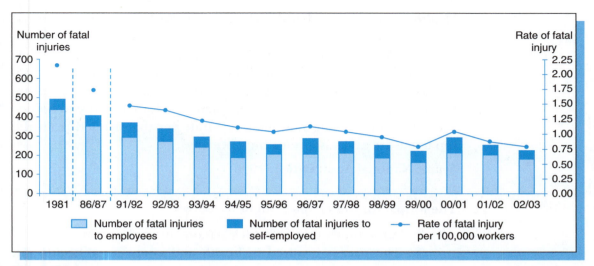

Figure 11.1
Fatal injuries to workers in works UK from 1981–2003

public. Days lost through injury at work and ill-health exceed 33 million and 6% of adults suffer from work-related ill health (HSE, 2004). A few high-profile tragedies take the headlines, such as the Piper Alpha oil rig fire in 1988 where 167 employees died, but most of the deaths and serious injuries are single, avoidable accidents.

The amount of money paid in insurance against employers' liability is astonishing. According to Trade Union Congress (TUC) statistics (BusinessEurope.com, 2002), employees were awarded over £1 billion in total in damages for work-related injury or ill-health, nearly double the figure compared to 5 years earlier. In January 1999, the High Court made awards that will eventually total over £5 million to 40,000 ex-miners who suffer from Vibration White Finger (Health and Safety, 1999). These payments put into the shade the court fines that are exacted where companies are found guilty of safety irregularities which, although rising steadily, still average less than £2000. You would expect hospitals to be the safest of places but this is not necessarily so as indicated in Focus on research 11.1.

Focus on research 11.1

Safety in hospitals

The National Audit carried out research into accidents in hospitals in 1997. They reviewed accidents and safety procedures in 30 National

Health Service (NHS) Trusts and found that 75% of accidents involved visitors or patients and most were caused by slips or falls. For staff, needlestick injuries and manual handling were the main culprits. They calculated that as many as 1 million people a year are injured in accidents in hospital at the total cost of £154 million. Their main recommendation was that hospital management needs to do more to reduce accidents, introducing hospital-wide strategies that are led from the top to ensure safety is given a high priority.

Source: National Audit Office (1996)

The format for this chapter will be as follows:

- An outline of the safety legislation currently in place.
- The parties involved in health and safety – the health and safety executive, safety inspectors, safety officers and safety representatives.
- Risk assessment and safety prevention.
- Welfare issues and services, including employee assistance programmes (EAPs), positive health programmes and counselling arrangements.
- The Role of the human resources department, including the development of health, safety and welfare policies.

Legal interventions

Origins of legislation

Since the onset of the industrial revolution, there have been calls for a better balance of responsibility between employer and employee over health and safety issues. In medieval times, it had been assumed that those who employed staff, mostly servants of course, could be relied upon to look after these staff in their own interests so that they could get a prolonged service. This had always been, in practice, somewhat patchy and the common law had never been too clear as to their precise responsibilities. By the late eighteenth century, when industrial and mining sites of 500 employees or more began to evolve, it became clear that employees were regarded, at best, as short-term investments who could easily be replaced, when no longer productive through accident or ill-health.

Legislation, promoted by dedicated humanitarians, such as Sir Robert Peel the Elder, father of the future Prime Minister, (who himself employed 15,000 'hands') and Lord Shaftesbury, began to be introduced from 1833 onwards through restricting hours of work, especially for women and young people. This was accompanied by regulations setting out minimum conditions of working practices through various Factory Acts. More important, they were backed up through enforcement agencies. Much of this was carried through despite considerable opposition from the industrialists. As the social historian, G.M. Trevelyan explained:

'In the earlier part of the nineteenth century, state control in the interests of the working classes was not an idea congenial to the rulers of Britain. They turned a deaf ear to Robert Owen when he pointed out to them that his own New Lanark mills were a model ready to hand, to teach the world how the new industrial system could be made the instrument of standardised improvement in sanitation, welfare, hours, wages and education, raising the conditions of working-class life to an average level that could never be attained under the domestic system ... The great opportunity that his vision had perceived was missed, until in the slow evolution, the state had come round to his doctrine of the control of factories and the condition of life for all employed therein.'

Trevelyan (1942, 4: p. 47)

In the first half of the twentieth century, the attention turned from the removal of the more obvious dangers and abuses in employment to an emphasis on the 'human relations' aspects, spearheaded by the work of Elton Mayo (1945) at the Hawthorne plant of the Western Electric Company. By paying attention to the physical and welfare needs of employees and providing a counselling service, productivity and morale could be both be raised leading to better profits for the owners.

Today, there are over 100 separate statutes in force relating to health, safety and welfare, the oldest dating back to the Explosives Act of 1875. Much of these are now 'relevant statutory provisions' under the Health and Safety at Work Act 1974 (HASAWA) and now enforced through the health and safety executive or local authority. There is not time or room in this publication to deal with more than a handful of the more recent acts or regulations (many of which stem from Europe) and only the most significant will be briefly addressed. You will find advice on where to investigate further on such legislation at the end of the chapter.

HASAWA

This influential legislation, borne of general consensus between the political parties, is essentially an 'enabling' act, with wide-ranging, if imprecise, provisions which require interpretation by the courts or putting into effect through Regulations sanctioned by Parliament. As put by Corbridge and Pilbeam:

'HASAWA represented a sea-change in the UK approach to health and safety legislation and was aimed at combating the endemic apathy towards health and safety provision, attributed to excessive, prescriptive and unintelligible law and compounded by ineffective policing and enforcement.'

Corbridge and Pilbeam (1998: p. 251)

Key directional changes included:

■ Providing support to voluntary effort and personal responsibility for health and safety rather than simply relying on detailed regulation.

■ Concentration on the protection of people, rather than buildings or machinery, and extending that protection to all people, including members of the public, and contractors on and off site, rather than just employees.

■ Trying to encourage industry self-regulation through such areas as developing codes of practice, rather than imposing them by government committee.

■ Providing a comprehensive cover through all industries and all employees under all conditions, building on and extending the common law provision. It has been estimated that as many as 3 million people came under the scope of safety legislation protection for the first time.

■ Imposing criminal liability to ensure compliance with its provisions.

There are duties placed essentially on employers, but the legislation also places duties on employees, designers, manufacturers, suppliers and equipment installers. We will look at each group in turn.

Duties on employers

The act lays down a fundamental *'duty of care'* towards the health, safety and welfare of all employees which is the starting point of all considerations (see Case study 11.1). As we shall see later, this duty has been interpreted in a much wider sense in recent years and now encompasses the duty to relieve stress where applicable.

Case study 11.1

Hickson and Welsh

In 1992, five workers were killed at the chemical company, Hickson and Welsh, in Castleford, West Yorkshire. The accident followed the first cleaning in 30 years of the sludge from a tank of volatile mono-nitroluene (MNT).

The job had not been properly assessed for risk and was left to a junior team leader who had only recently returned to the MNT section. Incorrect cleaning tools were used, a monitoring thermometer was inadequate, the sludge content had not been analysed and the whole approach had been 'casual'.

During the cleaning operation, a fireball suddenly burst from the tank, torching a frail control cabin next door and leaving the factory's main office block with shattered windows and burnt-out rooms.

The company was fined £250,000 with £150,000 costs in the High Court for breaches of their safety duties and face legal proceedings from the victims of the accident. Managers in the department were having to deal with several other problems and the company was in the middle of a management re-organisation. Dr Carter, head of the HSE field operations who reported 2 years later on the accident, said that 'the company had undergone a major management transformation and safety procedures had not caught up with that change'. Essential lessons for the chemical industry included basic reminders of proper practice, especially the vital need for rigorous planning before any unusual task was undertaken.

The manager director of the plant, the operations director and manager all left the company shortly after the accident.

Source: Wainwright (1994)

Section 2 sets out the general duties on employers, which cover:

1 The provision of systems of work, equipment and a workplace that are all safe.
2 Arrangements for the use, handling, storage and transport of articles and substances that are all safe.
3 Adequate and necessary information, supervision training and instruction to ensure effective employee safety.
4 Ensuring and there are safe means of getting into and out of premises.
5 Adequate welfare provision.

The duties also extend to sub-contractors working on their premises (see Case study 11.2) and to members of the public. Throughout this section of the act, the words '*as far as is reasonable practicable*' are mentioned for each clause. This limits the absolute responsibility to employers and allows them to achieve a balance between the assessed risk of an unsafe practice against the cost of avoiding that risk. Let us take an example. A factory is based alongside Heathrow Airport and there is a risk that a plane, one day, will crash into that factory. To avoid that risk, it is conceivable that the employer could build a cover to the factory that would protect the employees from the crash. Realistically, however, the cost of that cover would be colossal and could not be justified against the very low risk of the crash occurring. It would not be 'reasonably practical'.

This is a simple case; employers each day need to consider other cases that are far more evenly balanced. Should the 20-year-old machine be replaced this year before there is an accident or should we wait until we have generated more profits to invest in the new plant? The noise levels in the assembly area are rising with increased production. Should we investigate? If the results are not good, can we afford to invest in an acoustic control system? The old offices are getting stifling hot in summer. With an increase in numbers, do we need to invest in air-conditioning? These may be finely judged decisions and, ultimately, should an accident or incident arise before the employer has acted, it would then be down to the courts to decide if the action was 'reasonably practical' or not. If the court decided that the employer should have taken action as part of their 'duty of care' then the employer could be punished for its failure to carrying out its statutory duty.

Case study 11.2

Responsibility to sub-contractors

Joseph Jenkinson was a sub-contractor for construction company JDM Accord on a road maintenance contract. His main work was as a banksman, to direct the traffic on the site, but he had had no training in these duties and was directed to sweep and clear up the site. Jenkinson was struck and killed by a reversing trailer when he was involved in other work. The court found that there was no site management, no site inductions or any instructions to any of the operatives about traffic management and that drivers could make up their own system of work as they went along. JMD Accord was fined £100,000 with £32,000 costs.

Source: Health and Safety Practitioner (2004)

Other duties of employers include:

- Duty to persons other than employees, such as the public and contractors (Sections 3 and 4).
- The requirement to use 'best practical means' to solve safety problems. This is an ever-tightening noose trying to prevent employers from carrying out botched jobs or taking short cuts. In industries where safety is an absolute paramount, such as nuclear power or defence, then 'state of the art' safety systems are the expectation.
- The duty to prepare and update a written health and safety policy and communicate it properly to employees; to recognise the appointment of safety representatives and to form a safety committee if requested. (These duties will be examined later in the chapter.)

The duty of care extends to a degree of monitoring sickness, absence and health in the organisation. Each establishment has its own specific areas of danger and certain places are prone to a higher level of sickness if nothing is done. This includes those places where a 'sick building syndrome' occurs, through faults in the design, lighting or air conditioning (or lack of it) and management need to show that they are responding to these problems where evidence is brought forward. Another type of establishment where high absence has been a feature in recent years is a call centre where the nature of the work pressure is likely to increase the stress levels, as shown in Focus on research 11.2.

Focus on research 11.2

Health, sickness and absence management in a UK call centre

The health of employees at an energy call centre was investigated by researchers from Stirling University. They identified 17 symptoms of illness, including tiredness, stiff necks, sore eyes and backache and found that call handlers experienced a higher number of such symptoms than non-call handlers. While many of the symptoms were insufficiently serious on their own to cause absence from work, large numbers of workers experienced them in clusters. Forty per cent of employees experienced at least three symptoms either daily or several times a week. It was the way the call handlers' tasks were structured, organised and performed produced the greatest number of complaints and the most frequently reported cause of sickness. They had to answer queuing calls and meet targets so they only spent 4.7% of time away from their station, compared to 17% for non-call handlers and they had considerably less control over most of their aspects of work. More than two-thirds felt pressured as a result of work on a normal day.

Also reported was a 'draconian' absence policy which confused absence with absenteeism with a far from sympathetic employer who appeared to be uninterested in the reasons for absence. One respondent commented:

> 'You get upset when you don't meet the standards expected, the targets. That's when the stress factor goes up. After training, you are put on the phones and a lot of people don't know what to do … they get into a hole they can't get out of. Then they get stressed and depressed and they are soon on tablets, then they get put on a sickness review, feel under constant pressure and feel victimised.'

Following a series of recommendations, management complied with most of the environmental issues but were less inclined to revise the absence procedures. No action was taken on the target-driven model because of competitive pressures – the level of targets determined the volume of business that they would win.

Source: Taylor *et al*. (2003)

Duties on employees

The act recognised that responsibility for safety was not just one way. Confirming the common law-implied term of the employment contract that the employee is obliged to follow the safety instructions, Sections 7 and 8 of this act went further by stating that the employee must co-operate with safety initiatives and the training that accompanies them, to take reasonable care of their own health and safety and not recklessly interfere with machines, plant or processes so as to make them unsafe. The clear implications are that employees have to wear the required safety gear and follow all authorised safety rules. They also risk dismissal if they refuse to follow other important health and safety instructions (see Spotlight on the law 11.1).

Spotlight on the law 11.1

Smoking at work

O'Connell was employed at a branch of Marks and Spencer PLC. The staff regulations provided that smoking was allowed only in the staff lounge and the roof garden during specified hours and that there must be no smoking at any time in any other area of the store, including the yard and the perimeter of the store. It was expressly stated that failure to comply with the regulations would result in summary dismissal. O'Connell was on duty one night on a 12-hour shift with responsibility for ensuring that members of the public did not enter the premises and that contractors, working on new escalators, did not smoke inside the store.

During the course of his shift, O'Connell was observed smoking on the tiled area in front of the store. An investigation was conducted and he admitted that he had deliberately breached the smoking policy. He was instantly dismissed. On bringing a claim for unfair dismissal, the tribunal found that the employers had carried out a reasonable investigation and had a genuine belief that O'Connell had breached the serious safety regulation. However, evidence was given that contractors had no restrictions on smoking in the same area, nor did members of the public and, additionally, O'Connell had little opportunity to take a break. The tribunal also heard that the smoking ban was not total but one selectively applied for safety purposes to prevent fire hazards. They decided, given all the evidence, that dismissal was not a reasonable response and that the dismissal was unfair. The employers took the case to appeal.

Marks and Spencer PLC versus O'Connell, EAT 230/95
Source: IDS Brief 579, p. 14, December 1996

Duties on designers, manufacturers, suppliers and installers

Duties here under Section 6 include incorporating safety features at the design stage, testing for risks to health and providing full safety instruction and hazard details. Again, this aspect clarified the rather unspecific common law obligations and has made a large difference in the way products are designed and marketed. Since the act, for example, all commercial guillotines require the operator to have both hands on separate buttons for it to operate. Furthermore, one manufacturer of numerically controlled tools was successfully prosecuted because the design allowed the override of a guard while the machine was still working.

The Health and Safety Commission and Health and Safety Executive

Both the Health and Safety Commission and the Health and Safety executive were set up under HASAWA. The Commission is a quango, with between six and nine lay members drawn from bodies representing employers, trade unions and local authorities. It is primarily an advisory body and its main responsibility is for carrying out the policy of the act and providing advice to local authorities and others to enable them to discharge the responsibilities imposed upon then by the act. It reports to Parliament through the Secretary of State for Education and Employment. The Commission arranges for research to be carried out, submits proposals for new regulations, produces codes of practice and generally works to reassure the public that risks are being properly controlled through information and responsiveness to public concerns.

The health and safety executive are responsible for the policing and enforcement of the act and other acts involving safety. They employ a large staff of inspectors, whose duties are covered later in the chapter.

Control of Substances Hazardous to Health Regulations (COSHH) 1988

These influential regulations came into effect in 1989. They consist of nineteen regulations and four codes of practice and are designed to protect employees who work with any substances which could be hazardous to their health unless they are handled and utilised in a properly controlled way. They apply to all workplace, large and small and include all substances except for those where regulations were already in force, such as lead and asbestos.

The principal requirements in these regulations are five-fold (HSE, 1988):

■ A risk assessment must be made to identify all potentially hazardous substances and to set out the precautions required. For many manufacturing employers, this list of substances can be a very extensive list, stretching into four figures and much time has been taken up in producing the list. Criticisms have been made of the outcome of the regulations where lists need to include day to day common products, such as petrol, tippex and photo-copying fluid but many accidents and ill-health can arise from common causes such as misuse of products such as these. An amendment in 1992 required employers to carry out the risk assessment every 5 years.

■ A system must be put in place to prevent or control these risks. Consideration must be given to replace hazardous substances or to provide better controlled working arrangements where they are used.

■ Just as important, the employer must make sure these controls are effectively put to use and keep records of the monitoring process.

■ Employers must regularly conduct health surveillance of staff engaged in work associated with these substances where there is a known identifiable risk.

■ Employees must be informed of the hazards and trained in the control processes, including the precautions that they need to take.

Regulations arising from European Union Directives

It has been an objective from the early days of the European movement that laws relating to health and safety should be applied consistently across Europe. This ensures that the free market between states can operate efficiently without manufacturers and traders having to deal with different regulations in each country. The Framework Directive, implemented by member states in 1992, contained general safety principles and objectives, such as the prevention of occupational risks and providing balanced participation between the parties affected.

Additional regulations, known as 'daughter directives' covering specific areas have been issued within the framework of this directive and this programme will continue in the gradual move to ensure consistency across member states. They have been converted into regulations in the UK and the most important ones have been:

The Management of Health and Safety at Work Regulations 1992

These regulations take the requirements set out in HASAWA a stage further, making unqualified requirements on employers in areas such as carrying out risk assessments, providing training and establishing emergency procedures. Similarly, unconditional requirements have been made on employees to use equipment in the way they have been trained and to report any dangerous occurrence or gap that they see in the employer's systems.

The Workplace (Health, Safety and Welfare) Regulations 1992

These regulations require employers to provide a good working environment with appropriate temperature, ventilation and level of lighting, provision of rest rooms and no smoking areas.

The Manual Handling Operations Regulations 1992

These regulations make a clear requirement on the employer to reduce the risk of injuries by providing lifting gears where it is necessary and training employees on how to lift properly. The intention is to remove the 'macho lifting' culture and the operation of these regulations has helped to ensure that many more jobs involving lifting are open to women as well as men.

The Health and Safety (Display Screen Equipment) Regulations 1992

These regulations have had a major impact on the day to day operations of those who spend a great deal of their time in front of display screens. There is a requirement on employers to arrange for employees to have their eyes tested regularly, ensure that the work is planned to include breaks and changes of activity, appropriate training and the location of the units to prevent damage to employees' upper limbs.

The Working Time Regulations 1998

These regulations were implemented in the UK as a result of the Working Time Directive of November 1993. At first, the Conservative government refused to accept the directive as one of health and safety but the European Court of Justice decided against the UK. The arrival of the Labour government speeded up the process of acceptance resulting in the 1998 regulations. The essence of the Regulations is that employees cannot be forced to work in excess of 48 hours a week, averaged over 17 weeks. Employees should have 11 consecutive hours of rest in any 24 hours period and a 24 hours rest in every 7-day period, plus a 20 minutes break if the shift exceeds 6 hours. However, at this stage, employers and employees can agree to 'opt out' of the regulations and many employees, including most managers and, surprisingly, employees working in transport, are exempt for reasons that existing regulations are in place or that their time cannot be measured accurately.

In response to complaints concerning the extent of record-keeping, revised regulations were introduced in 1999 which reduced the need to keep records for those staff who had agreed to 'opt out'. However, there is still a duty of care on the part of the employer to monitor the hours actually worked. In 2004, following a complaint by the union Amicus, Britain was taken to the European Court of Justice under the infringement procedure because the UK Working Time Regulations do not insist on organisations ensuring that employees take their breaks and that too many employees were being allowed to work additional unrecorded hours.

The arrangement where employees can 'opt out' of the regulations is controversial. CIPD (2004) research found that long hours culture had caused problems to develop. Forty-seven per cent of respondents recorded strains on personal relationships, 17% reported mental health problems and 69% said that they missed out on leisure and hobby time, while 36% believed that they performed less efficiently. Thirty per cent claimed there was compulsion from their organisation to work long hours, up from 11% when the regulations were passed. However, 65% did not want the opting out clause to be outlawed. Although long hours are essentially the British phenomena, other organisations in Europe are increasing their opt-outs, especially in the light of a court ruling where stand-by hours were deemed to be part of working time under the regulations.

Regulations have also come into effect relating to the provision and use of protective equipment, the control of asbestos at work, measures to set minimum standards for the safe use of machines and equipment and the protection of young people and pregnant women in the workplace.

Reporting of Diseases and Dangerous Occurrences Regulations (RIDDOR) 1995

All statistics on safety arise from a system of reporting by employers and this revised system was introduced to produce more accurate information and extend it to dangerous situations where nobody was hurt. All deaths and serious injuries must be immediately reported and a written report sent within 10 days. Lesser accidents which cause an employee to be off work for more than 3 days must lead to a completed accident form to be sent to the enforcing authorities, as do some work-related diseases, such as skin cancer or dermatitis. In 1998–1999, there were 126,000 3 days or more absences reported (HSE, 1999).

A dangerous occurrence could be a situation where a truck with a platform for mending street lights travelled down a highway with the platform extended and brought down some telephone lines. No injury followed but it could well have caused a major traffic accident and the enforcing authorities would need to know how it came to happen and to ensure it is not repeated. There were 10,128 such cases reported in 1998–1999. Of these, 25% related to failure of lifting machinery and 13% to the release of dangerous substances (HSE, 1999). In 1996, an amendment was introduced requiring employers to report formally any incident of violence in the workplace, although no clear definition of violence has yet been issued at the time of writing.

Enforcing the law

There are two main groups who work to enforce the law: the *external authorities*, made up of *inspectors* who work for the health and safety executive and *local authority enforcement officers*; and the *internal authorities*, made up of *safety officers* and *safety representatives*.

External authorities

Local authority enforcement officers mostly deal with the service industries, such as hotels, restaurants, offices and warehouses while inspectors deal with factories, mines, railways, schools and hospitals. Their enforcement authority consist of rights to:

- enter premises, with or without notice, at any reasonable time (accompanied by the police, if obstructed);

- take samples, measurements and photographs or recordings;
- carry out tests;
- direct that work be left undisturbed;
- examine books and documents;
- take statements from any employee concerned.

Their main enforcement activities, after persuasion has not achieved the desired results, is to issue improvement notices and prohibition notices. *Improvement notices* are issued where the inspector is satisfied there has been a contravention of a statutory provision. The improvement notice will give the employer a certain time within which that contravention must be remedied. Work can continue in the meantime. A *prohibition notice*, which means the work must immediately cease, is issued when the inspector considers that the activity involves a risk of serious personal safety or of a severe safety hazard to the employees or the public. Around 15,000 notices are issued each year and the records of such notices are on public view for up to 3 years, providing a deterrent to safety transgressors. A diagrammatic illustration of this process is shown in Figure 11.2.

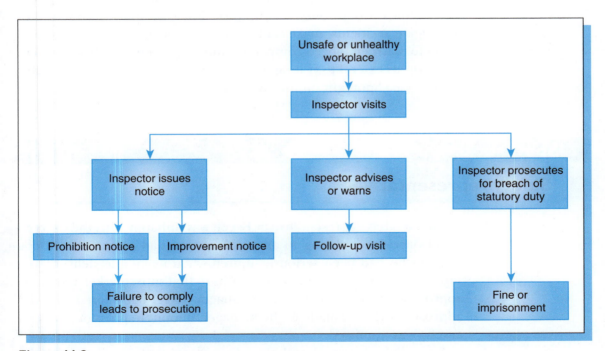

Figure 11.2
External monitoring process

Internal authorities

The main authorities within an organisation are *safety officers* and *safety representatives*. There is no specific requirement for an organisation to have a safety officer but most industrial sites employing over 200 usually have a full-time appointment. Smaller organisations may have a part-time employee or make use of consultants. The role of the safety officer is to ensure that the safety requirements imposed by legislation are met by the organisation. They will set up safe systems of work, carry out risk assessments, investigate accidents and dangerous occurrences and generally try to ensure that a 'safety culture' operates in the workplace. They are, however, employees of the organisation and their authority is limited by the position and influence they can wield.

Safety representatives are appointed or elected by the employees, either directly or through their trade union. Their rights were set down in HAWASA, and subsequently clarified by the Health and Safety (Consultation with Employees) Regulations 1996. They must be recognised by employers, involved in the consultation process through a safety committee and given reasonable paid time off to carry out their duties together with basic facilities, such as the use of a telephone and a filing cabinet. Their duties are, to a large extent, in tandem with the safety officer with whom they will work closely in practice, in that they investigate accidents, make regular safety inspections, assess risks and bring forward employee complaints and suggestions regarding safety. Their rights extend to visiting other companies to examine their safety systems (see Spotlight on the law 11.2).

Spotlight on the law 11.2

Safety representatives

Healey, a safety representative at Excel, was unhappy with the entry in Excel's accident relating to an accident that had occurred to a colleague who had been seriously injured when making as delivery to a supermarket. Healey made several visits to that supermarket and made approaches to the supermarket manager. Excel considered that the approaches Healey made to the manager amount to gross misconduct and he was dismissed.

The tribunal agreed with Excel's version that Healey had gone on a clandestine mission to the supermarket in order to pry into the supermarket's health and safety and his claim for unfair dismissal was dismissed. It could not be held to be a safety inspection as allowed under the Safety Representatives and Safety Committees Regulations 1977 because the supermarket was not under Excel's control.

Upon appeal, however, the Employment Appeals Tribunal (EAT) found that Healey had the right to 'inspect', 'investigate' and 'examine' in relation to safety issues concerning employees that he represented and a visit to the supermarket to look at the accident book was not an unreasonable part of such investigations. He was found to be unfairly dismissed.

Source: IDS (1998)

Safety committees

If two or more safety representatives request the formation of a safety committee then the employer must set one up. Most employers of a reasonable size do so without such a request, seeing it as an important vehicle for joint investigation and improvement. Membership usually consists of the safety representatives, the safety officer, management (in the form of the plant, maintenance or operations managers) the human resources officer and, in larger organisations, the company nurse or occupational health officer. The chair is usually a member of management who is knowledgeable on safety matters, such as the plant manager. Agenda items can include:

- Reporting and analysis of accidents and dangerous occurrences.
- Necessary revisions to safety policy and procedures.
- Discussion of reports on specific accidents, including contacts with factory inspectors.
- Investigation into safe systems of work, including general aspects, such as noise, temperature and use of protective equipment.
- Safety implications of new equipment or layouts.
- Monitoring of safety training.
- Publicity of safety issues.

Risk assessment

Risk assessment does not only apply to materials and substances under the COSHH regulations, although these regulations stimulated interest and experience in this process. Under the 1992 Code of Practice for the Management of Health and Safety at Work, it became a legal duty for employers to assess and record health and safety risks and requires the appointment of 'competent persons' to assist in this and other safety tasks.

There are three main stages in the process of assessing and controlling risks:

- Identifying hazards (the potential causes of harm).
- Assessing risks (the likelihood of harm occurring and its severity) and prioritising action.
- Designing, implementing and monitoring measures to eliminate or minimise risk.

Hazard identification can be carried out in a number of ways. Observation through, say, a regular safety tour of the plant by the safety officer and safety representatives for the areas, will bring to light poor housekeeping, such as accumulated rubbish or blocked fire exits, safety equipment not being worn and poor lighting or ventilation. Such hazards have to be considered as much for employees who may be aware of the dangers but also for visitors to the site and especially new employees who could be young and be completely unaware of potential dangers.

Longer investigations by trained technicians or by external agencies may be necessary to investigate the hazards of pollution, noise or noxious fumes and their degree of danger or to decide where, if at all, smoking can be allowed on the premises. Long-term projects will be needed to identify hazards in planned changes through new equipment, machinery, materials and lay-outs. A proper investigation here will involve the suppliers of the equipment, machinery and the materials.

When it comes to *assessing the risks*, it is useful to attempt to identify the severity of the hazard. Fowler (1995) set out a three-part rating scale for risk assessment (see Figure 11.3).

Using such a rating scale provides a consistent approach to identifying hazards and also provides help with prioritising safety action. It is not possible to eliminate every conceivable hazard. Where there are budgetary limits, the total hazard rating provides a league table of necessary action where those with the highest points get tackled first.

The final stage is to decide what can be done to *control or eliminate the risks*. Tightening up on housekeeping procedures should make the site cleaner, tidier and, therefore, safer. Supplying better protective equipment will serve to avoid the likelihood of injury to persons exposed to the risk. Replacing hazardous materials with safer replacements will

Likelihood of harm		
Certain	It is certain that harm will result whenever exposure to the hazard occurs	4 points
Probable	Harm will probably result in most cases when exposure to the hazard occurs, although there may be exceptions	3 points
Possible	Harm may occur in some cases when exposure to the hazard occurs, although there are likely to be many exceptions	2 points
Slight	Unlikely that harm will occur, except in a very small minority of cases	1 point
Severity		
Major	Death or major injury, as defined by RIDDOR, is probable	4 points
Serious	Injuries, though not necessarily formally classified as major, are likely to result in absences of more than 3 days	3 points
Minor	Injuries may cause some absence but probably for not more than 3 days	2 points
Slight	Any injuries are unlikely to result in time off work	1 point
Extent		
Very extensive	Likely to affect the whole workforce and/or significant numbers of the public	4 points
Extensive	Likely to affect a whole work group and might affect some members of the public	3 points
Limited	Likely to affect only a small number of either employees or members of the public	2 points
Very limited	Likely to affect only single individuals	1 point
RIDDOR: Reporting of diseases and dangerous occurrences regulations.		

Figure 11.3
Making risk assessments by rating hazards (Source: Fowler, 1995)

avoid or reduce the need to monitor and protect employees. Re-designing the production processes or layouts through such improvements as separating the operator from the risk by enclosing the process, using remote-control equipment, improving guarding and increasing extraction systems are all valuable investment in terms of hazard prevention. Automating lifting processes will also have a large effect on the incidences of employees injuring their backs, although fork-lift trucks and other devices also provides a further source of potential danger which needs to be assessed.

Risk assessment continues to be a matter of balance. The test of 'reasonably practical' is still used in the context of cost and difficulty balanced against likely danger. It is important, therefore, that organisations have set out policies and procedures which help them to achieve a fair balance and which will highlight actions that they have to take speedily.

Welfare issues and policies

It is no coincidence that the words 'health' and 'safety' are so closely linked. Encouraging employees to live and work in a healthy environment is as important as ensuring that the workplace is a safe environment. Employers need to take care, for example, over their smoking policy as shown in Spotlight on the law 11.3.

Spotlight on the law 11.3

Smoking at work

A non-smoking secretary worked in an office with colleagues who smoked. After a review, smoking was banned in her office but permitted in adjoining offices but she found this still unsatisfactory as ventilation in her office was poor and smoke still drifted in. She resigned and claimed constructive dismissal. The tribunal upheld her claim, ruling that the employers had been in breach of an implied term in her contract, namely a duty to provide and maintain a working environment that was reasonably tolerable to all employees. They pointed out that it would have been practicable for all smoking to be banned. This decision was upheld by EAT.

Waltons and Morse versus Dorrington (1997) reported in Croners Health and Safety Briefing, 26 January 1998

The emphasis is not just on healthy physical working conditions, such as heating, lighting, ventilation, sufficient space per employee and noise levels. There is an onus on employers to take initiatives to attempt to alleviate some of the sources of employee stress, which is estimated to be at the root cause of 60% of all work absence (HSE, 2002). These initiatives can be *individual*, looking at cases where employees appear to be suffering from occupational stress, or *group*, such as promoting healthy living or introducing an EAP.

Physical provision

A starting point is for the organisation to provide the appropriate medical facilities, given the nature of the business. In a large manufacturing or distribution site with over 1000 employees, these facilities would include a dedicated medical centre, trained for emergency care and immediate first aid and run by qualified medical staff; regular first aid training sessions and a well-monitored systems of first aid provision in all areas of the site; regular screening for employees who deal with any hazardous substances and voluntary screening for other ailments; medicals for all new employees.

Occupational stress

Stress has become one of the most serious health issues of recent years. A survey by the HSE (2002) estimates that stress costs nearly £4 billion per year in the UK, over 1% of Gross Domestic Product, or £150 per employee per year. The number of work-related stress cases reaching the courts has increased from 516 in 2002 to 6428 in 2003 (Palmer and Quinn, 2004); 150,000 employees take at least 1 month off for ailments caused by stress at work. Employees aged between 34 and 44 suffer the most, while the problems worsen the longer they stay in the same job.

The causes of occupational stress are numerous. They are associated with perceptions of job insecurity, increase in work intensity, aggressive management styles, lack of effective workplace communication, overt or insidious bullying and harassment, faulty selection for promotion or transfer and lack of guidance and training (Cartwright and Cooper, 1997). Employees may be exposed to situations which they find uncomfortable, such as continually dealing with customers, excessive computer work, repetitive or fragmented work or having to make regular public presentations. Probably the most common cause, however, is the constant fear of organisational change through re-structuring, takeovers, mergers or business process re-engineering. A lack of control over their work, their environment or their career progression can also be stressful (Rick *et al.*, 1997).

When a work environment containing these cultural aspects are added to personal problems, such as divorce or separation, ill or dying relatives, difficult housing conditions and financial problems, then it is not surprising that the employer will be faced with a good proportion of employees with stress-related problems.

Stress is manifested not only in high absence levels, although fatigue, increases in infections, backache and digestive illnesses are common. Irritation, hostility, anxiety and a state of panic can arise in the workplace with knock-on effects on working practices and relationships between employees. The end result may be that the employee is 'burnt-out', unable to cope with pressures that previously had been regarded as challenging and stimulating. Employees may also turn to palliatives, such as alcohol or drugs.

The CIPD (2003) have summarised these causes of stress into four categories as shown in Figure 11.4.

The employer who neglects the problem of occupational stress may face legal action. The first legal breakthrough for an employee was John Walker, a social work manager with Northumberland County Council who, having had a mental breakdown arising from his occupation, returned to his job but received no positive assistance from his employer to help him to cope successfully. His case against the Council succeeded (he was awarded £175,000) because it was held by the court that his employer was negligent with regard to the 'duty of care'. The judge held that here was no logical reason why the risk of psychiatric damage should be excluded from the scope of the duty of care and the risk of a further breakdown was reasonably foreseeable. Mr Walker had been driven to despair by his employer's failure to provide him with enough resources to satisfy urgent needs for the people in his area and thereby decrease his workload (*Walker versus Northumberland County Council*, 1995, IRLR 35/95).

Organisational problems	**Physical problems**
■ A training need ■ A relationship problem ■ Workload or pace ■ Loss of motivation	■ Physical illness ■ Design of workstation ■ Noise/lighting ■ Violent attack at work
Psychological problems	**Social problems**
■ Anxiety/depression ■ Phobias/panic attacks ■ Anger management ■ Addictive behaviours – alcoholism, gambling	■ Housing problems ■ Relationship difficulties ■ Financial problems ■ Legal problems – divorce, custody or crime

Figure 11.4
Causes of workplace stress (*Source*: CIPD, 2003)

Successive cases have included a primary school head who won £100,000 after suffering two nervous breakdowns allegedly caused by stress brought on from bullying and harassment, an out-of-court settlement was reached in 1998 between a NHS Trust and the bereaved spouse of an employee who committed suicide. In a later case, Birmingham City Council admitted liability for personal injury caused by stress where they moved a 39-year-old senior draughtsman to the post of a neighbourhood housing officer without sufficient training. The nature of the work was so different and the inter-personal demands so great that she had long periods of ill-health leading to early retirement on medical grounds. She was awarded £67,000 (Miller, 1999).

Greater clarification as to the employer's responsibility in the case of psychiatric injury based on exposure to unacceptable levels of stress was given by the Court of Appeal in 2002 (*Sutherland versus Hatton*). The court held that an employer was entitled to assume that an employee was able to withstand the normal pressures of the job and to take what the employee said about her own health at face value. It was only if there were indications which would lead a reasonable employer to realise that there was a problem that a duty to take action would arise. In terms of whether the injury to health was foreseeable, factors that should be taken into account include whether:

- The workload was abnormally heavy.
- The work was particularly intellectually or emotionally demanding.
- The demands were greater compared to similar employees.

If the only way of making the employee safe was to dismiss him or her, then there would be no breach of duty by letting the employee continue if he or she was willing to do so (IRS, 2002).

All of these cases show that employers need to carefully consider the way that the work demands affect their employees and ensure that they investigate each case, taking appropriate action to ameliorate potentially health damaging situations (Earnshaw and Cooper, 1996). A further consideration is the level of employees' expectations on welfare provision. It is a sure sign of a sympathetic and caring employer who will make special provision for the personal and individual needs of employees. Finally, an CIPD study (Tehrani, 2002) has shown that employers who have some form of 'wellness' programmes incurred annual employment costs of between £1335 and £2910 less per employee than employers who did not.

Employment Assistance Programmes (EAPs)

EAPs were first introduced in the US in the early part of the century, mainly to combat the problem of alcoholism among employees. The late 1980s saw a significant growth in the UK and there are currently around 1.2 million employees covered by 600 schemes (Merrick, 1998). Usage rates by employees are in the region of 4–8% and many are open to their relatives.

The types of services provided include:

- A confidential telephone help-line for personal emergencies.
- Workshops to help employees who have to cope with elderly relatives, marital breakdowns or financial pressures.
- Assistance in dealing with a work-related traumatic event, such as a major fire or an armed robbery.
- Confidential referrals to specialists dealing with drugs, HIV or alcohol problems.

Such services can be offered by in-house specialists in the occupational health department but it is much more common for the services to be outsourced. This ensures confidentiality and the opportunity to have contact with a wider set of expertise. Details of a long-established scheme at AstraZeneca are shown in Case study 11.3.

Other health initiatives can take the form of healthy food in the company canteens, assistance with membership fees for health clubs, the encouragement of outdoor exercise within a sporting and leisure club context and strict controls (or prohibition) on smoking in the workplace.

Case study 11.3

Counselling and life management (CALM) programme at AstraZeneca

Following 10 years of running stress management workshops, AstraZeneca set up the CALM programme in 1996 with the aim of promoting well-being and balanced living for their 10,000 UK employees. The programme is designed to encourage thought on life management – to help people recognise signs of stress and to provide routes of support. It includes:

- Advice and help for employees to try to achieve a sensible balance between home and work.

■ Advice and education on a range of topics, such as caring for aged relatives and dealing with childhood difficulties.

■ Confidential counselling service on any personal problems relating to bereavement, marital matters, drug and alcohol dependency, etc.

■ Short courses providing a 'personal MOT' encouraging employees to assess their health and life-style and to give advice on 'fine-tuning'.

■ Workshops on coping with pressure, including 'Believing in yourself' and 'Understanding other people' and 'Pressure Management'. A special series of one-to-one workshops for 150 top executives was initiated in 2001 for them to talk through their professional life and relationships with staff with several sessions over a 12-month period.

■ A website, leaflets and a small library loan service.

In 1999, members of the CALM team saw 9% of employees, an increase of 1.5% over 1998. The cost of CALM has been more than re-coupled by lower illness and a sustained reduction in absence from psychological conditions.

Source: IDS (2002)

Role of human resources

In the majority of organisations where separate human resource departments exist, they either have responsibility for health, safety and welfare issues in that organisation or they play a major part in those activities (Torrington and Hall, 1998). The main activities consist of:

■ formulating policy statements and procedures;
■ monitoring safety policy and procedures;
■ advising management and employees on safety legislation;
■ designing, providing and recording health and safety training;
■ liaising with the safety inspectorate and occupational health authorities;
■ helping create a healthy working environment.

These are the activities, which will be dealt with in turn. However, there is a larger job and that is to achieve an *effective health and safety culture* in the organisation. Gill and Martin (1976) pointed out that an effective safety culture does not necessarily follow from having in place a set of detailed and costly manuals catering for every contingency, produced by knowledgeable safety engineers. What matters if the action practice followed on the ground. Although difficult to pin down, the culture can be demonstrated by the behaviour of management, employees and their representatives. An indication of this culture operating can be seen by looking at how the parties behave in an *advanced safety culture*:

- *Management* carry out their safety activities not, primarily, because the law directs them to do so but because it is both good business practice and because it is ethically sound. Each accident or injury is seen as regrettable and a source of information which leads to its prevention in the future, and where disciplinary procedures are used as a last resort.
- *Employees* follow their safety instructions not just in terms of the way they carry out the work and the way they wear the required safety protective equipment; they also help to identify safety hazards, they encourage good housekeeping amongst themselves without being reminded and they co-operate with changing work practices where this leads to better safety provision.
- *Employee representatives* regard their task not as an opportunity to spend time away from the job or to score points against management but as an important part of the joint determination process, a partnership to help all parties gain in terms of less accidents, less cost and less disruption.

To achieve such a culture, human resource departments need to start by convincing management of the business and ethical cases. The business case rests essentially on the very high costs associated with poor health and safety. Accidents are expensive (a recent report by the HSE estimated that a average work-related vehicle accident is likely to cost an employer £16,000 on top of any repair costs), they cause considerable lost time by all parties – those injured, the management team in handling the aftermath and the loss of productivity by the rest of the work team. A reputation as an unsafe work site can raise the cost of recruitment, can cause a workforce to become de-motivated leading to falling productivity and eventually, if bad publicity occurs, can lead to customers choosing to go elsewhere. There are additional costs that can arise, such as higher insurance, fines arising from successful prosecutions and the costs of an extended investigation.

The ethical case stems from the need to treat employees fairly and to operate a true 'duty of care'. It is one of the saddest jobs of a human resource professional to have to visit the wife (or widow) of an employee recently killed or seriously injured in the workplace and to see the massive grief that this has caused. Management has to take ultimate responsibility for any such tragedy, even if the cause is a mixture of employee culpability and sheer bad luck and there is therefore a strong argument to divert resources to improve health and safety to as high a level as possible.

Formulating policies and procedures

This activity is more than a formality required by law. It is essential that new employees understand how safety works within a new organisation and the policies and procedures will set out how the safety responsibilities are structured, and the requirements from each employee. Specific references to areas (such as responsibility for checking lifting gear, or guards) should be clearly spelt out. The document should give a statement of management intent as to how safety issues will be treated in the workplace. Detailed procedures should be set out for dealing with emergencies, safety training, information arising from the investigations under COSHH, and procedures should be set out for all departments where hazards have been identified. Human resources should ensure that such documents are logical, readable and have been circulated correctly.

An example of a safety statement (which was published on notice boards around the hospital site) taken from a hospital policy document is given in Figure 11.5.

Monitoring policies and procedures

At regular intervals, all procedures need examining to see if they need updating to take account of new processes, materials and layouts. By attending management and safety meetings, human resources can ensure such necessary revisions can be identified and put into place.

Advising management and employees on safety legislation

New regulations continue to emerge, especially from Europe with different levels of importance and different implementation dates. By following regular bulletins, such as that provided by Croners, it is possible to provide a up to the minute service to all employees, including top

1   The hospital considers that the health and safety of its staff is of the greatest importance. It is necessary for management and staff to work together to reduce personal injuries and hazards to the health of staff and others to a minimum. For this reason, the hospital aims to achieve and maintain high standards of health and safety for its staff and members of the public who use its premises or equipment.

2   The hospital will fully comply with the current health and safety legislation and expects the full support of its staff in achieving this aim.

3   To ensure this happens the hospital will:
  ■ Observe in full the legislation and the hospital requirements relating to the health and safety of staff at work.
  ■ Ensure, as far as is possible, legislation is observed by all hospital staff and ensure adequate education and training.
  ■ Formulate and maintain health and safety plans by directorate that clearly set out the measures to be taken to safeguard staff and others affected by the hospital activities.
  ■ Produce, update and maintain for staff access, departmental health and safety policies, procedures and assessments.
  ■ Continually identify and eliminate or control hazards that present a risk to staff and other persons and possible damage to and loss of plant, equipment, property or service to clients.
  ■ Consider health and safety when planning new development, systems of work and when purchasing new equipment.
  ■ Keep and maintain accurate records of accidents, incidence, injuries and known exposure to health risks at work.
  ■ Take all practical steps to ensure adherence to this policy by all staff and other persons undertaking work on behalf of the hospital or who are on the premises.

4   Further information and details are included in the full health and safety policy document.

J. Caring   Chief Executive

Figure 11.5
Health and safety statement at Rising Hill Hospital (*This is not the name of the actual hospital*)

management, as to what actions are necessary and how these can be carried out.

Designing, providing and recording health and safety training

Systematic training is essential if procedures are to operate properly. It should start with induction training to ensure that employees who are involved in any hazardous operation have instruction in key areas before they set foot on the work site. Safety instruction should be incorporated into any new processes or where new materials are introduced onto site. New safety representatives have the right for time off for training and this should be encouraged by the organisation so they can operate efficiently.

Liaising with the safety inspectorate

Building a relationship with the enforcing authorities is essential. Making use of their advice and extensive knowledge can be valuable, especially where new processes or production lines are being planned. A list of necessary actions arising from a late visit by the factory inspector could cause an expensive delay to a new production facility.

Helping create a healthy working environment

All the research indicates that a healthy workforce will be a successful one and a higher performing one so being pro-active in introducing and encouraging initiatives to support health programmes can make a substantial difference to organisational performance, as shown in Case study 11.4.

Case study 11.4

Improving employee health at Kimberley-Clarke

Kimberley-Clarke, which makes products such as Kleenex and Huggies nappies, has made cost savings of £500,000 per annum and reduced long-term staff absence from 6.8% to 0.5% after launching schemes in 2002 aimed at improving the health of its 174 UK staff. Under the programme, the company introduced work-life balance coaching sessions, massages for desk workers and sleep management workshops to improve employees' sleep quality. It also provided free fruit twice a week to promote healthy eating. Evidence that the scheme was getting immediate results was that, after 6 months, only 19% admitted they suffered sleep problems, which was done from 68% before the scheme started.

Source: Watkins (2003)

Meteor case study

Shop stewards and safety

At one of the six-monthly meetings of human resource staff in the organisation, June, who was one of Sarah's opposite numbers at another site in the South of England, explained the severe difficulties they were having with two of their shop stewards who were also safety representatives. They took a great deal of time away from the workplace dealing with what were regarded as trivial safety issues and, when challenged, pointed out their legislative rights for time off with pay. As they were away so much, they had been moved to work that was not so essential, which only seemed to cause them to have even more time off. She recalled four specific episodes that had taken place over the last month:

- The stewards had advised their members to boycott a new piece of machinery because they were unhappy about the guarding arrangements. It was only after a visit by the factory inspector that the boycott had been lifted.
- One of the stewards had been away from his place of work for over an hour and was found in another department talking to one of his members about safety shoes. Supervisors from both departments were angry at the time that seemed to have been wasted in this case.
- A request had been made by one of the stewards to attend a union course on Abrasive Wheels Regulations when, only the previous year, they had attended the same type of course run by the company.
- The men insisted on making a safety inspection of the site every month even though it was pointed out to them that their rights extended only to an inspection every 3 months.

June knew that Sarah had become quite experienced in safety issues and asked her if she could provide some informal consulting. Sarah agreed to make a two-day visit the next month and prepared a list of questions for June to answer before she came. This included details of the safety record of the site, the safety organisation, the safety systems in place and the state of play on audits under COSHH and Display Screens Regulations.

This information arrived just before Sarah was due to visit and it made worrying reading. The accident record was poor, with the number of reportable accidents far in excess of Sarah's factory; two prosecutions had taken place over the previous 5 years, arising out of incidents where three serious injuries had occurred; details of the safety responsibilities were far from clear and the state of play on COSHH and Display Screens were not included.

Sarah realised that the situation may not be quite as straightforward as June indicated and knew she would have to prepare well for the visit to be able to provide the help required.

Summary

- The HASAWA and subsequent legislation has placed a responsibility and duty of care on employers to provide a safe place of work and on employees and sub-contractors to co-operate with all measures which reinforces this requirement.
- Important features of these duties include carrying out risk assessments, reporting accidents and dangerous occurrences and appropriate training.
- The enforcement process is shared between local authority enforcement officers and health and safety inspectors. They are able to issue improvement notices and prohibition notices. Within the organisation, employees can elect safety representatives who have rights and responsibilities supported by legislation.
- Occupational stress is increasingly being recognised as an illness and organisations are beginning to pay greater attention to their responsibilities in this area. Some are starting EAPs.
- Human resources have an important role in formulating policy, encouraging a safety culture, advising on legislation, designing training and communication and monitoring accidents and dangerous occurrences.

Student activities

1 In respect to the Meteor case study, what additional information will Sarah need to enable her to make a balanced judgement on the situation?
   - A meeting has been fixed between Sarah, June and the shop stewards. Role-play this meeting and subsequently discuss what Sarah's next move will be.
2 Carry out a risk assessment exercise for an activity that you take part in. It might be a local amateur football or netball team, drama event or similar.
3 What are the rights of smokers and non-smokers in employment? Investigate what is the 'best practice' by way of introducing no-smoking policies into the workplace.
4 Look up the references on stress in the workplace and summarise the actions that human resources need to carry out in this area.

5 Health and safety legislation shows no sign of abating. Debate whether you consider that excessive legislation merely creates confusion and bureaucracy and makes it more difficult for businesses to be run efficiently.

References

BusinessEurope.com (2004) TUC urges health and safety help for SMEs, 20 December.

Cartwright, S., Cooper, S. (1997) *Managing Workplace Stress.* Sage.

CIPD (2003) *Stress: Fact Sheet.* CIPD.

CIPD (2004) *Calling Time on Working Time.* CIPD.

Corbridge, M., Pilbeam, S. (1998) *Employee Resourcing.* Financial Times Management.

Earnshaw, J., Cooper, C. (1996) *Stress and Employer Liability.* IPD.

Fowler, A. (1995) How to make the workplace safer. *People Management,* 26 January, 38–39.

Gill, I., Martin, K. (1976) Safety management: reconciling rules with reality. *Personnel Management,* June.

Health and Safety (1999) Dead Hand ex-miners set for biggest compensation package. March, 8.

Health and Safety Practitioner (2004) 'Recipe for disaster' costs firm £132,000. April, 8.

Health and Safety Practitioner (2004) Farm contractor jailed for manslaughter, February, 8.

HSE (1988) *COSHH: a Brief Guide for Employers – The Requirements of the Control of Substances Hazardous to Health (COSHH) Regulations.* HMSO.

HSE (1996) *Good Health is Good Business.* Health and Safety Executive.

HSE (2002) *Tackling Work-related Stress: A Manager's Guide to Improving and Maintaining Employee Health and Well-being.* HSE.

HSE (2004) *Annual Report.* Health and Safety Executive.

IDS (1998) Duties of a health and safety practitioner. *Brief 622,* October, 5–6.

IDS (2002) Stress management. *Study,* **732,** July, 14–16.

IRS (2002) Court of appeal guidelines for stress at work cases. *Employment Law Review,* **748,** 25 March.

Miller, S. (1999) Council pays £67,000 for stress injury. *The Guardian,* 6 July, 4.

National Audit Office (1996) *Health and Safety in NHS Acute Hospitals in England.* HMSO (reported in Health and Safety at Work, January 1997, 5).

Palmer, B., Quinn, P. (2004) Protracted agony. *People Management,* 6 May, 17.

People Management (1996) 8 February, 9.

Rick, J. *et al.* (1997) *Stress: Big Issue, but what are the Problems?* Institute of Employment Studies Report 311, July.

Taylor, P., Baldry, C., Bain, P., Ellis, V. (2003) 'A unique working environment': health, sickness and absence management in UK call centres. *Work, Employment and Society,* **17**(3): 435–456.

Tehrani, N. (2002) *Managing Organisational Stress: A CIPD Guide to Improving and Maintaining Well-being.* CIPD.

Torrington, D., Hall, L. (1998) *Human Resource Management.* Prentice-Hall.

Trevelyan, G. (1942) *Illustrated English Social History.* Longmans, Green.

Wainwright, M. (1994) Mistakes led to chemical plant deaths. *Guardian,* 21 June, 8.

Watkins, J. (2003) Wellness beats output slump. *People Management,* 18 December, 12.

Whitfield, M. (1995) Negligent employers face charges of manslaughter. *People Management,* 10 August, 7–8.

Further reading

Earnshaw, J., Cooper, C. (2001) *Stress and Employer Liability.* CIPD.

IDS (2002) *Stress Management.* IDS Study 732.

Industrial Society (2001) *Occupational Stress: Managing Best Practice.* Industrial Society.

Stranks, J. (1997) *A Manager's Guide Top Health and Safety at Work.* Kogan Page.

For an examination of the reasons why *Wellness at Work Initiatives* have developed and further case studies in this area, see:

Manocha, R. (2004) Well adjusted. *People Management.* 8 April, 26–30.

Croner Publications produce a monthly Health and Safety at Work which contain general articles and a full list of current legislation.

Rick, J. (2004) *Evaluation of Reducing Risks.* HSE Research Report RR279.

Web sites

http://www.open.gov.uk.hse
The Health and Safety Executive web site which provides a comprehensive list of publications.

http://www.britishsafetycouncil.co.uk
Best practice from the British Safety Council.

http://www.rospa.co.uk
Occupational health and safety information from the Royal Society for the Prevention of Accidents.

CHAPTER 12

An international perspective

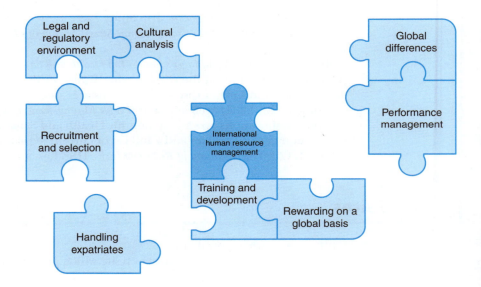

Globalisation is arguably among the most potent shaping forces of the contemporary study of business and management. Open any management or economics textbook and it will leap out at you from the pages; type the word 'globalisation' into the search engine of any business research database and you will get literally thousands of 'hits'. As we will consider shortly *Globalisation* is a highly contentious and indistinct concept and many commentators disagree on its extent, nature and virtue (Baalam and Veseth, 2005). However, there can be no doubt that in the last decades of the 20th century and the first of the 21st century, the international domain has become an increasingly more important dynamic in the work of those concerned with Human Resource Management (HRM) and workplace organisation. The prominence and importance of multi-national corporations (MNCs), the liberalisation of world markets, the integration of markets and business systems and the all-pervasive influence of information and communication technologies (ICTs) amongst many other factors have meant that the world has become more interconnected and in a metaphorical sense a smaller place. As a result, business and management activities, however localised, have an enhanced sensitivity to the potential impact of international phenomena. Furthermore, some commentators have argued that these developments have changed the operating environments of the world's 'developed' economies, industries and labour forces (such as the USA, the UK and Europe, and their manufacturing sectors) and increased the risks and challenges they face such as competition from other regions of the world and the imperative to innovate and find new 'flexible' ways of working in order to ensure competitiveness and survival (Eaton, 2000).

International trade

International trade and international organisations are nothing new. The very earliest civilisations traded goods and services to all parts of the known world and ever since the mightiest empires the world has known (e.g. Rome, Great Britain) have been built on a basis of not only military might but also the buying and selling of materials and goods from and to all parts of the known world. In the 20th century, the largest corporations in the world (e.g. Coca Cola, Ford, General Motors, Guinness breweries, IBM, ICI and numerous financial institutions to name but few) sought to increase the volume of their business by expanding operations to other lands from their country of origin (Tayeb, 1999). However, over the recent histories of these organisations, they have had to change the ways in which they organize their operations and thus how they organize and manage their workers. Economic and social pressures as well as opportunities presented by the relentless march of technological development and knowledge transfer have, according to many writers, taken away many of the relative certainties of management. For example, governments have been relinquishing many of the controls they previously placed on business in a bid to liberalise economies in order to make them more dynamic and competitive (Balaam and Vesteh, 2005). MNCs and their subsidiaries continue to be extremely powerful, by the reckoning of some they account for over a quarter of the economic output of the most developed countries, and important to local economies; but managers now have to consider the management of MNCs in this complex new environment and in particular the organisation of human resources on a much more strategic and sophisticated level.

One key element of this complexity is the fact that the nature of work and the behaviour of people in the workplace tends to differ from country to country, a phenomenon that is explained by the influence of *national culture* (Tayeb, 1999). Furthermore, the institutions of HRM that exist in one country may have similar terminology and basic *raisons d'être* to those in another country but may conduct their business in different ways and to different ends. For example, labour unions in France which are portrayed as militant and anti-establishment, and those of Japan which are organized on an enterprise level and tend to be subservient in the face of managerial prerogatives. These differences occur as a result of a complex mixture of historical, social and economic factors which we will consider in due course. Indeed to the observer in one country, the workplace practices in another might seem downright absurd. However, that observer might find that any attempt to impose the ways and methods that he or she knows best in that other national context might be doomed to failure.

International trade has long been premised on the fact that there are winners and losers in the economy, that is, that some countries will be developed and others developing and that the developed countries and their MNCs are in the 'driving seat' in terms of consolidating their influence. However, in recent decades, the economies of the developed world have been challenged by the emergence of new forces, especially in the Pacific Rim. Japan was the trailblazer with its economic miracle in the 1960s and 1970s but it has been followed more recently by Singapore, Malaysia and today the People's Republic of China is arguably the most talked about phenomenon in global business circles and has been enjoying staggering growth, and development of infrastructure. The consequence of this is that these emerging economies can compete with the developed world for manufacturing and even service jobs on the basis of having appropriate facilities, an educated workforce but far lower labour costs, and in a competitive global market this is an important consideration for MNCs and partners in joint ventures (Harzing, 1999).

In order to counter the challenges from emerging and established national competitors, some countries have put in place *supra-national* arrangements for creating economic relationships between themselves and other nations. This exists on the basis of trading blocs such as the World Trade Organization (WTO) whereby trade between member states is facilitated. However, rather more sophisticated relationships exist between the members of European Union (EU), whose institutions and functions are referred to in other sections of this book. The European Union (of which the UK is a prominent member) is worthy of close examination as not only does it establish economic interrelationships and interdependencies but it also seeks to impose a social dimension in order to not only bring about sustainable economic prosperity for its 25 member states but also political and social justice which seeks to guarantee rights and privileges for its citizens in the workplace and beyond.

These developments and phenomena give students of HRM and HR practitioners plenty to think about as these international forces have the potential to affect greatly the strategies and management techniques that are used to resource and organize work in the 21st century, and such is the pervasiveness of these forces, almost no organisation, however small it is or local its activities, is immune from the impact of international dynamics to some degree or another. An understanding of international HRM (IHRM) is therefore a vital aspect of the ideal knowledge set of those interested in the management and development of people in the workplace as international dimensions can be identified in all of the topics discussed in this book, from recruitment and selection to performance management and learning and development.

This chapter considers why the study of IHRM is important. It will firstly consider the context of IHRM, looking at the 'political economy' of global markets and how this impacts on the workplace. Secondly, it will look at appropriate ways of making sense and analysing IHRM looking in particular at institutional and cultural explanations of differences in workplace behaviours. Thirdly, we will feature ways and means of managing human resources across national boundaries in MNCs, looking in particular at resourcing and the use of expatriate workers. Fourthly, the extremely important issue of the growing influence of supra-national bodies, in particular the EU, in setting the agenda of HRM will be examined. Lastly, we look at how HRM interventions and regulations can seek to address some of the social and ethical issues that might arise out of exploitation of workers in the developing world in the competitive global economy.

The political economy of IHRM

By political economy we mean the general economic, social and political environment and structure of societies (Warhurst, 1997).

As we have discussed in Chapter 1 of this book, the environment of business has an impact on the way work is organized and how it is structured. Any HR manager must be aware of their organisation's environment and how it impacts of labour markets, skills needs, reward systems and so on. In an international context, these concerns become even more apparent and more complex. An understanding of the contextual domain of international business is therefore necessary in order to make sense of the role of the HR specialist in the global sphere.

The globalisation of markets

The great Scottish economist and philosopher Adam Smith was writing in his *Wealth of Nations* as long ago as 1776 (see Balaam and Veseth, 2005) about the need for international and national commerce to be organized on the basis of free and fair market competition. Smith described this concept in terms of the 'invisible hand' of the free market. However, this has never really been the case as powerful institutions such as governments have often intervened to manipulate economies for one reason or another by establishing laws and regulations, providing subsidies and even nationalising (i.e. taking ownership of) certain industries. The most extreme example of this occurred under communist regimes such as the Soviet Union and China where the state imposed heavy controls on the economy, industry and work systems out of ideological conviction; these systems were thought to be somewhat flawed and have be largely abandoned in favour of market capitalism. Even in Europe, North America and Japan, which are associated with a more liberal form of capitalism, governments have throughout the 20th century sought to intervene in the operations of business in order to attempt to ensure economic and social stability. Examples of this are regulations and tariffs on trade, laws guaranteeing rights for workers and the state ownership of corporations such as car manufacturers and airlines.

In the later part of the 20th century, a number of thinkers and politicians came to prominence who advocated a more liberal framework for business where governments would take a 'step back' and allow commerce to develop apparently along the lines envisaged by Smith some centuries ago. In the late 1970s and 1980s, the ideas of economists such as Milton Friedman and the policies of political leaders like Ronald Reagan (USA) and Margaret Thatcher (UK) heralded a change in how business was structured, allowing business to operate more freely both in national and international contexts. In the case of Margaret Thatcher's post 1979 Conservative administration in the UK, radical change occurred in the form of the privatisation of state industries – such as Rover Cars and British Airways (BA) and utilities such as gas, electricity and telecommunications – and the imposition of controls an the activities of trade unions in order to limit disruptions to production (see Chapter 7 of this book). These trends have been mirrored in many other national contexts, most notably in the fall of the communist Soviet Union and its Eastern European allies symbolised by the tumbling of the Berlin Wall in 1989. Thus a consensus has been reached by the world's major economic powers that industries should be freer to trade and compete internationally, a notion illustrated by the establishment of the WTO and the integration and expansion of the membership of the EU.

The consequence of these developments is that in the UK, the average company in the FSTE 100 (the top 100 UK companies quoted on the London Stock Exchange) earns half of its revenues abroad. Furthermore, foreign direct investment (FDI) has become increasingly more important to local economies in providing jobs and prosperity; in 1998 inward investment by the world's richest economies reached almost $500 billion (Ballaam and Vesath, 2005).

The liberalisation of trade has been a powerful force in affecting change in the world's economic landscape. However, it has also coincided with the rapid development of new technologies and in particular ICTs, the benefits of which you will be very familiar with from your use of e-mail and the Internet (or World Wide Web). Not only do these innovations allow you to keep in touch with loved ones and catch up with news of your favourite soccer team, but they also facilitate commerce and huge financial transactions; billions of dollars can now travel at the speed of light down a telephone line. Money has little regard for national borders also, zooming between London, New York, Cape Town and Hong Kong with ease depending on the state of the global financial markets. Also, it means that people can work together easily without even being located on the same continent.

These ongoing developments have in turn resulted in the development of previously poor countries and allowed them to compete with the older established powers. The countries of the Pacific Rim and even India are now synonymous with high-tech manufacturing and in 2001 China was admitted into the world's most exclusive economic club, the WTO. Furthermore, what these countries have in their favour are relatively low-labour costs; this has put the high-wage economies of the developed world under considerable pressure and has resulted in many manufacturing jobs being transferred from Western Europe and North America to China, the Pacific Rim and even South America. This phenomenon has resulted in obvious concerns for developed economies who have sought to either prevent MNCs moving jobs abroad or in the case of the UK to concentrate on service and 'knowledge' intensive industries.

The results of these 'paradigm shifts' and various other developments have been for the world, paraphrase the sociologist Anthony Giddens, to 'shrink' (Giddens, 1990). Indeed as long ago as 1958 the Canadian thinker Marshall McLuhan made reference to the 'Global Village' (see Giddens, 1990). We associate villages with being interconnected, mutually dependent where everyone knows everyone else's business. Has McLuhan's prophecy become a reality? If you consider that decisions can be made round a boardroom table in Detroit, Michigan that have a significant impact on the lives of many families in England. Indeed this happened recently when GM closed the Luton Vauxhall car plant in 2001 which had been in operation since 1907 and employed many thousands of workers.

Although globalisation as a tendency has many advocates, it should be noted that it also has many critics. For example, Beck (1991) talks of the emerging 'risk society' where many of the certainties of life have been removed and several eminent commentators in employee relations believe that globalisation has resulted in making workers more disposable and eroding their rights and well-being (Eaton, 1999). Furthermore, the perceived increasing dominance of large MNCs is seen as being a threat to democracy and civil society, as the imperatives of capitalism displace those of social justice. Indeed, the individual turnovers of the largest MNCs (e.g. GM, Mitsubishi, Wal-Mart) are bigger than the gross domestic products (GDPs) of most of the world's countries (Eaton, 2000)!

As we will see, these developments and controversies play a crucial role in shaping management imperatives and HRM policy and practice.

National business systems and HRM

If you have travelled to another country from the one in which you live, even if only to Spain on vacation, you will have been struck at how the whole feel of the place is different. The customs, habits and systems of that country may seem strange. You will therefore not be surprised to learn that in general, the nature of institutions, the structure of commerce and work organisation and the behaviour of people in the workplace differ from country to country. These national differences form a crucial part of our understanding of the IHRM, especially as we have observed above that the global domain is becoming more influential. We will consider some cultural explanations of differences in behaviour in the next section of this chapter, but for the time being we will look at how each country can be regarded as a national business system (NBS) (Warhurst, 1997: p. 214) where industry, work and economic activity are configured along distinctive lines having been shaped by national historical and political characteristics. Thus a number of factors and actors effectively contrive to 'negotiate' a system in accordance with a particular governing logic. As Almond *et al.* (2004: p. 589) illustrate:

> [F]or much of the twentieth century the US economy was characterised by a business system that emphasised very large vertically integrated firms engaged in the mass production and mass marketing of highly standardised products. In contrast to this, the British business system emphasised less standardised craft production by smaller, less integrated specialist firms which produced goods for distinct and more differentiated markets. Other economies, for example the German and Japanese economies, followed different paths that emphasised either high-quality system production or the production of standardised products that were continuously improved through the use of quality programmes.

So although most developed countries, their governments and the institutions and organisations that make up their systems are all governed by the rationale of wanting to achieve sustainable high economic performance within a broadly capitalist market framework, they follow different paths in attempting to achieve that goal. It follows that HRM phenomena and practices in each system will be informed by these factors. Dunlop (1958) used this systems analysis to build his influential 'industrial relations system' model where we can see that there are inputs which feed into processes and result in outcomes which Dunlop presented as rules.

A relevant example of systemic impact on HRM is the EU's 1998 Working Time Directive (see Chapter 11) where the EU decreed that its member states should introduce legislation to limit the number of hours employees should be expected to work each week. Each of the member states therefore had to set the limit that they believed was appropriate to their needs. The UK decided on 48 hours as being an acceptable limit (although this move was criticised by employers' organisations who claimed that it would make the UK economy uncompetitive). France on the other hand decided on a figure of 35 hours; a difference of 13 hours a week from their neighbours across the Channel! So why was there such a difference in outcome when the imperative came from a common source? There are perhaps two principal explanations which we can draw from our understanding of NBS. Firstly, trade unions in France are far more powerful and influential that their counterparts in the UK and were therefore better equipped to gain as favourable a settlement as possible for French workers. Secondly, France had, and continues to have, a chronic problem with long-term unemployment and the 35-hour week was seen by policymakers as a means of creating employment opportunities for more workers (Alis, 2003). The UK did not have this problem to the same extent.

Convergence and divergence

So we have established that policy and practice in HRM can differ between NBSs. However, because of the phenomena associated with globalisation, the environment of each NBS is highly dynamic and under continual pressure. Indeed, as the USA has emerged from the 1990s as the dominant world economy (especially in the light to the relative decline the fortunes of Japan) and that the doors opened by globalisation for the spread of capital, products, services and knowledge, could it be that the characteristics of the world's NBSs could be becoming more similar, basing themselves on the USA model? In his controversial book *The McDonaldization of Society*, Ritzer (1996) proposes that work routines and consumer experiences are becoming more standardised, routinised and degraded and that the spread of the McDonald's fast food chain is an illustration of this. However, commentators have been reporting a convergence of work systems for many years, long before McDonald's opened in your local High Street. Kerr *et al.* (1962) reported that as technological systems and industrial processes became more aligned, thus systems of employment and, by implication, HRM would also become more homogenised throughout the globe. In other words, the systems would gradually *converge*.

Anyone who observes popular culture would be forgiven for having some sympathy with the convergence thesis (e.g. the vast majority of Manchester United Football Club supporters live thousands of miles away from Old Trafford in East Asia). Also, many HRM techniques used in the UK originated in the USA or Japan (e.g. 360 degree feedback, quality circles). However, the convergence thesis has been criticised vigorously from a number of quarters. Much of the research into

IHRM has sought to demonstrate that although much change has taken place in national systems, their distinctiveness is still very durable and thus there are many continuities in the diversity of systems and that the fact that industrial and technological structures are becoming more similar in developed countries does not necessarily mean that management and HRM practices, nor employment laws and labour markets will necessarily converge with them (Muller, 1997). One explanation for these enduring differences is the behaviour of people in the workplace in respect of their collectively held values, expectations and attitudes; in other words, the culture. It is to this phenomenon that our attention now turns. A clear example of the tension between convergence and divergence is shown in Focus on research 12.1

Focus on research 12.1

Communication and consultation – a cross-national survey

The researchers from Oxford University investigated employee views on communications and consultation within very different institutional practices in France, Germany, Italy and the UK, contacting over 3500 employees. There was a general belief across the countries that employees felt they had little influence over important work decisions, despite the growing 'empowerment' initiatives over the last 20 years. Also, a perceived belief was widespread that representative channels of communications, (mostly through unions), was not very useful. However, there was general satisfaction over the amount of information provided by management.

Where the views differed across countries was in the degree of expectation over the consultation process. In the UK, employees expected few results from such exercises and they were not disappointed. They reported general disenchantment over communication initiatives and remained disengaged with the whole process. This is explained by the tradition that:

> .... British managers have traditionally sought to assert their prerogative at all levels of the organisation and, in the absence of any statutory or joint agreed obligation to communicate or consult, they have simply not done so .... (p. 530).

The views of the French are almost the reverse. They believe that upward communication should be useful, supported by strong statutory underpinning, such as at workplace level with the *groupes d'expression*.

However, the vast array of practices have led French employees to expect more and to foster disappointment when they do not receive it. For German employees, the position is even more extreme due to the degree of institutional power by employee groups, such as the *betriebsrat* and the role of worker directors. All the more disappointment, therefore, in recent years is when this power fails to restrict the growing round of redundancies and closures.

Source: Kessler *et al.* (2004)

National culture

Thinking once more of when you have visited other countries, or alternatively of friends that you might have who were born or raised in another country from you, do you think that there is anything about their national background that sets them apart in terms of their behaviour, philosophies and values? Of course, one must be careful not to stereotype. For instance the rather pernicious badinage of old music hall acts would often proclaim that the Irish were not very clever and the Scots were mean. In reality, educational attainment in the Republic of Ireland and Northern Ireland is amongst the most impressive in Europe and the Scots give more money to charity *per capita* than any other region of the UK. However, in the past few decades, a considerable amount of scientific research has been undertaken that seeks to prove and help us understand how the people in different countries have a collective programming that means that they are predisposed to behave in a certain way in the workplace. The work of these scholars has become highly influential in informing the strategies of managers in organisations that employ workers in more than one country.

Culture as a phenomenon in the study of human behaviour emerged in the late 19th century. The word was derived from one of German origin describing artificially bred biological cells. In 1871 the English anthropologist E. B. Tyler described culture as:

> 'that complex whole which includes knowledge, beliefs, art, morals, law, custom and any other capabilities and habits acquired by man as a member of society'
>
> Brown (1998: p. 4)

More recently, the study of organisations has used the concept of culture to explain how distinctive values and mores apply to individual organisations (Brown, 1999); In the 1960s when arguably the seeds of the gradual integration of the world's business systems were laid. Furthermore, the study of the social sciences adopted a more behavioural outlook, rather than concentrating on structures and systems. The behavioural and attitudinal differences of managers and workers in the workplace internationally became more apparent. Management studies started to undertake some small scale and limited research in the mid-1960s to attempt to explain what made managers and workers 'tick' in the workplace in different national contexts (Tayeb, 1999).

Hofstede and national culture

In 1968, the ambitious young Dutch social scientist Geert Hofstede secured the resources to undertake what was to become one of the largest ever single research projects. Using the US computer giant IBM and its numerous international branches and subsidiaries as his sample, he and his team surveyed over 116,000 employees in 50 different occupations in 66 countries with a questionnaire of approximately 150 questions about attitudes and values. The responses from these questionnaires were used to devise four indices that Hofstede believed were integral to the illustration of differences in national culture (Hofstede, 1980). The four resulting indices were as follows.

1 Power distance index

This index measures the extent to which people in a country tend to accept the act that power is distributed unevenly. For instance, in a country scoring highly on the power distance index (PDI) might feel less inclined to question the decisions of a manager. Counties in South-East Asia tend to score high whereas European countries tend to have lower scores.

High PDI	Low PDI	Selected others
Philippines (94)	Austria (11)	UK (35)
Mexico (81)	Israel (13)	USA (35)
India (77)	Denmark (18)	Germany FDR (35)
Singapore (74)	New Zealand (22)	France (68)

2 Uncertainty avoidance index

This index measures the extent to which people tend to be challenged by ambiguity. For example, people might be less inclined to take risks or they might develop beliefs and institutions that help counter these challenges, for example uniformity and formalised processes and structures in the workplace. The countries with the highest scores tend to be on mainland Europe. Interestingly, France has a high score and is renowned for its rigid bureaucratic structures and formalised work processes (Crozier, 1964). Singapore has by far the lowest score followed at some distance by a clutch of Northern European states.

High uncertainty avoidance index (UAI)	Low UAI	Selected others
Greece (112)	Singapore (8)	USA (46)
Portugal (104)	Denmark (23)	Germany (FDR) (65)
Belgium (94)	Sweden (29)	Australia (51)
France (92)	UK (35)	Italy (75)

3 Individualism index

This index measures the extent to which people in a particular country are more inclined to take care of themselves and their immediate families only. The opposite is 'collectivism' where people might have more pronounced mutual obligations with and to the wider community. Three 'Anglo-Saxon' societies top the table; the lowest positions tend to be held by South American countries where a more collectivist ethos prevails.

High individualism index (IDV)	Low IDV	Selected others
USA (91)	Venezuela (12)	France (71)
Australia (90)	Columbia (13)	Italy (76)
UK (89)	Pakistan (13)	India (48)
Netherlands (80)	Taiwan (17)	Singapore (20)

4 Masculinity index

This index is the most controversial of the four and considers the dichotomy between 'masculine' and 'feminine' values. Hofstede maintains that masculine values tend to be more assertive whereas feminine values are nurturing and caring. Also, people in countries scoring highly on this index would be more prone to overt materialistic displays of wealth and status. Japan ranks the highest whereas the lowest positions are held by Scandinavian countries.

High masculinity index (MAS)	Low MAS	Selected others
Japan (95)	Sweden (5)	UK (66)
Austria (79)	Norway (8)	USA (62)
Switzerland (70)	Netherlands (14)	France (43)
Mexico (69)	Denmark (16)	Australia (61)

Limitations of Hofstede's model and cross-cultural analysis

The scores from 40 of the countries in this sample were collated and ranked using the index, this providing an interesting means of comparing cultures as thus predicting how behaviours might differ in the workplace. However, it should be noted that Hofstede's original study, and those that he has subsequently undertaken to include countries originally excluded such as China, have been subject to a considerable degree of criticism on a number of grounds (Tayeb, 1999). The research is based on quantitative data derived from attitudinal questionnaire which is not necessarily the best way of studying something as abstract as culture. Also, the sample is rather narrow; are IBM employees typical of the entire working population of any country? As Tayeb explains:

> Given the complexity and dynamism of culture, it is arguable that Hofstede's findings reflect the values and attitudes of a large sample of employees in relation to their specific work environment at the time the study was conducted: nothing more, nothing less
>
> Tayeb (1999: p. 323)

The study takes little account of regional differences that can occur within a country (e.g. England, Scotland, Wales and Northern Ireland in the UK). However, perhaps one of the most profound criticisms of the study is that, as Hofstede concedes himself, the indices are derived from Western value sets and any attempt to measure countries in Asia, South America, Africa, etc. may distort the picture. This trait is known as *ethnocentrism* (Tayeb, 1999) which is an assumption that the values in which you have been socialised into are veritable and superior to those held by those in other countries.

In general, despite the engaging picture it paints of the differences between countries, cross-cultural analysis should be viewed with certain caveats in mind. Although behavioural differences between countries are undoubtedly evident, to it is far from certain whether culture matters as much as some scholars maintain. However, there are strong forces preventing the homogenisation of national systems and perhaps some explanations for this can be found in the behavioural attributes of people in the workplace in each national context.

HRM in multinational corporations

When future economic historians look back on the late 20th and early 21st centuries, they will surely all agree that the most distinctive and arguably most important characteristic of international commerce was the MNC. Their economic and social significance in global and local contexts cannot be understated. In essence, the MNC can be defined as an organisation that 'is physically active in more than one country' (Hollinshead and Leat, 1995: p. 78). Therefore, Ford can be put into the same category as a small wine-importing company. Although small businesses are important stakeholders in international business, it is the strategies of the larger organisations that tend to form a focus for analysis by those interested in HRM.

MNCs are an extremely important phenomenon in many of the world's developed and developing societies. They employ many millions of people and are therefore important players in national and local economies. MNCs can arguably be viewed as both a driving force and consequence of the phenomena associated with globalisation and their rise to prominence in economic and social studies, and the public consciousness has not been without controversy (Balaam and Veseth, 2005). MNCs tend to be the target of 'anti-globalisation' protests which have been occurring with increasing frequency; attacks on McDonald's restaurants and Starbuck's coffee shops have been two notable examples. The list of complaints against MNCs is a lengthy one but in particular, protesters and less militant critics tend to focus on damage caused by many MNCs to the physical environment and the manner in which suppliers in developing countries are often exploited and excluded from markets (see section on *Labour Standards and Social Responsibility* below). However, from an HRM perspective, the most interesting complaint is that due to their sheer economic power and influence they are able to exploit local workforces and indulge in 'social dumping,' for example, moving production to where labour costs are lower, avoiding labour unions or using certain subsidiaries for low-skilled production processes (Eaton, 2000). Indeed, as many of the world's MNCs are bigger than many of the world's countries in economic terms (turnover compared to GDP) they can often be in a position to influence government policy.

There is a significant probability that you will work for a MNC at some point in your career if you do not now or have not done so already (e.g. if you have worked in an ASDA supermarket, you have been part of Wal-Mart, one of the largest MNCs by Turnover and the largest private employer (1.5 million people)) (Balaam and Veseth, 2005). However, we must bear in mind that only a small proportion of any MNC's HRM function are likely to be concerned directly with international considerations such as the training and deployment of expatriate workers. However, an understanding of how MNCs formulate and implement HRM strategies is an important factor when analysing HRM practice at a local level.

IHRM models and strategies

It is only relatively recently that any importance has been attached to HRM in MNCs (Hollinshead and Leat, 1995). Corporate strategies, distribution chains and financial management have long been in the consciousness of senior executives. It is perhaps only since the apparent effects of Globalisation have emerged that the need for more integration of HRM considerations into the corporate agendas of MNCs have begun to be addressed (Almond *et al.*, 2004). Competitive pressures, regional economic development and the rapid development of more sophisticated technologies and production methods have prompted many of the most successful MNCs to think more carefully about aligning HRM more closely with other strategic considerations. Because of the complex operating environment of IHRM, HRM strategies in MNCs vary. Of course, there are a number of ambiguities around the notion of corporate strategy and in particular the notion of strategic HRM, let alone strategic IHRM. However, the challenge for senior executives, and managers and employees in local contexts, is to find an appropriate 'fit' for achieving organisational objectives which will depend on NBSs, product strategies, national and organisational cultures among a host of other complex factors (Warhurst, 1997).

In terms of formulating strategies for foreign subsidiary organisations, the key consideration for IHR managers in formulating strategies for

MNCs is striking a balance between the control necessary to ensure that corporate objectives are complied with and the flexibility required to respond to often dynamic and volatile local circumstances. Prahalad and Doz (1987) have presented this dilemma in terms of *integration* and *responsiveness*; the extent of centralisation and control that head office in the home country should be exerting over practices in foreign subsidiaries and in outsourced and 'partnership' organisations. On the one hand, if too much central control is exerted over HRM matters (e.g. recruitment and selection, pay and conditions, training and development, employment relations and collective bargaining), one runs the risk of compromising the necessary flexibility to make local decisions. Furthermore, head office may be implementing strategies that are not compatible with local cultures. On the other hand, MNCs need to create a well-coordinated and cohesive organisation that can grow and develop and learn best practice (Bartlett and Ghoshal, 1989).

Dowling and Schuller (1991) have developed a useful typology of strategies using the Prahald and Doz model as its inspiration. The Dowling and Schuller model is based on four broad approaches: *ethnocentric, polycentric, regiocentric* and *geocentric*. These are explained below:

1 *Ethnocentric*: In this approach, subsidiaries have little autonomy with strategic decisions being made at head office. HRM practices are likely to be prescribed in accordance with those that are customary in the home country. Expatriate managers are given little language or cross-cultural training. Japanese MNCs have often been characterised in this way (e.g. single union 'no-strike' agreements, team-working, commitment-based organisational culture).

2 *Polycentric*: Here, the MNC regards subsidiaries as distinct entities with some autonomy. Recruitment of staff will be conducted locally and the head office is less interested in imposing control and organisational culture on the subsidiary. Expatriate managers will be given some cross-cultural and language training.

3 *Regiocentric*: This approach focuses on regional values and ways of operating, drawing specialist employees and managers from a wider pool with a specific geographical zone (e.g. Europe, North America, the Pacific Rim).

4 *Geocentric* (or *Global*): According to expert opinion, this type is the one that contemporary MNCs should seek to emulate. The geocentric organisation is decentralised and flexible in its operations, but maintains an integrated set of values and mission. Managers are developed to be interchangeable between national contexts and promoted on the basis of merit. Networks

are established to spread knowledge and best practice through the global operation.

Although Dowling and Schuler's typology is engaging, it should be stressed that each strategy is an ideal type and it is unlikely that any one MNC would conform completely with their criteria. Neither is it the case that senior managers can simply wake up one morning and decide to pursue a particular route. An MNC's HRM strategy will emerge from a combination of evolution, management intervention and the interplay of a complex set of environmental forces.

MNCs and staffing

As you will have observed from the other chapters in this book, a key function of HRM is people resourcing, specifically the recruitment, selection, deployment and development of staff. In an international context, this process is arguably more complicated and crucial to the commercial success of the organisation (Hollinshead and Leat, 1995). In terms of the sources of staff for MNC subsidiaries, Hendry (1994) has categorised these into three types:

1 Parent-country nationals (PCNs) where staff come from the home country. An example of this would be British oil workers working for BP in the Gulf states. More generally, PCNs will be managerial and/or specialised technical staff.

2 Host-country nationals (HCNs) where staff are recruited locally from the country in which a subsidiary is based. The level and status of employee will depend greatly upon the quality of the local labour market; in many developing countries, those recruited will often be semi-skilled workers assigned to low-status, low-paid work this taking advantage of lower labour costs.

3 Third-country nationals (TCNs) where staffs are brought in to work in a foreign subsidiary, but are not originally from the country in which the subsidiary is located. Again, examples are to be found in the Gulf states where workers from India, Pakistan and Sri Lanka go to work in manual and semi-skilled capacities for much higher wages than they could earn in their country of origin; in doing so they are able to send money home to their families.

As managerial and technical/specialist employees are considered to add value to the organisation it is these expatriate employees who tend to receive the most attention in terms of cross-cultural training and support. The re-location of not only the employees but their families may be necessary, and if the employee's family experiences difficulties in settling in their new environment, this may affect the quality of the employee's work. Some MNCs go to great lengths to ensure that the transition from one culture to another is a smooth one.

MNCs, employee relations and trade unions

As detailed in Chapter 7, trades unions in the UK have faced numerous challenges in past quarter of a century. Membership has declined and unions are perceived as not enjoying as much power and influence as they once did. This trend is often attributed to the policies of the post 1979 Conservative government of Margaret Thatcher. However, similar patterns in the fortunes of unions can be charted in most if not all industrialised nations, albeit to varying degrees and in differing contexts. In contrast membership levels in Sweden have remained consistently high in the last 20 years, whereas in the UK and USA they have diminished sharply. This suggests more global factors are at play. As discussed earlier in this chapter, economic restructuring and technological change have brought about profound shifts in the way industry operates (e.g. decline of manufacturing, Japanese production techniques).

It should be emphasised that unions are not the same in every country, nor do they fulfil the same roles (Eaton, 2000). Also, as detailed above, each country has its own NBS and therefore the experiences of unions within each NBS has been different. However, certain general trends can be detected in union power and influence across national boundaries, which seem to suggest decline. The complex combination of social and economic shifts can be blamed for this. Perhaps a specific explanation can be found in the rise to prominence of the MNC. Whereas employers are able to function effectively across national boundaries, the unions who would seek to bargain do not generally do this. This is despite the existence of international trade union bodies such as the European Trade Union Confederation (ETUC) and the International Confederation of Free Trades Unions (ICFTU) (Hollinshead and Leat, 1995). Furthermore, many MNCs have been very effective in using strategies to avoid or marginalise trade unions by off-shoring production and introducing new production methods (Eaton, 2000).

However, the EU has been a source of some optimism for unions as they are involved in decision-making processes under the terms of the social dialogue and their activities supported by law. Furthermore, European Works Councils (EWCs) on which union representatives can sit can provide an outlet for union activities and voice in the EU member states.

Strategic alliances and 'off shoring'

For MNCs to operate effectively and flexibly, they often enter into partnerships with other organisations in other countries. There can be several reasons for doing this, such as to reduce risk, gain entry to restricted markets and to share and enhance knowledge and expertise (Tayeb, 1999). A famous example of this in the UK was the partnership of Rover and Honda which contributed greatly to Rover's survival during the very challenging times in the 1980s. However, the number of partnerships or 'strategic alliances' in world trade have grown considerably in the last decade. In particular, Chinese businesses have been involved in a number strategic alliances with Western firms such as Mercedes-Benz and Dell Computers (Balaam and Veseth, 2005).

The HRM implications of strategic alliances depend on the extent of the partnership. It could be that the arrangement exists merely to outsource a peripheral aspect of production, in which case the senior partner will be quite content to devolve HRM responsibility to the contractor. However, often, strategic alliances are used as an opportunity to exchange and enhance HRM practices. This was particularly the case with the example of River and Honda where the British firm learned a great deal from their Japanese counterparts.

The sorts of arrangements referred to above can also court controversy. Recently, there has been a string of features in the UK media about the increasingly common tendency of employers to move production (either in a manufacturing or service context) to other countries where wages are lower and employment rights seemingly less constraining. This trend can be seen as responsible to a considerable extent for the decline in manufacturing in developed countries (Balaam and Veseth, 2005). Often these jobs are low-skilled, low-discretion jobs, and are outsourced to a subcontractor. Some continental European nations such as France and Germany have introduced labour laws to prevent MNCs from taking jobs abroad. However, concerns have been raised recently in the UK about the fact that it is not merely manufacturing jobs that are moving abroad, but also service jobs, most notably call-centre customer-service work which certain economically depressed regions of the UK had come to depend on (Taylor and Bain, 1998).

In particular, financial institutions have moved jobs to India where there is a large potential labour market of English-speaking university graduates who see call-centre jobs as having prestige. Case study 12.1 explains how this has become a highly politicised issue in the UK. However, others, such as Riddell (2004) argues that the loss of call-centre jobs offshore is not necessarily so bad as this means that the imperative is created in the British labour market for the generation of higher skilled 'knowledge' jobs that create more wealth.

Case study 12.1

Insurer packs 7000 jobs off to India

Finance union Amicus condemned insurance giant Norwich Union yesterday over its 'devastating' decision to offshore 7000 British jobs to India. The massive jobs export comes from a company which has already exported 3700 jobs to India since December and will reduce its British workforce by 25% by 2007. Amicus national officer David Fleming said: 'Today's announcement of 950 jobs being offshored is not only devastating to the workforce, but the double whammy is the further 2.350 to go by 2007. In the first stage, 950 jobs will go to India and Sri Lanka next year, hitting workers, their families and communities in Norwich, York and Perth.' Mr Fleming said that it pointed to a 'bleak future' for Britain's financial services industry.

'We will not accept compulsory redundancies as a consequence of off shoring in any company and that will be fundamental to our negotiations with Norwich Union. Amicus will take whatever action our members request of us. All our options are open.'

Mr Fleming said that, in talks with the company, the union hopes to ensure maximum opportunities for retraining, job mobility and skills development for all staff affected. Looking across the financial services sector, he added that employees would now be 'bracing themselves' for 'thousands more' redundancies as companies 'show their off-shoring hand'.

Defending the announcement, Norwich Union chief Gary Withers insisted that it was a response to 'customers continually seeking better value for money and quality of service.'

Yesterday's blow confirmed a recent opinion survey carried out by Amicus among Norwich Union staff in which 99.9% of them feared further job cuts under the company's off shoring programme.

Tens of thousands of British jobs have been moved to India by banks, airlines, telecommunications firms and even national rail enquiries service, chasing wage cuts of up to 40%. But, aside from the devastation caused by the loss of jobs, there is also growing opposition from customers. Lloyds TSB customers backed by the bank's in-house staff association, are challenging its decision to shift jobs to India under the terms of the Data Protection Act.

Amicus has been at the forefront of campaigning to highlight the fundamental problems associated with off shoring – the lack of long-term business benefits and overall benefits to the customer. The union has also urged companies that export jobs to reinvest the cost savings made into developing their British workforce and generating numbers of skilled jobs.

However, according to Amicus, not a single company has yet been able to demonstrate a focus on reinvestment and corporate social responsibility.

Source: Stewart (2004)

Supra-national bodies and HRM

In the 20th century, the modus operandi for geopolitics has been that the nation state has normally been regarded as the most potent level of governance, making laws and seeking to defend and further the interests of its inhabitants, a duty that has often brought nations into conflict with each other. Of course, history has witnessed the efforts of some (usually big and powerful) nations seeking to influence others, either through colonisation or by more clandestine means. However, since the 1939–1945 war we have seen moves towards supra-national models of governance whereby national governments agree to be bound by rules and regulations that are formulated at a level beyond the nation state. There are now many alliances and trading blocs throughout the globe, but the organisations we are concerned with here are those that exert a direct and definite impact on the environment and on the environment of HRM. We will consider the following supra-national bodies:

- The International Labour Organization (ILO).
- EU.

The ILO

Although the UN concerns itself primarily with the resolution of international conflict, it also seeks to influence economic, social and workplace matters through its agencies. The ILO was founded in 1919 as part of the Treaty of Versailles and was incorporated into the UN in 1946. It seeks to promote fairness and human rights in the workplace through the promotion of a number of conventions that the members of the UN nominally adhere to (although even the most advanced nations often disregard them in practice).

The EU

If one were to read the British press, one would consider that the EU was a bureaucratic monstrosity that spends its time straightening bananas, worrying about the content of sausages and generally spending large sums of European taxpayers' money on number of pointless projects. The reality is actually quite far from these tabloid myths. The EU is a sophisticated and proactive set of institutions which since May 2004 has had a membership of 25 European nations. It seeks to create the conditions for economic prosperity and social justice for its members through policy and legislative interventions. Unlike other supra-national bodies, it is not merely a trading bloc but enacts social policies, many of which have a profound impact on the work of the HRM practitioners in the member states.

The social dialogue and the social partners

A core philosophy of the EU is the intention to resolve social and economic conflicts in European society through a process of dialogue and consensus. Thus, it brings together employer and trade union representatives (the social partners) to discuss matters of common concern such as economic performance, and living and working conditions. This process is aided by the activities of the economic and social committee.

The social charter

In 1972 the decision was taken by the members to address what were seen as gross disparities in living and working conditions in across the membership. Hence, a commitment was made to creating a set of fundamental social standards and rights. In 1989, after the signing of the important Single European Act in 1987, the Social Charter was adopted by all member states except for the UK, the British Conservative administration felt the regulation was excessive and would harm economic competitiveness. In 1992, it became the Social Chapter of the Maastricht Treaty and thus part of the core legislative framework of the EU. Again, the UK managed to opt out, although it did eventually sign up to it on the accession of the New Labour Administration in 1997.

The main provisions of the Social Charter are as follows:

1 Free movement of workers within the EU.
2 Fair remuneration of work (i.e. a minimum wage).
3 Improvement of living and working conditions (e.g. working time limits, paid leave, redundancy protection).
4 Social security protection (e.g. pensions, benefits).
5 Freedom and association and collective bargaining (i.e. the right to join a union and for your employer to recognise that union).
6 Vocational training (i.e. the access of every worker to training)
7 Gender equality.
8 Information, consultation and participation of workers.
9 Health protection and safety in the workplace.
10 Protection of children and adolescents in employment (e.g. minimum working age).
11 Elderly persons to enjoy decent standard of living post-retirement.
12 Equality for disabled persons.

It should be quite apparent how these provisions have a major impact on the HRM function. In a UK context, regulations have been introduced with regard to minimum wage payments and working time and the Employment Relations Act 1999 included the provisions relating to information and consultation and for recognition of trade unions. Equal opportunities legislation was already in existence in the UK for certain groups although this is subject to ongoing amendment in line with European Policy. Most notably has been the inclusion of sexuality and age discrimination as unlawful acts.

The Far East dimension

Japan

Although Japanese business methods and their associated human resources policies proved successful in an extraordinary way in the 1970s and 1980s, the 1990s have proved difficult years as other nations have copied those approaches and adjusted them equally successfully to their local environment. At the same time, the strength of the yen has made exporting increasingly difficult. To meet these challenges, Japanese employment systems are showing changes in five areas (Kyotani, 1999).

The first of these is the erosion of the *Nenko Wage system.* This was established in the 1920s and has given guarantees on regular pay increases for those 80% or more employees considered to be core employees. Since the 1970s, there has been a gradual erosion of this guarantee and, by the 1990s, over 80% of companies had either abandoned the guarantee, adjusted it or planned to do so shortly. The main adjustment is to make a proportion of the wage subject to the workings of a performance management process. For example, in NEC, over half of the wage is determined by the outcome of an annual appraisal.

So bad were the state of some industrial companies by the mid 1990s that unions agreed to a complete abolition of the guaranteed increase in Mitsui Metal company. In administrative jobs, this movement has occurred at a faster pace with many organisations now ignoring service as a determinant of pay. With inflation at nil, this is tantamount to a perpetual pay freeze for all but the above average performer. An interesting side effect of this changed policy is the widening of the pay differentials not just between good and poor performers but in the chain of command.

Associated with the Nenko system was the practice of *promotions based chiefly on service.* In recent years, however, the system of formal appraisal has taken over in most organisations, although some still keep a minimum service requirement, such as 5 years, before a promotion can be made. Within Japanese subsidiaries in other countries, career advancement for local managers is generally very limited indeed. The process of centralised decision-making requires Japanese expatriates to be in place to interpret correctly the decisions made at Head Office.

Shushin koyo – life-long employment – is another tradition that is on the wane. Core workers in large organisations continue to have this guarantee but over 90% of companies in a recent survey indicated their intention to start removing this guarantee. An estimate is made that only 30% of new employees receive a lifetime guarantee (Brewster and Tyson 1991). Due to the decline in internal demand, there is also a growing policy of encouraging early retirement and voluntary redundancy. Forty one per cent of companies have programmes for transferring employees to related firms, sometimes losing their major benefits in the transfer or reducing their hours or schemes to encourage employees to set up their own businesses. These processes (and the associated reduction of new hirings) have added to the growing unemployment rate which reached over 4% by 1999. A prime example of this policy was the announcement in October 1999 by Nissan car company that it would close five plants in Japan as part of a major rescue plant to prevent further escalation in losses, but at the expense of more than 15,000 job losses. Bannister, 1999) and a further example is shown in Case study 12.2.

There is also an interesting policy change in terms of *gender issues*. The overt policy stated by government, management and unions is to employ more female employees but this is not a general indication of equal opportunities. Since the establishment of the Equal Job Rights Law in 1996, many organisations have implemented the 'Job Career Path Programme' (Kosubetsu Koyo Seido). This divides employees into two groups. These are the 'general staff group' who are engaged in unskilled or repetitive jobs and who will never be promoted and the 'executive candidates group' who are expected to achieve managerial or professional status after experiencing various jobs in the organisation. In practice, this policy is working as a means of segregating male and female workers. Females go into the general staff group while the executive candidates group is almost entirely made up of men. Further more, the general staff group is increasingly being filled with temporary or agency staff, often provided by an associated company and at lower pay than for permanent employees. The position of women still continue to be seen as the helpers of men, making tea and doing typing. This helps to explain the recent high-profile legal suits against Japanese companies in America for sexual harassment and discrimination where multi-million pound settlements have been reached.

The fifth area is in the *loosening of regulations*. For example, the employment of agency staff used to be restricted to only a handful of job categories, such as catering and administration. This has now been extended and complete restrictions are likely to be lifted within the next few years. The restrictions on the employment of women for health and safety reasons, such as in night work, have also been lifted. Government regulations on the length of the working week are also in the process of being weakened. The overall outcome is that there is an increase in the flexibility of the workforce but one that appears to be achieved through the elimination of longer-term benefits and rights of the employees. This has drawn the country's working patterns closer to that of the West but it may also lead to a hardening of relations with the unions who have been largely subservient to date.

There are other areas of Japanese culture which continue to be successful with little change. Kaisen, the process of encouraging staff to contribute ideas on incremental improvements, has been copied throughout the world. Similarly, the emphasis on quality, just-in-time and team working have been replicated in all industrial countries.

Case study 12.2

Toyota cars

Toyota's 'Professional Contract Policy' implemented in 1994, specified that the employment terms of professionals, such as product designers, cannot be extended beyond five years. Although the number contracted in this way is small, Toyota is planning to hire more professionals in newly developed business fields such as communication equipment, aerospace vehicles and new transportation systems. By 2010, it is expected that fixed term contract employees will rise to 30% of the workforce.

Source: Kyotani (1999)

China

China's accession to the WTO in 2003 confirmed the almost unbelievable changes in the country's political and economic structure and strategy over the last 20 years. With a GDP growing at over 8% a year, it has been estimated that it will account for 25% of the total world economy by 2025. Western investment has surged (Motorola's investment has reached over £6 billion) and the Chinese government has responded by introducing initiatives to level out the playing field so foreign firms will enjoy similar benefits to locals (Sappal, 2003).

Traditional cultural values, however, are very different and slow to change. Many originated from Mao Tse Tung's 'iron rice bowl' regime and they provide a powerful influential on the working environment, such as:

- Fie fan wan – job for life.
- Da you fan – rewards unrelated to individual performance.
- Dan wei – cradle to grave welfare.
- Guanxi – the importance of relationships.
- Renquing – doing favours, which help to build relationships.
- Mianzi – saving face, often through reciprocating favours.
- Chang dei – respect for elders and seniority.

Operating many of these values in the work place had led to inefficiencies and corruption. Many managers are simply used to follow the orders so find it difficult to use their own initiative while major change programmes, especially those including redundancies, face severe obstacles in acceptance and implementation. Changing to Western-style employment relationships, therefore, remains a major step, although evidence is growing that Western practices, such as psychological testing and using references, are growing, especially in joint ventures. As Armstrong explains:

> 'When I was first there (in the early 1990s) … the Chinese were content to just have good economic growth and improve their education system. Now they want to reduce dependency on low-cost labour by raising added value and building human and intellectual capital…. More than 70% of people under 30 now speak English and Chinese firms have started to explore the HR agenda so they can compete head on with foreigners.'
>
> Sappal (2003: p. 37)

The adoption of Western HR practices varies according to a number of variables. The fastest movement have been implemented in subsidiaries of large Western-owned MNCs, but, even here, the speed of adoption is not predictable, being shaped by political and social realities, as explained in Focus on research 12.2.

Focus on research 12.2

Key factors influencing HRM practices in China

The researchers examined the HRM practices in 286 Chinese subsidiaries of US, German and Japanese companies and identified a series of influences which they divided into 'push' factors from the parent firm and 'pull' factors from the 'host country.'

The strongest 'push' factor was from financial control in subsidiary investment decision and joint venture structure where such decisions led to changing existing local practices to those closer to Western HRM practices. Little difference was identified in industry sector or the country of origin. In addition, many HRM practices may be converging to a more common universal form across different types of subsidiaries. Where the subsidiary was minority-owned, the degree of HRM practices was more limited.

Interestingly, there is a good evidence that parent firms start in China with global strategic imperatives for HRM practices but they become constrained by local environment and cultural conditions and make major modifications.

The largest direction of 'push' is towards a performance-oriented culture, including value systems that strive for efficiency and quality, employee appraisals focusing on financial performance and encouraging skills development. Where there is a greater pull factor from the local environment, (measured by longer time period of establishment in that locality), the practices tend to show a traditional flavour, such as provision for employee housing, consideration of the educational background for hiring managers and referrals. This is not to say that Western-style practices are absent, it is more a more hybrid system that has developed.

'As the competition in the Chinese market for skilled labour becomes stronger, many multinational firms are expected to adopt more "best" HRM practices that are not only results-oriented but also fit local cultural and social environments … Those managers adapting to the dual forces of "push" and "pull", linking global management policies and practices to the specific Chinese environments, sensitive to Chinese local culture and practices and willing to be flexible while maintaining professional standards may be most likely to succeed in the Chinese market.' (p. 702)

Source: Farley *et al.* (2004)

Labour standards and social responsibility

Although MNCs and governments are perceived as being all powerful and often portrayed as being reckless in the face of green and social issues in the pursuit of revenue, there has been something of a political and consumer backlash in recent years that has challenged some of the more unsavoury practices such as exploiting the populations in developing countries. Stories of how many MNCs, often household names such as Nike (Eaton, 2000), have been making large profits while using poorly paid labour, often working in terrible conditions. These problems are compounded further with reports of the use of child and forced prison labour, and the persecution of workers because of their membership of unions and opposition political parties (Tsogas, 1999).

In the face of these issues, the governments of developed nations, charitable agencies and non-governmental organizations (NGOs) and MNCs themselves have sought to develop frameworks that seek to address these concerns and oblige bad employers in developing (and some developed!) countries to improve the conditions of their workers. The frameworks tend to concern low wages, human rights and worker rights abuses, child labour and poor working conditions.

These frameworks tend to operate on three distinct levels:

- Unilateral national agreements, where countries enforce conditions on other countries and MNCs that they import from.
- Multilateral national agreements where countries agree trading conditions with other countries and MNCs in return for preferential tariff rates.
- Corporate codes of conduct where individual MNCs (or groups of MNCs) impose standards within their own organisations and on their suppliers and trading partners.

It is rather unfortunate that in the issue of labour standards, the righteous rhetoric of governments and MNCs is often not matched by reality. Standards are often not enforced as rigorously as they should be and major abuses of worker rights by MNCs continue to be a problem (Tsogas, 1999).

Meteor case study

Setting up a new unit in Belgium

Three years later, in line with the business strategy, Meteor was set to open a unit in mainland Europe and a site near Brussels had been chosen. Sarah was successful in her application to become the HR Manager for the site, her good knowledge of French being a crucial advantage. In setting out her human resources plan, she was aware that the system of pay determination and other HR practices in Belgium was highly centralised and regulated. The consensual nature of industrial relations was pivotal with the social partners in constant contact with each other through bipartite national and industry bodies, such as the Central Economic Council. Belgium's very open competitive stance this was reflected in the exchange of information between the partners, which has lead to reasonably harmonious agreements to protect jobs and guarantee incomes.

Sarah knew that she would have to work within national agreements reached in areas such as the average monthly minimum guaranteed income, introduced in 1975, which is linked to the national monthly consumer price index, and wage rates for employees under 21, both of which applied to the whole of Belgium. As a new employer, she needed to discover which, if any, national agreement had been reached in her industry over minimum rates as she learnt that such agreements, unlike the UK, were legally binding and which were also indexed. Her research found the appropriate national agreement and she was relieved to see that the indexation only applied to those employees on the national minimum wage.

These agreements were reached through sub-committees of the National Labour Council that dealt separately with agreements for blue and white-collar employees. For Sarah, this distinction provided difficulties as, in the UK, terms and conditions were harmonised without such a distinction. The national agreement produced considerable financial implications to the company for the transfer of blue-collar employees to white-collar status, due to higher payments for sickness and redundancy. Another issue she needed to carefully consider was the traditional nature of pay increments where some industries had as many as 20 automatic increments for white-collar employees from age 21 to 55. She found that it was a standard convention for most employees to receive a Christmas bonus equivalent to an additional month's pay. In fact, some senior employees in her industry were entitled to a 14th month's pay as well! There was also a minimum notice period of 28 days for blue collar workers.

Holiday entitlement was, she found, around the same as the UK in general but the payment surprised her in that most of the holiday had to be paid at double the wage rate. The outcome was that blue-collar employees receive a minimum of a total of 7 weeks and 2 days pay for 4 weeks leave. Sickness payments were also more generous for the employees in that minimum entitlement for all employees is one month, mostly paid by the employer, followed by the state sickness benefit, that pays around 60% of former earnings, although this figure is capped. From 1999, the statutory working week was reduced to 39 hours without loss of pay. There were complicated rules which restricted Sunday working. Considerably fewer employees had company cars, however, which relieved Sarah of a potential headache in terms of allocation and expensing. She was relieved that payment for managers and senior technologists remained outside of the scope of such agreements.

Also in her plan was the establishment of the Works Council, which was obligatory where there was more than 100 employees. She had no experience of such a body and spent some time fixing visits to see Councils in operation in the UK and Belgium, made through personal networking and the CIPD International Forum.

Overall, she was aware that the costs of employment were high as the employers' social security contributions were in the order of 25%, almost double the equivalent costs in the UK.

Additional source: IDS (1998)

Summary

- The workplace has become increasingly more exposed to international forces and knowledge of issues in international HRM is useful for practitioners.
- There is considerable variety in the way business operates within national contexts and therefore the environment of HRM tends to differ also.
- National culture can be a major determinant on the nature of workplace behaviour in different national contexts; when dealing in HRM matters with other countries, practitioners must be aware of these.
- MNCs are a very influential phenomenon in global trade. HRM practitioners should be aware of different strategies that can be deployed to manage people and what the key issues are (e.g. managing expatriate workers).
- Supra-national institutions and in particular the EU are very influential in HRM issues, especially with regard to the social and welfare aspects of HRM practice.
- Western-style HRM practices are being adopted in Far East countries but the speed of adoption and the degree of adaptation to local conditions varies greatly depending on differing factors.
- The internationalisation of business has had some unsavoury consequences such as exploitation and practitioners should be aware of their ethical and social responsibilities.

References

Alis, D. (2003) The 35 hour week in France: the French exception. *Personnel Review*, **32**(4): 510–525.

Almond, P., Clark, I., Treaskis, O. (2004) HRM in multinationals: a comparative international perspective. In: Beardwell, I., Holden, L., Claydon, T. (eds). *Human Resource Management: A Contemporary Approach*, 4th edition. London: FT/Prentice Hall.

Baalam, D., Veseth, M. (2005) *Introduction to International Political Economy*, 3rd edition Upper Saddle River, NJ: Pearson.

Bannister, N. (1999) 21,000 go in Nissan rescue. *Guardian*, 19 October, 22.

Bartlett, C., Ghoshal, S. (1989) *Managing Across Borders: The Transnational Solution*, Boston, MA: Harvard Business School Press.

Beck, U. (1991) *The Risk Society: Towards a New Modernity*. London: Sage.

Brown, A. (1998) *Organizational Culture*. London: Pitman.

Crozier, M. (1964) *The Bureaucratic Phenomenon*. Oxford: OUP.

Dowling, P., Schuller, R. (1991) *International Dimensions of Human Resource Management*. Boston: PWS-Kent.

Dunlop, J. (1958) *The Industrial Relations System*. Carbondale, Il: Southern Illinois University Press.

Eaton, J. (2000) *Comparative Employment Relations: An Introduction*. Polity: Cambridge.

Farley, J., Hoenig, S., Yang, J. (2004) Key factors influencing HRM practices of overseas subsidiaries in China's transition economy, International Journal of Human Resource Management, 15, 4 and 5, June and August, 688–704.

Giddens, A. (1990) *The Consequences of Modernity*, Cambridge: Polity.

Harzing, A-W. (1999) 'Structuring international organizations' in Tayeb, M. (ed.) *International Business: Theories, Policies and Practices*, London: FT/Prentice Hall.

Hendry, C. (1994) *Human Resource Strategies for International Growth*. London: Routledge.

Hofstede, G. (1980) *Culture's Consequences*, London: Sage.

Hollinshead, G., Leat, M. (1995) *Human Resource Management: An International and Comparative Perspective*. London: Pitman.

IDS (1998) *Pay and Conditions in Belgium*. Income Data Services.

Kerr, C., Dunlop, J., Harbison, F., Myers, C. (1962) *Industrialism and Industrial Man*. Boston: Harvard University Press.

Kessler, I., Undy, R., Heron, P. (2004) Employee perspectives on communication and consultation: findings from a cross-national survey. *International Journal of Human Resource Management*, **15**, 3 May, 512–532.

Kyotani, E. (1999) New managerial strategies of Japanese Corporations. In: Felstead, A., Jewson, N. (eds). *Global Trends in Flexible Labour*. Macmillan Business.

Muller, G. (1997) Institutional resilience in a changing world economy? The case of the German banking and chemical industries. *British Journal of Industrial Relations*, **35**(4): 954–985.

Prahalad, C., Doz, Y. (1987) *The Multinational Mission: Balancing Local Demands and Global Vision*. New York: The Free Press.

Riddell, P. (2004) The left is wrong to start a tug-of-war on call centres. *The Times*, 26/2/2004.

Ritzer, G. (1996) *The McDonaldization of Society*. London: Pine Forge.

Sappal, P. (2003) Cultural Evolution. *People Management*, 17 April, 33–28.

Stewart, K. (2004) Insurer packs 7000 jobs off to India. *Morning Star*, 23rd September, p. 1.

Tayeb, M. (1999) Understanding and managing the multicultural workforce. In: Tayeb, M. (ed.). *International Business: Theories, Policies and Practices*. London: FT/Prentice Hall.

Taylor, P., Bain, P. (1998) An assembly line in the head: the call centre labour process. *Industrial Relations Journal*, **30**(2): 101–117.

Tsogas, G. (1999) Labour standards, corporate codes of conduct and labour regulation in international trade. In: Tayeb, M. (ed). *International Business: Theories, Policies and Practices*. London: FT/Prentice Hall.

Warhurst, C. (1997) Political economy and the social organization of economic activity: a synthesis of neo-institutional and labour process analyses. *Competition and Change*, **2**: 213–246.

Subject Index

Author Index